Journey Through the Bible:
Lesson Plans to Teach and Study the Bible
Chapter by Chapter
Old Testament

Thomas E. Young, Sr., D. Min.

Acknowledgments

I would like to thank my granddaughter, Audrey LeeAnn Young Johnson, for taking on the complex task of organizing, coordinating, and researching the best approach for getting these 264 plus bonus Bible lessons on the Old Testament into the hands of God's children.

Also, I want to acknowledge the great value of the following resources that were available to me during over 21 years of teaching:

- Liberty University's Dr. Harold Wilmington's outstanding two-year Bible Course.

- From the "Word of Life Study Bible" copyright (c) 1993, by Thomas Nelson, Inc. Used by Permission. This Bible has excellent graphics and background notes to complement the individual lesson guide.

- Prophecy Study Bible, NKJV, John C. Hagee, General Editor, Thomas Nelson Publishers, Nashville. Copyright 1997. Scripture taken from the New King James, Copyright (c) 1979, 1980, 1982, by Thomas Nelson, Inc. Used by permission. All rights reserved.

- Perry Stone's teachings and studies on the Rapture and on the Book of Revelation and his many trips to the Holy Land.

- And to all who have not been mentioned but have contributed to my understanding of the Scriptures, our good Lord will acknowledge you and bless you when we all get home.

- A very special "thank you" to Lynda McFelia whose professional administrative skills have saved me close to two months in completing the Scripture Focus Chapters for the Old Testament Books.

- To Paul (P.W.) & Jeannie Currie, who assumed the leadership of the Friday Bible Study responsibility.

In addition, Mary Alice Padgett for all her special refreshments and baking for over 21 years, and all the ladies who substituted: Mary Donata, Melody Aversa, and Bonnie Webb for their Sunday brunches at Melody's home. All the ladies who provided the Friday Bible Study with special refreshments over our 21-year period made our studies a family setting and a blessing, and the Good Lord has all your names in His Book.

Thank you all,

Tom Young

Table of Contents

PREFACE

A Note from the Author: Every Church, every Denomination, every Pastor, every Family should have the Old and New Testament Lesson Plans available for the teaching of God's Word.

I believe it was in September 1997, when I went to a local Bible Study in my community. The Bible teaching minister did not show up because of the low-class attendance. This particular Friday, only a young lady (Mary Alice Padgett) and I were present. No teacher or leader.

I asked her, "What do we do?"

She said, "Let's read the Bible".

And that is what we did. I prepared future lessons and Mary Alice supplied the refreshments for the Bible Study for the next twenty-plus years. During the twenty-plus years, if Mary Alice or I were not present due to an illness or travel, volunteer Bible class members filled the gap by providing lessons and goodies.

The Bible Study grew, and attendees gravitated to an environment that allowed all of us to read and interpret the Scriptures weekly. After two decades (21 years and turning 88 years old), I stopped teaching the class, but it was recognized that what was created is a valuable tool that should be shared. The Bible Study continues today and is now taught by a younger Man of God with approximately 30 attendees each week, Thank God!

Additional copies of this resource along with the New Testament version can be ordered from Amazon.com in paperback, hardcover, and Kindle formats. Search "books" by Thomas E. Young Sr., or type the title, *Journey Through the Bible: Lesson Plans to Teach and Study the Bible Chapter by Chapter.*

INTRODUCTION

I desire to see the Word of God accessible to all and inexpensive for all. Why should those who desire to study the Bible have to pay $12.00 to $20.00 for a book to study the scripture of each book of the Bible? Why not just read the scripture itself and discuss it? Hence the creation of *Journey Through the Bible: Lesson Plans to Teach and Study the Bible Chapter by Chapter.*

This resource provides a framework for pastors, ministers, or individuals desiring to facilitate a Bible class or small group. Each book of the Old Testament is organized with a formatted Lesson Plan allowing the facilitator and student to read the scripture directly and be inspired by the Word of God.

Each Book of the Bible begins with an overview of the main components organized by chapter. After the general overview, each chapter is organized into individual lessons with a Lesson Plan providing the format to study that particular section. I recommend that the facilitator provide a copy of each Lesson Plan to the students so that everyone can actively participate, take notes, and have the lesson available after the class.

How to Use this Resource to Facilitate Bible Study Groups/Classes

1. *Open in Prayer (thanksgiving for our health, family, our Country, our leaders, for those that we know may be sick or in need of prayer, and for a deeper understanding of God's Word).*

2. *Welcome each student by asking them to introduce themselves (just sharing their names).*

3. *Read through the lessons in the Lesson Plan aloud so that everyone is aware of how, where, and what will be discussed.*

4. *After walking through the Lesson Plan, read each of the scriptures noted (encourage participants to volunteer to read scripture aloud to the group). After each scripture, ask for comments and/ or questions.*

5. *Close in prayer.*

Each class should last about an hour. Ideally, 1–1.5 hours is great for morning or evening Bible studies in homes or churches. If possible, allow time for fellowship.

The Lesson Plans end with the same two scriptures for specific reasons.

2 Chronicles 7:14:

About 2900+ years ago (2952 years), God appeared to Solomon just after he had completed the Temple and offered him the promise of Conditional Covenant for His people. God knew there would be wars, pestilence, famines, persecutions, and lack of rain (see 2 Chronicles 7:13) and therefore was giving us (you and me and His chosen people) an opportunity to have our land healed. He had covenants with Abraham, Noah, David, etc., and here He was offering us a conditional promise or covenant.

There are approximately 37,000 Catholic Priests, about 109,000 pastors/clergy, and countless Bible teachers who should be leading the sheep/flock in taking advantage of God's conditional promise to heal our land. We are suffering because we are not taking advantage of God's promise in II Chronicles 7:14.

Psalm 122:6:

This psalm is not a suggestion. It is a command from God. Thus, we should heed His command. His Son will reign from Jerusalem for a thousand years during the millennium so we should be praying for its tranquility.

CHRONOLOGY OF SIGNIFICANT EVENTS

The following chronological listing is provided in order to show the general flow of major events. Although the events recorded by divine revelation are anchored in history, it is not always possible to ascertain precisely when each event occurred. Where dates are less certain—particularly in the earlier centuries—approximate dates are given in order to maintain a frame of reference for added understanding.

The Beginning	Creation	750 B.C.	Uzziah and Jotham
The Beginning	Adam and Eve		in Judah
3000-2500 B.C.	Noah and the flood	740 B.C.	Isaiah begins ministry
2400 B.C.	Tower of Babel	735 B.C.	Micah's prophecy
2091 B.C.	Call of Abraham	723-721 B.C.	Israel falls to Assyria
2066 B.C.	Isaac born	701 B.C.	Sennacherib invades
2006 B.C.	Jacob and Esau born		Judah
1885 B.C.	Joseph in Egypt	650 B.C.	Nahum's prophecy
1876 B.C.	Israel settles in Egypt	639 B.C.	Josiah king of Judah
1526 B.C.	Moses born	635 B.C.	Zephaniah's prophecy
1446 B.C.	Ten plagues	626 B.C.	Jeremiah begins
1446 B.C.	Exodus from Egypt		Ministry
1445 B.C.	Ten Commandments	621 B.C.	Book of Law found
1445 B.C.	Tabernacle built	610 B.C.	Habakkuk's
1445 B.C.	Israelites numbered		Questioning
1445-1406 B.C.	Laws of Moses	604 B.C.	Daniel taken captive
1406 B.C.	Joshua crosses Jordan	601 B.C.	Nebuchadnezzar
1406-1400 B.C.	Promised land		has dream
	Conquered	597 B.C.	Great Deportation
1400-1380 B.C.	Period of the elders	592 B.C.	Ezekiel prophesies
1380 B.C.	Rise of the judges		in exile
1100 B.C.	Ruth the Moabite	588 B.C.	Jerusalem under
1090 B.C.	Samson the		siege
	Strongman	587 B.C.	Jeremiah confined
1050 B.C.	Samuel brings	586 B.C.	Babylonia captures
	transition		Jerusalem
1043 B.C.	Saul anointed king	586 B.C.	Jeremiah's
1004 B.C.	David becomes king		Lamentations
971 B.C.	Solomon made king	584 B.C.	Shadrach, Meshach,
967-960 B.C.	Solomon's temple		Abednego
	Built	572 B.C.	Ezekiel's temple
931 B.C.	The kingdom divides		vision
870 B.C.	Elijah the prophet	562 B.C.	Nebuchadnezzar's
852 B.C.	Elisha begins ministry		insanity

845 B.C.	Obadiah's prophecy	552 B.C.	Daniel's apocalyptic
835 B.C.	Joash in Judah		visions
825 B.C.	Prophecy of Joel	542 B.C.	Writing on the wall
781 B.C.	Jeroboam II in Israel	541 B.C.	Daniel in the lions'
775 B.C.	Jonah preaches in		den
	Nineveh	539 B.C.	Cyrus' decree
770 B.C.	Prophecy of Hosea	538 B.C.	Return to Jerusalem
765 B.C.	Prophecy of Amos	536 B.C.	Daniel's last vision
520 B.C.	Haggai and	A.D. 30	Holy Spirit on
	Zechariah		Pentecost
516 B.C.	New temple	A.D. 32-37	Stephen martyred
	Completed	A.D. 32-37	Saul (Paul) converted
480 B.C.	Esther and Mordecai	A.D. 34-38	Gentiles become
465 B.C.	Malachi's prophecy		Christians
458 B.C.	Ezra returns from	A.D. 45-47	Paul's first journey
	exile	A.D. 48-50	Jerusalem conference
444 B.C.	Nehemiah rebuilds	A.D. 50	Letter to Galatians
	wall	A.D. 50-51	Paul's second
425 B.C.	Dedication of the		journey
	wall	A.D. 51	Letters to
424 B.C.	Artaxerxes dies in		Thessalonians
	Persia	A.D. 53	Paul's third journey
330 B.C.	Persia falls to		begins
	Alexander	A.D. 55-57	Letters to the
323 B.C.	Rise of the Ptolemais		Corinthians
201 B.C.	Rome defeats	A.D. 58	Letter to the Romans
	Hannibal	A.D. 50-60	James' letter
190 B.C.	Antiochus Epiphanes	A.D. 58	Paul arrested
163-143 B.C.	Maccabean revolt	A.D. 58-60	Paul before Felix
135 B.C.	Jewish rule under		and Festus
	Hyrcanus	A.D. 60	Paul's voyage to
63 B.C.	Pompey invades		Rome
	Palestine	A.D. 61-63	Paul under house
47 B.C.	Caesar appoints		arrest
	Antipater	A.D. 61-63	Letter to Colossians
37 B.C.	Herod king of Judea	A.D. 61-63	Letter to Philemon
27 B.C.	Augustus Caesar,	A.D. 61-63	Letter Ephesians
	Pax Romana	A.D. 61-63	Letter to Philippians
6-4 B.C.	Messiah's Birth	A.D. 50-64	Peter's two letters
	Announced	A.D. 63-64	Paul's last travels
5-3 B.C.	Jesus is born	A.D. 63-64	First letter to

4-2 B.C.	Wise men worship		Timothy
	Jesus	A.D. 63-64	Letter to Titus
4-2 B.C.	Flight into Egypt	A.D. 64-67	Paul's final
3-1 B.C.	Return to Nazareth		imprisonment
A.D. 27	John the Baptist	A.D. 64-67	Second letter to
A.D. 27	Jesus begins ministry		Timothy
A.D. 28	Opposition to Jesus	A.D. 60-80	Jude's letter
A.D. 29	Feeding of 5000	A.D. 65-70	Writing to the
A.D. 30	Jesus' crucifixion		Hebrews
A.D. 30	Jesus' resurrection	A.D. 90-95	John's three letters
A.D. 30	Ascension of Jesus	A.D. 95-96	Revelation to John

Obtained from The DAILY BIBLE, Guideposts edition; Copyright 1984 by Harvest House Publishers

The Book of Genesis

Scripture Focus Chapters 1-50

Objective: To get an understanding of the creation, the fall, and the consequences mankind faces in the future.

Objective Breakdown:

1.	God Creates the World	Chapter 1:1-5
2.	The Sky Is Formed	Chapter 1:6-8
3.	The Land and Water Are Separated	Chapter 1:9-13
4.	The Stars and Planets Are Created	Chapter 1:14-19
5.	The Living Creatures Are Created	Chapter 1:20-25
6.	God Creates People –Male and Female	Chapter 1:26-31
7.	God Rests from His Work	Chapter 2:1-3
8.	A Second Account of Human Creation	Chapter 2:4-9
9.	God Places the Man in Eden	Chapter 2:10-17
10.	Woman Is Created and Marriage Is Established	Chapter 2:18-25
11.	Adam and Eve Disobey	Chapter 3:1-7
12.	Adam and Eve Hide from God	Chapter 3:8-13
13.	Curses from God	Chapter 3:14-19
14.	God Sends Adam and Eve Out of the Garden	Chapter 3:20-24
15.	Cain Kills Abel	Chapter 4:1-8
16.	Cain Is Cursed but Protected	Chapter 4:9-15
17.	Cain's Descendants	Chapter 4:16-24
18.	Eve Bears Another Son	Chapter 4:25-26
19.	From Adam to Seth	Chapter 5:1-5
20.	From Seth to Enoch	Chapter 5:6-20

The Twelve Tribes of the Children of Israel

Listed in Old Testament in order of Birth

1. Reuben
2. Simeon
3. Levi
4. Judah
5. Dan
6. Naphtali
7. Gad
8. Asher
9. Issachar
10. Zebulun
11. Joseph
12. Benjamin

Listed in New Testament as 144,000 Witnesses

1. Judah
2. Reuben
3. Gad
4. Asher
5. Naphtali
6. Manasseh
7. Simeon
8. Levi
9. Issachar
10. Zebulun
11. Joseph
12. Benjamin

Note: Dan was replaced by Manasseh in the New Testament (Revelation Chapter 7) most likely since they were the first to go into Idolatry. The Twelve tribes in the New Testament were witnesses, thus the tribe of Dan as idolaters were not good witnesses. However, In the Book of Ezekiel (Chapter 47) the Tribe of Dan was also given land as an inheritance in the Millennium period.

Lesson Plan 1

The Book of Genesis

Chapter 1

Objective: To give an understanding of our Origin and the Creation of our World.

Objective Breakdown:

1. Introduction

2. God Creates the World   Genesis 1:1-5

3. The Sky is Formed   Genesis 1:6-8

4. Land and Water Are Separated   Genesis 1:9-13

5. Stars and Planets Are Created   Genesis 1:14-19

6. Living Creatures Are Created   Genesis 1:20-25

7. God Creates People Male & Female   Genesis 1:26-31

Introduction:

The word Genesis means "origin." This title is closely related to the first words in the book, "In the beginning" (Genesis 1:1). Origination is the theme of Genesis, which relates the beginnings of:

1. The Universe (Genesis 1). The eternal God created time-and-space universe. Genesis tells us what happened. That means we can trust what happened. However, the book does not necessarily tell us how it happened. That means we can trust the account, even if we are still trying to understand the mechanics of what was involved.

2. The World (Genesis 1-2). Earth and its creatures were created by God. Thus, the Earth belongs to Him. God is sovereign over the world and accomplishes His purposes in it.

3. People (Genesis 1-2). We were created in the image of God. In its account of Eden, Genesis gives us a glimpse of what God originally intended for us, and how we were to relate to Him and to each other (see "made in His Image" Genesis 1: 26-30).

4. Work (Genesis 2:8-17). Humans were created to carry out God's work in the world. Genesis shows that the gift of work was given prior to the Fall.

5. The Family (Genesis 2-4). God created male and female and established the institution of the family. However, families in Genesis (as throughout the Bible) are not just under one roof but extend across generational and even geographical lines. This makes roots important. The families in Genesis established roots by such means of naming their children, digging wells, and naming them.

6. Evil and Sin (Genesis 3). When God made the world, He declared it to be "very good" (Genesis 1:31). But evil entered this perfect creation when Adam and Eve chose to disobey God (Genesis 3:1-7). Genesis reveals the tragic consequences of that choice, known as "the Fall" (see "What the Curse Tells us about God" at Genesis 3:14-19). It shows that sin gives people the terrible ability to misuse every good thing, brings shame and guilt, unleashes trouble in all human relationships, and eventually results in death.

7. Salvation and Redemption (Genesis 3, 12). God's ultimate response to sin was to overcome it through Jesus' death on the Cross. God's plan to rescue the world and its people began immediately after the Fall (see Genesis 3:14-19).

The time frame of Genesis divides neatly into three geographical settings:

(1) The Fertile Crescent (chapters 1-11)

(2) Israel (chapters 12-36)

(3) Egypt (chapters 37-50)

The settings of the first eleven chapters' changes rapidly as it spans more than two thousand years and fifteen hundred miles, and paints the majestic acts of Creation, the garden of Eden, the Noahic Flood, and the towering citadel of Babel.

The middle section of Genesis (chapters 12-36) rapidly funnels down from the broad brim of the two millennia spent in the Fertile Crescent to less than two hundred years into the little country of Canaan. Surrounded by the rampant immorality and idolatry of the Canaanites, the godliness of some of Abraham's descendants rapidly degenerated into gross immorality.

In the last fourteen chapters, God dramatically saves the small Israelite nation from extinction by transferring the "seventy souls" (Jacob's family) to Egypt so that they may grow and multiply.

Genesis spans more time than any other book in the Bible. In fact, it covers more time than sixty- five other books of the Bible put together. Utilizing the same three-fold division noted above. The following dates can be assigned:

A. 2,000 or more years, 4000-2090 B.C.   (Genesis 1-11)

    1. Creation, 4000 B.C. or earlier   (Genesis 1:1)

    2. Death of Terah, 2090B.C.   (Genesis 11:32)

B. 193 years, 2090-1897 B.C.   (Genesis 11:32)

    1. Death of Terah, 2090 B.C.   (Genesis 11:32)

    2. Joseph to Egypt, 1897 B.C.   (Genesis 37:2)

C. 93 years 1897-1804 B.C.   (Genesis 37-50)

    1. Joseph to Egypt, 1897 B.C.   (Genesis 37:2)

    2. Death of Joseph, 1804 B.C.   (Genesis 50:26)

2 Chronicles 7:14

If my people who are called by my name will humble themselves, and pray and seek my face, and turn from their wicked ways, then I will hear from heaven, and will forgive their sin and heal their land.

Psalm 122:6

Pray for the peace of Jerusalem: May they prosper that love thee.

Lesson Plan 2

The Book of Genesis

Chapter 2

Objective: To give an understanding of our Origin and the Creation of our World

Objective Breakdown:

1. Introduction

2. God Rests from His Work   Genesis 2:1-3

3. A Second Account of Human Creation   Genesis 2:4-9

4. God Places Man in Eden   Genesis 2:10-17

5. Woman Is Created and Marriage Is Established   Genesis 2:18-25

Introduction:

As the Book of Genesis is the "book of beginnings," it is not surprising that it presents the beginnings of three fundamental institutions of society: the family, the state, and the community of faith. The family is the primary institution established by God (Genesis 2:23). Before there were any nations, cities, or other human communities, there was a family. Logically and chronologically, family comes first.

But when the world's first family began to break down because of sin, God established the state. After Cain killed Abel (Genesis 4:8), his judgment and punishment came from God (Genesis 4:9-15). There was no court of law or other governmental authority to deal with the case. But when God placed a mark on Cain as a peace-bond, He gave a law to prevent other members of the family from killing Cain (Genesis 4:15). The rule of law was the beginning of the state. As in the case of the family, however, it was not long before sinful people began to corrupt the state as well (Genesis 4:23-24).

But a third institution can also trace its beginnings to the early days of the world. After righteous Abel was buried, Adam and Eve had another son named Seth. This man and his son Enosh were linked with an increasing tendency of people to "call on the name of the Lord" (Genesis 4:26). This kind of commitment to righteousness was preserved in Noah (Genesis 6:8), and continued later with Abraham, through whom God promised to "bless all families of the earth" (Genesis 12:1-3).

The promise to Abraham was fulfilled in Jesus Christ. He has brought the blessing of salvation from sin. He had also brought the blessings of a community based on common faith, known as the church

(Ephesians 2:14-22).

Ideally, these three institutions—the family, based on biological unity; the state, based on geographical unity; and the church, based on spiritual unity are intended to reinforce each other and be mutually dependent. Each one needs the other two to function in an effective Godly way.

2 Chronicles 7:14

If my people who are called by my name will humble themselves, and pray and seek my face, and turn from their wicked ways, then I will hear from heaven, and will forgive their sin and heal their land.

Psalm 122:6

Pray for the peace of Jerusalem: May they prosper that love thee.

Lesson Plan 3

The Book of Genesis

Chapter 3

Objective: To give an understanding of our origin, the creation of our world, and the fall of mankind

Objective Breakdown:

1. Introduction

2. Adam and Eve Disobey God   Genesis 3:1-7

3. Adam and Eve Hide from God   Genesis 3:6-13

4. Curses from God   Genesis 3:14-19

5. God Sends Adam and Eve Out of the Garden   Genesis 3:20-24

Introduction:

What the curse tells us about God. A snake is made to crawl on its belly (Genesis 3:14-15). A woman's birth pangs will be multiplied (Genesis 3:16). A man's work will turn into toil (Genesis 3:17-19). These curses would be a blast of vindictive retaliation from the mouth of someone less than God. But when God pronounces these words, He reveals something important about His character. He is a God of justice who takes seriously matters of right and wrong.

As sinful humans we may look the other way when moral issues are at stake. But God is Holy and Righteous. He does not wink at sin. In the Curse He shows us that sin has consequences. Those consequences are a sad outcome for what was declared no less than seven times to be a good creation (Genesis 1:4, 10, 12, 18, 21, 25, 31).

However, God did set limits on the effects of the Curse. For example, after Cain killed Abel, God marked him for protection and set up a deterrent against anyone killing him (Genesis 4:10-15). Later, Christ established final and absolute limit on sin's consequences by taking the curse and its penalties on Himself (Galatians 3:13). Eventually, after its purposes are complete, the Curse will be removed from the earth and lifted from God's people forever (Romans 8:18-25; Revelation 22:3).

God doesn't enjoy the Curse any more than those of us who suffer under it. In fact, from the outset, He knew that His judgment would ultimately fall on His Own Son (Ephesians 1:4-10). Yet His very character demanded that justice be satisfied.

We may grieve over the outcome of Adam and Eve's disobedience. But we can also be thankful that their sentence (and ours) was set by a God of Justice who is also a God of Love.

2 Chronicles 7:14

If My people who are called by My name will humble themselves, and pray and seek My face, and turn from their wicked ways, then I will hear from heaven, and will forgive their sin and heal their land.

Psalm 122:6

Pray for the peace of Jerusalem: May they prosper that love thee.

Note: As one commentary stated: "What does not agree with Scripture does not come from God!"

Lesson Plan 4

The Book of Genesis

Chapter 4

Objective: To give an understanding of our origin, the creation of our world, and the fall of mankind.

Objective Breakdown:

1. Introduction

2. Cain Kills Abel   Genesis 4:1-8

3. Cain Is Cursed but Protected   Genesis 4:9-15

4. Cain's Descendants   Genesis 4:16-24

5. Eve Bears Another Son   Genesis 4:25-26

Introduction:

The first couple (Adam and Eve) gained a terrible new knowledge by breaking the rules. After eating the fruit, Adam and Eve, who had previously known only good, now came to know evil (Genesis 3:22). One of the results of their newfound "knowledge" was that they were no longer unashamed of who they were as creatures made in God's image. Instead, they felt shame in their naked condition and immediately covered themselves (Genesis 3:7; see Genesis 2:25).

What a sad gain—self disrespect! And that was the beginning of humanity's troubles for acting on the serpent's deception. Soon the loss of respect for God's ways and for human dignity led to rampant evil in God's good creation (Genesis 6:5-6).

God's response to the intrusion of sin into His World and into the lives of His human coworkers was to put limits on the evil. He refused to let it go unchecked. Notice several restraints that God appears to have imposed:

(1) He provided clothing, perhaps to limit lust and sexual abuses (Genesis 3:21).

(2) He drove Adam and Eve out of the Garden, depriving them of access to the Tree of Life and thereby preventing them from living forever in a fallen condition (Genesis 3:22-24).

(3) He prevented Cain, the first murderer, from continuing to farm the earth and benefit from its systems as before, possibly to keep him from using the world's resources to wreak further havoc (Genesis 4:11-

12).

(4) He sent a flood to check the wickedness of Noah's generation, but preserved Noah and his family in order to repopulate the earth for an obedient people (Genesis 6:1-22).

(5) After the Flood He kept limits on what Noah and his descendants could eat and established a penalty for murder, and perhaps (by extension) for other abuses of people against people (Genesis 9:1-7).

(6) When evil once again gained momentum and the people of Babel worked together to establish their supremacy over the rest of the world, God frustrated their plans by confusing their languages and limited their ability to build a tower (Genesis 11:1-9).

God will not allow evil to completely undo what He loves and wishes to redeem. This is cause for hope in a world that cries with pain, violence, and immorality. Sometimes evil and wickedness seem out of control, but the Bible continually reminds us of God's continual and intervening love.

2 Chronicles 7:14

If My people who are called by My name will humble themselves, and pray and seek My face, and turn from their wicked ways, then I will hear from heaven, and will forgive their sin and heal their land.

Psalm 122:6

Pray for the peace of Jerusalem: May they prosper that love thee.

Lesson Plan 5

The Book of Genesis

Chapters 5, 6, 7, & 8

Objective: To give an understanding of our origin, the creation of our world, and the fall of mankind.

Objective Breakdown:

1. Introduction

2. From Adam to Seth   Genesis 5:1-5

3. From Seth to Enoch   Genesis 5:6:20

4. From Enoch to Noah   Genesis 5:21-32

5. Wickedness Brings Sorrow to God   Genesis 6:1-8

6. Noah Builds the Ark   Genesis 6:9-22

7. The Ark Is Entered   Genesis 7:1-16

8. The Flood   Genesis 7:17-24

9. The Flooding Stops   Genesis 8:1-5

10. The Water Recedes   Genesis 8:6-12

11. Noah and His Family Leave the Ark   Genesis 8:13-22

Introduction:

Was the Birth of a City Good or Bad? Many of us are familiar with Cain, the world's first murderer. But how many are aware that Cain was also the first known builder of a city, and that ironically, from this violent man's lineage came the signs of civilization?

Cain's motivation to find a settled town may have sprung from the punishment he received for killing his brother Abel. God placed a curse on Cain and forced him to wander the earth (Genesis 4:10-12). But he feared for his life, so God marked him to protect him from enemies (Genesis 4:13-15). Still, he wandered east of Eden ("Delight") to a land of Nod ("Wandering") - a stark contrast!

Perhaps to end his fugitive status, offset the effects of God's judgment, and maybe even recapture something of the original Eden, Cain founded Enoch. It is interesting that he names the settlement after his first-born son.

Although Cain's descendants brought much good into the world, though none of them escaped the effect of either Adam's fall or curse placed on Cain. Cain's lineage included Irad (meaning "uncertain"), Mehujael ("smitten of God") Methushael ("man of God") and Lamech (meaning "unknown"), Genesis 4:18.

The three sons born to Lamech included another nomad or wanderer, Jabal ("nomadic"), but also a musician, Jubal ("playing"), and a skilled craftsman, especially in metals, Tubal-Cain ("smith" or "striker," Genesis 4:20-22). Thus, from Cain came both pastoral and urban descendants, with the artist perhaps moving between both worlds. Their sister was named Naamah ("lovely" or "graceful"), reinforcing the idea that these were relatively cultured people.

Yet before long another tragedy struck the Cain family. Lamech came to his two wives one day and admitted to murder. But Lamech pled self-defense as his reason for killing a man (Genesis 4:23-24). He insisted that he had avenged ten times as much as his ancestor Cain, who committed premeditated murder. In this way Lamech took the law into his own hands, perpetuating the violence and the "Curse of Cain." So, in the end, Cain left a legacy of good as well as evil.

2 Chronicles 7:14

If My people who are called by My name will humble themselves, and pray and seek My face, and turn from their wicked ways, then I will hear from heaven, and will forgive their sin and heal their land.

Psalm 122:6

Pray for the peace of Jerusalem: May they prosper that love thee.

Lesson Plan 6

The Book of Genesis

Chapters 9, 10, & 11

Objective: To give an understanding of our origin, the creation of our world, and the fall of mankind.

Objective Breakdown:

1. Introduction

2. God's Covenant with Noah   Genesis 9:1-11

3. The sign of the Rainbow   Genesis 9:12-17

4. A Curse and Blessings on Noah's sons   Genesis 9:18-28

5. The Descendants of Japheth   Genesis 10:1-5

6. The Descendants of Ham   Genesis 10:6-20

7. The Descendants of Shem   Genesis 10:21-32

8. The Tower of Babel   Genesis 11:1-9

9. From Shem to Terah   Genesis 11:10-25

10. Terah Moves His Family to Haran   Genesis 11:26-32

Introduction:

Noah and the Nations. The story of the Flood, with waters that prevailed and greatly increased, covering even mountains of the earth (Genesis 7:10-24), recalls the creation account, in which waters were gathered together in one place as "Seas" to cover the earth (Genesis 1:9-10) a reassuring thought. Yet God used Noah to save both people and animals.

God promised never again to completely destroy the human race with flood (9:15)—a reassuring thought. The story of Noah assures us that all forms of life share a common fated in this world, as well as a common concern from God. After the Flood, He sent forth people and animals to repopulate the earth. In Genesis 10, we find Noah's sons producing families, cities-states, and even entire nations. Ultimately all the peoples of the world descend from one righteous man, Noah, (Genesis 9:1).

When we consider the awesome effects of a natural phenomenon, such as a volcano eruption or a powerful hurricane, to imagine the massive destruction that must have occurred as a result of a flood. Yet after the waters subsided, Noah led his family in worship and thanksgiving (Genesis 8:20). In doing so he reaffirmed for the next generation the value of life and the need for people to follow God's ways.

In response, the Lord resolved never again to curse the ground or destroy every living thing. He also promised to renew the cycle of the seasons (Genesis 8:21-22). Then God created a memorial or sign of His promise—a beautiful rainbow as a permanent reminder of His covenant with every living creature (Genesis 9:12-17).

2 Chronicles 7:14

If My people who are called by My name will humble themselves, and pray and seek My face, and turn from their wicked ways, then I will hear from heaven, and will forgive their sin and heal their land.

Psalm 122:6

Pray for the peace of Jerusalem: May they prosper that love thee.

If we don't speak out in support of Christian matters, we forfeit our authority given us by God!

Lesson Plan 7

The Book of Genesis

Chapters 12, 13, & 14

Objective: To give an understanding of our origin, the creation of our world, and the fall of mankind.

Objective Breakdown:

1. Introduction & Background

2. God calls Abram   Genesis 12:1-3

3. Abrams Journeys South   Genesis 12:4-9

4. Famine Drives Abram to Egypt   Genesis 12:10-20

5. Abram and Lot Separate   Genesis 13:1-13

6. God Promises the Land to Abram   Genesis 13:14-16

7. Melchizedek Blesses Abram   Genesis 13:17-18

8. The War of Kings   Genesis 14:1-12

9. Abram Rescues Lot   Genesis 14:13-16

10. Melchizedek Blesses Abram   Genesis 14:17-24

Introduction & Background:

A major turning point in the Book of Genesis occurs in chapter 11. For the second time, a new beginning is called for in the aftermath of God's judgment on a sinful humanity. Notice the two cycles of Genesis 1-11.

First cycle:

God creates the world and its people (Genesis 1:1-2:25).

Sin enters the world, and people become increasingly wicked; finally, God destroys them through the Flood (Genesis 3:1 through 7:24).

Second cycle:

God starts over again with Noah and his family (Genesis 9:1-19); Noah's descendants multiply (Genesis

10:1-32).

Eventually they resist God's mandate to "fill the earth" (Genesis 1:28; 9:7); finally, God's forces them to scatter abroad through the confusion of languages at Babel (Genesis 11:1-9)

What will God do next? Once again, He singles out one man and his family through whom to accomplish His purposes—the family of Abram (later renamed Abraham), a descendant of Shem (Genesis 11:10-26). This call of Abram narrows the focus of the Old Testament to one family, but through them all families of the earth are blessed (Genesis 12:3). Thus, God's long-term strategy to bring blessing on the entire world goes forward.

God's intention has always been to bring people into a right relationship with him. Ultimately that plan was fulfilled in Abram's descendant, Jesus Christ (Ephesians 1:3-4, 7-12; Colossians 1:26-27). Through Him, anyone can start over again in knowing God and living as God originally intended (2 Corinthians 5:17).

We see the Tower of Babel in Genesis chapter 11, and we also see that the whole earth had one language and one speech, and they (the inhabitants) said let us build a city for ourselves and a tower whose top is in the heavens. Let us make a name for ourselves lest we be scattered abroad over the face of the whole earth."

The Lord came down from Heaven to see the city and the tower which the sons of men had built. And the Lord said, "Indeed the people are one and they all have one language, and this is what they begin to do; now nothing that they propose to do will be withheld from them. Let us go down there and confuse their language, that they may not understand one another's speech." So, the Lord scattered them abroad from over the face of all the earth, and they ceased building the city. Therefore, its name is called Babel (Genesis 11:1-9).

Babel. The name means "gate of God," also "confusion."

Elsewhere in the Old Testament the name is rendered as Babylon.

Some background:

Founded by Nimrod, the mighty hunter (Genesis 10:10).

Site of the Tower of Babel (11:1-9), which may have been similar to the ziggurats common to the Sumerians, Babylonians and Assyrians, lofty structures resembling pyramids, built in successive stages with an outside staircase and a religious shrine at the top.

Became a world-renowned city under Hammurabi (about 1728-1686 B.C.), who made the city the home of Marduk, chief god in a pantheon of 1300 deities. Assumed empire status under Chaldean kings (625-539), especially Nebuchadnezzar (605-563 B.C.).

Well-known for its wealth, commercial trade, and royal splendor. The city walls were so thick that chariots could pass each other on them going in opposite directions. Private homes were also large, some with as many as 26 rooms and several courtyards.

Babel or Babylon was also noted for its development of mythology, philosophy, medicine, mathematics, and astronomy.

2 Chronicles 7:14

If My people who are called by My name will humble themselves, and pray and seek My face, and turn from their wicked ways, then I will hear from heaven, and will forgive their sin and heal their land.

Psalm 122:6

Pray for the peace of Jerusalem: May they prosper that love thee.

Note: If we don't speak out in support of Christian matters, we will forfeit our authority given to us by God!

Lesson Plan 8

The Book of Genesis

Chapters 15, 16, & 17

Objective: To give an understanding of our origin, the creation of our world, and the fall of mankind.

Objective Breakdown:

1. Introduction

2. God Promises Descendants to Abram   Genesis 15:1-11

3. God Makes a Covenant with Abram   Genesis 15:12-21

4. Sarai Gives Hagar to Abram   Genesis 16:1-6

5. God Makes a Promise to Hagar   Genesis 16:7-14

6. Ishmael Is Born to Hagar   Genesis 16:15-16

7. Abram Is Renamed Abraham   Genesis 17:1-8

8. The Sign of Circumcision   Genesis 17:9-14

9. Sarai, Renamed Sarah, Will Bear a Son   Genesis 17:15-27

Introduction:

God's Purpose for the Amorites. In making promises to Abraham and foretelling his descendants' destiny, God was mindful to mention the Amorites (Genesis 15:16). The Amorites were a nomadic, barbarous people living in Canaan (Genesis 10:16; Deuteronomy 1:27), or what is now Palestine, western Saudi Arabia, and southern Syria. Shortly before 2000 B.C., their ancestors migrated from the West (Amorites means "westerners") and overran the kingdoms and cities of the Fertile Crescent as far as Mesopotamia. They dominated the region until about 1850 B.C., when they were brought under Babylonian control.

Throughout Old Testament times, Amorites remained in Syria, Phoenicia, and the desert regions of the South (Joshua 13:4). A significant number, however, settled in Palestine (Judges 11:19-22). They spoke a language that closely related to Canaanite and Hebrew. The Old Testament frequently uses "Amorites as a synonym for Canaanites in general, as is the case here in Genesis 15. Canaan, the grandson of Noah, was the father of the Amorites (Genesis 10:16).

God allowed the Amorites, or Canaanites, to live in the Promised Land for many years despite their idolatry and immorality. But His patience was not limitless. He would soon cast them out, as His promise to Abraham indicated. Many Amorites cities would be conquered under Joshua. In fact, the first Israelite victories came against the Amorite kings Sihon and Og, who ruled much of the Promised Land east of the Jordan River (Joshua 12:1-6). The survivors became servants to the Israelites (1 Kings 9:20-21). Thus, Noah's curse of Canaan was fulfilled (Genesis 9:25-27) as well as God's promise to Abraham (Genesis 15:16).

The Lord's message here indicates that He was guiding Israel and the Amorites toward a goal. God was fitting the nations of the ancient Near East into His master plan.

2 Chronicles 7:14

If My people who are called by My name will humble themselves, and pray and seek My face, and turn from their wicked ways, then I will hear from heaven, and will forgive their sin and heal their land.

Psalm 122:6

Pray for the peace of Jerusalem: May they prosper that love thee.

Note: If we don't speak out in support of Christian matters, we will forfeit our authority given to us by God!! We as the "Church" and "Ambassadors" should not hide.

We should "Shine" because there can be beautiful miracles in our mouth. Amen!

Lesson Plan 9

The Book of Genesis

Chapters 18 & 19

Objective: To give an understanding of our origin, the creation of our world, and the fall of mankind.

Objective Breakdown:

1. Introduction
2. Abraham Receives Visitors   Genesis 18:1-8
3. Sarah learns She Will Conceive   Genesis 18:9-15
4. God Considers Sodom and Gomorrah   Genesis 18:16-21
5. Abraham Intercedes for Sodom   Genesis 18:22-33
6. Angels Come to Lot in Sodom   Genesis 19:1-11
7. Lot Flees from Sodom   Genesis 19:12-22
8. Sodom and Gomorrah Are Destroyed   Genesis 19:23-26
9. Abraham Surveys the Destruction   Genesis 19:27-29
10. Lot Lies with His Daughters   Genesis 19:30-38

Introduction:

Throughout Scripture and in countless extra biblical works, Sodom and Gomorrah and other cities of the plain (Genesis 13:12) stand as a symbol of divine judgment for collective wickedness. What was once a well-watered, fertile region is today barren, full of tar pits, mounds of asphalt, and marsh. These ill-fated cities remind us that wickedness will not go unpunished. They also show that God not only judges sinful individuals, such as Lot's wife (Genesis 19:26), but also entire cities and their surroundings.

However, the story is not all bad news. After the tragic end of Sodom and Gomorrah, "God remembered Abraham" (Genesis 19:29). When we remember the patriarch's righteous example, several lessons of the story become clear: Prayer makes a difference. Abraham shows us that it is legitimate to pray for cities, as he did (Genesis 18:22-33). We may not always be able to go to a city, but we can still pray for it. Abraham prayed more for a place than for individual people. He prayed persistently for an entire city, believing that nothing was too hard for the Lord (Genesis 18:14). Moreover, he prayed for justice in the city as well as for its peace and salvation. His example challenges us to ask are we praying for cities or countries today? If so, what are we asking God to do? Save the city or judge it?

Pride goes before a fall. Sodom was destroyed not only because of sexual sin (Genesis 19:1-17, Jude 7), but because it had pride and a surplus of wealth yet failed to care for its poor and needy (Ezekiel 16:48-50). Its example challenges us: What are we doing with the resources God has put under our control?

2 Chronicles 7:14

If My people who are called by My name will humble themselves, and pray and seek My face, and turn from their wicked ways, then I will hear from heaven, and will forgive their sin and heal their land.

Psalm 122:6

Pray for the peace of Jerusalem: May they prosper that love thee.

Note: If we don't speak out in support of Christian matters or we will forfeit our authority given to us by God!! We as the "Church" and "Ambassadors" should not hide. We should "Shine" because there can be beautiful miracles in your mouth. Amen!

Lesson Plan 10

The Book of Genesis

Chapters 20, 21, & 22

Objective: To give an understanding of our origin, the creation of our world, and the fall of mankind.

Objective Breakdown:

1. Introduction

2. Abraham Deceives Abimelech   Genesis 20:1-7

3. Abimelech's Situation Is Resolved   Genesis 20:8-18

4. Isaac Is Born to Sarah   Genesis 21:1-8

5. Hagar and Ishmael Are Sent Away   Genesis 21:9-21

6. Abraham's Well at Beersheba   Genesis 21:22-34

7. Abraham and Isaac Journey to Moriah   Genesis 22:1-8

8. Abraham Prepares to Sacrifice Isaac   Genesis 22:9-10

9. God Intervenes to Spare Isaac   Genesis 22:11-19

10. Children of Abraham's Brother   Genesis 22:20-24

Introduction:

It seems incredible that God would tell Abraham to "take your son, only son Isaac, whom you love," and offer him up as a sacrifice (Genesis 22:2). What sort of God would ask such a thing? What sort of God would test a man's faith with such a weighty request? It was severe test of Abraham's faith. Most of us would have failed the test. We might even reject God as cruel and blood thirsty. But Abraham believed God. Though the sacrifice of Isaac seemed to go against God's promise of an heir, Abraham believed God would still fulfill His Word, even if it required Him to raise Isaac from the dead (Romans 4:17).

The request was also a harsh lesson that all of life comes from and belongs to God (Genesis 2:7; Job 27:3; 33:4). In essence life is merely a loan to us, both as parents and children. God can ask for its return at any time. So, in that respect, the request to slay Isaac was similar to the difficult period that Abram and Sarai endured as they waited for the birth of this very son (Genesis 18:1-15;21: 1-7). Their lives and the lives of any children they might have were in the hands of God.

He is also the God of Wisdom. He sometimes makes what to us may seem like strange requests, but if like Abraham we will believe and obey, He will reward our faith with His goodness and righteousness.

Words to Live By:

Ephesians 4:29, Let not any filthy word go out of your mouth, but if any *is* good to building up *in respect of* need, that it may give grace to the ones hearing.

Ephesians 4:30, And do not grieve the Holy Spirit of God, by whom you are sealed until *the* day of redemption.

Ephesians 4:31, Let all bitterness and wrath and anger and tumult and evil speaking be put away from you, with all malice.

Ephesians 4:32, And be kind to one another, tenderhearted, forgiving one another, even as God for Christ's sake has forgiven you.

2 Chronicles 7:14

If my people who are called by my name will humble themselves, and pray and seek my face, and turn from their wicked ways, then I will hear from heaven, and will forgive their sin and heal their land.

Psalm 122:6

Pray for the peace of Jerusalem: May they prosper that love thee.

Note: If we don't speak out in support of Christian matters or we will forfeit our authority given to us by God!! We as the "Church" and "Ambassadors" should not hide. We should "Shine" because there can be beautiful miracles in your mouth. Amen!

Lesson Plan 11

The Book of Genesis

Chapters 23, 24, & 25

Objective: To give an understanding of our origin, the creation of our world, and the fall of mankind.

Objective Breakdown:

1. Introduction

2. Sarah Dies   Genesis 23:1-9

3. Abraham Buys a Burial Site   Genesis 23:10-20

4. Abraham Commissions His Servant   Genesis 24:1-9

5. The Servant Seeks a Bride for Isaac   Genesis 24:10-28

6. The Servant Negotiates with Laban   Genesis 24:29-49

7. Rebekah Is Given to Be Isaac's Bride   Genesis 24:50-60

8. Isaac and Rebekah Are Married   Genesis 24:61-67

9. Abraham's Legacy and Death   Genesis 25:1-11

10. The Descendants of Ishmael   Genesis 25:12-18

11. Esau and Jacob Are Born to Rebekah   Genesis 25:19-26

12. Esau Sells His Birthright to Jacob   Genesis 25:27-34

Introduction:

Hebron. Burial place of the Patriarchs. One of the oldest cities of Palestine, occupied since at least 3000 B.C., at the southern end of the Judean hill country, 23 miles south of Jerusalem. Originally known as Kirjath Arba or four cities (Genesis 23:2; Joshua 20:7). Hebron ("league or "confederacy") implied military importance and historic connections. Settled by the Hittites (sons of Heth" Genesis 23:7-8) and the Amorites. Hebron is situated in the valley of Eschol ("cluster of grapes") which boasted vineyards, orchards, olive groves and several wells and pools of water. It is also a site of numerous biblical events and highly symbolic for the Israelites.

Abraham purchased of the field of Ephron was a public transaction, as is evident from the phrase, "before all who went in at the gate of his city" (Genesis 23:18). In the Middle East, a city's gates were where much of its civic business was conducted.

Words to Live By:

Ephesians 4:29, Let not any filthy word go out of your mouth, but if any *is* good to building up *in respect of* need, that it may give grace to the ones hearing.

Ephesians 4:30, And do not grieve the Holy Spirit of God, by whom you are sealed until *the* day of redemption.

Ephesians 4:31, Let all bitterness and wrath and anger and tumult and evil speaking be put away from you, with all malice.

Ephesians 4:32, And be kind to one another, tenderhearted, forgiving one another, even as God for Christ's sake has forgiven you.

2 Chronicles 7:14

If my people who are called by my name will humble themselves, and pray and seek my face, and turn from their wicked ways, then I will hear from heaven, and will forgive their sin and heal their land.

Psalm 122:6

Pray for the peace of Jerusalem: May they prosper that love thee.

Note: If we don't speak out in support of Christian matters, we will forfeit our authority given to us by God!! We as the "Church" and "Ambassadors" should not hide. We should "Shine" because there can be beautiful miracles in our mouth. Amen!

Lesson Plan 12

The Book of Genesis

Chapters 26, 27, & 28

Objective: To give an understanding of our origin, the creation of our world, and the fall of mankind

Objective Breakdown:

1. Introduction

2. Isaac Survives a Famine Through Deception   Genesis 26:1-11

3. Isaac Prospers in the Land   Genesis 26:12-16

4. Isaac Digs a Well   Genesis 26:17-25

5. Isaac and Abimelech Make a Treaty   Genesis 26:26-33

6. Esau's Wives   Genesis 26:34-35

7. Isaac Plans to Bless Esau   Genesis 27:1-4

8. Rebekah Plots to Get Jacob Blessed   Genesis 27:5-17

9. Jacob Deceives His Father   Genesis 27:18-29

10. Esau Discovers Jacob's Treachery   Genesis 27:30-46

11. Isaac Sends Jacob to Get a Wife   Genesis 28:1-5

12. Esau Takes an Ishmaelite Wife   Genesis 28:6-9

13. Jacob Dreams and Hears God's Promise   Genesis 28:10-17

14. Jacob Names the Place Bethel   Genesis 28:18-22

Introduction:

You can't unravel sin. Esau had been cheated by schemes of his mother and brother (Genesis 27:1-39). When he realized what had been done to him, he was outraged—some would say justifiably so (Genesis 27:34-36). Yet how did he deal with his anger and hurt? He nursed it into a grudge and determined to retaliate by killing his brother after his father was dead (Genesis 30:41). See Hebrews 12:16-17.

However, Esau failed to take into account the complicity of his mother. When she learned of Esau's plan, she helped Jacob's escape. And rather than confront the deception that she and Jacob had committed, and apologize to Esau, she merely suggested that time would heal all wounds (Genesis 30:42-45).

The patterns of trickery and manipulation continued into the next generation. Jacob's sons committed such evils as destroying an entire city out of revenge (Genesis 34:1-31) and selling one of their brothers into slavery and then lying to their father about what happened (Genesis 37:23-28, 31-35). Apparently, they had learned from their grandfather and grandmother that the way to deal with sin was not to acknowledge it but hide it.

The conflict between Esau and Jacob (Genesis 27:41) was eventually patched up (Genesis 33:4, 10-11). Nevertheless, the two brothers set a precedent for their descendants that grew into centuries-long feud between the Edomites and the Israelites.

Words to Live By:

Ephesians 4:29, Let not any filthy word go out of your mouth, but if any *is* good to building up *in respect of* need, that it may give grace to the ones hearing.

Ephesians 4:30, And do not grieve the Holy Spirit of God, by whom you are sealed until *the* day of redemption.

Ephesians 4:31, Let all bitterness and wrath and anger and tumult and evil speaking be put away from you, with all malice.

Ephesians 4:32, And be kind to one another, tenderhearted, forgiving one another, even as God for Christ's sake has forgiven you.

2 Chronicles 7:14

If my people who are called by my name will humble themselves, and pray and seek my face, and turn from their wicked ways, then I will hear from heaven, and will forgive their sin and heal their land.

Psalm 122:6

Pray for the peace of Jerusalem: May they prosper that love thee.

Note: If we don't speak out in support of Christian matters, we will forfeit our authority given to us by God!! We as the "Church" and "Ambassadors" should not hide. We should "Shine" because there can be beautiful miracles in our mouth. Amen!

Lesson Plan 13

The Book of Genesis

Chapters 29 & 30

Objective: To give an understanding of our origin, the creation of our world, and the fall of mankind.

Objective Breakdown:

1. Introduction

2. Jacob Meets Rachel   Genesis 29:1-12

3. Laban Deceives Jacob   Genesis 29:13-30

4. Four Sons Are Born to Leah   Genesis 29:31-35

5. Rachel Gives Bilhah to Jacob   Genesis 30:1-8

6. Leah Gives Zilpah to Jacob   Genesis 30:9-13

7. More Sons Are Born to Leah   Genesis 30:14-21

8. Joseph is Born to Rachel   Genesis 30:22-24

9. Jacob Seeks Release from Service   Genesis 30:25-36

10. Jacob's Flocks Increase   Genesis 30:37-43

Introduction:

Bethel is the site of "Jacobs Ladder." Wherever God touches the world, that place becomes a sacred place. That was the experience of Jacob. Waking from a dream in which he saw and heard the Lord, he cried, "surely the LORD is in this place" (Genesis 28:16). It was sacred because God had been there. Likewise, Abraham had previously built an altar near Bethel to remember that God was very present to him there (Genesis 13:3-4).

This Old Testament concept of sacred place takes on a greater meaning in the New Testament. There we read that God Himself "became flesh and dwelt among us" (John 1:14). He not only touched the Earth, He came to live on it for a while and in the person of Jesus. Jesus alluded to this Bethel-like visitation as He spoke with Nathanael, a man who He recruited as one of His followers. Just as Jacob had seen angels ascending and descending on a ladder between heaven and earth, so Nathanael would see "heaven open, and the angels of God ascending and descending upon the Son of Man" (John 1:51).

Jesus' words to Nathanael had been preliminary fulfilled at Jesus' Baptism, when the Spirit descended upon Him like a dove (Matthew 3:16). Wherever Jesus went, God went. Whatever place Jesus visited became Bethel, or a sacred place. But the idea of a sacred place does not end there. Jesus told His followers, including believers today, that He would send His Spirit, not only to be with them, but live in them (John 14:16-17). In other words, the believers have become the "House of God," the place where God Lives (see 1 Corinthians 6:19-20). Where we go, God goes. As Christ lives in us and we live in the world, every place we go is a place where God can do His work.

Words to Live By:

Ephesians 4:29, Let not any filthy word go out of your mouth, but if any *is* good to building up *in respect of* need, that it may give grace to the ones hearing.

Ephesians 4:30, And do not grieve the Holy Spirit of God, by whom you are sealed until *the* day of redemption.

Ephesians 4:31, Let all bitterness and wrath and anger and tumult and evil speaking be put away from you, with all malice.

Ephesians 4:32, And be kind to one another, tenderhearted, forgiving one another, even as God for Christ's sake has forgiven you.

2 Chronicles 7:14

If my people who are called by my name will humble themselves, and pray, and seek my face, and turn from their wicked ways, then I will hear from heaven, and will forgive their sin and heal their land.

Psalm 122:6

Pray for the peace of Jerusalem: May they prosper that love thee.

Note: If we don't speak out in support of Christian matters, we will forfeit our authority given to us by God!! We as the "Church" and "Ambassadors" should not hide. We should "Shine" because there can be beautiful miracles in our mouth. Amen!

Lesson Plan 14

The Book of Genesis

Chapters 31, 32, & 33

Objective: To give an understanding of our origin, the creation of our world, and the fall of mankind.

Objective Breakdown:

1. Introduction
2. Jacob Decides to Return to Canaan   Genesis 31:1-16
3. Jacob and His Wives Leave Secretly   Genesis 31:17-21
4. Laban's Pursuit   Genesis 31:22-32
5. Laban Searches for His Idols   Genesis 31:33-35
6. Jacob Defends His Honor   Genesis 31:36-42
7. Jacob and Laban Make a Treaty   Genesis 31:43-55
8. Jacob Prepares to Meet Esau   Genesis 32:1-12
9. Jacob Arranges Gifts for Esau   Genesis 32:13-21
10. Jacob Wrestles with God   Genesis 32:22-32
11. Esau Welcomes His Brother   Genesis 33:1-17
12. Jacob Arrives Safely in Canaan   Genesis 33:18-20

Introduction:

Sometimes good happens to us when we least expect it. Sometimes we receive far more good than we deserve.

When Jacob learned that Esau was approaching (Genesis 32:6), he was terrified. Here was the older twin brother—the brother he and his mother had cheated out of rightful portion of the family inheritance (Genesis 27:1-29) coming toward him with 400 men. Jacob assumed the worst. He cried out to God for mercy and deliverance (Genesis,32:9-12) and sent his own extended family and his possessions to his brother's "welcoming committee" (Genesis 32:13-23).

Yet to Jacob's surprise, Esau ran to him, embraced him, kissed him, and wept (Genesis 33:4). This kind of grace was completely unexpected. It proved disarming to Jacob, and he could only respond by pressing his gifts on Esau, perhaps a small remuneration for the lost inheritance (Genesis 33:8-11).

Words to Live By:

Ephesians 4:29, Let not any filthy word go out of your mouth, but if any *is* good to building up *in respect of* need, that it may give grace to the ones hearing.

Ephesians 4:30, And do not grieve the Holy Spirit of God, by whom you are sealed until *the* day of redemption.

Ephesians 4:31, Let all bitterness and wrath and anger and tumult and evil speaking be put away from you, with all malice.

Ephesians 4:32, And be kind to one another, tenderhearted, forgiving one another, even as God for Christ's sake has forgiven you.

2 Chronicles 7:14

If My people who are called by My name will humble themselves, and pray, and seek my face, and turn from their wicked ways, then I will hear from heaven, and will forgive their sin and heal their land.

Psalm 122:6

Pray for the peace of Jerusalem: May they prosper that love thee.

Note: If we don't speak out in support of Christian matters, we will forfeit our authority given to us by God!! We as the "Church" and "Ambassadors" should not hide. We should "Shine" because there can be beautiful miracles in our mouth. Amen!

Lesson Plan 15

The Book of Genesis

Chapters 34, 35, & 36

Objective: To give an understanding of our origin, the creation of our world, and the fall of mankind.

Objective Breakdown:

1. Introduction

2. Shechem Violates Dinah   Genesis 34:1-4

3. The Families Discuss a Settlement   Genesis 34:5-12

4. Jacob's Sons Plot Revenge   Genesis 34:13-24

5. Hamor and His Sons Are Killed   Genesis 34:25-35

6. Jacob Prepares to Go to Bethel   Genesis 35:1-4

7. The Journey to Bethel   Genesis 35:5-8

8. Jacob is Renamed Israel   Genesis 35:9-15

9. Rachel Dies Bearing Benjamin   Genesis 35:16-20

10. Reuben Sins Against Israel   Genesis 35:21-22

11. The Sons of Jacob   Genesis 35:23-26

12. Isaac Dies   Genesis 35:27-29

13. The Family of Esau   Genesis 36:1-5

14. Esau Relocates to Edom   Genesis 36:6-8

15. Esau's Descendants   Genesis 36:9-30

16. Rulers in Edom   Genesis 36:31-43

Introduction:

Unbridled sexual desire. Personal pleasure makes a good slave but a poor master. When our primary focus is on self-gratification the results can be destructive, not only for us, but for everyone around us

(Titus 3:3; James 4:1-4). Scripture makes it clear that living for our own pleasures is both unacceptable and unhealthy. The outcome of Shechem (Genesis 34:2) illustrates this point. When young Shechem saw the beautiful girl Dinah, he allowed his lust to rule his behavior, and raped her, like an animal, he let his hormones run his life, so sexual gratification became more important than Dinah's dignity as a person. By contrast, Scripture challenges God's people to exercise control over their sexuality (1Thessalonians 4:3-4).

Words to Live By:

Ephesians 4:29, Let not any filthy word go out of your mouth, but what is good for necessary

edification, that it may impart grace to the hearers

Ephesians 4:30, And do not grieve the Holy Spirit of God, by whom you are sealed until *the* day of redemption.

Ephesians 4:31, Let all bitterness and wrath and anger and tumult and evil speaking be put away from you, with all malice.

Ephesians 4:32, And be kind to one another, tenderhearted, forgiving one another, even as God for Christ's sake has forgiven you.

2 Chronicles 7:14

If My people who are called by My name will humble themselves, and pray, and seek My face, and turn from their wicked ways, then I will hear from heaven, and will forgive their sin and heal their land.

Psalm 122:6

Pray for the peace of Jerusalem: May they prosper that love thee.

Note: If we don't speak out in support of Christian matters, we will forfeit our authority given to us by God!! We as the "Church" and "Ambassadors" should not hide. We should "Shine" because there can be beautiful miracles in our mouth. Amen!

Lesson Plan 16

The Book of Genesis

Chapters 37, 38, & 39

Objective: To give an understanding of our origin, the creation of our world, and the fall of mankind

Objective Breakdown:

1. Introduction

2. Israel Favors Joseph   Genesis 37:1-4

3. Joseph's Brothers Resent His Dream   Genesis 37:5-11

4. Joseph Goes to Observe His Brothers   Genesis 37:12-17

5. Joseph's Brothers Conspire   Genesis 37:18-24

6. Joseph Is Sold into Slavery   Genesis 37:25-36

7. Judah Fathers Three Sons   Genesis 38:1-5

8. Tamar Is Left a Widow   Genesis 38:6-11

9. Tamar Poses as a Prostitute   Genesis 38:12-19

10. Tamaar Bears Judah Two Sons   Genesis 38:20-30

11. Potiphar Favors Joseph   Genesis 39:1-6

12. Potiphar's Wife Tries to Seduce Joseph   Genesis 39:7-18

13. Joseph Is Put in Prison   Genesis 39:19-23

Introduction:

Excellence is good anywhere. Many of us will do our best as long as circumstances rewards our efforts. But what happens if we work for a less than ideal boss, or if our company seems satisfied with mediocrity, or we are treated unjustly? Are we as willing to pursue excellence when things aren't going our way?

Joseph is an encouragement to anyone who lives and labor in a less than perfect world. Unjustly jailed because he spurned the advances of his boss's wife (Genesis 39:6-18), he soon became a warden assistant in the prison to which he was sent (Genesis 39:21-23). His proven ability was so strong that his keepers did not even bother to check his work. They trusted him implicitly.

Joseph maintained such a pursuit of excellence applying himself to the task at hand rather than focusing on how he had been framed. As a slave he probably had no means of appeal anyway. So, he turned hardship of his life into opportunities for diligence and focus.

God honored this attitude with achievements that would be considered amazing under any circumstances. Ultimately, Joseph the minority slave rose to power and status as the nation's second in command (Genesis 41:41-45). So, if you honor God in your work and pursue an attitude of excellence, will God reward you with power and prestige? There is no guarantee of that; however, Scripture does make a promise and a strong recommendation: "Whatever you do, do it heartily, as to the Lord and not to men, knowing that from the Lord you will receive the reward of inheritance" (Colossians 3:23-24). God will reward you according to how you do your work. He challenges you to excellence!

Words to Live By:

Ephesians 4:29, Let not any filthy word go out of your mouth, but what is good for necessary edification, that it may impart grace to the hearers.

Ephesians 4:30, And do not grieve the Holy Spirit of God, by whom you are sealed until *the* day of redemption.

Ephesians 4:31, Let all bitterness and wrath and anger and tumult and evil speaking be put away from you, with all malice.

Ephesians 4:32, And be kind to one another, tenderhearted, forgiving one another, even as God for Christ's sake has forgiven you.

2 Chronicles 7:14

If my people who are called by my name will humble themselves, and pray, and seek my face, and turn from their wicked ways, then I will hear from heaven, and will forgive their sin and heal their land.

Psalm 122:6

Pray for the peace of Jerusalem: May they prosper that love thee.

Note: If we don't speak out in support of Christian matters, we will forfeit our authority given to us by God!! We as the "Church" and "Ambassadors" should not hide. We should "Shine" because there can be beautiful miracles in our mouth. Amen!

Some Thoughts on Our Future with God

Five Pictures of God's Ultimate World Order:

1. It Will Be a Time of Peace

One Thousand years of Peace (Psalm 72:7).

Nations will not make war against each other (Micah 4:3).

2. It Will Be a Time of Prosperity

The wilderness and waste lands shall bloom abundantly; there will be streams in the desert (Isaiah 35:1-2).

3. It Will be a Time of Purity

Justice will be pure, no conflicting or competing ideologies (Zechariah 13:2).

4. It Will Be a Time of Prolonged Life

Persons who are 100 years old will be considered young (Isaiah 65:20).

There will be rapid multiplication of the human race. (Jeremiah 30:19b).

5. It Will Be a Time of Personal Joy

God will multiply joy among the Nations (Isaiah 9:3).

The whole Earth will break forth in singing (Isaiah 14:7).

Tears will be wiped away (Isaiah 25:8-9).

New songs will be sung (Isaiah 42:10-12).

WOW!!

Lesson Plan 17

The Book of Genesis

Chapters 40, 41, & 42

Objective: To give an understanding of our origin, the creation of our world, and the fall of mankind.

Objective Breakdown:

1. Introduction

2. Joseph Meets a Butler and a Baker   Genesis 40:1-8

3. The Butler's Dream   Genesis 40:9-15

4. The Baker's Dream   Genesis 40:16-23

5. Pharaoh Is Troubled by His Dreams   Genesis 41:1-8

6. The Butler Remembers Joseph   Genesis 41:9-13

7. Joseph is Brought to Pharaoh   Genesis 41:14-24

8. Joseph Interprets the Dreams   Genesis 41:25-32

9. Joseph Recommends a Plan   Genesis 41:33-36

10. Pharaoh Makes Joseph Prime Minister   Genesis 41:37-45

11. Joseph Oversees Grain Storage   Genesis 41:46-49

12. Joseph Fathers Two Sons   Genesis 41:50-52

13. Famine Begins   Genesis 41:53-57

14. Joseph's Brothers Come to Egypt   Genesis 42:1-5

15. The Brothers Do Not Recognize Joseph   Genesis 42:6-17

16. Joseph Tests His Brothers   Genesis 42:18-24

17. The Brothers' Money Is Refunded   Genesis 42:25-28

18. Jacob Refuses to Send Benjamin   Genesis 42:29-38

Introduction:

The Pharaoh. The man identified as Pharaoh (Genesis 41:1) was probably one of the rulers in what is called the Hyksos period of Egyptian history (1786-1570 B.C.). Pharaoh ("great house") was not a name, but a title given to Egyptian Kings. We do not know the name of the pharaoh under whom Joseph served or exactly when he ruled.

However, we do know that the Hyksos ("rulers of foreign lands") were semitic-Asiatics who wrestle control from earlier pharaohs, most likely through a coup. The Hyksos did not interfere with Egyptian culture. However, they ruled in a manner that was far more benevolent to outsiders than either their predecessors or their successors, such as the oppressive pharaoh of Moses' day. They are known for having introduced the chariot and the horse, the compound bow, battle axes, and advanced fortification techniques.

The main link between the various pharaohs was not the bloodline but religious tradition. The pharaoh was considered a god among men and a man among gods, performing a priestly and magisterial role. Temples, statues, and pyramid tombs built in the rulers' honor attest to the strong religious link that the Egyptians believed between the dead kings, known as the Royal Ancestors, and gods as they supposedly worked together for the welfare of the Egyptians.

Words to Live By:

Ephesians 4:29, Let not any filthy word go out of your mouth, but what is good for necessary edification, that it may impart grace to the hearers.

Ephesians 4:30, And do not grieve the Holy Spirit of God, by whom you are sealed until *the* day of redemption.

Ephesians 4:31, Let all bitterness and wrath and anger and tumult and evil speaking be put away from you, with all malice.

Ephesians 4:32, And be kind to one another, tenderhearted, forgiving one another, even as God for Christ's sake has forgiven you.

2 Chronicles 7:14

If my people who are called by my name will humble themselves, and pray, and seek my face, and turn from their wicked ways, then I will hear from heaven, and will forgive their sin and heal their land.

Psalm 122:6

Pray for the peace of Jerusalem: May they prosper that love thee.

Note: If we don't speak out in support of Christian matters, we will forfeit our authority given to us by

God!! We as the "Church" and "Ambassadors" should not hide. We should "Shine" because there can be beautiful miracles in our mouth. Amen!

Lesson Plan 18

The Book of Genesis

Chapters 43, 44, & 45

Objective: To give an understanding of our origin, the creation of our world, and the fall of mankind.

Objective Breakdown:

1. Introduction

2. The Famine Grows Worse   Genesis 43:1-10

3. Jacob Agrees to Let Benjamin Go   Genesis 43:11-14

4. Joseph Is Kind to His Brothers   Genesis 43:15-25

5. A Banquet Is Served   Genesis 43:26-34

6. More Refunds and a Silver Cup   Genesis 44:1-5

7. The Brothers Are Brought Back   Genesis 44:6-13

8. Joseph Frightens His Brothers   Genesis 44:14-17

9. Judah Pleads for Mercy   Genesis 44:18-34

10. Joseph Reveals His Identity   Genesis 45:1-15

11. Pharaoh Honors Joseph's Family   Genesis 45:16-20

12. The Brothers Return to Jacob   Genesis 45:21-28

Introduction:

Bread for the World. Joseph's well-executed strategy ended up feeding the entire Middle East during a seven-year famine (Genesis 41-57). His economic plans, which helped to revitalize cities and alleviate world hunger, appears as mere background details in the larger account of how he reconciled to his brothers (Genesis 41:46- 47:27). But his example as a ruler—and in effect a manager—invites believers today to work in and through corporate and political structures on behalf of humans needs, particularly hunger.

Consider Joseph's accomplishment: he leveraged the massive institutions of pagan government to develop two seven-year plans—one for a budget surplus, and the other for a budget deficit. During the years of plenty, Egypt set aside 20% of its crops in preparation for the coming years of scarcity, thanks to Joseph's initiative (Genesis 41:34-36). When the seven years of famine finally came, as predicted, the deficits were unusually severe, yet Joseph and the people found creative, cooperative ways to beat the hunger. He managed what we would call a food cooperative, a world food bank, a land bank, and urban housing projects (Genesis 47:13-26).

Joseph's strategy utilized strong, centralized government control. However, the key was not the control but the effective planning, a result of God's hand upon Joseph, working through him to carry out His purposes.

Words to Live By:

Ephesians 4:29, Let not any filthy word go out of your mouth, but what is good for necessary edification, that it may impart grace to the hearers.

Ephesians 4:30, And do not grieve the Holy Spirit of God, by whom you are sealed until *the* day of redemption.

Ephesians 4:31, Let all bitterness and wrath and anger and tumult and evil speaking be put away from you, with all malice.

Ephesians 4:32, And be kind to one another, tenderhearted, forgiving one another, even as God for Christ's sake has forgiven you.

2 Chronicles 7:14

If my people who are called by my name will humble themselves, and pray, and seek my face, and turn from their wicked ways, then I will hear from heaven, and will forgive their sin and heal their land.

Psalm 122:6

Pray for the peace of Jerusalem: May they prosper that love thee.

Note: If we don't speak out in support of Christian matters, we will forfeit our authority given to us by God!! We as the "Church" and "Ambassadors" should not hide. We should "Shine" because there can be beautiful miracles in our mouth. Amen!

Lesson Plan 19

The Book of Genesis

Chapters 46, 47, & 48

Objective: To give an understanding of our origin, the creation of our world, and the fall of mankind.

Objective Breakdown:

1. Introduction

2. Israel's Journeys to Egypt   Genesis 46:1-7

3. The Family of Israel   Genesis 46:8-27

4. Joseph and His Father Are Reunited   Genesis 46:28-34

5. Israel Gets Land in Goshen   Genesis 47:1-12

6. Egypt Is Made Poor by Famine   Genesis 47:13-22

7. Pharaoh's Share of the Harvest   Genesis 47:23-26

8. Israel Demands Burial with His Fathers   Genesis 47:27-31

9. Jacob Accepts Joseph's Sons   Genesis 48:1-7

10. Joseph's Sons Are Blessed   Genesis 48:8-22

Introduction:

Sometimes God puts an opportunity in one's way that could advance a career and brings prosperity. That is what happened to Jacob and his sons when they migrated to Egypt. Of course, they were hardly looking for a career move; mainly they wanted to escape the famine in Canaan, and they ended up relocating largely at the request of Joseph. But once they arrived, circumstances created a unique opportunity.

Joseph was faced with a bit of a problem, how to introduce his long-lost family to Pharaoh. Pharaoh had an extremely high regard for Joseph. But what would be his reaction when he learned that Jacob and his sons were shepherds and ranchers? Those occupations were an "abomination: to the Egyptians (Genesis 46:34), fit only for slaves. One can gain some idea of how detestable they were, noting that when brothers came on their second journey to Egypt, bringing Benjamin with them, they were forced to eat by themselves, away from the Egyptians (Genesis 43:32). Apparently, Hebrews and Shepherds were synonymous in the Egyptian mind.

But Joseph turned his embarrassment into an opportunity. He instructed his brothers to boldly claim their skills rather than downplay their occupation. He knew that Pharaoh would probably never change his opinion of Shepherds, but most likely the ruler would at least allow the family to live by themselves in the Goshen District.

That exactly how the plan worked out (Genesis 47:1-6), but in addition, Pharaoh's respect for Joseph led to a request that the brothers have oversight over Pharaoh's own livestock. He still detested shepherds but when it came to care of his own animals apparently, he preferred to employ the kin of someone he trusted. The assignment matched the skills and experience of the brothers. Like many immigrants around the world today, they were willing and able to do work that people in host cultures find unacceptable. As a result, they prospered in the land (Genesis 47:27).

Words to Live By:

Ephesians 4:29, Let not any filthy word go out of your mouth, but what is good for necessary edification, that it may impart grace to the hearers.

Ephesians 4:30, And do not grieve the Holy Spirit of God, by whom you are sealed until *the* day of redemption.

Ephesians 4:31, Let all bitterness and wrath and anger and tumult and evil speaking be put away from you, with all malice.

Ephesians 4:32, And be kind to one another, tenderhearted, forgiving one another, even as God for Christ's sake has forgiven you.

2 Chronicles 7:14

If my people who are called by my name will humble themselves, and pray, and seek my face, and turn from their wicked ways, then I will hear from heaven, and will forgive their sin and heal their land.

Psalm 122:6

Pray for the peace of Jerusalem: May they prosper that love thee.

Note: If we don't speak out in support of Christian matters, we will forfeit our authority given to us by God!! We as the "Church" and "Ambassadors" should not hide. We should "Shine" because there can be beautiful miracles in our mouth. Amen!

Lesson Plan 20

The Book of Genesis

Chapters 49 & 50

Objective: To give an understanding of our origin, the creation of our world, and the fall of mankind.

Objective Breakdown:

1. Introduction

2. Jacob's Last Words to His Sons   Genesis 49:1-4

3. Simeon and Levi   Genesis 49:5-7

4. Judah   Genesis 49:8-12

5. Zebulun   Genesis 49:13

6. Issachar   Genesis 49:14-15

6. Dan   Genesis 49:16-18

7. Gad   Genesis 49:19

8. Asher   Genesis 49:20

9. Naphtali   Genesis 49:21

10. Joseph   Genesis 49:22-26

11. Benjamin   Genesis 49:27-28

12. Jacob's Final Charge and Death   Genesis 49:29-33

13. Jacob's Body Is Embalmed   Genesis 50:1-3

14. Jacob Is Buried in Canaan   Genesis 50:4-14

15. Joseph Is Reconciled with his Brothers   Genesis 50:15-21

16. Joseph Dies   Genesis 50:22-26

Introduction:

Sometimes God puts an opportunity in one's way that could advance a career and bring prosperity.

That is what happened to Jacob and his sons when they migrated to Egypt. Of course, they were hardly looking for a career move; they wanted to escape the famine in Canaan, and they ended up relocating largely at the request of Joseph. But once they arrived, circumstances created a unique opportunity.

Joseph was faced with a bit of a problem: how to introduce his long-lost family to Pharaoh. Pharaoh had a high regard for Joseph. But what would his reaction be when he learned that Jacob and his sons were shepherds and ranchers? Those occupations were an abomination to the Egyptians (Genesis 46:34), fit only for slaves. One can gain some idea of how detestable they were by noting that when the brothers came on their second journey to Egypt bringing their brother Benjamin with them, they were forced to eat by themselves, away from the Egyptians (Genesis 43:32). Apparently, Hebrews and Shepherds were synonymous in the Egyptian mind.

But Joseph turned this potential embarrassment into an opportunity. He instructed his brothers to boldly proclaim their skills rather than downplay their occupation. He knew Pharaoh would probably never change his opinion of shepherds, but most likely the ruler would at least allow the family to live by themselves in the Goshen District. That is exactly how the plan worked out (Genesis 47:1-6). But in addition, Pharaoh respect for Joseph led to a request that the brothers have oversight of Pharaoh's own livestock. He still detested shepherds, but when it came to the care of his own animals apparently, he preferred to employ the kin of someone he trusted. The assignment matched the skills and experience of the brothers.

Words to Live By:

Ephesians 4:29, Let not any filthy word go out of your mouth, but what is good for necessary edification, that it may impart grace to the hearers.

Ephesians 4:30, And do not grieve the Holy Spirit of God, by whom you are sealed until *the* day of redemption.

Ephesians 4:31, Let all bitterness and wrath and anger and tumult and evil speaking be put away from you, with all malice.

Ephesians 4:32, And be kind to one another, tenderhearted, forgiving one another, even as God for Christ's sake has forgiven you.

2 Chronicles 7:14

If my people who are called by my name will humble themselves, and pray, and seek my face, and turn from their wicked ways, then I will hear from heaven, and will forgive their sin and heal their land.

Psalm 122:6

Pray for the peace of Jerusalem: May they prosper that love thee.

Note: If we don't speak out in support of Christian matters, we will forfeit our authority given to us by God!! We as the "Church" and "Ambassadors" should not hide. We should "Shine" because there can be beautiful miracles in our mouth. Amen!

The Book of Exodus

Scripture Focus Chapters 1-40

Objective: To get an understanding of the creation, the fall, and the consequences mankind faces in the future.

Objective Breakdown:

1.	Israel's Rapid Multiplication	Chapter 1:1-7
2.	Israel's Severe Affliction	Chapter 1:8-14
3.	Midwives Planned Extinction	Chapter 1:15-22
4.	Moses is Redeemed from Murder	Chapter 2:1-4
5.	Pharaoh Daughter Adopts Moses	Chapter 2:5-10
6.	Moses Kill a Man and Flees	Chapter 2:11-15
7.	Moses Starts a Family	Chapter 2:16-22
8.	God Hears the Israelites	Chapter 2:23-25
9.	God Speaks from a Burning Bush	Chapter 3:1-6
10.	God Sends Moses as a Deliverer	Chapter 3:7-10
11.	Who AM I	Chapter 3:11-12
12.	What Is his Name	Chapter 3:13-22
13.	They Will Not Believe Me	Chapter 4:1-9
14.	I Am Slow of Speech	Chapter 4:10-17
15.	Moses Returns to Egypt	Chapter 4:18-23
16.	Moses Reinstitutes Circumcision	Chapter 4:24-26
17.	Israel Accepts the Call of Moses as Deliverer	Chapter 4:27-31
18.	Moses to Pharaoh: "Let My People Go"	Chapter 5:1-14
19.	Israel Rejects Moses	Chapter 5:15-21
20.	Moses Questions God's Plan Out to God	Chapter 5:22-23

Lesson Plan 21

The Book of Exodus

Chapters 1, 2, & 3

Objective: To gain an understanding of Israel's delivery from slavery in Egypt.

Objective Breakdown:

1. Israel's Children Multiply	Exodus 1:1-7
2. The Israelites Are Enslaved	Exodus 1:8-14
3. Midwives Refuse to Kill Babies	Exodus 1:15-22
4. Moses Is Born and Hidden	Exodus 2:1-4
5. Pharaoh's Daughter adopts Moses	Exodus 2:5-22
6. God Hears the Israelites	Exodus 2:23-25
7. God Speaks from a Burning Bush	Exodus 3:1-6
8. God Sends Moses as a Deliver	Exodus 3:7-10
9. God Promises to Be with Moses	Exodus 3:11-22

Introduction:

Israel's deliverance from slavery in Egypt was one of the defining moments in world history. It established a model of liberation from which countless oppressed people have drawn hope. This Exodus became the benchmark for later incidents in which God delivered His people, especially the deliverance by Jesus Christ from sin.

Exodus begins by looking back some 400 hundred years to Genesis, to the time when Jacob relocated his family to Egypt, where his son Joseph ruled as second in command (Exodus 1:1-7; Genesis 41:39-41; 46:1-7). This relocation was a master plan of God Which God had revealed to Abraham (Genesis 15:12-21).

During the centuries that Israel was growing from a family into a nation, Egypt was in transition from a Middle Kingdom to the New Kingdom (1800-1400 B.C.). A group of foreigners called the Hyksos was driven out, the country became united again, and Egypt attained a high-water mark of its ancient history. The nation's new Pharaoh embarked on ambitious building programs, and they conscripted the minority Israelites as workers. Before long, the Hebrews had become slaves to the Egyptian taskmasters, and they cried out to God for deliverance (Exodus 18:14; 2:23). Exodus tells us that God responded to their pleas (Exodus 2:24-25). First, He raised up a leader, Moses, to whom He revealed Himself by His name, "I AM WHO I AM" (Exodus 3:14). Then He showed His power to the Egyptians through a series of ten plagues which must have devastated the economy and ecology of Egypt (Exodus 11:11).

Finally, Pharaoh gave permission for the Israelites to leave, but then changed his mind and pursued them as far as the Red Sea. In a miraculous display of power God parted the Red Sea for the Israelites to cross but released the waters to drown the Egyptian charioteers and secure His people's freedom.

God is a God of justice. He can be counted on to right the world's wrongs. Today, when there is so much emphasis on God's love, grace, and mercy, is it possible that we have forgotten that God is to be feared (respected)? We should always approach our God in prayer with awe and humbleness and with thanksgiving and praise for His wonderful compassion love and care.

Two women whose commitment to God led to an act of civil disobedience (Exodus 1:15-21). Thus, Israel's deliverance from oppression began with two brave midwives who refused to do Pharaoh's bidding.

Also, we will see Moses' mother Jochebed, determined to save her newborn son from infanticide. Her determination led to a clever plan to hide the baby along the Nile River (Exodus 2:10; 6:20), where he was discovered by Pharaoh's daughter. Forty years as the adopted son of Pharaoh's daughter, helped this man (Moses) to become the leader of God's people.

The setting for the Book of Exodus is two areas in the Middle East: the Nile Delta in Egypt and the Sinai Peninsula. The Exodus covers a time span of a little more than 80 years, beginning with the birth of Moses and ending with the early portion of the Israelites journey to the Promised Land, sometime around 1400 B.C.

Words to Live By:

Ephesians 4:29, Let not any filthy word go out of your mouth, but what is good for necessary edification, that it may impart grace to the hearers.

Ephesians 4:30, And do not grieve the Holy Spirit of God, by whom you are sealed until *the* day of redemption.

Ephesians 4:31, Let all bitterness and wrath and anger and tumult and evil speaking be put away from you, with all malice.

Ephesians 4:32, And be kind to one another, tenderhearted, forgiving one another, even as God for

Christ's sake has forgiven you.

2 Chronicles 7:14

If my people who are called by my name will humble themselves, and pray, and seek my face, and turn from their wicked ways, then I will hear from heaven, and will forgive their sin and heal their land.

Psalm 122:6

Pray for the peace of Jerusalem: May they prosper that love thee.

Note: If we don't speak out in support of Christian matters, we will forfeit our authority given to us by God!! We as the "Church" and "Ambassadors" should not hide. We should "Shine" because there can be beautiful miracles in our mouth. Amen!

Lesson Plan 22

The Book of Exodus

Chapters 4, 5, & 6

Objective: To gain an understanding of Israel's delivery from slavery in Egypt.

Objective Breakdown:

1. Introduction

2. Moses Doubts His Qualifications   Exodus 4:1-12

3. God will Make Aaron a Spokesman   Exodus 4:13-17

4. Moses Returns to Egypt   Exodus 4:18-20

5. God Will Harden Pharaoh's Heart   Exodus 4:21-26

6. Moses and Aaron speak to the Israelites   Exodus 4:27-31

7. Moses' to Pharaoh: "Let My People Go"   Exodus 5:1-5

8. Pharaoh Increases the Burden   Exodus 5:6-19

9. Hebrew Leaders Complain to Moses   Exodus 5:20-21

10. Moses Cries Out to God   Exodus 5:22-23

11. God Reaffirms His Promises   Exodus 6:1-13

12. The Background of Moses and Aaron   Exodus 6:14-27

13. God Again Sends Moses to Pharaoh   Exodus 6:28-30

Introduction:

The Pharaoh before whom Moses and Aaron appeared (Exodus 5:1) was a different ruler than Pharaoh "who did not know Joseph" (Exodus 1:8) and in whose court Moses had been raised (Exodus 2:8-10). That king who wanted to execute Moses for murdering an Egyptian, had died while Moses was in Midian (Exodus 2:15, 23). Both rulers were called Pharaoh as a title, not a name. No one knows the name of either of the two rulers who played such a significant role in Moses' life.

One of the most widespread motivations in the workplaces of the world today is also one of the most destructive and that is fear. Workers fear losing their jobs. Managers fear a loss of productivity and profits. Investors and owners fear a loss of capital. Yet fear as a dominating force in the work world is nothing new, as the conflict between Pharaoh and the children of Israel illustrates. The situation was fraught with tension and anxiety on both sides. A crushing demand for increased output (Exodus 5:6-9) was just one of the tragic ingredients. Fear influenced the three main parties involved.

Pharaoh was a hard taskmaster, but his power and anger were ultimately the result of fear. The Egyptians watched as the Israelites multiplied rapidly, and the account says they were literally "in dread of what might happen in an event of war" (Exodus 1:10, 12). So, when Moses the Hebrew spokesman, asked for a long weekend holiday for the laborers, the Egyptians' fears conditioned Pharaoh's response (Exodus 5:4-5). The brick makers were given an increased workload with no increase in supply of basic resources or extension of deadlines. Clearly the last thing Pharaoh wanted to do was to do was to empower his workers. Instead, he wanted to dominate them because he was driven by fear.

The Israelites, especially their supervisors, reacted to Pharaoh new production policy by verbally attacking their own leader, Moses (Exodus 5:15-21). They knew the people could not meet Pharaoh's impossible demand, and they feared what would happen as a result (Exodus 5:19).

Moses responded to the Hebrew supervisors' rebuke by turning to God, challenging His Word and His purposes, and complaining that he was the wrong man for the job (Exodus 5:22-23). Although, the text doesn't say explicitly, it is easy to see that Moses deeply feared the rejection of the people and the prospect that his mission might end in failure.

Fear distorted reality for all three parties in the Exodus account—managers, workers, and spokesman. Ultimately God's plan prevailed.

Words to Live By:

Ephesians 4:29, Let not any filthy word go out of your mouth, but what is good for necessary edification, that it may impart grace to the hearers.

Ephesians 4:30, And do not grieve the Holy Spirit of God, by whom you are sealed until *the* day of redemption.

Ephesians 4:31, Let all bitterness and wrath and anger and tumult and evil speaking be put away from you, with all malice.

Ephesians 4:32, And be kind to one another, tenderhearted, forgiving one another, even as God for Christ's sake has forgiven you.

2 Chronicles 7:14

If my people who are called by my name will humble themselves, and pray, and seek my face, and turn from their wicked ways, then I will hear from heaven, and will forgive their sin and heal their land.

Psalm 122:6

Pray for the peace of Jerusalem: May they prosper that love thee.

Note: If we don't speak out in support of Christian matters, we will forfeit our authority given to us by God!! We as the "Church" and "Ambassadors" should not hide. We should "Shine" because there can be beautiful miracles in our mouth. Amen!

Homework: Read Psalms 15 through 22 and Proverbs 5 and 6.

Lesson Plan 23

The Book of Exodus

Chapters 7, 8, & 9

Objective: To gain an understanding of Israel's delivery from slavery in Egypt.

Objective Breakdown:

1. Introduction

2. Moses as God   Exodus 7:1-7

3. Moses' Rod Becomes a Snake   Exodus 7:8-13

4. Egypt's Water Turns to Blood   Exodus 7:14-21

5. Pharaoh Remains Unmoved   Exodus 7:22-24

6. Frogs Cover Egypt   Exodus 8:1-7

7. Pharaoh Gets Relief but Is Unmoved   Exodus 8:8-15

8. Egypt's Dust Turns to Lice   Exodus 8:16-19

9. Swarms of Flies Afflict Egypt   Exodus 8:20-24

10. Pharaoh Gives in, Then Backs Out   Exodus 8:25-32

11. The Livestock of Egypt Die   Exodus 9:1-7

12. The Egyptians Break Out in Boils   Exodus 9:8-12

13. Hail Falls on Egypt   Exodus 9:13-26

14. Pharaoh Confesses but Sins Yet More   Exodus 9:27-35

Introduction:

The Lord's statement to Moses that "I have made you as God to Pharaoh" (Exodus 7:1) may seem puzzling to a modern reader. But is helps realize that the Egyptian pharaohs were considered gods, and their words seen as divine pronouncements. Thus, they held absolute sway over the people.

Moses had been raised in a Pharaoh's Court (Exodus 2:8-10), so he was well aware that Pharaoh would pay little attention to the statements of an ordinary human. Thus, the Lord's message was a reassuring promise to Moses. God would persuade the ruler that in Moses he was dealing with someone who deserved a hearing.

It is not enough to be called a leader; one must act as a leader to expect results. That's the challenge that Moses and Aaron faced as they appeared to meet with Pharaoh (Exodus 7:2). God had already given them authority to speak on His behalf. We might call that positional authority, the sort of status that rank might confer. But actions speak louder than words. So now their task was to communicate to Pharaoh to Pharaoh the authority they had been given, and to do so clearly with power.

Words to Live By:

Ephesians 4:29, Let not any filthy word go out of your mouth, but what is good for necessary edification, that it may impart grace to the hearers.

Ephesians 4:30, And do not grieve the Holy Spirit of God, by whom you are sealed until *the* day of redemption.

Ephesians 4:31, Let all bitterness and wrath and anger and tumult and evil speaking be put away from you, with all malice.

Ephesians 4:32, And be kind to one another, tenderhearted, forgiving one another, even as God for Christ's sake has forgiven you.

2 Chronicles 7:14

If my people who are called by my name will humble themselves, and pray, and seek my face, and turn from their wicked ways, then I will hear from heaven, and will forgive their sin and heal their land.

Psalm 122:6

Pray for the peace of Jerusalem: May they prosper that love thee.

Note: If we don't speak out in support of Christian matters, we will forfeit our authority given to us by God!! We as the "Church" and "Ambassadors" should not hide. We should "Shine" because there can be beautiful miracles in our mouth. Amen!

Homework: Read Psalms 23 through 28 and Proverbs 7 and 8.

Lesson Plan 24

The Book of Exodus

Chapters 10, 11, & 12

Objective: To gain an understanding of Israel's delivery from slavery in Egypt.

Objective Breakdown:

1. Introduction

2. Moses Warns of a Plague of Locusts   Exodus 10:1-6

3. Pharaoh Agrees to Let Only Men Go   Exodus 10:7-11

4. The East Wind Brings the Locust   Exodus 10:12-15

5. Pharaoh Flip Flops Again   Exodus 10:16-20

6. Darkness Descends on Egypt   Exodus 10:21-29

7. God Will Slay Egypt's Firstborn   Exodus 11:1-10

8. God Commands the Sacrifice of Lambs   Exodus 12:1-13

9. Annual Observance of the Passover   Exodus 12:14-20

10. Israel Prepares the Passover   Exodus 12:21-28

11. The Firstborn Slain, Pharaoh Relents   Exodus 12:29-32

12. The Israelites Are Driven Out   Exodus 12:33-39

13. The Passover Is Instituted   Exodus 12:40-51

Introduction:

The Egyptians believed that Pharaoh was the Divine Son of the God Ra. After living in Egypt for many generations, every Jews knew that this belief was the official state policy, as well as the religious belief of the Egyptian people. To empower the people with enough trust in the God of Israel, it was necessary to publicly defeat and humiliate the Divine Pharaoh himself.

This is why the Bible says more than a dozen times that God hardened Pharaoh's heart, so that he could be knocked down again and again. Each time Pharaoh is defeated, the Jewish people and many

Egyptians too became committed to the God of Israel.

The infestation of frogs (Exodus 8:8-15) and the other nine plagues that God visited on Egypt created an ecological nightmare. The Nile and related waterways, the air over Egypt, the flora and fauna of the region, and many other natural systems were degraded by the upset of the region's ecological balance. However, let there be no mistake; the responsibility for these natural disasters was Pharaoh's not God's. The ruler's refusal to obey God, or even to treat the Hebrew laborers with simple compassion, brought about the ten judgments.

Indeed, several statements in the Bible show the growing split among the Egyptians. As plague followed plague many Egyptians did not follow Pharaoh's stubborn path, and thus escaped his fate." Those officials of Pharaoh who feared the word of the LORD hurried to bring their slaves and their livestock inside. But those who ignored the word of the LORD left their slaves and livestock in the field." (Exodus 9:20-21) and suffered death.

Words to Live By:

Ephesians 4:29, Let not any filthy word go out of your mouth, but what is good for necessary edification, that it may impart grace to the hearers.

Ephesians 4:30, And do not grieve the Holy Spirit of God, by whom you are sealed until *the* day of redemption.

Ephesians 4:31, Let all bitterness and wrath and anger and tumult and evil speaking be put away from you, with all malice.

Ephesians 4:32, And be kind to one another, tenderhearted, forgiving one another, even as God for Christ's sake has forgiven you.

2 Chronicles 7:14

If my people who are called by my name will humble themselves, and pray, and seek my face, and turn from their wicked ways, then I will hear from heaven, and will forgive their sin and heal their land.

Psalm 122:6

Pray for the peace of Jerusalem: May they prosper that love thee.

Note: If we don't speak out in support of Christian matters, we will forfeit our authority given to us by God!! We as the "Church" and "Ambassadors" should not hide. We should "Shine" because there can be beautiful miracles in our mouth. Amen! **If we are not part of the solution, we are part of the problem.**

Homework: Read Psalms 29 through 35 and Proverbs 9 and 10.

Lesson Plan 25

The Book of Exodus

Chapters 13, 14, & 15

Objective: To gain an understanding of Israel's delivery from slavery in Egypt.

Objective Breakdown:

1. Introduction

2. The Feast of Unleavened Bread   Exodus 13:1-10

3. Setting Apart the First-Born   Exodus 13:11-16

4. The Journey Begins   Exodus 13:17-22

5. Pharaoh's Army Gives Pursuit   Exodus 14:1-9

6. The People Cry Against Moses   Exodus 14:10-14

7. God Says to Go Forward   Exodus 14:15-20

8. The Miraculous Red Sea Crossing   Exodus 14:21-31

9. The People Celebrate with Song   Exodus 15:1-19

10. Miriam and the Women Dance   Exodus 15:20-21

11. God Provides Water   Exodus 15:22-27

Introduction:

It would be natural to assume that Pharaoh's grief over the loss of his firstborn child (Exodus 12:29) was what finally motivated him to let the Hebrews go (Exodus 12:31-32). But his decision was probably less the product of emotion than it was of politics and religion, for the tenth plague was the finale in a titanic contest to see whose god was more powerful, Egypt's or Israel's.

To the Egyptians, Pharaoh was a god whose fate determined their fate. So, when Moses and Aaron came, claiming to speak for a new god whom they called "LORD," Pharaoh wanted to know, "Who is the LORD, that I should obey his voice" (Exodus 5:2). In effect, he was throwing down a challenge to the Lord to prove Himself.

God accepted his challenge and brought nine catastrophic plagues on Egypt to demonstrate His power (see the Ecological Disaster Exodus 8: 8-15). Nevertheless, Pharaoh resisted all nine. But in the tenth plague, God struck down Pharaoh's supposedly divine child. That was the ultimate blow. It undercut Pharaoh's credibility and authority as a god. As pointed out in the text, this powerful, godlike ruler was suddenly no different than the lowest prisoner in his dungeon, or for that matter, than the animals in the field (Exodus 2:29).

No wonder the last words of Pharaoh convey submission and humility: "Be gone; and bless me also" Exodus 12:32). Realizing that he had been bested, the supposedly divine king of Egypt was asking for pity and help from the God he now knew to be supreme.

Words to Live By:

Ephesians 4:29, Let not any filthy word go out of your mouth, but what is good for necessary edification, that it may impart grace to the hearers.

Ephesians 4:30, And do not grieve the Holy Spirit of God, by whom you are sealed until *the* day of redemption.

Ephesians 4:31, Let all bitterness and wrath and anger and tumult and evil speaking be put away from you, with all malice.

Ephesians 4:32, And be kind to one another, tenderhearted, forgiving one another, even as God for Christ's sake has forgiven you.

Matthew 12:25, And Jesus knew their thoughts and said to them, every kingdom divided against itself is brought to desolation. And every city or house divided against itself shall not stand.

Mark 3:24, And if a kingdom is divided against itself, that kingdom cannot stand.

2 Chronicles 7:14

If my people who are called by my name will humble themselves, and pray, and seek my face, and turn from their wicked ways, then I will hear from heaven, and forgive their sin and heal their land.

Psalm 122:6

Pray for the peace of Jerusalem: May they prosper that love thee.

Note: If we don't speak out in support of Christian matters, we will forfeit our authority given to us by God!! We as the "Church" and "Ambassadors" should not hide. We should "Shine" because there can be beautiful miracles in our mouth. Amen!

If we are not part of the solution, then we are part of the problem.

Homework: Read Psalms 36 through 42 and Proverbs 11 and 12.

Lesson Plan 26

The Book of Exodus

Chapters 16, 17, & 18

Objective: To gain an understanding of Israel's delivery from slavery in Egypt.

Objective Breakdown:

1. Introduction

2. The People Complain of Hunger   Exodus 16:1-3

3. God Promises to Send Food   Exodus 16:4-12

4. God Provides Quail and Bread   Exodus 16:13-30

5. The Bread Is Called Manna   Exodus 16:31-36

6. Moses Get Water from a Rock   Exodus 17:1-7

7. War with the Amalekites   Exodus 17:8-16

8. Moses Is Reunited with His Family   Exodus 18:1-12

9. Moses Is Advised to Delegate   Exodus 18:13-27

Introduction:

Some people see two Gods in the Bible. According to this view, the "God of the Old Testament" is violent and retaliatory, while the "God of the New Testament" is a God of love and peace. However, the whole of Scripture clearly reveals one God who is good, true, powerful, pure, and compassionate—but never vindictive or brutal.

For example, Moses' song to the Lord describes God as:

Powerful (Exodus 15:6) Moses praises God's triumph in war, but this is to be seen in the light of the horribly evil record of Pharaoh (Exodus chapters 1-14). God is a God of justice, and that justice is meted out toward all sinners, not just Pharaoh; ultimately it led to the sacrifice of God's own Son on behalf of sinners (John 3:16-21; Romans 5:8, 18-21).

Pure (Exodus 15:11) God's character is holy or morally perfect—a unique quality that sets Him apart from all other so-called gods (1Samuel 2:2; Revelation 25:4). Holiness demands that sin be punished

(Psalm 96:13; 98:9; John 3:17-21), and so there are consequences for sinful rebellion. A holy God also desires His people to be holy and righteous (Isaiah1:10-14; Micah 6:6-8; Matthew 12:7).

Compassionate (Exodus 15:13) God shows love and mercy toward us even though we have turned away from Him and disobeyed (Daniel 9:9; 1Timothy 1:13, 16), and none of us deserve it (Romans 3:9-20; 9:14-18). That kind of love can only come from God (John 3:11-21). It is the sort of compassion demonstrated by Christ dying for us while we were sinners fully deserving condemnation (Romans 5:6-11). Without question, the Old Testament story is at times cruel and ugly. But the ugliness does not come from God, it comes from sin and rebellion of the people. Nor does the New Testament tell only a peaceful and pleasant tale: Jesus' voluntary death on behalf of guilty sinners is a brutal account as can be.

Words to Live By:

Ephesians 4:29, Let not any filthy word go out of your mouth, but what is good for necessary edification, that it may impart grace to the hearers.

Ephesians 4:30, And do not grieve the Holy Spirit of God, by whom you are sealed until *the* day of redemption.

Ephesians 4:31, Let all bitterness and wrath and anger and tumult and evil speaking be put away from you, with all malice.

Ephesians 4:32, And be kind to one another, tenderhearted, forgiving one another, even as God for Christ's sake has forgiven you.

Matthew 12:25, And Jesus knew their thoughts and said to them, every kingdom divided against itself is brought to desolation. And every city or house divided against itself shall not stand.

Mark 3:24, And if a kingdom is divided against itself, that kingdom cannot stand.

2 Chronicles 7:14

If my people who are called by my name will humble themselves, and pray, and seek my face, and turn from their wicked ways, then I will hear from heaven, and forgive their sin and heal their land.

Psalm 122:6

Pray for the peace of Jerusalem: May they prosper that love thee.

Note: If we don't speak out in support of Christian matters, we will forfeit our authority given to us by God!! We as the "Church" and "Ambassadors" should not hide. We should "Shine" because there can be beautiful miracles in our mouth. Amen!

If we are not part of the solution, then we are part of the problem.

Homework: Read Psalms 43-Through 49 and Proverbs 13 and 14.

Lesson Plan 27

The Book of Exodus

Chapters 19, 20, & 21

Objective: To gain an understanding of Israel's delivery from slavery in Egypt

Objective Breakdown:

1. Introduction

2. God and the People Make a Covenant   Exodus 19:1-9

3. The People Prepare for God   Exodus 19:10-15

4. God Comes Down to Mount Sinai   Exodus 19:16-25

5. God Gives the Ten Commandments   Exodus 20:1-17

6. The People Fear God   Exodus 20:18-21

7. A Warning Against Idols   Exodus 20:22-26

8. Servants and Masters   Exodus 21:1-11

9. Personal Injuries   Exodus 21:12-27

10. Injuries Involving Animals   Exodus 21:28-36

Introduction:

Moses was a classic case of a workaholic heading toward burnout. Fortunately, he had in Jethro an astute father-in-law who could see what Moses could not—that eventually his failure to delegate would wear himself and his people out (Exodus 18:18). Jethro had the courage to speak up and warn his son-in-law about the looming danger. Such drastic action is often necessary with alcoholics because they are often the last to see the damage their compulsive habits are doing to themselves and other around them. When things are not working out, their tendency is to work harder, making the problem even worse. Moses responded right away to Jethro's suggestions (Exodus 18:24).

Today, we have caring relatives and friends of people who are addicted to various substances and or habits and the intervention by these relatives and friends can literally make the difference between life and death.

Might you be a Jethro in someone's life by taking the person aside and explaining the damage that excessive work is causing.

Words to Live By:

Ephesians 4:29, Let not any filthy word go out of your mouth, but what is good for necessary edification, that it may impart grace to the hearers.

Ephesians 4:30, And do not grieve the Holy Spirit of God, by whom you are sealed until *the* day of redemption.

Ephesians 4:31, Let all bitterness and wrath and anger and tumult and evil speaking be put away from you, with all malice.

Ephesians 4:32, And be kind to one another, tenderhearted, forgiving one another, even as God for Christ's sake has forgiven you.

Matthew 12:25, And Jesus knew their thoughts and said to them, every kingdom divided against itself is brought to desolation. And every city or house divided against itself shall not stand.

Mark 3:24, And if a kingdom is divided against itself, that kingdom cannot stand.

2 Chronicles 7:14

If my people who are called by my name will humble themselves, and pray, and seek my face, and turn from their wicked ways, then I will hear from heaven, and forgive their sin and heal their land.

Psalm 122:6

Pray for the peace of Jerusalem: May they prosper that love thee.

Note: If we don't speak out in support of Christian matters, we will forfeit our authority given to us by God!! We as the "Church" and "Ambassadors" should not hide. We should "Shine" because there can be beautiful miracles in our mouth. Amen!

If we are not part of the solution, then we are part of the problem.

Homework: Read Psalms 50-56 through 49 and Proverbs 15 and 16.

Lesson Plan 28

The Book of Exodus

Chapters 22, 23, & 24

Objective: To gain an understanding of Israel's delivery from slavery in Egypt.

Objective Breakdown:

1. Introduction

2. Personal Property   Exodus 22:1-15

3. Treatment of People   Exodus 22:16-31

5. Measures to Ensure Justice   Exodus 23:1-9

6. The Sabbath Year   Exodus 23:10-13

4. Three Major Feasts   Exodus 23:14-19

5. The Promised Land   Exodus 23:20-33

6. The Leaders Worship God   Exodus 24:1-11

7. Moses Goes Up the Mountain   Exodus 24:12-18

Introduction:

The Law made provision for people to have one day of rest each week (Exodus 23:12). God knew the makeup of His creatures. Neither human nor beast was capable of working endlessly like a machine. Yet today, when more people work with machines than animals, there is a tendency to start seeing people as machines rather as human beings with a need for rest and refreshment. This trend is accelerated by a common view of the world that reduces everything to the material and ignores the spiritual side of life. The Law's amplification of the fourth commandment, which concerns the Sabbath (Exodus 20:8-11), reflects not only a godly view of work, but a godly view of humanity. We are more than just sophisticated pieces of technology.

We are living souls made in the image of God (Genesis 2:7). Therefore, as He rested from His work we should do likewise.

Words to Live By:

Ephesians 4:29, Let not any filthy word go out of your mouth, but what is good for necessary edification, that it may impart grace to the hearers.

Ephesians 4:30, And do not grieve the Holy Spirit of God, by whom you are sealed until *the* day of redemption.

Ephesians 4:31, Let all bitterness and wrath and anger and tumult and evil speaking be put away from you, with all malice.

Ephesians 4:32, And be kind to one another, tenderhearted, forgiving one another, even as God for Christ's sake has forgiven you.

Matthew 12:25, And Jesus knew their thoughts and said to them, every kingdom divided against itself is brought to desolation. And every city or house divided against itself shall not stand.

Mark 3:24, And if a kingdom is divided against itself, that kingdom cannot stand.

2 Chronicles 7:14

If my people who are called by my name will humble themselves, and pray, and seek my face, and turn from their wicked ways, then I will hear from heaven, and forgive their sin and heal their land.

Psalm 122:6

Pray for the peace of Jerusalem: May they prosper that love thee.

Note: If we don't speak out in support of Christian matters, we will forfeit our authority given to us by God!! We as the "Church" and "Ambassadors" should not hide. We should "Shine" because there can be beautiful miracles in our mouth. Amen!

If we are not part of the solution, then we are part of the problem.

Homework: Read Psalms 57 through 63 and Proverbs 17 and 18.

Lesson Plan 29

The Book of Exodus

Chapters 25, 26, & 27

Objective: To gain an understanding of Israel's delivery from slavery in Egypt.

Objective Breakdown:

1. Introduction

2. Contributions for a Sanctuary   Exodus 25:1-9

3. The Arch of the Covenant Described   Exodus 25:10-22

4. The Table for the Show Bread   Exodus 25:23-30

5. The Golden Lamp Stand   Exodus 25:31-40

6. Curtains of Linen   Exodus 26:1-6

7. Curtains of Goat Hair   Exodus 26:7-14

8. Boards and Bars Overlaid with Gold   Exodus 26:15-30

9. The Veil and the Screen   Exodus 26:31-37

10. The Altar   Exodus 27:1-8

11. The Court of the Tabernacle   Exodus 27:9-19

12. Olive Oil for the Lamp Stand   Exodus 27:20-21

Introduction:

A worship center in the wilderness. Sometimes people speak of a sanctuary, or place of worship, as "God's' house." That can be a bit misleading, for the Lord does not need a house to live in. He is Spirit and is everywhere present (Psalm 139:7-10; John 4:24).

Why, then, did God instruct His people to build a worship center, "that I may dwell among them" (Exodus 25:8)? Perhaps it was not because He needed a place to live, but because they needed a place to worship. The sanctuary, or tabernacle, was for their benefit more than His—as becomes more apparent when we look at the minute details given for the construction (Chapters 25-31).

The former slaves of Egypt had probably seen incredible temples and monuments in the empire along the Nile, and indeed the Israelites may have helped to construct some of them. Now they were refugees in the wilderness, with no centralized location at which to worship the God who had delivered them from bondage. So, they must have been awed to hear God's plan for a beautiful worship center of their own, complete with finely crafted accessories.

Not only was the tabernacle a work of art, but its construction involved the entire community. In fact, it showed that the ordained priests were not the only spirit-filled leaders in Israel; so were the artists and craftsmen who led the project (Exodus 31:1-11). It was their wisdom, management ability, and technical expertise, not just Moses, that made it possible to do the work (Exodus 39:42).

Likewise, the financing of the tabernacle was also a community effort. It is interesting that Moses proposed both a free-will donation, or love offering (Exodus 25:2-9), a flat tax (Exodus 30:12-16) to pay for the project. As a result, rich and poor alike shared the cost—and therefore the ownership. Thus, everyone can know that they have built a sanctuary for God, and He will come to dwell among them.

Words to Live By:

Ephesians 4:29, Let not any filthy word go out of your mouth, but what is good for necessary edification, that it may impart grace to the hearers.

Ephesians 4:30, And do not grieve the Holy Spirit of God, by whom you are sealed until *the* day of redemption.

Ephesians 4:31, Let all bitterness and wrath and anger and tumult and evil speaking be put away from you, with all malice.

Ephesians 4:32, And be kind to one another, tenderhearted, forgiving one another, even as God for Christ's sake has forgiven you.

Matthew 12:25, And Jesus knew their thoughts and said to them, every kingdom divided against itself is brought to desolation. And every city or house divided against itself shall not stand.

Mark 3:24, And if a kingdom is divided against itself, that kingdom cannot stand.

2 Chronicles 7:14

If my people who are called by my name will humble themselves, and pray, and seek my face, and turn from their wicked ways, then I will hear from heaven, and forgive their sin and heal their land.

Psalm 122:6

Pray for the peace of Jerusalem: May they prosper that love thee.

Note: If we don't speak out in support of Christian, matters we will forfeit our authority given to us by God!! We as the "Church" and "Ambassadors" should not hide. We should "Shine" because there can be beautiful miracles in our mouth. Amen!

If we are not part of the solution, then we are part of the problem.

Homework: Read Psalms 64 through 69 and Proverbs 19 and 20.

Who is the angel that is being referred to in Exodus 23:20? Is it the pre-incarnate Jesus?

(My Answer: No, I believe it may the Arch Angel Michael or at the least the Arch Angel Gabriel, but not the pre-incarnate Jesus.)

Exodus 23:20: "Behold I send an <u>Angel</u> before thee, to keep thee in the way, and to bring thee into the place which I have prepared." KJV by Power Publishing Corp, 2006

Exodus 23:20: "See, I am sending an <u>angel</u> ahead of you to guard you along the way and to bring you to the place I have prepared." NIV Zondervan Bible Publishers 1981

Exodus 23:20: "See, I am sending an <u>Angel</u> before you to lead you safely to the land I have prepared for you." Living Bible Zondervan Bible Publishers 1981

Exodus 23:20: "Behold, I send an <u>angel</u> before you, to guard you on the way and to bring you to the place which I have prepared." Revised Standard Bible Zondervan Bible Publishers 1981

Exodus 23:20: "I am sending an <u>angel</u> before you to guard you on your way and bring you to the place that I have made ready." Hebrew-English Tanakh

Acts 12:7, And, behold, the angel of the Lord came upon *him,* and a light shined in the prison: and he smote Peter on the side, and raised him up, saying, Arise up quickly. And his chains fell off from *his* hands.

2 Corinthians 11:14, And no marvel; for Satan himself is transformed into an angel of light.

Lesson Plan 30

The Book of Exodus

Chapters 28, 29, & 30

Objective: To gain an understanding of Israel's delivery from slavery in Egypt.

Objective Breakdown:

1.	Introduction & Background	
2.	Garments for the Priests	Exodus 28:1-4
3.	The Ephod	Exodus 28:5-14
4.	The Breastplate	Exodus 28:15-28
5.	The Urim and Thummim	Exodus 28:29-30
6.	The Robe of the Ephod	Exodus 28:31-35
7.	The Priestly Turban and Tunic	Exodus 28:36
8.	Holiness of the LORD	Exodus 28:37-43
9.	Preparing Priests for Their Work	Exodus 29:1-9
10.	Sacrifices of a Bull and Two Rams	Exodus 29:10-21
11.	A Wave Offering	Exodus 29:22-25
12.	The Priest's Portions	Exodus 29:26-34
13.	Daily Sacrifices	Exodus 29:35-46
14.	The Altar of Incense	Exodus 30:1-10
15.	The Half-Shekel Offering	Exodus 30:11-16
16.	The Laver for Washing	Exodus 30:17-21
17.	Spiced Oil for Anointing	Exodus 30:22-33
18.	Fragrant Incense	Exodus 30:34-38

Words to Live By:

Ephesians 4:29, Let not any filthy word go out of your mouth, but what is good for necessary edification, that it may impart grace to the hearers.

Ephesians 4:30, And do not grieve the Holy Spirit of God, by whom you are sealed until *the* day of redemption.

Ephesians 4:31, Let all bitterness and wrath and anger and tumult and evil speaking be put away from you, with all malice.

Ephesians 4:32, And be kind to one another, tenderhearted, forgiving one another, even as God for Christ's sake has forgiven you.

Matthew 12:25, And Jesus knew their thoughts and said to them, every kingdom divided against itself is brought to desolation. And every city or house divided against itself shall not stand.

Mark 3:24, And if a kingdom is divided against itself, that kingdom cannot stand.

2 Chronicles 7:14

If my people who are called by my name will humble themselves, and pray, and seek my face, and turn from their wicked ways, then I will hear from heaven, and forgive their sin and heal their land.

Psalm 122:6

Pray for the peace of Jerusalem: May they prosper that love thee.

Note: If we don't speak out in support of Christian matters, we will forfeit our authority given to us by God!! We as the "Church" and "Ambassadors" should not hide. We should "Shine" because there can be beautiful miracles in our mouth. Amen!

If we are not part of the solution, then we are part of the problem.

Homework: Read Psalms 70 through 76 and Proverbs 21 and 22.

Lesson Plan 31

The Book of Exodus

Chapters 31, 32, & 33

Objective: To gain an understanding of Israel's delivery from slavery in Egypt.

Objective Breakdown:

1. Introduction

2. God Appoints Craftsmen   Exodus 31:1-11

3. A Warning to Keep the Sabbath   Exodus 31:12-18

4. Aaron and the People Make a Golden Calf   Exodus 32:1-6

5. God Threatens to Destroy the People   Exodus 32:7-10

6. Moses Asks God to Withhold His Wrath   Exodus 32:11-14

7. Moses Destroys the Tablets and the Calf   Exodus 32:15-21

8. Aaron Tries to Excuse Himself   Exodus 32:22-24

9. The People Are Punished   Exodus 32:25-29

10. Moses Returns to the Lord   Exodus 32:30-35

11. The People Mourn   Exodus 33:1-6

12. Moses' Tent for Meeting with God   Exodus 33:7-11

13. God Promises to Go with Moses   Exodus 33:12-17

14. Moses Asks to See God's Glory   Exodus 33:18-23

Introduction:

How many times have we heard people say words to the effect of "I would believe in God If I could only see Him?" According to this common excuse, a person's unwillingness to put wholehearted trust in God is actually God's fault: He hasn't revealed Himself plainly. If He would, such people would instantly believe in Him and start following Him. But the experience of the people of Israel at Mount Sinai refutes this sort of reasoning. If ever there were an occasion on which God revealed Himself to human beings, it was at Mount Sinai. For many days God's presence descended on the mountain, producing a spectacular display of thunder, lightning, trumpet sounds and smoke. In fact, the sight was so overwhelming that the people trembled with fear (Exodus 19:16; 20:18) clearly, they were convinced that they were standing before God Himself.

Yet did that cause them to believe in Him? No, it may have verified His existence for them, but it did not change their hearts. In fact, while the Lord's presence was still hovering over the mountain, the Israelites fashioned an idol and began worshiping it in riotous abandon (Exodus 32:1-6). What an incredible rejection of God!

History contains ample evidence of God's revelation of Himself to humanity. The creation reveals His existence (Psalm 19:1-4; Romans 1:19-20), the Bible reveals His will (John 5:46-47), and Jesus Christ has revealed His person (John 1:14; 14:7-11). If these and countless other attesting signs are not enough to persuade someone to turn to the Lord in faith and obedience, probably nothing else will. No bolt of lightning, not the thunder of His voice, not even someone rising from the dead (Luke 16:31).

Words to Live By:

Ephesians 4:29, Let not any filthy word go out of your mouth, but what is good for necessary edification, that it may impart grace to the hearers.

Ephesians 4:30, And do not grieve the Holy Spirit of God, by whom you are sealed until *the* day of redemption.

Ephesians 4:31, Let all bitterness and wrath and anger and tumult and evil speaking be put away from you, with all malice.

Ephesians 4:32, And be kind to one another, tenderhearted, forgiving one another, even as God for Christ's sake has forgiven you.

Matthew 12:25, And Jesus knew their thoughts and said to them, every kingdom divided against itself is brought to desolation. And every city or house divided against itself shall not stand.

Mark 3:24, And if a kingdom is divided against itself, that kingdom cannot stand.

Romans 13:1, Let every soul be subject unto the higher powers. For there is no power but of God: the powers that be are ordained of God.

Commentary: God is the ultimate authority. Government as an institution has been established by God. God raises up and does away with leaders.

Romans 13:2, Whosoever therefore resisteth the power, resisteth the ordinance of God: and they that resist shall receive to themselves damnation.

Commentary: Government as an institution has been established by God to serve His purposes. Both followers and leaders are ultimately accountable to God. Submission to human authority as it aligns with God's Word reflects our submission to God's authority. We must serve the highest of all authorities, God Himself.

2 Chronicles 7:14

If my people who are called by my name will humble themselves, and pray, and seek my face, and turn from their wicked ways, then I will hear from heaven, and forgive their sin and heal their land.

Psalm 122:6

Pray for the peace of Jerusalem: May they prosper that love thee.

Note: If we don't speak out in support of Christian matters, we will forfeit our authority given to us by God!! We as the "Church" and "Ambassadors" should not hide. We should "Shine" because there can be beautiful miracles in our mouth. Amen!

If we are not part of the solution, then we are part of the problem.

Homework: Read Psalms 70 through 76 and Proverbs 21 and 22.

Lesson Plan 32

The Book of Exodus

Chapters 34, 35, & 36

Objective: To gain an understanding of Israel's delivery from slavery in Egypt.

Objective Breakdown:

1. Introduction

2. New Stone Tablets   Exodus 34:1-4

3. God Descends to the Mountain   Exodus 34:5-9

4. God Renews the Covenant   Exodus 34:10-17

5. Various Observances Are Restated   Exodus 34:18-28

6. Moses' Face Shines   Exodus 34:29-35

7. The Sabbath Is Renewed   Exodus 35:1-3

8. Moses Seeks Gifts for the Tabernacle   Exodus 35:4-19

9. The People Respond Generously   Exodus 35:20-29

10. The Craftsmen Assemble   Exodus 35:30-35

11. The Contributions Are More than Enough   Exodus 36:1-7

12. Curtains of Linen   Exodus 36:8-13

13. Curtains of Goats Hair   Exodus 36:14-19

14. Boards and Bars Overlaid with Gold   Exodus 36:20-34

15. The Veil and the Screen   Exodus 36:35-38

Introduction:

What does God look like? The saying that "seeing is believing" describes some people's attitude toward God. "I can't believe in a God I can't see," they say. "If God truly exists, why doesn't HE SHOW Himself?" Yet the question makes some unwarranted assumptions about the nature of God and the capacity of people to experience Him. As God told Moses, no Human being can see God and live

(Exodus 33:20).

The infinite God exceeds our limited ability to know him. That is why no one knows exactly what God looks like. In fact, we cannot even say that He "looks like anything, for He has no body, He is a Spirit (John 4:24).

Yet Scripture tells of a number of people who had encounters with God in which they saw manifestations of Him, even if they did not see Him directly. For example, Moses was able to see God's "back" (Exodus 33:23). Isaiah saw the Lord sitting on His throne (Isaiah 6:1-8). And Ezekiel had a vision in which God appeared like a man clothed in the fire standing above a storm cloud resembling a chariot (Ezekiel 1:1-28). In reading about encounters like these, it's important to keep in mind that the writers were relating what they experienced, as best as they could, in human terms. However, their reports cannot fully describe or explain God, as He exceeds human comprehension.

Thus, there are limits to knowing God. Fortunately, God has transcended those limits by sending Jesus, who is God in human form (John 1:14; 14:8-9; Colossians 1:1-15). Through Him, we can believe in a God we cannot see, and relate to a God who goes beyond our knowledge (John 20:29; Ephesians 1:15-21; 3:14-19).

Words to Live By:

Ephesians 4:29, Let not any filthy word go out of your mouth, but what is good for necessary edification, that it may impart grace to the hearers.

Ephesians 4:30, And do not grieve the Holy Spirit of God, by whom you are sealed until *the* day of redemption.

Ephesians 4:31, Let all bitterness and wrath and anger and tumult and evil speaking be put away from you, with all malice.

Ephesians 4:32, And be kind to one another, tenderhearted, forgiving one another, even as God for Christ's sake has forgiven you.

Matthew 12:25, And Jesus knew their thoughts and said to them, every kingdom divided against itself is brought to desolation. And every city or house divided against itself shall not stand.

Mark 3:24, And if a kingdom is divided against itself, that kingdom cannot stand.

Romans 13:1, Let every soul be subject unto the higher powers. For there is no power but of God: the powers that be are ordained of God.

Commentary: God is the ultimate authority. Government as an institution has been established by God. God raises up and does away with leaders.

Romans 13:2, Whosoever therefore resisteth the power, resisteth the ordinance of God: and they that resist shall receive to themselves damnation.

Commentary: Government as an institution has been established by God to serve His purposes. Both followers and leaders are ultimately accountable to God. Submission to human authority as it aligns with God's Word reflects our submission to God's authority. We must serve the highest of all authorities, God Himself.

2 Chronicles 7:14

If my people who are called by my name will humble themselves, and pray, and seek my face, and turn from their wicked ways, then I will hear from Heaven, and forgive their sin and heal their land.

Psalm 122:6

Pray for the peace of Jerusalem: May they prosper that love thee.

Note: If we don't speak out in support of Christian matters, we will forfeit our authority given to us by God!! We as the "Church" and "Ambassadors" should not hide. We should "Shine"!! Because there can be beautiful miracles in our mouth. Amen!

If we are not part of the solution, then we are part of the problem.

Homework: Read Psalms 77 through 83 and Proverbs 23 and 24.

Lesson Plan 33

The Book of Exodus

Chapters 37, 38, 39, & 40

Objective: To gain an understanding of Israel's delivery from slavery in Egypt.

Objective Breakdown:

1. Introduction

2. The Ark of the Covenant   Exodus 37:1-9

3. The Table for the Show Bread   Exodus 37:10-16

4. The Golden Lamp Stand   Exodus 37:17-24

5. The Altar of Incense   Exodus 37:25-28

6. Anointing Oil & Incense   Exodus 37:29

7. The Altar   Exodus 38:1-7

8. The Laver for Washing   Exodus 38:8

8. The Court of the Tabernacle   Exodus 38:9-20

9. Adding Up the Costs   Exodus 38:21-29

10. Garments for the Priests   Exodus 39:1-7

11. The Breastplate   Exodus 39:8-21

12. The Robe of the Ephod   Exodus 39:22-29

13. The Priestly Turban   Exodus 39:30

14. Holiness to the Lord   Exodus 39:31

15. The Work Is Finished   Exodus 39:32-43

16. God Says to Set Up the Tabernacle   Exodus 40:1-8

17. Preparations for Dedication   Exodus 40:9-15

18. The Tabernacle Is Erected   Exodus 40:16-33

Introduction:

From conflict to cohesion. After escaping from Egypt, the children of Israel struggled with numerous problems in the desert that threatened the cohesiveness of their community:

The complained over a lack of good food (Exodus 16:2-3).

They quarreled with Moses over water Exodus 17:2-3).

Their many needs for arbitration brought Moses to the point of exhaustion (Exodus 18:13-27).

Impatient over their Leader's absence during his stay on Mount Sinai, they fell into idolatry resulting in judgment from God (Exodus 32:1-35).

So, when Moses finally "broke ground" on the monumental task of building the tabernacle and its furnishing, it gave the people a unifying cause to rally around and unleashed a tide of generosity (Exodus 36:2-7). As a result, the entire community came together in some encouraging ways. Suddenly, the people showed willing hearts (Exodus 35:21, 26), diligence in the work, and generosity that exceeded the needs of the project. In fact, their leaders had to restrain the people from bringing more resources.

The world has never lacked for talented people. God has placed among humans a marvelous diversity of gifts and skills to accomplish meaningful work in the world. The experience of Israel in the wildness is testimony to this fact. First, God gave Moses to Israel, a gifted leader. However, when it came to the time to construct the tabernacle, Moses did not have the skills required. He was not a craftsman in the building trades. But God had already provided among the people migrating from Egypt skilled workers such as Bezalel, Aholiab (Exodus 36:1), and countless unnamed others such as the women who wove yarns and fine linen (Exodus 35:25-26) and those who gave freely and worked hard (Exodus 35:10, 21, 29; 36:3-7). All of these worked according to abilities that the Spirit had given them.

In looking over God's instructions to Moses concerning these workers, one notices that he was to (1) identify them a skilled people, (2) affirm them in their responsibilities in the task, and (3) free them to do their work jobs under the supervision of others who knew the trades. In carrying out this delegation of work Moses had a good example to follow in God, who delegated responsibility to people at the beginning of creation. He declared, "I have given it to you," and "it shall be yours" (Genesis 1:29; 9:2-3; 12:7; 13:15-17).

Words to Live By:

Ephesians 4:29, Let not any filthy word go out of your mouth, but what is good for necessary edification, that it may impart grace to the hearers.

Ephesians 4:30, And do not grieve the Holy Spirit of God, by whom you are sealed until *the* day of redemption.

Ephesians 4:31, Let all bitterness and wrath and anger and tumult and evil speaking be put away from you, with all malice.

Ephesians 4:32, And be kind to one another, tenderhearted, forgiving one another, even as God for Christ's sake has forgiven you.

Matthew 12:25, And Jesus knew their thoughts and said to them, every kingdom divided against itself is brought to desolation. And every city or house divided against itself shall not stand.

Mark 3:24, And if a kingdom is divided against itself, that kingdom cannot stand.

Romans 13:1, Let every soul be subject unto the higher powers. For there is no power but of God: the powers that be are ordained of God.

Commentary: God is the ultimate authority. Government as an institution has been established by God. God raises up and does away with leaders.

Romans 13:2, Whosoever therefore resisteth the power, resisteth the ordinance of God: and they that resist shall receive to themselves damnation.

Commentary: Government as an institution has been established by God to serve His purposes. Both followers and leaders are ultimately accountable to God. Submission to human authority as it aligns with God's Word reflects our submission to God's authority. We must serve the highest of all authorities, God Himself.

2 Chronicles 7:14

If my people who are called by my name will humble themselves, and pray, and seek my face, and turn from their wicked ways, then I will hear from heaven, and forgive their sin and heal their land.

Psalm 122:6

Pray for the peace of Jerusalem: May they prosper that love thee.

Note: If we don't speak out in support of Christian matters, we will forfeit our authority given to us by God!! We as the "Church" and "Ambassadors" should not hide. We should "Shine" because there can be beautiful miracles in our mouth. Amen!

If we are not part of the solution, then we are part of the problem.

Homework: Read Psalms 84 through 90 and Proverbs 25 and 26.

The Book of Leviticus

Scripture Focus Chapters 1-27

Objective: To gain an understanding of God's guidebook for His newly redeemed people, showing them how to worship, serve, and obey a Holy God.

Objective Breakdown:

1. Burnt Offering	Chapter 1:1-17
2. The Grain Offering	Chapter 2:1-16
3. The Peace Offering	Chapter 3:1-17
4. The Sin Offering	Chapter 4:1-35
5. The Sin Offering (cont.)	Chapter 5:1-13
6. The Trespass Offering	Chapter 5:14-19
7. The Trespass Offering (cont.)	Chapter 6:1-7
8. The Burnt Offering	Chapter 6:8-13
9. The Grain Offering	Chapter 6:14-23
10. The Sin Offering	Chapter 6:24-30
11. The Trespass Offering	Chapter 7:1-10
12. The Peace Offering	Chapter 7:11-36
13. The Summary of the Offerings	Chapter 7:37-38
14. Consecration Commanded by God	Chapter 8:1-5
15. Cleansing the Priest with Water	Chapter 8:6
16. Special Garments	Chapter 8:7-9
17. Anointing with Oil	Chapter 8:10-13
18. Consecrating with Blood	Chapter 8:14-30
19. The Priest Are to Remain in the Tabernacle	Chapter 8:31-36
20. Offerings for the Priest	Chapter 9:1-14

Lesson Plan 34

The Book of Leviticus

Chapters 1, 2, 3, 4, & 5

Objective: To gain an understanding of God's guidebook for His newly redeemed people, showing them how to worship, serve, and obey a Holy God.

Objective Breakdown:

1. Introduction

2. Burnt Offering   Chapter 1:1-17

3. The Grain Offering   Chapter 2:1-16

4. The Peace Offering   Chapter 3:1-17

5. The Sin Offering   Chapter 4:1-35

6. The Sin Offering (cont.)   Chapter 5:1-13

7. The Trespass Offering   Chapter 5:14-19

Introduction:

The word "Leviticus" means "pertaining to Levites," that is, the Book contains the System of Laws, administered by the Levitical Priesthood, under which the Hebrew nation lived. These laws were given mostly at Mt. Sinai with additions, repetitions, and explanations, throughout the Wilderness wanderings.

Levites, one tribe out of the Twelve, were set apart for the work of God. They were supported by Tithes; and had 48 cities (Numbers 35:7; Joshua 21:19).

One family of Levites, Aaron and sons, were set apart to be Priests. The rest of the Levites were to be Assistants to the Priests. Their duties were the care of the Tabernacle, and, later, the care of the Temple; and to be Teachers, Scribes, Musicians, Officers and Judges (see I Chronicles 23).

Chapters 1 to 5. Various Kinds of Offerings

Burnt-Offerings: of Bullocks, Rams, Goats, Doves, Pigeons: were wholly burned, signifying entire Self-Dedication to God.

Meal-Offerings: of Grain, Flour or Cakes, without leaven: a handful was burned: the rest was for priests.

Peace-Offerings: of Cattle, Sheep or Goats: the fat was burned: the rest, eaten, partly by offerers.

Sin-Offerings and Trespass-Offerings: different offerings for different sins: fat was burned: the rest, in some cases was burned without the camp.

2 Chronicles 7:14

If my people who are called by my name, shall humble themselves, and pray, and seek my face, and turn from their wicked ways; then will I hear from heaven, and will forgive their sin, and heal their land.

Psalm 122:6

Pray for the peace of Jerusalem; they shall prosper who love thee.

Lesson Plan 35

The Book of Leviticus

Chapters 6 & 7

Objective: To gain an understanding of God's guidebook for His newly redeemed people, showing them how to worship, serve, and obey a Holy God.

Objective Breakdown:

1. Introduction

2. The Trespass Offering (cont.)   Chapter 6:1-7

3. The Burnt Offering   Chapter 6:8-13

4. The Grain Offering   Chapter 6:14-23

5. The Sin Offering   Chapter 6:24-30

6. The Trespass Offering   Chapter 7:1-10

7. The Peace Offering   Chapter 7:11-36

8. The Summary of the Offerings   Chapter 7:37-38

Introduction:

Most of the religions of the ancient world made a distinction between sacred and the profane. However, the gods of these pagan religions were usually seen as behaving little better than human beings, and often quite a bit worse. Furthermore, the rituals of many of these religions were often cruel, degrading, and dehumanizing (see Leviticus 18:24-30).

God did not want His people Israel to practice those things. He was not a God to be worshiped in that way. So, when the Israelites left Egypt, He gave them careful instructions for how they were to worship Him. Most of these religious laws are contained in the Book of Leviticus which means "the book of the Levites." The Levites were the descendants of Levi who were called to be priests and religious leaders. Thus, Leviticus could be said to be Israel's manual for worship and religious life. Another term by which Leviticus is often known is the Holiness Code. It spells out what it means to worship and serve a Holy God.

Categories of instruction include:

Worship through offerings and sacrifices (Chapters 1-7).

The relationship between physical and biological matters and religious life (Chapters 11-15).

The Day of Atonement, the annual occasion in which the nation's sin was dealt with (Chapter 16).

The spiritual implications of day-to-day life (Chapters 17-24).

The Year of Jubilee, involving the return of property and lands to their owners and servants to their families (Chapter 25).

The implications of obeying or disobeying the Law (Chapter 26).

Vows (Chapter 27).

2 Chronicles 7: 14

If my people who are called by my name, shall humble themselves, and pray, and seek my face, and turn from their wicked ways; then will I hear from heaven, and will forgive their sin, and heal their land.

Psalm 122:6

Pray for the peace of Jerusalem; they shall prosper who love thee.

Lesson Plan 36

The Book of Leviticus

Chapters 8, 9, 10, & 11

Objective: To gain an understanding of God's guidebook for His newly redeemed people, showing them how to worship, serve, and obey a Holy God.

Objective Breakdown:

1. Introduction

2. Consecration Commanded by God   Chapter 8:1-5

3. Cleansing the Priest with Water   Chapter 8:6

4. Special Garments   Chapter 8:7-9

5. Anointing with Oil   Chapter 8:10-13

6. Consecrating with Blood   Chapter 8:14-30

7. The Priest Are to Remain in the Tabernacle   Chapter 8:31-36

8. Offerings for the Priest   Chapter 9:1-14

9. Offerings for the People   Chapter 9:15-21

10. The Lord Accepts the Offerings   Chapter 9:22-24

11. The Sin of Nadab and Abihu   Chapter 10:1-11

12. The Sin of Eleazar and Ithamar   Chapter 10:12-20

13. Animals of the Earth   Chapter 11:1-8

14. Living Things in the Waters   Chapter 11:9-12

15. Birds of the Air   Chapter 11:13-19

16. Winged Insects   Chapter 11:20-23

17. The Carcasses of the Unclean Animals   Chapter 11:24-28

18. Creeping Things   Chapter 11:29-38

Introduction: Chapters 8, 9. Consecrations of Aaron

Previous to the time of Moses, sacrifices were offered by Heads of Families. But now the nation organized, a place set apart for sacrifice, and a ritual prescribed, a special Hereditary Order of men was created, in solemn ceremony, for the service.

The Levitical Priesthood

Was divinely ordained as mediator between God and the Hebrew nation in the ministry of Animal Sacrifices. Animal Sacrifices Are No Longer Necessary. Christ Himself is the Great High-Priest for Man: The Only Mediator between God and Man. Hebrews 8, 9, 10, makes this very clear.

Chapter 10. Nadab and Abihu

Their swift and terrible punishment was a warning against high-handed treatment God's ordinances; even to Church Leaders who distort the Gospel of Christ with all kinds of Human Traditions.

Chapter 11. Clean and Unclean Animals

There was a distinction before the Flood between Clean and Unclean animals (Genesis 7:2). Moses enacted this distinction into law. Jesus abrogated the distinction (Mark 7:19), "making all meats clean."

2 Chronicles 7: 14

If my people who are called by my name, shall humble themselves, and pray, and seek my face, and turn from their wicked ways; then will I hear from Heaven, and will forgive their sin, and heal their land.

Psalm 122:6

Pray for the peace of Jerusalem; they shall prosper who love thee.

Lesson Plan 37

The Book of Leviticus

Chapters 12, 13, 14, & 15

Objective: To gain an understanding of God's guidebook for His newly redeemed people, showing them how to worship, serve, and obey a Holy God.

Objective Breakdown:

1. Introduction

2. The Laws Concerning Childbirth   Chapter 12:1-8

3. Examination of People   Chapter 13:1-46

4. Examination of Garments   Chapter 13:47-59

5. Cleansing of People   Chapter 14:1-32

6. Cleansing of Houses   Chapter 14:33-53

7. Purpose of the Laws of Leprosy   Chapter 14:54-57

8. Discharges of the Man   Chapter 15:1-18

9. Discharges of the Woman   Chapter 15:19-30

10. The Purpose of the Laws of Discharges   Chapter 15:31-33

Introduction:

You are an example—good or bad. People in authority always set an example be it good or bad. Nadab and Abihu (Leviticus 10:3) were judged severely by God not only because they had offered "profane fire" to the Lord, but also because in doing so they had dishonored God before "all the people" (Leviticus 10:3). God was well aware that people tend to follow leaders not on the basis of what those leaders say, but on the basis of what they do. The same is true for Christians who have been called to act as light in the world (Matthew 5:14-16). As followers of Christ, we are under particular scrutiny, especially by people who do not share our faith. God wants us to take seriously the privilege of representing Christ in our Community and workplace.

Chapter 12.

Purification of Mothers after Childbirth. In Leviticus, God linked clean and unclean with foods laws. In effect, this action of the Law formed the basis for Israel's national health policy. It not only addressed questions about food (Leviticus Chapter 11) but also certain childbirth issues (Leviticus Chapter 12), bodily functions (Leviticus Chapter 15), contagious skin diseases, especially leprosy (Leviticus Chapters 13 & 14), and related matters such as mildew and toxic environment.

Chapters 13, 14. Test of Leprosy

These regulations were for the purpose of controlling the spread of one of the most loathsome and dreaded diseases.

Chapter 15. Uncleanness

The elaborate system of specifications as to how a person could become ceremonially "uncleaned," and the requirements concerning it were it seems, designed to promote personal physical cleanliness, and continual recognition of God in all the ways of life.

2 Chronicles 7: 14

If my people who are called by my name, shall humble themselves, and pray, and seek my face, and turn from their wicked ways; then will I hear from heaven, and will forgive their sin, and heal their land.

Psalm 122:6

Pray for the peace of Jerusalem; they shall prosper who love thee.

Lesson Plan 38

The Book of Leviticus

Chapters 16, 17, 18, 19, & 20

Objective: To gain an understanding of God's guidebook for His newly redeemed people, showing them how to worship, serve, and obey a Holy God.

Objective Breakdown:

1. Introduction

2. Preparation of the High Priest   Chapter 16:1-5

3. Identification of Sacrifices   Chapter 16:6-10

4. Atonement or the Priest   Chapter 16:11-14

5. Atonement for the Tabernacle   Chapter 16:15-19

6. Atonement for the People   Chapter 16:20-28

9. Purpose of the Day of Atonement   Chapter 16:29-34

10. Laws Concerning the Location of Sacrifices   Chapter 17:1-9

11. Laws Concerning the Use of Blood   Chapter 17:10-16

12. Laws of Sexual Sins   Chapter 18:1-30

13. Laws of Social Order   Chapter 19:1-37

14. The Penalty of Worshiping Molech   Chapter 20:1-5

15. The Penalty for Consulting Spirits   Chapter 20:6-8

16. The Penalty for Cursing Parents   Chapter 20:9

17. The Penalty for Committing Sexual Sins   Chapter 20:10-21

18. The Purpose of the Laws of Sanctification of the People   Chapter 20:22-27

Introduction:

Chapter 16. Annual Atonement

This was on the 10th day of the 7th month. Most solemn day of the year. The removal of sin was only for a year (Hebrews 10-3), but it pointed forward to eternal removal (Zechariah 3:4, 8, 9; 13:1; Hebrews 10:14).

Chapter 17. Manner of Sacrifice

The law required presentation of animals at the door of the Tabernacle. Eating of Blood was strictly forbidden (3:17; 7:26, 27; 17:10-16; Genesis 9:4; Deuteronomy 12:16, 23-25); and still is (Acts 15:29).

Chapter 18. Canaanite Abominations

If we wonder that some of these things: Incest, Sodomy, Cohabitation with animals: are even mentioned, it was because they were in common practice among Israel's neighbors. Human sexuality is one of the most powerful dimensions of human life. Sexual union can create incredible bonds between a loving couple. It can lead to the birth of a baby, producing another human being in the image of God. Yet sex can also bring horrible devastation when misused—for example, through violence of rape, the out-of-control obsession of sexual addiction, or the tragic sexual abuse of another human. God gave humankind the gift of sexuality and is very concerned that people understand its proper and fulfilling use. So, He included clear warnings about its misuse (Leviticus 18:6-30).

Chapters 19, 20. Miscellaneous Laws

About the Sabbath, Idolatry, Peace-Offerings, Gleanings, Stealing, Swearing, Wages, Courts, Tale-Bearing, Brotherly Love, Diverse Breeding and Planting, Adultery, Orchards, Augury, Marred Beards and Flesh Cuttings, Harlotry, Respect for the Aged, Kindness to Strangers, Just Weights, Parents, Incest, Sodomy, Animals, Cleanliness and Uncleanliness.

Thou Shalt Love Thy Neighbor as Thyself, 19:18

Concubinage, Polygamy, Divorce, Slavery

These were allowed, but greatly restricted (19:20; Deuteronomy 21:15; 24:1-4; Exodus 21:2-11). Moses' law lifted marriage to a far higher level than existed in surrounding nations.

2 Chronicles 7:14

If my people who are called by my name, shall humble themselves, and pray, and seek my face, and turn from their wicked ways; then will I hear from heaven, and will forgive their sin, and heal their land.

Pray for the peace of Jerusalem; they shall prosper who love thee.

Lesson Plan 39

The Book of Leviticus

Chapters 21, 22, 23, 24, & 25

Objective: To gain an understanding of God's guidebook for His newly redeemed people, showing them how to worship, serve, and obey a Holy God.

Objective Breakdown:

1. Introduction

2. Laws Concerning Priests   Chapter 21:1-9

3. Laws Concerning High Priests   Chapter 21:10-15

4. People Prohibited from the Priesthood   Chapter 21:16-24

5. Things Prohibited of the Priesthood   Chapter 22:1-16

6. Sacrifices Prohibited by the Priesthood   Chapter 22:17-30

7. Purpose of the Laws of the Priesthood   Chapter 22:31-33

8. The Weekly Sabbath   Chapter 23:1-3

9. Passover   Chapter 23:4-5

10. Unleavened Bread   Chapter 23:6-8

11. First Fruits   Chapter 23:9-14

12. Pentecost   Chapter 23:15-22

13. Trumpets   Chapter 23:23-25

14.. Day of Atonement   Chapter 23:26-32

15. Tabernacles   Chapter 23:33-44

16. Oil for the Lamps   Chapter 24:1-4

17. The Showbread   Chapter 24:5-9

18. Law of the Sanctified Name of God   Chapter 24:10-23

Introduction:

Give God your best. When it came to sacrifices, offerings, and the payment of vows, God required that the Israelites bring their best animals and goods to Him. Nothing with a defect was allowed (Leviticus 22:20-23). This was because God is a Holy, perfect God. He is worthy of the best His people had to offer. In the end all that they had belonged to Him anyway (see Deuteronomy 8:18; 1 Chronicles 29:14-15). In light of this command to bring God the best believers today do well to consider:

Do we honor God with the best of what we have—in terms of our time, talent and treasure or do we just offer our "leftovers"?

Do we serve God at work with our best effort utilizing the resources and abilities that He has given us as best we can?

Do we worship God in an alert, active way, paying attention and entering into His presence with all we have—mind, emotion and will?

Do we treat others—who are made in God's image—with the best intentions, showing honor, respect, and love toward them as we would toward Christ?

Offenses punishable with death include murder (Genesis 9:6; Exodus 21:12).

Chapters 21, 22. Priests and Sacrifices

An expansion of the provisions of chapters 1 to 9. Priests must be without physical blemish and may marry only a virgin. Sacrificial animals must be without blemish, and at least 8 days old.

Chapters 23, 24. Feasts, Lamp, Shewbread, Blasphemy

Capital Punishment (Leviticus Chapter 24:10-23)

Chapter 25. Sabbatical Year. Year of Jubilee Chapter 25.

Sabbatic Year was every 7th year. The land was to lie fallow. No sowing, no reaping, no pruning of vineyards. Spontaneous produce was to be left for the poor and the sojourner. God promised enough in the 6th year to carry over. Debts of fellow Jews were to be canceled.

Jubilee Year was every 50th year. It followed the 7th Sabbatic Year, making two rest years come together. It began on the Day of Atonement. All debts were canceled, slaves set free, and lands that had been sold returned. Jesus seemed to regard it as a sort of picture of the Grand Jubilee which He came to proclaim (Leviticus 25:10; Luke 4:19).

Ownership of Land

The Land of Canaan was divided among the 12 tribes, and, in the tribes, among families. With certain exceptions, it could not be sold in perpetuity out of the families. A sale amounted to a lease till Jubilee when it would be returned to original family.

The Number Seven

Every 7th day a Sabbath.

Every 7th year a Sabbatic year.

Every 7th Sabbatic year was followed by a Jubilee year.

Every 7th month was especially holy, having 3 feasts.

There were 7 weeks between Passover and Pentecost.

Passover Feast lasted 7 days.

Tabernacles Feast lasted 7 days.

At Passover 14 lambs (twice 7) were offered daily.

At Tabernacles 14 lambs (twice 7), daily, and 70 bullocks.

At Pentecost 7 lambs were offered.

2 Chronicles 7: 14

If my people who are called by my name, shall humble themselves, and pray, and seek my face, and turn from their wicked ways; then will I hear from heaven, and will forgive their sin, and heal their land.

Psalm 122:6

Pray for the peace of Jerusalem; they shall prosper who love thee.

Lesson Plan 40

The Book of Leviticus

Chapters 26 & 27

Objective: To gain an understanding of God's guidebook for His newly redeemed people, showing them how to worship, serve, and obey a Holy God.

Objective Breakdown:

1. Introduction

2. Basic Requirements of Obedience   Chapter 26:1-2

3. Conditions and Results of Obedience   Chapter 26:3-13

4. Conditions and Results of Disobedience   Chapter 26:14-39

5. The Promise of Restoration   Chapter 26:40-46

6. Consecration of Persons   Chapter 27:1-8

7. Consecration of Animals   Chapter 27:9-13

8. Consecration of Houses   Chapter 27:14-15

9. Consecration of Fields   Chapter 27:16-25

10. Firstborn Clean Animals   Chapter 27:26-27

11. Devoted Things   Chapter 27:28-29

12. Tithes   Chapter 27:30-33

13. The Conclusion of Leviticus   Chapter 27:1-34

Introduction:

The redeeming relative. To whom would you turn to if you fell on hard times financially? Many people resort to family and close relatives. But more and more people today have no one to turn to if they need help. In ancient Israel, by contrast, people generally could count on some family member to step forward with financial support if poverty forced them into slavery or caused them to lose their land. This relative was called a "redeeming relative" (Leviticus 25:25) or "kinsman-redeemer."

The redeeming relative was usually a male relation—a brother, an uncle, a cousin (Leviticus 25:48-49) provided to protect the clan. The Hebrew word used for this kinsman means one who has the right to redeem. An Israelite could sell himself, his family, or his land (Leviticus 25:3943) in case of poverty. But the redeeming relative had first option by law to buy back any land or person being sold, thus allowing ownership to be kept within the clan (Leviticus 25:23-28; Jeremiah 32:6-10). Thus, the redeeming relative was an important figure in Israelite culture.

In the New Testament, Jesus is described as our brother who redeems us from the power of sin (Hebrews 2:11-12, 17).

Chapter 26. Obedience or Disobedience

Note: This chapter 26, like Deuteronomy 28, of magnificent promises and frightful warnings, is one of the great chapters of the Bible.

Chapter 27. Making Vows to the Lord

Chapter 27:1-34

2 Chronicles 7:14

If my people, which are called by my name, shall humble themselves, and pray, and seek my face, and turn from their wicked ways; then will I hear from heaven, and will forgive their sin, and will heal their land.

Psalm 122:6

Pray for the Peace of Jerusalem; May they prosper who love thee.

The Book of Numbers

Scripture Focus Chapters 1-36

Objective: To gain an understanding of the challenges the Israelites faced in the wilderness and why.

Objective Breakdown:

1.	Introduction	
2.	God Tells Moses to Take Census	Chapter 1:1-4
3.	Leaders of the Twelve Tribes	Chapter 1:5-16
4.	The Numbering Begins	Chapter 1:17-43
5.	All but the Levites Are Numbered	Chapter 1:44-54
6.	Three Tribes Are to Camp on the East	Chapter 2:1-9
7.	Three Tribes Are to Camp on the South	Chapter 2:10-17
8.	Three Tribes Are to Camp on the West	Chapter 2:18-24
9	Three Tribes Are to Camp on the North	Chapter 2:25-34
10.	Priests and Levites	Chapter 3:1-13
11.	Levites Are Numbered and Given Duties	Chapter 3:14-39
12.	Duties of the Ones of Kohath	Chapter 4:1-20
13.	Duties of the Sons of Gershon	Chapter 4:21-28
14.	Duties of the Sons of Merari	Chapter 4:29-33
15.	Moses Numbers the Sons of Kohath	Chapter 4:34-37
16	Moses Numbers the Sons of Gershon	Chapter 4:38-41
17.	Moses Numbers the Sons of Merari	Chapter 4:42-49
18.	Removal of Unclean Persons	Chapter 5:1-1-4
19.	Restitution for Wrongdoing	Chapter 5:5-10
20.	Trying a Woman for Adultery	Chapter 5:11-31
21.	The Vow of the Nazirite	Chapter 6:1-12

121

Lesson Plan 41

The Book of Numbers

Chapter 1

Objective: To gain an understanding of the challenges the Israelites faced in the wilderness and why.

Objective Breakdown:

1. Introduction

2. God Tells Moses to Take Census   Chapter 1:1-4

3. Leaders of the Twelve Tribes   Chapter 1:5-16

4. The Numbering Begins   Chapter 1:17-43

5. All But the Levites Are Numbered   Chapter 1:44-54

Introduction:

Leviticus covers one month, but Numbers covers almost thirty-nine years (1444-1405 B.C.). It records Israel's movement from the last twenty days at Mt Sinai (1:1; 10:11), the wandering around Kadesh Barnea, and finally the arrival in the plains of Moab in the fortieth year (Chapters 22:1; 26:3; 33:50; Deuteronomy 1:3).

Their tents covered several square miles whenever they camped since there are approximately two-and half million people (based on the census figures in Numbers 1 and 26). God miraculously feeds and sub-stains them in the desert. He preserves their clothing and gives them manna, meat, water, and a promise (Numbers 14:34).

Israel was made up of twelve tribes descended from the twelve sons of Jacob. However, the tribe of Joseph (Numbers 1:32) was considered two distinct tribes, Ephraim, and Manasseh, named after Joseph's sons (Genesis 48: 8-16). (Note: The Levites were not counted formally as a tribe.)

God Tells Moses to Take Census	Chapter 1:1-4
Leaders of the Twelve Tribes	Chapter 1:5-16
The Numbering Begins	Chapter 1:17-43
All But the Levites Are Numbered	Chapter 1:44-54

2 Chronicles 7:14

If my people, which are called by my name, shall humble themselves, and pray, and seek my face, and turn from their wicked ways; then will I hear from heaven, and will forgive their sin, and will heal their land.

Psalm 122:6

Pray for the Peace of Jerusalem; May they prosper who love thee.

Lesson Plan 42

The Book of Numbers

Chapters 2, 3, & 4

Objective: To gain an understanding of the challenges the Israelites faced in the wilderness.

Objective Breakdown:

1. Introduction

2. Three Tribes Are to Camp on the East   Chapter 2:1-9

3. Three Tribes Are to Camp on the South   Chapter 2:10-17

4. Three Tribes Are to Camp on the West   Chapter 2:18-24

5. Three Tribes Are to Camp on the North   Chapter 2:25-34

6. Priests and Levites   Chapter 3:1-13

7. Levites Are Numbered and Given Duties   Chapter 3:14-39

8. The Firstborn Are Redeemed   Chapter 3:40-51

9. Duties of the Sons of Kohath   Chapter 4:1-20

10. Duties of the Sons of Gershon   Chapter 4:21-28

11. Duties of the Sons of Merari   Chapter 4:29-33

12. Moses Numbers the Sons of Kohath   Chapter 4:34-37

13. Moses Numbers the Sons of Gershon   Chapter 4:38-41

14. Moses Numbers the Sons of Merari   Chapter 4:42-49

Introduction:

Organizing the encampment. As the Israelites traveled across the Sinai, they strayed in the tents that were arranged into sections or "neighborhoods" by tribes and family (Numbers 2:2). The Bible does not say why God specified the layout of the encampment as He did. Perhaps He wished to keep the tribes together as much as possible because the nation's warriors were organized by tribe (Numbers 1:2–4; 2:2–3). Or it may be that the arrangement was intended to make the tabernacle as accessible as possible.

Organizing for a big project:

One good way is to organize teams around specific tasks. That is how God instructed Moses to handle the mammoth task of moving Israel's house of worship the tabernacle. It was a delicate but important job. Notice the work teams assigned to the task:

Aaron and the priests carefully prepared the ark, the lampstands, utensils, and furniture for the move. Each piece had specific wrapping requirements (Numbers 4:5-16). The Kohathite division was assigned transportation of the items that Aaron and the priests had packed. This team could not go to work until the tabernacle's holy things were completely wrapped and ready to be placed on the carrying poles (Numbers 4:15).

The Gershonite Unit then collected and carried all the hangings, screens, and remaining utensils. Their work was carried out under strict supervision (Numbers 4:21-28).

The Merarite Group loaded and carried all bases, pillar, bars, cords, and pegs under the supervision of the priests, who were careful to name each worker assigned to carry each individual item (Numbers 4:29-33).

This kind of careful precision can be continued today among believers as they serve God. We can serve God by working together, planning systems carefully, and overcoming tendencies of competition and conflict.

2 Chronicles 7:14

If my people, which are called by my name, shall humble themselves, and pray, and seek my face, and turn from their wicked ways; then will I hear from heaven, and will forgive their sin, and will heal their land.

Psalm 122:6

Pray for the peace of Jerusalem; they will prosper who love thee.

Lesson Plan 43

The Book of Numbers

Chapters 5 & 6

Objective: To gain an understanding of the challenges the Israelites faced in the wilderness.

Objective Breakdown:

1. Introduction

2. Removal of Unclean Persons   Chapter 5:1-4

3. Restitution for Wrongdoing   Chapter 5:5-10

4. Trying a Woman for Adultery   Chapter 5:11-31

5. The Vow of the Nazirite   Chapter 6:1-12

6. Paying the Nazirite Vow   Chapter 6:13-21

7. A Blessing for Israel   Chapter 6:22-27

Introduction:

Jailing criminals may protect society and punish offenders, but what does it do for the victim of crimes? Wandering Israel had no jails, so it punished criminals in other ways. However, a major part of serving justice was for the offender to make restitution to the wronged person (Numbers 5:70). Restitution involved restoring or repaying losses in a way that made amends for the crime. In that way the law considered both criminal and victim. Ultimately it regarded crimes against property and persons to be "unfaithfulness against the Lord."

Modern day laws handle crimes and restitution much differently. But quite apart from the criminal justice system are there situations in you past or present in which paying someone back you have wronged would be appropriate, no matter how difficult?

What does a spouse do when the marriage partner breaks faith in the relationship? What can other believers do to address the wrong which has been done and see that justice is accomplished? In the case of an Israelite's wife suspected of adultery, the law acknowledged the pain of the offended spouse (Numbers 5: 14). It recognized the destructive potential of jealousy. So, it instructed an offended husband to bring his wife before the priest, who in turn would "set her before the Lord" (Numbers 5:15-16), who was the only One to be trusted to properly detect the sin.

The implication is clear: people are not likely to exhibit much justice when they are angry, or jealous. Ultimately, revenge belongs only to a Holy and righteous God. Only He can be trusted to mete out an absolutely fair punishment (Deuteronomy 32:35-39; Romans 12:19).

2 Chronicles 7:14

If my people, which are called by my name, shall humble themselves, and pray, and seek my face, and turn from their wicked ways; then will I hear from heaven, and will forgive their sin, and will heal their land.

Psalm 122:6

Pray for the peace of Jerusalem; they will prosper who love thee.

Lesson Plan 44

The Book of Numbers

Chapters 7 & 8

Objective: To gain an understanding of the challenges the Israelites faced in the wilderness.

Objective Breakdown:

1. Introduction

2. Leaders Bring Dedication Offerings   Chapter 7:1-11

3. From Judah   Chapter 7:12-17

4. From Issachar   Chapter 7:18-23

5. From Zebulun   Chapter 7:24-29

6. From Reuben   Chapter 7:30-35

7. From Simeon   Chapter 7:36-41

8. From Gad   Chapter 7:42-47

9. From Ephraim   Chapter 7:48-53

10. From Manasseh   Chapter 7:54-59

11. From Benjamin   Chapter 7:60-65

12. From Dan   Chapter 7:66-71

13. From Asher   Chapter 7:72-77

14. From Naphtali   Chapter 7:78-83

15. The Dedication Offering Is Summarized   Chapter 7:84-89

16. The Golden Lampstand   Chapter 8:1-4

17. Levites Are Cleansed for Service   Chapter 8:5-22

18. Age Qualification for Levites   Chapter 8:23-26

Introduction:

Have you ever felt a desire to dedicate yourself to the Lord in some special way for a period of time? The Nazarite vow (Numbers 6:2) was a very special way for the ancient Hebrews to do that. Just as they were encouraged to pay vows of their possessions (see "Learning to Say Thank You" at Levites 27:1-25), they could also make a vow of their own lives.

The term Nazirite meant "one separated or consecrated." Thus, a person taking a Nazirite vow devoted himself to God. As a sign of his commitment, the Nazirite abstained from all products of the vine—grapes, raisins, wine, and vinegar—from the use of a razor, from touching a dead body, even that of a family member (Numbers 6:3-7).

The scripture does not explain why a person would make such a vow. But many believe that it was an act of devotion, or possibly of penitence after atonement for a sin. It is also possible that one became a Nizirite as a way of expressing single minded commitment to some important task. Along these lines, parents were known to make a Nazirite vow on behalf of their unborn children. For example, Hannah pledged that she would dedicate to the Lord any child that He might give her (1 Samuel 1:11, 27-28). In a similar case, the Angel of the Lord told Manoah that his wife would bear a son who would be a Nazirite. Thus, the judge Samson was born (Judges 13:3-5).

These vows appear to be exceptional. Numbers implies that the Nazarite vow normally lasted for a fixed period of time (Numbers 6:13). If so, that would make it accessible to the average person. One could show devotion to God for several days, weeks, months, or perhaps even years. So, there was no need to drop out of society or practice extreme forms of abstinence.

2 Chronicles 7:14

If my people, which are called by my name, shall humble themselves, and pray, and seek my face, and turn from their wicked ways; then will I hear from heaven, and will forgive their sin, and will heal their land.

Psalm 122:6

Pray for the peace of Jerusalem; they will prosper who love thee.

Lesson Plan 45

The Book of Numbers

Chapters 9 & 10

Objective: To gain an understanding of the challenges the Israelites faced in the wilderness.

Objective Breakdown:

1. Introduction

2. The People Keep the Passover   Chapter 9:1-5

3. Passover for Special Cases   Chapter 9:6-14

4. God Uses a Cloud to Lead Israel   Chapter 9:15-23

5. Trumpets Are Used as Signals   Chapter 10:1-10

6. The People Start Out   Chapter 10:11-13

7. The Order to March   Chapter 10:14-28

8. Hobab Is Recruited as a Guide   Chapter 10:29-32

9. A Three-Day Journey   Chapter 10:33-36

Introduction:

Knowing when to start and stop. As God led Israel through the wilderness, He used the cloud of His presence to indicate starts and stops (Numbers 9:15-23). Today believers have the Word of God to guide them through. Yet even so, we still need wise leaders who have a good sense of timing for when to get something started and when to bring a halt to activity.

God was Israelites' guide. Is He ours? Do we follow the basic guidelines of His Word and then make wise, responsible choices?

The congregation which Moses was to call by blowing the silver trumpets (Numbers 10:2-3) included the entire population of Israel as God's chosen people. Often this group was referred to as the "assembly," especially as it came to gathering at an appointed time (for example, on the Sabbath or a feast day and the "tabernacle of meeting") (Numbers 10:3) for religious purposes.

Centuries later, when the synagogue was developed (see Mark 1:21), the group that gathered at the synagogue was referred to as the "assembly." The Hebrew word for assembly was often rendered ekklesia, a term that early Christians adopted. Eventually ekklesia was translated into English a "church."

2 Chronicles 7:14

If my people, which are called by my name, shall humble themselves, and pray, and seek my face, and turn from their wicked ways; then will I hear from heaven, and will forgive their sin, and will heal their land.

Psalm 122:6

Pray for the peace of Jerusalem; they will prosper who love thee.

Lesson Plan 46

The Book of Numbers

Chapters 11 & 12

Objective: To gain an understanding of the challenges the Israelites faced in the wilderness.

Objective Breakdown:

1. Introduction

2. Complaining Is Punished   Chapter 11:1-3

3. The People Crave Meat   Chapter 11:4-9

4. Moses Cried Out to the Lord   Chapter 11:10-23

5. Seventy Elders Prophesy   Chapter 11:24-30

6. God Sends Quail and a Plague   Chapter 11:31-35

7. Miriam and Aaron Speak Against Moses   Chapter 12:1-3

8. God Responds   Chapter 12:4-9

9. Miriam Is Stricken with Leprosy   Chapter 12:9-16

Introduction:

In Numbers 12:3 it states that Moses was the humblest man on the face of the earth. In any case Moses put up with a great deal of grief and rarely complained. His example gives us a challenge on how we should respond to harsh treatment.

Some families seem destined to leadership. The family of Moses, Aaron, and Miriam was such a family. Yet a crisis developed when the two older siblings turned on their younger brother Moses (Numbers 12:1-2). The text suggests that the root of the problem may have been racial intolerance toward Moses' Ethiopian wife. Ethiopia, sometimes referred to as Nubia or Cush, was south of Egypt.

Sooner or later every authority figure will probably face a challenge of authority. Moses faced one from two major Israelite leaders, who happened to be his sister and brother. How he handled the situation, including his plea for God to deliver his sister, Miriam, from Leprosy (Numbers 12:13) proves instructive. There are several lessons to be gained about the nature of Godly authority and the challenges people in authority face.

Was the attack of Miriam and Aaron solely a racial issue? Was it possibly also a case of sibling rivalry, such as Cain and Able experienced in Genesis 4:1-16. Were the older brother and sister competing for leadership over Israel, much like James and John argued over who was closest to Jesus (Mark 10:35-44)? In any case Miriam was stricken with Leprosy for her rebellion and Aaron repented and pleaded for mercy for himself and his sister Miriam. Moses, then cried out to the Lord for mercy and for healing (Numbers 12:9-15).

2 Chronicles 7:14

If my people, which are called by my name, shall humble themselves, and pray, and seek my face, and turn from their wicked ways; then will I hear from heaven, and will forgive their sin, and will heal their land.

Psalm 122:6

Pray for the peace of Jerusalem; they will prosper who love thee.

Lesson Plan 47

The Book of Numbers

Chapters 13 & 14

Objective: To gain an understanding of the challenges the Israelites faced in the wilderness.

Objective Breakdown:

Introduction:

Our world has entered the "information age." Never before has humanity known so much. Yet as Moses and the Israelites discovered at Kadesh Barnea, possessing facts does not necessarily lead to wisdom. For what we need is leaders with vision.

Apparently only two of the men that Israel sent to spy the land of Canaan (Numbers 13:2,17) were visionary leaders. The rest became depressed by their data. Actually, the English term "spy" is a bit misleading. They were not engaged in cloak-and dagger espionage. They were more like explorers and land surveyors. Many of the details of their work are laid out in Numbers chapters 34 and became the basis for apportioning the land 40 years later.

But as chapters 13-14 show, even though these men had the technical skill to access the lay of the land, most of them lacked the vision and the courage to take hold of it. Despite God's repeated promises to help His people by driving out the Canaanites, these men lost faith in Him. Indeed, lost faith in themselves. "We were like grasshoppers in our own sight" (Numbers 13:13).

Thus, twelve experts read the same data, but ten reached a different conclusion than the other two. What was the difference? Vision. All twelve could see that this was indeed a "land flowing with milk and honey." All twelve could see the powerful obstacles to overcome, but only two put their faith in God who is more powerful than all the Canaanites put together. Had God not defeated the Egyptians? The God who had pledged Himself to deliver the land to His people.

2 Chronicles 7:14

If my people, which are called by my name, shall humble themselves, and pray, and seek my face, and turn from their wicked ways; then will I hear from heaven, and will forgive their sin, and will heal their land.

Psalm 122:6

Pray for the peace of Jerusalem; they will prosper who love thee.

Lesson Plan 48

The Book of Numbers

Chapters 15 & 16

Objective: To gain an understanding of the challenges the Israelites faced in the wilderness.

Objective Breakdown:

1. Introduction

2. Instructions About Offerings   Chapter 15:1-21

3. Unintentional Sins   Chapter 15:22-29

4. Presumptuous Sins   Chapter 15:30-31

5. A Sabbath Violator Is Stoned   Chapter 15:32-36

6. Fringes as a Reminder   Chapter 15:37-41

7. Korah Leads a Rebellion   Chapter 16:1-3

8. Moses Calls a Meeting   Chapter 16:4-19

9. Korah's People Are Set Apart   Chapter 16:20-30

10. God's Judgment Falls   Chapter 16:31-40

11. A Plague Is Stopped   Chapter 16:41-50

Introduction:

Some passages in the bible are difficult, not because they are hard to understand, but because they are hard to accept. The condemnation and execution of a man for picking up sticks on the Sabbath (Numbers 15:32-36) is one of them.

To our way of thinking, this incident may seem like an abuse of authorityon God's part. Put s man to death for picking up sticks? I seem like an incredible case of overkill. Yet it's important to put this incident in perspective. (Like a similar case in Scripture: Ananias and Sapphira, Acts 5:1-11).

God decided to make an example of this individual for ignoring God's instructions. It's instructive to notice that his offense followed God's Word regarding presumptive sins (Numbers 15:30-31). Apparently, this man willfully and knowingly ignored God's explicit instruction concerning the Sabbath

(Exodus 20:8-10).

In a sense God had to act decisively and firmly at some point. Otherwise, the people might have well concluded that God's laws were of little consequence, and they could do as they pleased. What does this say about following God today? If we step out of line, should we expect Him to react? The Old Testament including Numbers 15, was written for our instruction (see Romans 15:4; 1 Corinthians 10:6, 11). We should read and heed what God has said, realizing that what God is trying to show us should not be trifled with. Obey God and His Word it is the safest and most desirable way to please our Creator and spend eternity with Him.

2 Chronicles 7:14

If my people, which are called by my name, shall humble themselves, and pray, and seek my face, and turn from their wicked ways; then will I hear from heaven, and will forgive their sin, and will heal their land.

Psalm 122:6

Pray for the peace of Jerusalem, they will prosper who love thee.

Lesson Plan 49

The Book of Numbers

Chapters 17, 18, 19, & 20

Objective: To gain an understanding of the challenges the Israelites faced in the wilderness.

Objective Breakdown:

1. Introduction

2. Aaron's Rod Blossoms   Chapter 17:1-12

3. Priestly Privileges   Chapter 18:1-7

4. Offerings for the Use of the Priests   Chapter 18:8-19

5. Tithes and Tenths of Tithes   Chapter 18:20-32

6. The Ordinance of the Red Heifer   Chapter 19:1-10

7. Using the Heifers' Ashes to Purify   Chapter 19:11-22

8. Miriam Dies   Chapter 20:1

9. The People Cry Out for Water   Chapter 20:2-6

10. Moses Strikes a Rock in Error   Chapter 20:7-13

11. Edom Refuses Israel's Passage   Chapter 20:14-21

12. Aaron Dies   Chapter 20:22-29

Introduction:

When a relationship has broken down, what can be done? When broken promises separate friends, how can the two people be reunited? It helps when a third party can be found to mediate a settlement. That was the function of the priests in ancient Israel. By favoring Aaron's rod over the others, God made it clear who should stand between Him and the people (Numbers 17:10-11).

God's relationship with Israel repeatedly broke down as a result of violated commandments and rebellious complaints on the part of the Israelites. Sometimes the offenses were so substantial that God immediately punished the offenders (Numbers 14:40; 15:3-36; 16:31-35). Yet even when His character was violated and the people deserved judgment God listened to Moses and Aaron as they intervened on behalf of the people (Numbers 16:22, 46-48).

After Korah was taken away, the situation continued to deteriorate (Numbers 16:41). Apparently, the people had already forgotten whom God had already placed in charge and made priests. So, the Lord devised a plan to again make it clear that one group—the sons of Aaron—were to act as intermediaries or priests between Him and the rebellious nation (Numbers 17:1-11). In the New Testament Jesus Christ is the intermediary or advocate between God and sinful people.

2 Chronicles 7:14

If my people, which are called by my name, shall humble themselves, and pray, and seek my face, and turn from their wicked ways; then will I hear from heaven, and will forgive their sin, and will heal their land.

Psalm 122:6

Pray for the peace of Jerusalem; they will prosper who love thee.

Lesson Plan 50

The Book of Numbers

Chapters 21 & 22

Objective: To gain an understanding of the challenges the Israelites faced in the wilderness.

Objective Breakdown:

1. Introduction

2. Victory over the King of Arad   Chapter 21:1-3

3. A Bronze Serpent on a Pole   Chapter 21:4-9

4. The Journey Continues   Chapter 21:10-20

5. Victory Over the Amorites   Chapter 21:21-30

6. Victory Over Bashan   Chapter 21:31-35

7. Balaam Refuses to Side with Balak   Chapter 22:1-14

8. God Let Balaam Go to Balak   Chapter 22:15-21

9. Balaam Learns a Lesson   Chapter 22:22-35

10. Balaam Arrives at Moab   Chapter 22:36-41

Introduction:

The transfer of authority is always a difficult task. Changing leaders can be a time of great stress for an organization of old alliances and political forces with new ones to determine who will share the future.

The death of Aaron (Numbers 20:22-29) was a major event in the life of Israel. He was not only high priest for the nation of Israel but the nation's first high priest. Furthermore, he had been Moses's primary spokesman (Exodus 4:16; 7:1). He was also Moses' brother.

Aaron's successor, Eleazar was his third son. Nadab and Abihu, Aaron's two older sons, had been consumed in the Lord's anger after offering "profane fire" before the Lord (Leviticus 10:1-3). Thus, Eleazar was in in a sense, the third choice for the position of high priest.

Despite these other factors, the transition from Aaron to Eleazar went smoothly. Perhaps because God Himself oversaw the transfer of power.

2 Chronicles 7:14

If my people, which are called by my name, shall humble themselves, and pray, and seek my face, and turn from their wicked ways; then will I hear from heaven, and will forgive their sin, and will heal their land.

Psalm 122:6

Pray for the peace of Jerusalem; they will prosper who love thee.

Lesson Plan 51

The Book of Numbers

Chapters 23 & 24

Objective: To gain an understanding of the challenges the Israelites faced in the wilderness.

Objective Breakdown:

1. Introduction

2. Balaam Blesses Israel   Chapter 23:1-12

3. Balaam Blesses Israel Again   Chapter 23:13-26

4. Balaam Blesses Israel Yet Again   Chapter 23:27-30

5. Balaam Blesses Israel Yet Again (cont.)   Chapter 24:1-11

6. The Oracle of Balaam   Chapter 24:12-25

Introduction:

Given the fact that the number of Israelites traveling through the Sinai Desert probably numbered in the millions, the Exodus journey could be considered something of a miracle. The amount of water and food required to feed such a multitude was not readily available in the natural environment, which was wilderness (Numbers 21:11). God had to provide for His people during the forty years that it took them to reach the Promised Land.

This not to suggest that the Sinai wilderness was completely void of resources. The Egyptians, Midianites, and other groups had long sent caravans across these wastes, establishing well-worn routes. Seasoned traders knew where oases were, and how to find water by following the many wades, or dry riverbeds, that occasionally turned into gushing streams during a rare downpour, especially near mountains. They also knew that a few feet under the desert sand lay deposits of limestone, which collected water that cold sometime be brought to the surface.

The water table helped a number of hardy plants to grow such as the acacia tree (see Exodus 25:10) and desert grasses. This vegetation supported not only insects and reptiles, but mammals such as lions, gazelles, desert hares, antelopes, and wild bulls, as well as birds such as quail and ostriches.

Life in the wilderness was not easy for the Israelites, but it was not impossible either. With both natural and supernatural resources to draw upon, the nation survived the journey in the process, they learned the lesson that man does not live by bread alone, but by "every word that proceeds from the mouth of the Lord" (Deuteronomy 8:3).

2 Chronicles 7:14

If my people, which are called by my name, shall humble themselves, and pray, and seek my face, and turn from their wicked ways; then will I hear from heaven, and will forgive their sin, and will heal their land.

Psalm 122:6

Pray for the peace of Jerusalem; they will prosper who love thee.

Lesson Plan 52

The Book of Numbers

Chapters 25 & 26

Objective: To gain an understanding of the challenges the Israelites faced in the wilderness.

Objective Breakdown:

1. Introduction

2. Israel's Immorality with Moab   Chapter 25:1-5

3. The Zeal of Phinehas   Chapter 25:6-9

4. God Makes a Covenant of Peace   Chapter 25:10-18

5. A Second Census Is Commanded   Chapter 26:1-4

6. Reuben   Chapter 26:5-11

7. Simeon   Chapter 26:12-14

8. Gad   Chapter 26:15-18

9. Judah   Chapter 26:19-22

10. Issachar   Chapter 26:23-25

11. Zebulun   Chapter 26:26-27

12. Manasseh   Chapter 26:28-34

13. Ephraim   Chapter 26:35-37

14. Benjamin   Chapter 26:38-41

15. Dan   Chapter 26:42-43

16. Asher   Chapter 26:44-47

17. Naphtali   Chapter 26:48-51

18. Principles for Dividing the Land   Chapter 26:52-56

19. The Levites Are Numbered   Chapter 26:57-62

Introduction:

Balaam (Numbers 22:5) is one of the most intriguing characters in Scripture, and in study contrasts. He was a priest or seer who could bless or curse people (Numbers 22:6). Even though he was not a Hebrew he communicated with their God (Numbers 22:8-12). He was known to work for a fee (Numbers 22:7, 16-18).

He lived at Pethor, a town on the Euphrates River in Mesopotamia, yet his fame was apparently widespread enough that King Belak in Moab and his Midianites allies sent to him for help (Numbers 22:4-5). He was explicitly prevented by God from cursing the Israelites, yet he kept trying to find a way to satisfy the Moabites' request and perhaps earn himself a handsome fee (Numbers 22:12, 20-21).

He eventually succeeded in causing Israel trouble, yet it cost him his own life (see Numbers 31:15-16).

Even though Balaam was a Gentile, he apparently knew and to some extent served the living God, in that way he was like other ancient priests like Moses' father-in-law, Reuel (or Jethro Exodus 2:16-18), and possible Job (Job 42:8-9).

Actually, Balaam had little choice but to bless Israel three times. After all, God had already pronounced blessings on Abraham's descendants (Numbers 22:12), and Balaam could not counter that (Numbers 22:18; 24:12-13).

2 Chronicles 7:14

If my people, which are called by my name, shall humble themselves, and pray, and seek my face, and turn from their wicked ways; then will I hear from heaven, and will forgive their sin, and will heal their land.

Psalm 122:6

Pray for the peace of Jerusalem; they will prosper who love thee.

Lesson Plan 53

The Book of Numbers

Chapters 27 & 28

Objective: To gain an understanding of the challenges the Israelites faced in the wilderness.

Objective Breakdown:

1. Introduction

2. Zelophehad's Daughters Request Land   Chapter 27:1-11

3. God Tells Moses to Prepare to Die   Chapter 27:12-14

4. Moses Commissions Joshua   Chapter 27:15-23

5. Daily Offerings   Chapter 28:1-8

6. Sabbath Offerings   Chapter 28:9-10

7. Monthly Offerings   Chapter 28:11-15

8. Offerings at Passover   Chapter 28:16-25

9. Offerings at the Feast of Weeks   Chapter 28:26-31

Introduction:

Often when vast new resources become available, new rules must be written to manage the distribution of those resources. Sometimes new systems are required to ensure the fairness and mediate among competing interests.

Israel faced such a situation as it prepared to enter the "land of milk and honey," the daughters of Zelophehad (Numbers 27:1) had listened while Moses reviewed the laws of inheritance (Numbers 26:53-56). These laws must have been of keen interest to every family, for soon each one's inheritance would include a portion of the promised.

The rule of thumb in settling an estate was to divide the land among the sons of each clan (Deuteronomy 21:15-17). This kept the land within the family throughout the generations. Daughters, who were among most likely married within the family throughout the generations. Daughters, who were more likely to marry outside the clan, were not included in the settlement of the estate. This was not only true of the Hebrews but of the surrounding Near Eastern cultures. Instead of inherited land daughters received

150

dowries at the time of marriage for example, Judges 1:13-15; 1 Kings 9:16).

However, the daughters of Zelophehad brought an appeal to Moses because their father had died without leaving sons to inherit any land that would come the family's way. They pointed out that in fairness they be given their father's allotment (Numbers 26:33-34; 27:4). Moses enacted a new law, and the daughters received the land. Thus, new legislation and new resources led to a reexamination of old values and revised legislation.

2 Chronicles 7:14

If my people, which are called by my name, shall humble themselves, and pray, and seek my face, and turn from their wicked ways; then will I hear from heaven, and will forgive their sin, and will heal their land.

Psalm 122:6

Pray for the peace of Jerusalem; they will prosper who love thee.

Lesson Plan 54

The Book of Numbers

Chapters 29 & 30

Objective: To gain an understanding of the challenges the Israelites faced in the wilderness.

Objective Breakdown:

1. Introduction

2. Offerings at the Feast of Trumpets   Chapter 29:1-6

3 Offerings at the Day of Atonement   Chapter 29:7-11

4. Offerings at the Feast of Tabernacles   Chapter 29:12-40

5. Vows Made by Men   Chapter 30:1-2

6. Vows Made by Women   Chapter 30:3-16

Introduction:

Learning to pray. Prayer is a scary, awkward proposition for many people. It's the kind of activity that they would just as soon leave to religious professionals. But Scripture encourages with numerous examples of people who demonstrate that prayer is an everyday activity for everyday people. Moses, who asked God for a successor (Numbers 27:15-17), is a case in point.

Moses was a hard-working man. He went through at least three different careers--privileged ruler in Egypt, forgotten shepherd in Midian, and a national liberator and leader of the Israelites.

Throughout these pursuits, Moses regularly turned to God in prayer. Consider the following conversations that he had with God:

He debated with God about his fitness to lead Israel out of Egypt (Exodus 3:11-4:17; 6:28-7:7)

He interceded on behalf of the Egyptians (Exodus 8:9-13).

He asked for water for his thirsty nation of refugee people (Exodus 15:24-25).

He pleaded with God about sinful Hebrews and what God would do to them (Exodus 32:11-13, 31-34).

He interceded with God concerning his sister's leprosy, after she exhibited prejudice against

Moses' foreign-born spouse (Numbers 12:4-15).

He prayed for the transition of Leadership to Joshua (Numbers 27:15-23).

He appealed to God to allow him to join his people in their entrance to the Promised Land (Deuteronomy 3:23-25; 34:1-4).

Moses demonstrated the often forgotten truth that God is more than ready to hear our complaints, appeals, and frustrations. Are you willing to approach God in Prayer about the problems that vex you? Why not pause to do so right now?

2 Chronicles 7:14

If my people, which are called by my name, shall humble themselves, and pray, and seek my face, and turn from their wicked ways; then will I hear from heaven, and will forgive their sin, and will heal their land.

Psalm 122:6

Pray for the peace of Jerusalem; they will prosper who love thee.

Lesson Plan 55

The Book of Numbers

Chapters 31 & 32

Objective: To gain an understanding of the challenges the Israelites faced in the wilderness.

Objective Breakdown:

Introduction:

Playing with fire. The man who blessed thee Israelites three times ended up bringing a curse upon them—and on himself. The seer Balaam (Numbers 31:16) is a tragic lesson in how playing with fire can lead to getting burned.

Balaam played with fire by listening to the tempting offers of Balak, King of Moab (Numbers 22:16-17). Balak wanted Balaam to curse Israel. But the priest blessed Go's people three times (Numbers 23:7-11, 18-25; 24:3-10). However, Balaam never forgot Balak's offer. Sometime after returning home, he came up with the clever idea. He himself was forbidden by God to curse Israel, but what if the Israelites brought a curse upon themselves? To cause that Balaam apparently told Balak to use Moabite women to tempt the men of Israel into immorality and idolatry (Numbers 25:1-3; 31:15-16).

Israel fell into sin and the "anger of the Lord was aroused," resulting in a plague (Numbers 25:3, 8-9). We don't know what payment Balaam may have received for this plot. But when Israel eventually overran Midian, Balaam was killed as an enemy—despite the previous blessings he had uttered (Numbers 31:8).

Balaam was not the only one to get burned by playing with fire. Having once again toyed with idolatry, the Hebrews brought God's wrath upon themselves, resulting in 24,000 deaths (Numbers 25:9). Likewise, the Moabites and Midianites suffered militarily at the hands of the Israelites (Numbers 25:16-18; 31:1-18).

With what tempting fires do you play with? Sexual immorality? Financial impropriety? And theological novelty? If you are pushing past the limits of godliness, watch out! "Our God is a consuming fire" (Hebrews 12:29).

2 Chronicles 7:14

If my people, which are called by my name, shall humble themselves, and pray, and seek my face, and turn from their wicked ways; then will I hear from heaven, and will forgive their sin, and will heal their land.

Psalm 122:6

Pray for the peace of Jerusalem; they will prosper who love thee.

Lesson Plan 56

The Book of Numbers

Chapters 33 & 34

Objective: To gain an understanding of the challenges the Israelites faced in the wilderness.

Objective Breakdown:

1. Introduction

2. Israel's Journey   Chapter 33:1-2

3. From Rameses to Rephidim   Chapter 33:3-14

4. From Rephidim to Mount Hor   Chapter 33:15-39

5. From Mount Hor to Moab   Chapter 33:40-56

6. The Borders of Canaan   Chapter 34:1-15

7. Leaders Are Named to Divide the Land   Chapter 34:16-29

Introduction:

The journeys of Israel. No one knows the exact route that Israel took from Egypt to Canaan (Numbers 33:1). However, it was not a direct journey. After the people left Egypt, they traveled south to Mount Sinai, where they received the Law. Then they eventually made their way North to Kadesh (see Numbers 13:26), from which they sent spies to survey Promised Land. They lost faith in the Lord's promises. As a result, Israel spent the next forty years "wandering" through the wilderness while an entire generation died off. (Numbers 14:34-35).

Actually, the term "wandering" is a misnomer. The multitude was led by God Himself who gave His people a cloud to follow by day and a fiery cloud by night (Exodus 13:21-22). The next major leg in the journey was the attempt to pass through Edom (see "Hurt Can Lead to Prejudice" at Numbers 20:14-21). Because the King of Edom refused access to the King's Highway, Israel was forced to take a route around Edom in order to travel North for the Transjordan valley east of Canaan. It was from this area that they eventually began the conquest of the land.

The list in Numbers 33 includes many of the sites that the Israelites visited, however, not many have been positively identified by modern-day archaeologists.

If my people, which are called by my name, shall humble themselves, and pray, and seek my face, and turn from their wicked ways; then will I hear from heaven, and will forgive their sin, and will heal their land.

Psalm 122:6.

Pray for the peace of Jerusalem; they will prosper who love thee.

Lesson Plan 57

The Book of Numbers

Chapters 35 & 36

Objective: To gain an understanding of the challenges the Israelites faced in the wilderness.

Objective Breakdown:

1. Introduction

Introduction:

What shall we call the land? God promised to give the entire "land of Canaan" to the Israelites (Numbers 34:2). That promise began to be fulfilled around 1400 B. C. when Joshua and the people crossed the Jordan River and began conquering Canaan cities (Joshua 12:43). Long after that campaign was over, however, the territory seems to have continued to be called "the land of Canaan" (Judges 21:12). In fact, it was not until the later period of the Judges that it began to be called Israel (Ruth 4:7, 14; 1 Samuel 3:11; 11:3).

During the monarchy, the kingdom was called Israel until it divided in two. Then the ten Northern tribes which rebelled against Solomon's son Rehoboam kept the name Israel (1 Kings 12:18-19), while the kingdom of the two Southern tribes was known as Judah (1 Kings 12:21, 14:29). Israel eventually fell to the Assyrians (722 B.C.), and Judah to the Babylonians (586 B.C.). After the Babylonian exile, the district around Jerusalem continued to be called Judah (Nehemiah 1:2; Haggai 1:1).

However, a change had occurred by the time of Christ. The Romans then dominated the region, referring to the former territory of Canaan generally as Judea. For administrative purposes, though, they divided the into several districts: Judea, Idumea, Samaria, Galilee, and Perea. But the Jews in these districts maintained a sense of ethnic and religious unity by referring to themselves collectively as Israel (Matthew 8:10; 10:23).

It is interesting that the name Palestine was never used for the territory of Israel during the Biblical area.

It was only after the Romans destroyed Jerusalem in A.D. 70 that they renamed the land Palaestina, apparently as an insult to the Jews. The name is Latin for Palistia—a designation that recalled Israel's long-standing and detested enemies the Philistines (see Judges 13:1).

2 Chronicles 7:14

If my people, which are called by my name, shall humble themselves, and pray, and seek my face, and turn from their wicked ways; then will I hear from heaven, and will forgive their sin, and will heal their land.

Psalm 122:6

Pray for the peace of Jerusalem; they will prosper who love thee.

The Book of Deuteronomy

Scripture Focus Chapters 1-34

Objective: To gain an understanding of the warnings and blessings of the covenant which Moses spoke to all Israel during the forty years of their wandering in the desert.

Introduction:

What will you be remembered for?

What statements of yours will your children's children pass onto succeeding generations?

In the Book of Deuteronomy, we have Moses' farewell address to the people of Israel. Knowing that they would soon enter Canaan without him, Moses was responsible for reminding them of the binding agreement, or covenant, that their parents had made with the Lord at Mount Sinai. A great many of those who heard Moses' speech had not even been born when the original covenant was made. Now young adults, they needed to know what was expected of them as they entered the Promised Land.

Deuteronomy is not just a repeat of Exodus and Leviticus. It is the summary of a godly heritage, a record of God's faithfulness during more than forty difficult years. It is also the final pronouncement of a great leader.

As you read Deuteronomy, put yourself in Moses' shoes, and then in the shoes of his listeners. Either way, you'll see the importance of telling future generations about the works and words of God.

1.	Introduction	
2.	Moses Addresses Israel	Chapter 1:1-4
3.	The Journey from Horeb to Kadesh Barnea	Chapter 1:5-28
4.	The People's Disbelief	Chapter 1:29-40
5.	Israel's Defeat by the Amorites	Chapter 1:41-46
6.	The Bypassing of Seir and Moab	Chapter 2:1-12
7.	The Wilderness Journey	Chapter 2:13-23
8.	The Defeat of Sihon and the Amorites	Chapter 2:24-37
9.	The Defeat of Og, King of Bashan	Chapter 3:1-11
10.	The Division of Eastern Lands	Chapter 3:12-22

Lesson Plan 58

The Book of Deuteronomy

Chapters 1 & 2

Objective: To gain an understanding of a summary of a godly heritage, a record of God's faithfulness during more than 40 difficult years of wandering in the desert.

Objective Breakdown:

1. Introduction

2. Moses Addresses Israel   Chapter 1:1-4

3. The Journey from Horeb to Kadesh Barnea   Chapter 1:5-28

4. The People's Disbelief   Chapter 1:29-40

5. Israel's Defeat by the Amorites   Chapter 1:41-46

6. The Bypassing of Seir and Moab   Chapter 2:1-12

7. The Wilderness Journey   Chapter 2:13-23

8. The Defeat of Sihon and the Amorites   Chapter 2:24-37

Introduction:

Moses must have had his tongue planted firmly in his cheek as he wrote that Kadesh was separated from Horeb (Mount Sinai) by only a11 days of travel (Deuteronomy 1:2). Israel had spent 40 years getting from Kadesh to the plains of Moab on the eastern side of Canaan. Why the delay?

Moses told the twelve men to spy out the land of Canaan, and said to them (Numbers 12:17-23) "Go up this way into the South, and go up to the mountains, and see what the land is like: whether the people who dwell in it are strong or weak; a few or many; whether the land they dwell in is good or bad; whether the cities they inhabit are like camps or strongholds; whether the land is rich or poor; whether there is forest there or not. Be of good courage. And bring some of the fruit of the land."

Because ten of the twelve men that were sent to spy out (explore) the Land reported back that they are giants in the land and that we the spies or explorers (scouts) were like grasshoppers in comparison to the giants that we saw in the land.

Only Joshua and Caleb were convinced that they could take the land. And only Joshua and Caleb and those under 20 years of age were ultimately permitted by God to enter the Promised Land. All the others, 20 years and older, perished in the wilderness. They perished in the desert because of their unbelief in the promises of God.

2 Chronicles 7:14

If my people, which are called by my name, shall humble themselves, and pray, and seek my face, and turn from their wicked ways; then will I hear from heaven, and will forgive their sin, and will heal their land.

Psalm 122:6

Pray for the peace of Jerusalem; they will prosper who love thee.

Lesson Plan 59

The Book of Deuteronomy

Chapters 3 & 4

Objective: To gain an understanding of a summary of a godly heritage, a record of God's faithfulness during more than 40 difficult years of wandering in the desert.

Objective Breakdown:

1. Introduction

2. The Defeat of Og, King of Bashan   Chapter 3:1-11

3. The Division of Eastern Lands   Chapter 3:12-22

4. God's Prohibition of Moses' Entry   Chapter 3:23-29

5. Israel Must Keep the Law   Chapter 4:1-6

6. The Nation Is Favored by God   Chapter 4:7-10

7. God's Covenant with Israel   Chapter 4:11-14

8. Israel Is Told to Reject False Gods   Chapter 4:15-24

9. God Will Punish Idolatry   Chapter 4:25-31

10. God's Dealing with Israel Are Unique   Chapter 4:32-40

11. Three Cities of Refuge Are Set Apart   Chapter 4:41-43

12. Preface to the Restatement of the Law   Chapter 4:44-49

Introduction:

Words of encouragement. Some people spend their whole life working in obscurity, with little to show for their efforts despite years of toil. The Hebrews fit that profile after trudging through the wilderness for forty years (Deuteronomy 2:7).

The nations decades-long detour on the way to the Holy Land resulted from crisis of faith at Kadesh Barnea. Everyone 20 years of age and older was condemned to die in the wilderness, except Joshua and Caleb (Numbers 14:29-30). Thus, many who were children when they came out of Egypt were now in their forties, fifties, and perhaps even sixties. Yet what had they done with their lives but "wander" through desert, wastes waiting for their parents' generation to expire?

Thus, Moses' word that the "Lord your God knows your trudging this wilderness (Deuteronomy 2:7) must have come as a great encouragement. God has not forgotten this new generation. He was mindful of the "work of their hands" which amounted to the task of surviving the wilderness journey.

In the same way God is mindful of you if you are toiling away with little or no recognition, through tough times and good times. He knows what you have been through and whether you have been recognized or not and has been there with you every step of the way.

2 Chronicles 7:14

If my people, which are called by my name, shall humble themselves, and pray, and seek my face, and turn from their wicked ways; then will I hear from heaven, and will forgive their sin, and will heal their land.

Psalm 122:6

Pray for the peace of Jerusalem; they will prosper who love thee.

Lesson Plan 60

The Book of Deuteronomy

Chapters 5, 6, & 7

Objective: To gain an understanding of a summary of a godly heritage, a record of God's faithfulness during more than 40 difficult years of wandering in the desert.

Objective Breakdown:

1. Introduction

2. The Ten Commandment   Chapter 5:1-22

3. The People Fear God's Presence   Chapter 5:23-33

4. Hear O Israel   Chapter 6:1-9

5. The People Are to Remember God   Chapter 6:10-19

6. The Law Is to Be Taught   Chapter 6:20-25

7. The People Must Be Holy   Chapter 7:1-11

8. Obedience Will Bring Blessing   Chapter 7:12-16

9. Israel Will Conquer the Canaanites   Chapter 7:17-26

Introduction:

Moses' prophetic words about the Lord scattering the Israelites among the peoples (Deuteronomy 4:27-28) were fulfilled centuries later. After the Hebrews turned away from the Lord more and more to serve idols and acted more corruptly than the Canaanites whom they had displaced, God allowed foreigners to capture their cities and take them away to foreign lands. Jeremiah chapter 9:16 tells us "I will scatter them also among the Gentiles, whom neither they nor their fathers have known. And I will send a sword after them until I have consumed them." Also in Jeremiah chapter 52:28-30, God's words confirm that Nebuchadnezzar carried away captive in the seventh year, three thousand and twenty-three Jews; and in the eighteenth year He carried away another eight hundred and thirty-two people; in the twenty third year he carried away seven hundred forty-five persons for a total of four thousand six hundred all from Jerusalem.

The world is a complex place. Many things vie for our attention. As a result, no matter how much we want to honor God, it is easy to become distracted and even confused. It is easy to forget what is really matters. Moses made it clear to the Israelites what really mattered and therefore what they needed to stay focused on. After briefly reviewing how God had delivered them from Egypt and kept them alive during their desert journeys, he challenged the people to keep their attention focused on the statutes and judgments of the Lord (Deuteronomy 5:1). He urged them: to hear, to learn, to be careful and observe.

Moses reviewed the Ten Commandments (Deuteronomy 5:6-21), the spine of the law, then he called for a three-part response: Be careful to do them, not to turn aside from them and to walk in all their ways.

2 Chronicles 7:14

If my people, which are called by my name, shall humble themselves, and pray, and seek my face, and turn from their wicked ways; then will I hear from heaven, and will forgive their sin, and will heal their land.

Psalm 122:6

Pray for the peace of Jerusalem; they will prosper who love thee.

Lesson Plan 61

The Book of Deuteronomy

Chapters 8, 9, & 10

Objective: To gain an understanding of a summary of a godly heritage, a record of God's faithfulness during more than 40 difficult years of wandering in the desert.

Objective Breakdown:

1. Introduction

2. God Is Bringing Israel into the Land   Chapter 8:1-10

3. The Perils of Prosperity   Chapter 8:11-20

4. God Is the Sole Reason for Victory   Chapter 9:1-6

5. Israel's History of Stubbornness   Chapter 9:7-14

6. The Golden Calf Is Remembered   Chapter 9:15-21

7. Moses' Intercession   Chapter 9:22-29

8. The Second Set of Tablets   Chapter 10:1-11

9. God's Criteria for Israel   Chapter 10:12-22

Introduction:

The need for clear understanding. Too often when people make commitments, they fail to clearly spell out the terms of agreement. In God's covenant with Israel, He clearly stated what would happen to the nation if it obeyed or disobeyed His Law. If the people obeyed, He would bless them with prosperity; if they disobeyed, He would bring judgment upon them (Deuteronomy 7:9-11 and blessings for obedience Leviticus 26:1-13). If only people could be as clear and straight forward in their agreements.

Human beings tend to think of mercy as ignoring, excusing, indulging, or even approving of wrongdoing. God never does that. Indeed, He is of purer eyes than to behold evil, and cannot look on wickedness (Habakkuk 1:13). Thus, when He withholds punishment, it is not because He is indulgent, but because He is patiently waiting for repentance, allowing people ample time to change their ways (Isaiah 30:18; 2 Peter 3:9, 15). However, if repentance from sin never comes, the Lord's very mercy moves Him to enforce justice (Deuteronomy 5:9; 7:9-11).

171

Perhaps a modern way to describe this response is tough love. Thus, sometimes love must act punitively in order to bring about, if possible, the best in and for the beloved. God loves us too much to let us drown in our own sin. His infinite love sometimes moves Him to judgment when we refuse to seek His best.

2 Chronicles 7:14

If my people, which are called by my name, shall humble themselves, and pray, and seek my face, and turn from their wicked ways; then will I hear from heaven, and will forgive their sin, and will heal their land.

Psalm 122:6

Pray for the peace of Jerusalem; they will prosper who love thee.

Lesson Plan 62

The Book of Deuteronomy

Chapters 11, 12, & 13

Objective: To gain an understanding of a summary of a godly heritage, a record of God's faithfulness during more than 40 difficult years of wandering in the desert.

Objective Breakdown:

1. Introduction

2. Love the Lord and Keep His Commandments   Chapter 11:1-12

3. Prosperity is Promised for Obedience   Chapter 11:13-21

4. Obedience Will Bring Victory   Chapter 11:22-25

5. A Choice Between a Blessing and a Curse   Chapter 11:26-32

6. Pagan Alters Are to Be Destroyed   Chapter 12:1-4

7. God Will Select the Place for Sacrifices   Chapter 12:5-14

8. Eating Certain Foods   Chapter 12:15-28

9. Imitating the Canaanites Is Forbidden   Chapter 12:29-32

10. Idolaters Are to be Put to Death   Chapter 13:1-11

11. Idolatrous Cities Are to Be Destroyed   Chapter 13:12-18

Introduction:

Among the inhabitants of Canaan before the invasion of the Israelites were the decedents of Anak, or Anakim (Deuteronomy 9:2). Little is known about this group except that they were great and tall. In fact, whenever the Old Testament mentions them, it usually comments on their stature.

How big were the Anakim? The spies sent into Canaan from Kadesh Barnea reported that they saw giants (Nephilim), and the text explains that the Anakim were descended from the giants (Numbers 13:33). The spies claimed to have felt like grasshoppers in front of them, but this is probably not a literal comparison of stature. Otherwise, the Anakim would have been nearly 200 feet tall.

More likely, the Anakims were an extremely large and tall people, not unlike the philistine champion

Goliath who was six cubits and a span, or about 9 feet and nine inches tall (1 Samuel 17:4). A person this size would have been an imposing human being, of whom the proverb justified "Who can stand before the descendants of Anak?" (Deuteronomy 9:2).

The Anakim were settled in the hill country of Southern Canaan. The city of Kirjath Arba, later known as Hebron (see Genesis 23:19), may have been their principal city. Most of them were killed or driven out during the early campaigns of Joshua's conquest (Joshua 11:21-22), and Caleb finished the job when he was allotted Hebron (Joshua 21:11-12; Judges 1:20).

2 Chronicles 7:14

If my people, which are called by my name, shall humble themselves, and pray, and seek my face, and turn from their wicked ways; then will I hear from heaven, and will forgive their sin, and will heal their land.

Psalm 122:6

Pray for the peace of Jerusalem; they will prosper who love thee.

Lesson Plan 63

The Book of Deuteronomy

Chapters 14, 15, & 16

Objective: To gain an understanding of a summary of a godly heritage, a record of God's faithfulness during more than 40 difficult years of wandering in the desert.

Objective Breakdown:

1. Introduction

2. Unacceptable Signs of Grief   Chapter 14:1-2

3. Clean and Unclean Meats   Chapter 14:3-21

4. Paying Tithes   Chapter 14:22-29

5. Release of Debts   Chapter 15:1- 6

6. Treatment of Poor Israelites   Chapter 15:7-11

7. Treatment of Hebrew Servants   Chapter 15:12-18

8. Dedication of First-Born Males   Chapter 15:19-23

9. Keeping the Passover   Chapter 16:1-8

10. Keeping the Feast of Weeks   Chapter 16:9-12

11. Keeping the Feast of Tabernacles   Chapter 16:13-17

12. Ensuring Justice   Chapter 16:18-20

13. Honoring God's Holiness   Chapter 16:21

Introduction:

In a world where the motto often seems to be "do your own thing" people frequently develop self-styled religious beliefs and practices. For some reason this means taking a pick-and-choose, take-it-or-leave-it approach to established Christianity. For others it means coming up with outlandish ideas about God and eccentric ways of living. Either way, the ultimate authority seems to be the individual, who assumes the prerogative of ignoring any demands or discipline that feels limiting or imposing.

A somewhat similar attitude seems to have characterized the Israelites as they prepared to enter the Promised Land. Apparently, they were doing whatever was right in their own eyes when it came to religious observances of worship (Deuteronomy 12:8). Not that they were turning away from God, but the lack of a permanently located worship center seems to bring about a degree of laxness in regard to the ritual obligations of the Law.

Moses warned them that must change once they enter the land that God designated a site for worshiping Him (Deuteronomy 12:13-14). They were to follow the detailed instructions of the Law concerning sacrifices, holy days, tithes and offerings, and other elements of religious life.

2 Chronicles 7:14

If my people, which are called by my name, shall humble themselves, and pray, and seek my face, and turn from their wicked ways; then will I hear from heaven, and will forgive their sin, and will heal their land.

Psalm 122:6

Pray for the peace of Jerusalem; they will prosper who love thee.

Lesson Plan 64

The Book of Deuteronomy

Chapters 17, 18, 19, & 20

Objective: To gain an understanding of a summary of a godly heritage, a record of God's faithfulness during more than 40 difficult years of wandering in the desert.

Objective Breakdown:

1. Introduction

2. Honoring God's Holiness (continued)   Chapter 17:1

3. Idolaters Are to Be Stoned   Chapter 17:2-7

4. A Supreme Court of Judgment   Chapter 17:8-13

5. Instructions for a King   Chapter 17:14-20

6. Provisions for Priests and Levites   Chapter 18:1-8

7. Canaanites Abominations   Chapter 18:9-14

8. A Prophet Like Moses Will Arise   Chapter 18:15-22

9. Six Cities of Refuge   Chapter 19:1-13

10. Property Boundaries   Chapter 19:14

11. Eye for Eye, Tooth for a Tooth   Chapter 19:15-21

12. God Will Go with Israel in Battle   Chapter 20:1-9

13. Policies for Waging War   Chapter 20:10-20

Introduction:

The third-year tithe and the poor. One of the most difficult issues for any nation to face is what to do about the poor people. One view is saying to let the poor fend for themselves and not become a burden on society. Another view holds that humane governments have a responsibility to help all of their citizens, and especially those who are unable to provide for their own needs. Is there a place for government-sponsored assistance to the poor, according to the Bible?

The question is not easily settled. But it might help to consider what the lord told the Israelites to do (Deuteronomy 14:28-29). The Law assumed certain classes of people would be at an economic disadvantage in Hebrew society: Levites, "strangers" or non-Israelites, foreigners, orphans, and widows.

To help these groups, the Law said that a tithe (a ten percent) of every third year's produce should be set aside for their use. It was to be stored "within your gates" (Deuteronomy 14:28), indicating that the aid should be collected and administered by towns and cities, not by individual's households. Thus, the third-year tithe was a form of community charity.

However, the system was designed to prevent chronic dependence or laziness, the poor were welcome to eat what they needed from the supplies. But by storing up the food, a city could prevent inappropriate distribution. In addition, the beneficiaries of this aid were to be living within your gates (Deuteronomy 14:29). Thus, it would not be possible for someone to travel from town-to-town freeloading.

2 Chronicles 7:14

If my people, which are called by my name, shall humble themselves, and pray, and seek my face, and turn from their wicked ways; then will I hear from heaven, and will forgive their sin, and will heal their land.

Psalm 122:6

Pray for the peace of Jerusalem; they will prosper who love thee.

Lesson Plan 65

The Book of Deuteronomy

Chapters 21, 22, & 23

Objective: To gain an understanding of a summary of a godly heritage, a record of God's faithfulness during more than 40 difficult years of wandering in the desert.

Objective Breakdown:

1. Introduction

2. Clearing the Innocent of Bloodguilt   Chapter 21:1-9

3. Marriage to Captives   Chapter 21:10-17

4. Dealing with a Rebellious Son   Chapter 21:18-23

5. Domestic and Personal Matters   Chapter 22:1-12

6. Purity at Marriage   Chapter 22:13-21

7. Adultery   Chapter 22:22-30

8. Fitness for Worship Participation   Chapter 23:1-8

9. Maintaining Holiness   Chapter 23:9-18

10. Loans and Vows   Chapter 23:19-25

Introduction:

Holy warfare in ancient Israel. Wars are fought for many reasons, but the Israelites' war against Canaanites was fought because God told them to fight it (Deuteronomy 20:16). This means that the campaign fit the definition of a "holy war," a war that God declares, fights, leads, and wins. Similar engagements were carried out against the Amorites (Exodus 17:16) and Midianites (Numbers 31:1-3).

Ancient Israel did not have a standing army like the Egyptians, Assyrians, or Babylonians. Nor did it have chariots or horses, or sophisticated weaponry prior to the monarchy. Instead, the Israelites were to trust in the Lord, who promised to fight on their behalf. In fact, even after Israel acquired military hardware and expertise, the nation was still told to rely on God to bring the victory.

The Lord Himself would be the defender of Israel. Even though the nation's men were often mustered to battle, it was the Lord fighting through them, as well as for them. In fact, defeat actually occurred as a result of disobedience against God.

For this reason, Israelite warriors were expected to consecrate themselves to God. Often, they were to do so by abstaining from certain activities, such as drinking or sexual relations. And those who distracted by fear, a recent marriage, a new house, or a newly planted vineyard were told to remain home (Deuteronomy 20:5-9).

Because a holy war was primarily God's war, certain rules of engagement applied. For example, if a besieged city surrendered, the occupants were to be spared, thought they would become servants of the Israelites (Deuteronomy 20:10-11). Likewise, the natural environment of the battlefield was to be preserved as much as possible (Deuteronomy 20:11-20).

2 Chronicles 7:14

If my people, which are called by my name, shall humble themselves, and pray, and seek my face, and turn from their wicked ways; then will I hear from heaven, and will forgive their sin, and will heal their land.

Psalm 122:6

Pray for the peace of Jerusalem; they will prosper who love thee.

Lesson Plan 66

The Book of Deuteronomy

Chapters 24, 25, & 26

Objective: To gain an understanding of a summary of a godly heritage, a record of God's faithfulness during more than 40 difficult years of wandering in the desert.

Objective Breakdown:

1.	Introduction	
2.	Divorce	Chapter 24:1-4
3.	Miscellaneous Matters	Chapter 24:5-15
4.	Individual Responsibility	Chapter 24:16
5.	Provisions for the Poor	Chapter 24:17-22
6.	Limits on Punishment	Chapter 25:1-3
7.	A Variety of Subjects	Chapter 25:4-19
8.	Offering the First of the Produce	Chapter 26:1-11
9.	A Prayer for Blessing	Chapter 26:12-15
10.	Israel's Obedience is Exhorted	Chapter 26:16-19

Introduction:

An economic safety net. In developed nations today, economic assistance is generally handled by a network of government agencies and nonprofit organizations. In ancient Israel, private citizens themselves were expected to help the poor. One of the primary means for that was gleaning (Deuteronomy 24:19-21). Gleaning allowed the poor to go through a field, orchard, or vineyard after the main harvest and gather whatever the harvesters had missed or intentionally left for them. The Law encouraged landowners not to be overly zealous in gathering produce from their fields, but to purposely leave some behind for the poor. The point was not to hand the poor a free meal but to provide them away from keep from starving. Thus, gleaning was an economic safety net.

Deuteronomy names three type of people who were likely to be poor: the stranger, the fatherless, and the widow. Strangers, or sojourners were non-Jews who came to live in Canaan for a period of time.

Although foreigners enjoyed numerous privileges among the Hebrews, they did not own their own land. Thus, they tended to live in poverty.

The fatherless and widows also tended to be poor since they lacked a male to work the land, provide for their needs and look out for their rights.

2 Chronicles 7:14

If my people, which are called by my name, shall humble themselves, and pray, and seek my face, and turn from their wicked ways; then will I hear from heaven, and will forgive their sin, and will heal their land.

Psalm 122:6

Pray for the peace of Jerusalem; they will prosper who love thee.

Lesson Plan 67

The Book of Deuteronomy

Chapters 27, 28, 29, 30

Objective: To gain an understanding of a summary of a godly heritage, a record of God's faithfulness during more than 40 difficult years of wandering in the desert.

Objective Breakdown:

1. Introduction

2. A Plan to Raise a Memorial   Deuteronomy 27:1-10

3. Curses Are Proclaimed   Deuteronomy 27:11-26

4. Blessings for Obedience   Deuteronomy 28:1-14

5. Curses for Disobedience   Deuteronomy 28:15-46

6. Invasion by Enemies   Deuteronomy 28:47-57

7. Diseases and Enslavement   Deuteronomy 28:58-68

8. A Covenant Between God & People   Deuteronomy 29:1-13

9. A Testimony for Coming Generations   Deuteronomy 29:14-29

10. Repentance Will Restore Blessings   Deuteronomy 30:1-10

11. A Choice Between Life and Death   Deuteronomy 30:11-20

Introduction:

Every modern-day contract includes blanks for the principals making the contract to sign. Their signatures attest that they agree to the terms of the contract, and by signing on the line they confirm the agreement. A much more elaborate and memorable way was devised for Israel to sign off on the agreement (or covenant, or the Law) by which they would inhabit the Promised Land as the Lord's people. The plan involved two mountains in central Canaan, Mount Gerizim, and Mount Ebal (Deuteronomy 27:12-13).

Earlier, Moses had designated these two mountains as the site for the occasion (Deuteronomy 11:26-32). Six tribes were to stand on Mount Gerizim and six on Mount Ebal. The valley in between was a natural amphitheater such that a speaker on either mountain could be easily heard on the other. A monument was to be erected on Mount Ebal on which the Law was to be written, and then sacrifices were to be offered (Deuteronomy 27:1-8).

After that, the blessings for obedience were to be read, which the tribes on Mount Gerizim were to affirm and agree by saying, "Amen." Then the curses for disobedience were to read, which tribes on Mount Ebal were to affirm by saying, "Amen." Finally, the Levites were to state specific sins that would bring a curse, to which all people on both mountains were to say, "Amen." This ceremony was held after the Israelites took possession of central Palestine (Joshua 8:30-35).

2 Chronicles 7:14

If my people, which are called by my name, shall humble themselves, and pray, and seek my face, and turn from their wicked ways; then will I hear from heaven, and will forgive their sin, and will heal their land.

Psalm 122:6

Pray for the peace of Jerusalem; they will prosper who love thee.

Lesson Plan 68

The Book of Deuteronomy

Chapters 31, 32, 33, & 34

Objective: To gain an understanding of a summary of a godly heritage, a record of God's faithfulness during more than 40 difficult years of wandering in the desert.

Objective Breakdown:

1. Introduction

2. Moses Passes Leadership to Joshua   Deuteronomy 31:1-13

3. God Speaks to Moses and Joshua   Deuteronomy 31:14-18

4. God Gives Moses a Song   Deuteronomy 31:19-23

5. Moses Warns the Levites   Deuteronomy 31:24-30

6. The Song of Moses   Deuteronomy 32:1-43

7. Moses Teaches His Song to The People   Deuteronomy 32:44-47

8. Moses Prepares to Die on Mount Nebo   Deuteronomy 32:48-52

9. Moses Blesses the Tribes   Deuteronomy 33:1-29

10. Moses Views the Promised Land   Deuteronomy 34:1-4

11. Moses Dies   Deuteronomy 34:5-8

12. Joshua Succeeds Moses   Deuteronomy 34:9-12

Introduction:

The consequence of sin. God never delights in sin, but He does delight in forgiving sin (John 3:16-18; John 1:9). He promised to remove the believers' guilt "as far as the East is from the West" (Psalm 103:12). Yet even though God deals with the wages of sin (Romans 6:23), He often leaves us to faces the tragic consequences of sin.

Moses and Aaron committed acts that cost the participation in the "land of milk and honey" (Deuteronomy 32:48-52). Even though they doubtless confessed their sins and offered the required sacrifices to atone for them, they still had to face the consequences of their disobedience.

This is a sobering lesson for all of us. Like Moses and Aaron, we can find forgiveness of sin from God. But we are not immune to the practical effects of our sin. For example, to recover from some sins we may have to live under strong disciplines to avoid repeating the mistakes of the past. Some sins produce indelible physical or emotional marks. Or like Zacchaeus, we may need to make costly restitution to those we have wronged (Luke 19:1-11). In some cases, we may have to let go of certain relationships that are permanently broken. At least in this world as a result of what we have done (Revelation 21:4). Sin does have a price. Christ paid the ultimate penalty for sin on the cross. But when it comes to the practical consequences of our actions, we can often expect to pay those ourselves.

Words to Live By:

Ephesians 4:29, Let not any filthy word go out of your mouth, but what is good for necessary edification, that it may impart grace to the hearers.

Ephesians 4:30, And do not grieve the Holy Spirit of God, by whom you are sealed until *the* day of redemption.

Ephesians 4:31, Let all bitterness and wrath and anger and tumult and evil speaking be put away from you, with all malice.

Ephesians 4:32, And be kind to one another, tenderhearted, forgiving one another, even as God For Christ's sake has forgiven you.

Matthew 12:25, And Jesus knew their thoughts and said to them, every kingdom divided against itself is brought to desolation. And every city or house divided against itself shall not stand.

Mark 3:24, And if a kingdom is divided against itself, that kingdom cannot stand.

Romans 13:1, Let every soul be subject unto the higher powers. For there is no power but of God: the powers that be are ordained of God.

Commentary: God is the ultimate authority. Government as an institution has been established by God. God raises up and does away with leaders.

Romans 13:2, Whosoever therefore resisteth the power, resisteth the ordinance of God: and they that resist shall receive to themselves damnation.

Commentary: Government as an institution has been established by God to serve His purposes.

Both followers and leaders are ultimately accountable to God. Submission to human authority as it aligns with God's Word reflects our submission to God's authority. We must serve the highest of all authorities, God Himself.

2 Chronicles 7:14

If my people, which are called by my name, shall humble themselves, and pray, and seek my face, and turn from their wicked ways; then will I hear from heaven, and will forgive their sin, and will heal their land.

Psalm 122:6

Pray for the peace of Jerusalem; they will prosper who love thee.

Note: If we don't speak out in support of Christian matters, we will forfeit our authority given to us by God!! We as the "Church" and "Ambassadors" should not hide. We should "Shine"!! Because there can be beautiful miracles in our mouth. Amen!

If we are not part of the solution, then we are part of the problem.

Homework: Read Psalms 112 through 118 and 1 Peter Chapter 5.

Time is of the Essence to Be Born Again!!

The Book of Joshua

Scripture Focus Chapters 1-24

Objective: To gain an understanding of Israelites taking possession of Canaan, known as the Promised Land, and what the land should be called.

Objective Breakdown:

1. Introduction

2. God Commissions Joshua   Chapter 1:1-9

3 Joshua Prepares the People   Chapter 1:10-18

4. Two Spies Are Sent to Jericho   Chapter 2:1-7

5. Rahab Gets Protection for Her Family   Chapter 2:8-14

6. Rahab Sends the Spies Away to Safety   Chapter 2:15-21

7. Spies Report Back to Joshua   Chapter 2:22-24

8. The People Prepare to March   Chapter 3:1-6

9. Israel Crosses the Jordan on Dry Ground   Chapter 3:7-17

10. Tribal Representatives Gather Stones   Chapter 4:1-7

11. A Memorial Is Erected in the Jordan   Chapter 4:8-14

12. The Meaning of the Memorial   Chapter 4:15-24

13. Fear Strikes the Canaanites   Chapter 5:1-9

14. Passover Is Kept and the Manna Ceases   Chapter 5:10-12

15. The Commander of God's Army Appears   Chapter 5:13-15

16. The Conquest of Jericho Begins   Chapter 6:1-11

17. The Walls of Jericho Falls   Chapter 6:12-21

18. Rehab and Her Family Are Spared   Chapter 6:22-27

19. Achan's Disobedience Brings Defeat   Chapter 7:1-5

20. Joshua Prays   Chapter 7:6-15

Lesson Plan 69

The Book of Joshua

Chapters 1, 2, & 3

Objective: To gain an understanding of the leadership of Joshua and the courageous faith that enabled the Israelites in taking possession of Canaan.

Objective Breakdown:

1.	Introduction	
2.	God Commissions Joshua	Chapter 1:1-9
3	Joshua Prepares the People	Chapter 1:10-18
4.	Two Spies Are Sent to Jericho	Chapter 2:1-7
5.	Rahab Gets Protection for Her Family	Chapter 2:8-14
6.	Rahab Sends the Spies Away to Safety	Chapter 2:15-21
7.	Spies Report Back to Joshua	Chapter 2:22-24
8.	The people Prepare to March	Chapter 3:1-6
9.	Israel Crosses the Jordan on Dry Ground	Chapter 3:7-17

Introduction:

The Book of Joshua takes its name from the man who is regarded as its author. Joshua was the successor to Moses (Deuteronomy 34:9; Joshua 1:1-2), and he serves as the central figure in this account of Israel's conquest of Canaan.

The time span of this book begins just after the death of Moses (Joshua 1:1) and ends with the death of Joshua (Joshua 24:29; Judges 1:1), a period of about 30 years, sometime around 1400 B.C. The book begins with the Israelites in the plains of Moab, but they soon cross over the Jordan River and move North and South throughout the territory of Canaan.

The Book of Joshua tells about the Israelites taking possession of Canaan, known as the Promised Land. God told the Israelites to drive out or destroy the tribes already living in the land, known as the Canaanites. The Canaanites had a fairly advanced culture, organized into city-states. They were among the most active merchants and traders in the ancient Middle East. But they stood under the judgment of God because of their idolatrous religious practices which the Lord condemned as abominations. The Israelite invasion was God's means of judging these pagan tribes.

The Book of Joshua gives an account of Joshua's leadership, including 1) entry into the Promised Land (Joshua chapters 1-5); 2) the capture of the first city, Jericho (Joshua chapters 6 and 7); 3) the Southern campaign (Joshua chapters 11 and 12); 4) the division of the Land among the 12 tribes (Joshua chapters 13-21); 5) the renewal of the covenant at Shechem and Joshua's farewell address (Joshua chapters 22-24).

2 Chronicles 7:14

If my people, which are called by my name, shall humble themselves, and pray, and seek my face, and turn from their wicked ways; then will I hear from heaven, and will forgive their sin, and will heal their land.

Psalm 122:6

Pray for the peace of Jerusalem; they will prosper who love thee.

Lesson Plan 70

The Book of Joshua

Chapters 4, 5, & 6

Objective: To gain an understanding of the leadership of Joshua and the courageous faith that enabled the Israelites in taking possession of Canaan.

Objective Breakdown:

1. Introduction

2. Tribal Representatives Gather Stones   Chapter 4:1-7

3. A Memorial Is Erected in the Jordan   Chapter 4:8-14

4. The Meaning of the Memorial   Chapter 4:15-24

5. Fear Strikes the Canaanites   Chapter 5:1-9

6. Passover Is Kept and the Manna Ceases   Chapter 5:10-12

7. The Commander of God's Army Appears   Chapter 5:13-15

8. The Conquest of Jericho Begins   Chapter 6:1-11

9. The Walls of Jericho Falls   Chapter 6.12-21

10. Rehab and Her Family Are Spared   Chapter 6:22-27

Introduction:

Stand strong and hang on! Was Joshua hard of hearing? The Lord reminded him three times to be "strong" and "courageous" (Joshua 6:7, 9). There must have been an important in those words. The Hebrew word for "strong" refers to sound legs while the word for courage refers having a good grasp. The point is clear; God was telling Joshua that his success as a leader depended on whether he could stand strong and hold on tightly!

Joshua had already experienced situations in which he was forced to take a strong stand in the face of opposition. For instance, when the Israelites were poised to enter Canaan 40 years earlier, Joshua had been one of two men who insisted that the nation should move forward under God's power (Numbers 13:1-14:45).

What was Joshua to keep a secure grasp on? God's plans, purposes, and values as found in the Book of the Law (Joshua 1:8). Joshua example urges believers to consider: what do we stand for—and on what are we holding onto with a secure grasp?

Perhaps two million or more people left Egypt at the start of the Exodus. Of the grown men who began only two men made it to Canaan. Joshua was one of those men, Caleb was the other (Numbers 13:30-33; 14:6, 29-30, 38). Their minority report after spying out the land showed a trust in God that resulted in an exemption from the sentence passed on the other Hebrews age 20 and older; 40 years in the wilderness until death took them before they could enter the Promised Land.

Even Moses was not to reach Canaan (Deuteronomy 34:1-6). Shortly before his death he passed the of military, political and spiritual leadership to Joshua who was full of the spirit of wisdom (Deuteronomy 34:9).

2 Chronicles 7:14

If my people, which are called by my name, shall humble themselves, and pray, and seek my face, and turn from their wicked ways; then will I hear from heaven, and will forgive their sin, and will heal their land.

Psalm 122:6

Pray for the peace of Jerusalem; they will prosper who love thee.

Lesson Plan 71

The Book of Joshua

Chapters 7, 8, & 9

Objective: To gain an understanding of the leadership of Joshua and the courageous faith that enabled the Israelites in taking possession of Canaan.

Objective Breakdown:

1. Introduction

2. Achan's Disobedience Brings Defeat   Chapter 7:1-5

3. Joshua Prays   Chapter 7:6-15

4. Achan Is Identified and Executed   Chapter 7:16-26

5. Israel Prepares to Attack Ai   Chapter 8:1-8

6. The Men of Ai Are Fooled by an Ambush   Chapter 8:9-17

7. Ai Is Destroyed   Chapter 8:18-29

8. Joshua Builds an Altar and Reads the Law   Chapter 8:30-35

9. The Gibeonites' Deception   Chapter 9:1-15

10. Israel Still Honors the Agreement   Chapter 9:16-27

Introduction:

By referring to the Amorites and Canaanites (Joshua 5:1). Scripture was indicating all peoples living in Canaan between Jordan River and the Mediterranean Sea. Both were descendants of Canaan (Genesis 10:15-20), and both were facing the Lord's judgment for their idolatry and immorality.

The Amorites referred to here were a nomadic people who lived in the hill country on both sides of the Jordan. The Israelites had already encountered the tribes living to the East. In fact, a miscalculation by of their kings, Sihon, enabled the Hebrews to gain a strategic foothold in the Transjordan area. The Amorites not only fought Israel, but they also fought among themselves. Gibeon, a prominent Amorite city north of Jerusalem (Joshua 10:4), made peace with the Israelites, in doing so, they alienated a league of five other Amorite cities, whose kings declared war. Thus, now Israel was forced into a conflict, but God used the incident to deliver the Amorites into their hands (Joshua 10:1-30).

The people called Canaanites included a group of nations throughout Palestine and Phoenica. They lived on the coastal plains and excelled at trade. Like the Amorites, their communities were organized into cities-states led by regional kings. Reconnaissance had reported the Canaanites as "giants' to be feared (Numbers 13:31-33). Yet after Israel's miraculous crossing of the Jordan River, it was the Canaanites whose hearts and spirits melted in fear (Joshua 5:1). They were hearing about a new God who was far more powerful than any of their own gods.

2 Chronicles 7:14

If my people, which are called by my name, shall humble themselves, and pray, and seek my face, and turn from their wicked ways; then will I hear from heaven, and will forgive their sin, and will heal their land.

Psalm 122:6

Pray for the peace of Jerusalem; they will prosper who love thee.

Lesson Plan 72

The Book of Joshua

Chapters 10 & 11

Objective: To gain an understanding of the leadership of Joshua and the courageous faith that enabled the Israelites in taking possession of Canaan.

Objective Breakdown:

1. Introduction

2. The Israelites Defend Gibeon   Chapter 10:1-11

3. The Sun Stands Still   Chapter 10:12-15

4. Five Kings Are Captured at Makkedah   Chapter 10:16-28

5. Libnah, Lachish, Horam, and Eglon Fall   Chapter 10:29-35

6. Hebron, Debir, and the South Are Taken   Chapter 10:36-43

7. Northern Kings Combine Against Israel   Chapter 11:1-5

8. Israel Is Victorious and Takes Hazor   Chapter 11:6-15

9. A Summary of Captured Territories   Chapter 11:16-23

Introduction:

Leadership often involves negotiation, diplomacy, and keeping the peace. But peace alone is not a worthwhile goal, as a treaty with the Gibeonites suggests (Joshua 9:15). God had instructed Israel to destroy the Canaanites. How, then did Joshua fail in that assignment with the people of Gibeon? Three lessons of leadership can be seen:

(1) The decision was made on the basis of appearances rather than careful study, and investigation (Joshua 9:12-14). The text suggests that Joshua and the elders of Israel came to a hasty decision. They failed to check the facts of the Gibeonites' story and were apparently satisfied with circumstantial evidence.

(2) The decision was made without seeking counsel from the Lord (Joshua 9:14). This was Israel's gravest mistake. Normally Joshua was known as a leader who moved only after worshiping God and seeking His direction (for example, Joshua 5:13-15; 8:35; 11:15). But on this occasion, he acted on his own, with the result being a bad bargain.

(3) The decision was poor, but the deal was honored nevertheless (Joshua 9:18-20). To the nation's credit, it followed through on its commitment to spare the lives of the Gibeonites.

The decision challenges us to ask: on what basis am I making decisions? Am I seeking God's wisdom and timing?

2 Chronicles 7:14

If my people, which are called by my name, shall humble themselves, and pray, and seek my face, and turn from their wicked ways; then will I hear from heaven, and will forgive their sin, and will heal their land.

Psalm 122:6

Pray for the peace of Jerusalem; they will prosper who love thee.

Lesson Plan 73

The Book of Joshua

Chapters 12, 13, & 14

Objective: To gain an understanding of the leadership of Joshua and the courageous faith that enabled the Israelites in taking possession of Canaan.

Objective Breakdown:

1.	Introduction	
2.	Kings Defeated Under Moses	Chapter 12:1-6
3.	Kings Defeated Under Joshua	Chapter 12:7-24
4.	Land Remaining to Be Possessed	Chapter 13:1-7
5.	Land of the Eastern Tribes	Chapter 13:8-14
6.	The Territory of Reuben	Chapter 13:15-23
7.	The Territory of Gad	Chapter 13:24-28
8.	The Territory of Half of Manasseh	Chapter 13:29-33
9.	The Division of the Land of Canaan	Chapter 14:1-5
10.	Caleb's Inheritance	Chapter 14:6-15

Introduction:

Kadesh is a royal city of the Canaanites (Joshua 12:22) in the mountainous territory allotted to Naphtali (Joshua 19:37), 15 miles North of the Sea of Galilee. The name means holy. It was made a Levitical city (Joshua 21:1-3) and a city of refuge (Numbers 35:11) west of the Jordan River. Headquarters for Barak, Israel's commander under Judge Deborah, who defeated the Canaanite General Sisera with 10,000 men (Judges 4:6-16).

Moses had promised that Reuben and Gad could have the lush mountainous region of Gilead East of the Jordan River if they faithfully helped the other tribes conquer the lands to the West (Numbers 32:28-30). The two tribes honored their commitment and so, along with Half of the Manasseh, they were given Gilead, including its principal city, Heshbon (Joshua 13:10). Heshbon means stronghold (Numbers 21:26).

Jazer area was ideal for ranching. Just a few miles North of Hesbon, Jazer (Joshua 13:25) was an enviable city to own. It was well fortified and surrounded by valuable grazing land, which is what made it attractive to the Gadites in the first place (Numbers 32:1-5).

The Heights of Mizpah. Ramath Mizpah (Joshua 13:26) is sometimes identified with Ramoth Gilead, a major commercial center on the North-South route connecting Syria to the King's Highway (Numbers 20:17). Because of its importance it was site of many battles between Israel and Syria and changed hands frequently.

2 Chronicles 7:14

If my people, which are called by my name, shall humble themselves, and pray, and seek my face, and turn from their wicked ways; then will I hear from heaven, and will forgive their sin, and will heal their land.

Psalm 122:6

Pray for the peace of Jerusalem; they will prosper who love thee.

Lesson Plan 74

The Book of Joshua

Chapters 15, 16, & 17

Objective: To gain an understanding of the leadership of Joshua and the courageous faith that enabled the Israelites in taking possession of Canaan.

Objective Breakdown:

1. Introduction

2. The Territory of Judah   Chapter 15:1-12

3. Caleb Takes His Land   Chapter 15:13-19

4. Southern and Lowland Cities of Judah   Chapter 15:20-47

5. Hill and Wildness Cities of Judah   Chapter 15:28-63

6. The Inheritance of Joseph's Children   Chapter 16:1-10

7. The Inheritance of Joseph's Children (continued)   Chapter 17:1-2

8. Land for Zelophehad's Descendants   Chapter 17:3-6

9. The Territory of Ephraim and Manasseh   Chapter 17:7-13

10. More Land for Ephraim and Manasseh   Chapter 17:14-18

Introduction:

"Give me this mountain!" Caleb is a case study in unflinching faithfulness and seasoned courage. When the entire nation wanted to quit its journey at Kadesh Barnea and return to Egypt, he and Joshua stood against them, convinced that God would deliver on His promise to give them the land (Numbers 13:30; 14:6-9). As an older man, Caleb was probably the spokesperson, even though Joshua became the successor to Moses.

As a result of his courageous stand for God, Caleb not only entered Canaan but helped Moses divide the land (Numbers 34:16, 19) and led his people, Judah, in the possession of their territory. God seemed to prolong Caleb's life as a reminder to a younger generation that He fulfills His word.

Convinced of that truth, 85-year-old Caleb could be heard to cry, "Give me this mountain!" as he looked upon Mount Hebron (Joshua 14:12; see Genesis 23:19). Once granted his request, he boldly drove out the Anakim who lived there (Joshua 15:13-14)—a direct response to the timidity shown by his peers 40 years earlier at Kadesh, who wailed about "giants" in the land (Numbers 13:31-33). In the end, Caleb's persevering faith won out over both the size of his enemies and the fear of his friends.

2 Chronicles 7:14

If my people, which are called by my name, shall humble themselves, and pray, and seek my face, and turn from their wicked ways; then will I hear from heaven, and will forgive their sin, and will heal their land.

Psalm 122:6

Pray for the peace of Jerusalem; they will prosper who love thee.

Lesson Plan 75

The Book of Joshua

Chapters 18, 19, 20, & 21

Objective: To gain an understanding of the leadership of Joshua and the courageous faith that enabled the Israelites in taking possession of Canaan.

Objective Breakdown:

1. Introduction

2. Surveyors from Seven Tribes Are Sent   Chapter 18:1-10

3. The Territory of Benjamin   Chapter 18:11-20

4. Benjamin Cities   Chapter 18:21-27

5. The Territory of Simeon   Chapter 19:1-9

6. The Territory of Zebulun   Chapter 19:10-16

7. The Territory of Issachar   Chapter 19:17-23

8. The Territory of Asher   Chapter 19:24-31

9. The Territory of Naphtali   Chapter 19:32-39

10. The Territory of Dan   Chapter 19:40-48

11. The City of Joshua   Chapter 19:49-51

12. Cities of Refuge Are Assigned   Chapter 20:1-9

13. Levitical Cities Are Distributed   Chapter 21:1-7

14. Cities for the Kohathites   Chapter 21:8-26

15. Cities for the Gershonites   Chapter 21:27-33

16. Cities for the Merarites   Chapter 21:34-42

17. The Distribution Is Completed   Chapter 21:43-45

Introduction:

Imagine being in Joshua's shoes, the responsibility of helping the tribes of Israel divide up the land of Canaan among themselves. At your direction, seven tribes who have not yet received their inheritance send out surveyors to inspect their allotted territories. After they report back, your job is to use the information they gathered to divide the lands proportionately. How would you go about making your final decisions?

Joshua elected to cast lots (Joshua 18:8-10). No one knows the exact method he used, but apparently an element of chance was involved. Should he have used a more direct communication from God?

Actually, the text says that Joshua cast the lots "before the Lord in Shiloh" (Joshua 18:8,10) that is, at the tabernacle that was permanently set up there (Joshua 18:1). It may be that God was superintending the outcome of the lots, so actually there was no chance involved. Some believe that he items known as the Urim and Thummum were used in that manner. (Exodus 28:30). Urim and Thummum were stones carried by High priests to determine God's will.

2 Chronicles 7:14

If my people, which are called by my name, shall humble themselves, and pray, and seek my face, and turn from their wicked ways; then will I hear from heaven, and will forgive their sin, and will heal their land.

Psalm 122:6

Pray for the peace of Jerusalem; they will prosper who love thee.

Lesson Plan 76

The Book of Joshua

Chapters 22, 23, & 24

Objective: To gain an understanding of the leadership of Joshua and the courageous faith that enabled the Israelites in taking possession of Canaan.

Objective Breakdown:

1. Introduction
2. The Eastern Tribes Return to their Lands   Chapter 22:1-9
3. An Offensive Altar Is Built   Chapter 22:10-20
4. The Eastern Tribes Explain Themselves   Chapter 22:21-29
5. Phinehas Gives Affirmation   Chapter 22:30-34
6. Joshua Farewell Address   Chapter 23:1-16
7. Joshua Reviews Israel's History   Chapter 24:1-13
8. Choose Whom You Will Serve   Chapter 24:14-18
9. People Say They Will Serve the Lord   Chapter 24:19-28
10. Joshua and Eleazer Are Laid to Rest   Chapter 24:29-33

Introduction:

An inheritance can be a blessing to a family, but it can also be a curse that divides family members. A lot can depend on who manages the disbursement of the assets and how well they do their job.

When Israel divided Canaan, it was Joshua's job to act somewhat like a trustee of an estate making sure that each tribe receive the lands to which it was entitled. It was a delicate job that required him to act with great integrity. Otherwise, he might be charge with being unfair in assigning boundaries or neglecting commitments previously made by Moses.

Joshua handled his responsibilities seeking the welfare of the Twelve Tribes before asking for land for himself (Joshua 19: 49-50). In doing so, he ran the risk of having to settle for a leftover, second-best portion of Canaan. But he avoided any question of impropriety.

This policy was in marked contrast to that of the Canaanite and Amorite kings of the city-state that the Israelites were inheriting. The pagan kings generally lorded over their people, choosing for themselves the first and the best. Joshua of a servant leader, forsaking greed and self interest in order to seek the highest good for his people (see Matthew 20:25-28).

Joshua's example is worth emulating today. As we accept responsibilities and make decisions that affects others, our challenge is to do the right thing by seeking justice, trusting God to work the details of our own welfare.

2 Chronicles 7:14

If my people, which are called by my name, shall humble themselves, and pray, and seek my face, and turn from their wicked ways; then will I hear from heaven, and will forgive their sin, and will heal their land.

Psalm 122:6

Pray for the peace of Jerusalem; they will prosper who love thee.

The Book of Judges

Scripture Focus Chapters 1-21

Objective: To gain insight on the twelve judges and their responsibilities.

Objective Breakdown:

1. Introduction

2. Judah Conquers Jerusalem   Chapter 1:1-10

3. Caleb Gives Achsah to Othniel   Chapter 1:11-15

4. Judah Gains More Cities   Chapter 1:16-21

5. Bethel Is Taken   Chapter 1:22-26

6. Cities Not Taken   Chapter 1:27-36

7. The Reasons for Defeats   Chapter 2:1-6

8. Joshua Dies   Chapter 2:7-10

9. Israel Turns Away from God   Chapter 2:11-23

10. Nations Are Left to Test Israel   Chapter 3:1-6

11. Othniel Judges Israel   Chapter 3:7-11

12. Ehud Kills Eglon King of Moab   Chapter 3:12-30

13. Shamgar Delivers Israel   Chapter 3:31

14. Deborah Judges Israel   Chapter 4:1-10

15. Barak's Men Put Sisera to Flight   Chapter 4:11-16

16. Jael Kills Sisera with a Tent Peg   Chapter 4:17-24

17. Deborah and Barak Sing   Chapter 5:1-11

18. The Victory Is Recounted   Chapter 5:12-23

19. Jael Is Praised for Her Courage   Chapter 5:24-31

20. Israel's Rebellion Brings Oppression   Chapter 6:1-6

Lesson Plan 77

The Book of Judges

Chapters 1, 2, & 3

Objective: To gain insight and an understanding of the twelve judges of Israel and of their responsibilities and accomplishments.

Objective Breakdown:

1. Introduction

2. Judah Conquers Jerusalem   Chapter 1:1-10

3. Caleb Gives Achsah to Othniel   Chapter 1:11-15

4. Judah Gains More Cities   Chapter 1:16-21

5. Bethel Is Taken   Chapter 1:22-26

6. Cities Not Taken   Chapter 1:27-36

7. The Reasons for Defeats   Chapter 2:1-6

8. Joshua Dies   Chapter 2:7-10

9. Israel Turns Away from God   Chapter 2:11-23

10. Nations Are Left to Test Israel   Chapter 3:1-6

11. Othniel Judges Israel   Chapter 3:7-11

12. Ehud Kills Eglon King of Moab   Chapter 3:12-30

13. Shamgar Delivers Israel   Chapter 3:31

Introduction:

From conquest to chaos. For both individuals and nations, the period just after great victory is usually a time of great vulnerability. It seems that when people have overcome an obstacle, survived a great threat, or defeated a dangerous enemy, they tend to let down their guard and relax. That puts them at great risk, not just for external attack but for internal decay.

This was the experience of Israel during the period of the Judges. His was just the experience of Israel during the period of the judges. Having achieved impressive military victories under Joshua, the Israelites succumbed to moral and civil anarchy after Joshua's death. The root of their troubles was chronic disobedience in regard to the Law, and repeated departure from the Lord.

Judges makes for trouble reading because it shows a nation in moral and spiritual decline. This period in Israelite history, which has been called Israel's Dark Age, was a time in which everyone did what was right in their own eyes (Judges 21:25). Could the troubles of modern society be the result of a similar pattern of open, self-willed rebellion against God?

2 Chronicles 7:14

If my people, which are called by my name, shall humble themselves, and pray, and seek my face, and turn from their wicked ways; then will I hear from heaven, and will forgive their sin, and will heal their land.

Psalm 122:6

Pray for the peace of Jerusalem; they will prosper who love thee.

Lesson Plan 78

The Book of Judges

Chapters 4, 5, & 6

Objective: To gain insight and an understanding of the twelve judges of Israel of their responsibilities and accomplishments.

Objective Breakdown:

1. Introduction

2. Deborah Judges Israel   Chapter 4:1-10

3. Barak's Men Put Sisera to Flight   Chapter 4:11-16

4. Jael Kills Sisera with a Tent Peg   Chapter 4:17-24

5. Deborah and Barak Sing   Chapter 5:1-11

6. The Victory Is Recounted   Chapter 5:12-23

7. Jael Is Praised for Her Courage   Chapter 5:24-31

8. Israel's Rebellion Brings Oppression   Chapter 6:1-6

9. A Prophet Chides Israel   Chapter 6:7-10

10. The Angel of the Lord Visits Gideon   Chapter 6:11-24

11. Gideon Tears Down the Altar of Baal   Chapter 6:25-27

12. The Men of Ophrah Are Angered   Chapter 6:28-32

13. Gideon Assembles an Army   Chapter 6:33-35

14. Gideon Questions God with a Fleece   Chapter 6:36-40

Introduction:

Who were the Judges? During the period between 1380 and 1050 B.C. (according to one commonly accepted estimate), Israel was led by a series of national leaders called Judges (Judges 2:16). These man and women were generally military heroes sometimes called deliverers (Judges 3:9,15), who were called by God to rally the people against oppressive enemies and stimulate them toward spiritual revival.

Judge	Duration of Leadership	Major Accomplishments
Othniel King of Judges 3:7-11	40 years	Caleb's nephew, defeated Mesopotamia
Ehud king Judges 3:12-30	80 years	Left-handed; Killed Eglon, of Moab, and subdued the Moabites
Shamgar Judges 3:31	Unknown	Killed 600 Philistines
Deborah Israelite Judges 4:4-5:31	40 years	Recruited Barak to lead warriors to victory over a Canaanite king, Jabin, and his general Siera.
Gideon Judges 6:11-8:32	40 years	With an army of only 300, defeated the Midianites
Tola Judges 10:1-2	23 years	Unknown
Jair Judges 10:3-5	22 years	Unknown
Jephthah but at Judges 11:1-12:7	6 years	Subdued the Ammonites, the cost of his daughter whom he vowed to sacrifice as a burnt offering, disciplined the Ephramites.
Ibzan Judges 12:8-10	7 years	Unknown
Elon Judges 12:11-12	10 years	Unknown
Abdon Judges 12:13-15	8 years	Unknown
Samson de-Judges 13:2-16:31	20 years	Harassed the Philistines, destroyed a pagan temple and killed many at the cost of his own life.

2 Chronicles 7:14

If my people, which are called by my name, shall humble themselves, and pray, and seek my face, and turn from their wicked ways; then will I hear from heaven, and will forgive their sin, and will heal their land.

Psalm 122:6

Pray for the peace of Jerusalem; they will prosper who love thee.

Lesson Plan 79

The Book of Judges

Chapters 7, 8, & 9

Objective: To gain insight and an understanding of the twelve judges of Israel and of their responsibilities and accomplishments.

Objective Breakdown:

1. Introduction
2. Gideon's Army Is Cut to Three Hundred   Chapter 7:1- 8
3. Gideon Prepares for Battle   Chapter 7:9-18
4. The Midianites Are Defeated   Chapter 7:19-25
5. The Men of Ephraim Complain   Chapter 8:1-3
6. Succoth and Penuel Refuse to Help   Chapter 8:4-12
7. Gideon Takes Revenge   Chapter 8:13-21
8. Gideon Makes an Ephod for Israel   Chapter 8:22-28
9. Gideon Dies and Israel Reverts   Chapter 8:29-35
10. Abimelech Becomes King Through Murder   Chapter 9:1-6
11. Jotham Speaks a Parable Against Shechem   Chapter 9:7-21
12. Gaal Challenges Abimelech   Chapter 9:22-33
13. Gaal Is Defeated   Chapter 9:34-41
14. Abimelech Defeats Shechem   Chapter 9:42-49
15. Abimelech Is Killed Besieging Thebez   Chapter 9:50-57

Introduction:

The man who would be king. After Gideon defeated the Midianites, the people of Israel wanted to make him their king, but he refused the title (Judges 8:22-23). Apparently, his son, Abimelech, was not so humble. Even though it meant the brutal murder of his seventy half-brothers, he arranged to have himself crowned king of Shechem.

Yet Abimelech's glory was as limited in scope as it was in duration. His influence probably never extended more than ten miles, even though he was said to have reigned over Israel (Judges 9:22). And after three years he was driven from Shechem by the very people who had aided him his rise to power. He sought safer quarters several miles south at Arumah (Judges 9:39-41).

An Abimelech's grasp on the region began to slip, he resorted to more violence in a desperate bid to retain control (Judges 9:42-52). But in the end, having been rejected by Gideon's family, by his mother's family, and by the citizens of his kingdom, he found himself dying in shame. True to form, he made one last request to preserve what little reputation he had left by compelling one of his men to run him through with a sword (Judges 9:53-54).

2 Chronicles 7:14

If my people, which are called by my name, shall humble themselves, and pray, and seek my face, and turn from their wicked ways; then will I hear from heaven, and will forgive their sin, and will heal their land.

Psalm 122:6

Pray for the peace of Jerusalem; they will prosper who love thee.

Lesson Plan 80

The Book of Judges

Chapters 10, 11, & 12

Objective: To gain insight and an understanding of the twelve judges of Israel and of their responsibilities and accomplishments.

Objective Breakdown:

1. Introduction

2. Tola and Jair Judge Israel   Chapter 10:1-5

3. Israel Sins and Is Oppressed   Chapter 10:6-16

4. The Ammonites Come Against Israel   Chapter 10:17-18

5. Jephthah's Background   Chapter 11:1-3

6. The People Turn to Jephthah   Chapter 11:4-11

7. Jephthah Disputes with the Ammonites   Chapter 11:12-28

8. A Battle Is Won and a Daughter Is Lost   Chapter 11:29-40

9. Gilead and Ephraim Battle Each Other   Chapter 12:1-7

10. Ibzan, Elon, and Abdon Judge Israel   Chapter 12:8-15

Introduction:

Ashtoreth, pagan fertility goddess. The goddess of love and fertility worshiped by many Semitic peoples of the ancient world was called Astoreth by Canaanites and later by the Israelites (Judges 10:6). Other names given her were Astarte (Phoenicians), Inana (Sumerians), Ishtar (Babylonians), Aphrodite (Greeks), and Venus (Romans). She was often depicted as a naked female figure.

Among the Canaanites extremely depraved behavior, including intercourse with temple prostitutes—one reason why the Canaanites stood under the Lord's judgment (see "the Abominations of the Canaanites" at Leviticus 18:24-30). Nevertheless, soon after the conquest of Canaan, the Israelites rather quickly succumbed to idolatry involving Ashtoreth (Judges 2:13).

This worship persisted into the days of Samuel, who put a temporary stop to it. (1 Samuel 7:3-4; 12:10).

But the cult quickly revived later when Solomon, whose many foreign wives turned his heart away from the Lord, erected a public altar to Ashtoreth and began worshiping there personally (1 Kings 11:5; 2 Kings 23:13). Ritual prostitution has been part of religious worship since at least 3000 B. C. (Judges 16:1)

2 Chronicles 7:14

If my people, which are called by my name, shall humble themselves, and pray, and seek my face, and turn from their wicked ways; then will I hear from heaven, and will forgive their sin, and will heal their land.

Psalm 122:6

Pray for the peace of Jerusalem; they will prosper who love thee.

Lesson Plan 81

The Book of Judges

Chapters 13, 14, 15, & 16

Objective: To gain insight and an understanding of the twelve judges of Israel and of their responsibilities and accomplishments.

Objective Breakdown:

Introduction

Introduction:

The Philistines. The conflict between the Israelites and the Philistines that preceded the birth of Samson (Judges 13:1) was one of many that occurred between the two peoples throughout biblical history. Probably no other group was so much a thorn in the side of the Israelites as their neighbors along the southwestern Mediterranean coast in the land known as Philistia (see the Philistine Threat at 1 Samuel 28:4-5).

It is hard to say for sure where Philistines originated. They were descendants of Noah's son Ham through his son Mizraim and grandson Casluhim (Genesis 10:13-14). The name Philistines was used by the Egyptian pharaoh Ramses III to describe one of the sea peoples a coalition of invaders which he repelled in a naval battle in about 1188 B.C.

The Bible regularly associates the Philistines with the Land of Caphtor, believed to be Crete, and its inhabitants, the Caphtorim (1 Chronicles 1:12; Jeremiah 47:4; Amos 9:7). This is consistent with the view that the Greeks moved into the Aegean area beginning about 1500 B.C., the Philistines and other sea people migrated south and east. Some eventually settled on the southwestern coast of Canaan.

2 Chronicles 7:14

If my people, which are called by my name, shall humble themselves, and pray, and seek my face, and turn from their wicked ways; then will I hear from heaven, and will forgive their sin, and will heal their land.

Psalm 122:6

Pray for the peace of Jerusalem; they will prosper who love thee.

Lesson Plan 82

The Book of Judges

Chapters 17, 18, & 19

Objective: To gain insight and an understanding of the twelve judges of Israel and of their responsibilities and accomplishments.

Objective Breakdown:

1. Introduction

2. Micah and His Mother Obtain an Idol   Chapter 17:1-6

3. Micah Hires a Levite as Priest   Chapter 17:7-13

4. Men from Dan Visit the Priest   Chapter 18:1-6

5 The Priest Joins the Danites   Chapter 18:7-20

6. The Danites Conquer Laish   Chapter 18:21-31

7. A Levite Retrieves His Concubine   Chapter 19:1-9

8. The Two Stay with an Old Man at Gibeah   Chapter 19:10-21

9. Men Rape and Torment the Concubine   Chapter 19:22-26

Introduction:

Moral decadence in the book of Judges. The book of Judges begins on a high note, with the people of Israel continuing Joshua's legacy, taking possession of more and more territory in the Promised Land (Judges 1). Yet the book ends on a depressing note with the nation sinking in a moral cesspool of depravity, anarchy, and a civil war touched off by the rape of the Levite's concubine (Judges 19:25).

How can one account for this widespread, rapid decline in light of the lofty standards of the Law envisioned in Exodus, Leviticus, and Deuteronomy? One answer is given in Romans 7, where Paul points out that the Law itself is powerless to produce righteousness. Instead, it exposes sin (Romans 7:7-12).

This is important to remember as we face moral decline in society today. Passing more laws may have a value, but laws alone cannot change behavior; they can only help to distinguish right from wrong. People must choose whether or not they will do what is right.

The ancient Israelites chose to turn away from God. Which way are you choosing to live?

2 Chronicles 7:14

If my people, which are called by my name, shall humble themselves, and pray, and seek my face, and turn from their wicked ways; then will I hear from heaven, and will forgive their sin, and will heal their land.

Psalm 122:6

Pray for the peace of Jerusalem; they will prosper who love thee.

Lesson Plan 83

The Book of Judges

Chapters 20 & 21

Objective: To gain insight and an understanding of the twelve judges of Israel and of their responsibilities and accomplishments.

Objective Breakdown:

1. Introduction

2. All Israel Gathers Against Gibeah   Chapter 20:1-11

3. Thousands of Israelites Are Killed   Chapter 20:12-23

4. Israel Ambushes Gibeah   Chapter 20:24-35

5. Israel Defeats the Benjamites   Chapter 20:36-48

6. Wives Are Needed for the Benjamites   Chapter 21:1-7

7. Jabesh Gilead Is Punished   Chapter 21:8-12

8. Jabesh Gilead and Shiloh Yield Wives   Chapter 21:13-25

Introduction:

Overcoming a tough start. What hope is there to a child born to a prostitute? Society tends to have low expectations—sometimes downright hostility—for people born out of wedlock. Such was the case for Jephthah (Judges 11:1).

The product of his father's dalliance with a prostitute, Jephthah was not only excluded but expelled from his more respectable family (Judges 11:2). Like many rejects, he led the life of a criminal (Judges 11:3), though he and his gang may have harassed the Ammonites more than the Israelites.

The irony of Jephthah's life was that when Israel faced war with Ammon, the leaders of his hometown came looking for Jephthah to deliver them! They offered no apology; they merely appealed for help. To his credit, Jephthah agreed to help them after negotiating his terms (Judges 11:9-11), and God gave him the victory (Judges 11:33).

2 Chronicles 7:14

If my people, which are called by my name, shall humble themselves, and pray, and seek my face, and turn from their wicked ways; then will I hear from heaven, and will forgive their sin, and will heal their land.

Psalm 122:6

Pray for the peace of Jerusalem; they will prosper who love thee.

The Book of Ruth

Scripture Focus Chapters 1-4

Objective: To gain insight on the book of Ruth and how God used an unknown widow from a foreign nation to produce a king for His people.

Objective Breakdown:

1. Introduction

2 Chronicles 7:14

If my people, which are called by my name, shall humble themselves, and pray, and seek my face, and turn from their wicked ways; then will I hear from heaven, and will forgive their sin, and will heal their land.

Psalm 122:6

Pray for the peace of Jerusalem; they will prosper who love thee.

Lesson Plan 84

The Book of Ruth

Chapter 1 & 2

Objective: To gain insight on the book of Ruth and how God used an unknown widow from a foreign nation to produce a king for His people.

Objective Breakdown:

1. Introduction

2. Naomi Predicament   Chapter 1:1-5

3. Naomi Sends Her Daughter Away   Chapter 1:6-14

4. Ruth Refuses to Leave Naomi   Chapter 1:15-22

5. Ruth Gleans in Boaz's Field   Chapter 2:1-7

6. Boaz Praises Ruth   Chapter 2:8-13

7. Ruth Tells Naomi About Boaz   Chapter 2:14-23

Introduction:

A spark of hope. If you ever feel like you are living in dark time, the story of Ruth can provide encouragement. It stands as an important afterword to the book of Judges. The book of Ruth tells how God used an unknown widow from a foreign nation to produce a king for His people. Against the backdrop of Judges, Ruth's faith shines like a point of light in spiritual darkness of that era.

In reading Ruth's story, you can take hope from the fact that no matter how terrible the times may be, God has His people, and He is always carrying out His purposes. Are you aware that the Lord wants to use you? The impact of your faithfulness may seem small and insignificant, but as Ruth shows, that hardly matters. Any spark of faith can light a fire of righteousness.

Ruth insisted that her mother-in-law Naomi allow her to come to Bethlehem, in order that Naomi's people, the Israelites could become Ruth's people and Naomi's God, Ruth's God (Ruth 1:6-17).

The story of Ruth begins in Moab, a land on the eastern shore of the Dead Sea, and ends in Bethlehem, a city of Judah five miles south of Jebus (later Jerusalem).

The events take place against a backdrop of Judges, a time of moral and spiritual decadence when there is no king in Israel. Ironically, there is a famine in Bethlehem ("a house of bread"). A man named "God is my King" goes to pagan Moab to find bread, only to die there. His wife Naomi is left a single parent with two sons, who eventually marry Moabite women, Orpah and Ruth.

After ten years, the two sons die, leaving the three women to fend for themselves. Naomi determines to return to Bethlehem. Orpah stays behind in Moab while Ruth steadfastly follows Naomi. Once in Israel Ruth meets Boaz who negotiates as a "redeeming relative to take her as his wife. Through her a son is born who grandson is David, God's answer to Israel's need for a king. Through David, the King of kings is descended, God's answer to the world's need for a Savior.

2 Chronicles 7:14

If my people, which are called by my name, shall humble themselves, and pray, and seek my face, and turn from their wicked ways; then will I hear from heaven, and will forgive their sin, and will heal their land.

Psalm 122:6

Pray for the peace of Jerusalem; they will prosper who love thee.

Lesson Plan 85

The Book of Ruth

Chapters 3 & 4

Objective: To gain insight on the book of Ruth and how God used an unknown widow from a foreign nation to produce a king for His people.

Objective Breakdown:

1. Introduction

2. Ruth Seeks Security from Boaz   Chapter 3:1-13

3. Ruth Returns to Naomi with Barley   Chapter 3:14-18

4. Boaz and the Kinsman Negotiate   Chapter 4:1-6

5. The Transaction Is Accomplished   Chapter 4:7-12

6. Ruth Marries Boaz and Bears a Son   Chapter 4:13-17

7. Line Through Boaz to David   Chapter 4:18-22

Introduction:

Can anything good come from Moab? The name Moab (Ruth 1:1) recalls two unpleasant incidents from earlier in the Old Testament: the birth of Moab and the trouble his descendants caused Israel during their wilderness journey to the Promised Land.

Moab was born in the aftermath of Sodom and Gomorrah. Lot fled Sodom with his family and in effect, took the sin from the city with him into the wilderness. His wife disobeyed God's instruction and was turned into a pillar of salt (Genesis 19:26). Lot's daughters plotted to get their father drunk so that he might commit incest with them and father their children. One daughter gave birth to Moab, and the other to Ammon (Genesis 19:30-38). In time, their descendants grew into rival nations that have contended with Israel to this day.

One of the most grievous offenses that Moab committed occurred during Israel's wilderness wanderings. The king of Moab attempted to hire Balaam the seer to curse the Israelites, but Balaam blessed them instead (Numbers chapters 22-24). However, the seer came up with a plan to seduce God's people into idolatry by sending Moabite women to entice them. The plan worked perfectly, and 24,000 people died as a result (Numbers 25:3, and Numbers 31:15-16).

No wonder the Law prohibited a Moabite or Ammonite from ever becoming a member of the Israelite community (Deuteronomy 23:3).

Thus, the question raised by opening the book of Ruth—can anything good come from Moab? The answer is a resounding yes! From Moab comes Ruth—and from Ruth, Obed; from Obed comes Jesse, then David (Ruth 4:18-22); and from David comes Jesus Christ (Matthew 1:1, 5-6). Amen!

2 Chronicles 7:14

If my people, which are called by my name, shall humble themselves, and pray, and seek my face, and turn from their wicked ways; then will I hear from heaven, and will forgive their sin, and will heal their land.

Psalm 122:6

Pray for the peace of Jerusalem; they will prosper who love thee.

The Book of 1 Samuel

Scripture Focus Chapters 1-31

Objective: To gain insight on the book of 1 Samuel and the transition from the time of Judges to the monarchy.

Objective Breakdown:

1. Introduction

2. Childless Hannah Prays for a Son   Chapter 1:1-11

3. Eli Misjudges the Situation   Chapter 1:12-18

4. Hannah Dedicates Samuel to the Lord   Chapter 1:19-28

5. Hannah's Prayer of Thankfulness   Chapter 2:1-11

6. Eli's Wicked Sons   Chapter 2:12-17

7. Samuel Grows and Honors the Lord   Chapter 2:18-26

8. God Promises to Judge Eli and His Sons   Chapter 2:27-36

9. A Voice in the Night Awakens Samuel   Chapter 3:1-9

10. The Lord Speaks to Samuel   Chapter 3:10-18

11. Samuel is Confirmed as a Prophet   Chapter 3:19-21

12. The Philistines Capture the Ark   Chapter 4:1-11

13. Eli Hears the Bad News and Dies   Chapter 4:12-18

14. The Birth of Ichabod   Chapter 4:19-22

15. Dagon Is Broken Before the Ark   Chapter 5:1-5

16. The Ark Afflicts Its Philistine Keepers   Chapter 5:6-12

17. The Philistines Plans to Return the Ark   Chapter 6:1-9

18. The Ark Is Carried Back to Israel   Chapter 6:10-16

19. The Men of Beth Shemesh Are Punished   Chapter 6:17-21

20. The Ark Remains at Kirjath Jearim   Chapter 7:1-2

Lesson Plan 86

The Book of 1 Samuel

Chapters 1, 2, & 3

Objective: To gain insight on the book of Samuel and the transition between the period of Judges and the monarchy.

Objective Breakdown:

1. Introduction

2. Childless Hannah Prays for a Son   Chapter 1:1-11

3. Eli Misjudges the Situation   Chapter 1:12-18

4. Hannah Dedicates Samuel to the Lord   Chapter 1:19-28

5. Hannah's Prayer of Thankfulness   Chapter 2:1-11

6. Eli's Wicked Sons   Chapter 2:12-17

7. Samuel Grows and Honors the Lord   Chapter 2:18-26

8. God Promises to Judge Eli and His Sons   Chapter 2:27-36

9. A Voice in the Night Awakens Samuel   Chapter 3:1-9

10. The Lord Speaks to Samuel   Chapter 3:10-18

11. Samuel Is Confirmed as a Prophet   Chapter 3:19-21

Introduction:

The books of 1 and 2 Samuel were originally one book which gave an account of the transition between the period of Judges and the Monarchy. First Samuel tells of the rise of David to the throne, and 2 Samuel deals with the reign of David.

The demand for a king was based on the chronic moral and spiritual breakdowns that occurred under the Judges. As 1 Samuel opens, we find Israel once again drifting under ineffective leadership. Eventually disaster strikes as the ark is captured by the Philistines.

God graciously brought the ark back to His people and raised up Samuel as their Judge. But as Samuel grew older, a debate for and against a monarchy. Samuel's sons were not worthy to succeed him, and there seemed to be no other leadership on the horizon. Consequently, the people insisted on having a king, and God finally granted the people's wish. Yet Scripture says that this request was a great wickedness in that it was a denial of the Lord's right to rule over His people (1 Samuel 8:7; 10:19; 12:12; 12:17-20).

The problem was not that Israel did not need a king, but that the Israelites were not willing to serve the king that they already had—the Lord. How, then, would they follow a human king who had faults and failures?

Ironically, God was already at work to produce a ruler of His own choosing when the people demanded a king. He allowed Saul to be anointed and reign temporarily, but his own plans called for David. First Samuel tells the story of how God brought David to the throne in spite of Saul's effort to the contrary.

Second Samuel continues with an account of David's reign. At first, he was king over Judah only, which he ruled for seven- and one-half years. During much of this period, he fought a war with the successors of Saul, until he finally gained control over all of Israel (see 2 Samuel 2:9-20).

2 Chronicles 7:14

If my people, which are called by my name, shall humble themselves, and pray, and seek my face, and turn from their wicked ways; then will I hear from heaven, and will forgive their sin, and will heal their land.

Psalm 122:6

Pray for the peace of Jerusalem; they will prosper who love thee.

Lesson Plan 87

The Book of 1 Samuel

Chapters 4, 5, & 6

Objective: To gain insight on the book of Samuel and the transition between the period of Judges and the monarchy.

Objective Breakdown:

1. Introduction

2. The Philistines Capture the Ark   Chapter 4:1-11

3. Eli Hears the Bad News and Dies   Chapter 4:12-18

4. The Birth of Ichabod   Chapter 4:19-22

5. Dagon Is Broken Before the Ark   Chapter 5:1-5

6. The Ark Afflicts Its Philistine Keepers   Chapter 5:6-12

7. The Philistines Plans to Return the Ark   Chapter 6:1-9

8. The Ark Is Carried Back to Israel   Chapter 6:10-16

9. The Men of Beth Shemesh Are Punished   Chapter 6:17-21

Introduction:

Praising the King. Many people today debate the potential as well as the limits of big government. The books of 1 and 2 Samuel make interesting reading in light of that discussion, for they offer an account of Israel's transition from rule by judges to a Jerusalem based monarchy.

Under the judges, the nation went through periods of political and spiritual health. But, for most part, the people turned away from God (Judges 21:25). Would they do better under kings?

Hannah's song (1 Samuel 2:1-10) answers that question from the outset of the book: no matter who rules Israel, whether judge or king, the Lord is Israel's true king (1 Samuel 2:3, 10), salvation is from Him (1 Samuel 2:1), and God's concern is often for the outsiders, the poor—people on the bottom of the heap (1 Samuel 2:4-9).

The rest of 1 and 2 Samuel as well as 1 and 2 Kings, bears out these truths:

When the people demanded a king (1 Samuel 8:4-5), the Lord said that it was because they rejected Him as their King (1 Samuel 8:7).

When he nation faced crises, it was not their king who delivered them, but the Lord (for example, 1 Samuel 11:13; 17:46; 2 Samuel 5:22-25).

It was not Saul, the people's favorite, who firmly established the monarchy, but David, the eighth and youngest son of Jesse, a shepherd of Bethlehem (1 Samuel 16:7, 9-13; 2 Samuel 7:12-16).

Thus, Hannah's song is a helpful corrective to overconfidence in government of any kind, all governments is ultimately established by God (Romans 13:1-7).

2 Chronicles 7:14

If my people, which are called by my name, shall humble themselves, and pray, and seek my face, and turn from their wicked ways; then will I hear from heaven, and will forgive their sin, and will heal their land.

Psalm 122:6

Pray for the peace of Jerusalem; they will prosper who love thee.

Lesson Plan 88

The Book of 1 Samuel

Chapters 7, 8, & 9

Objective: To gain insight on the book of Samuel and the transition between the period of Judges and the monarchy.

Objective Breakdown:

1. Introduction

2. The Ark Remains at Kirjath Jearim   Chapter 7:1-2

3. Israel Repents at Mizpah   Chapter 7:3-8

4. Samuel Sets Up the Stone Ebenezer   Chapter 7:9-14

5. Samuel to Judge Over Israel   Chapter 7:15-17

6. The People Demand a King   Chapter 8:1-9

7. Samuel Warns the People   Chapter 8:10-18

8. People Refuse to Heed Samuel   Chapter 8:19-22

9. Saul Searches for His Father's Donkeys   Chapter 9:1-10

10. Saul Encounters Samuel   Chapter 9:11-21

11. Samuel and Saul Eat a Meal Together   Chapter 9:22-27

Introduction:

The capture and return of the Ark. He captures and return of the Ark of the Covenant by the Philistines (1 Samuel 4:11; 5:1-12) was as much a spiritual defeat for Israel as it was a political and military loss. It should have been a "wake up call" to the nation, which languished for years in spiritual ambivalence, moral anarchy, and civil chaos (Judges 21:25; 1 Samuel 2:27-36; 3:11-14).

The Ark was carried into battle ass good luck charm and was captured by the Philistines near Aphek (1 Samuel 4:1, 10-11). The Ark was placed in the temple of Dagon at Ashdod until the idol was toppled and the people were struck with tumors (perhaps bubonic plague). Then it was sent to Gath (1 Samuel 5:1-8). At Gath, "Tumors" again struck the people, and the Ark was sent to Ekron (1 Samuel 5:9-10).

After a brief stop at Ekron, where it caused more disease and death, the Ark was sen on an unmanned cart back to the Israelites (1 Samuel 5:10; 6:12). The Ark stayed with the tabernacle in Shiloh until Eli's two sons foolishly carried it into battle (Joshua 18:1; 1 Samuel 4:4).

The Ark was removed to Kirjath Jearim, where it remained for twenty years (1 Samuel 7:1-2) until David finally relocated it to Jerusalem (2 Samuel 6). The cart bearing the Ark stopped briefly in a field near Beth Shemesh, but was sent on after people looked inside and were struck dead (1 Samuel 6:13-20).

2 Chronicles 7:14

If my people, which are called by my name, shall humble themselves, and pray, and seek my face, and turn from their wicked ways; then will I hear from heaven, and will forgive their sin, and will heal their land.

Psalm 122:6

Pray for the peace of Jerusalem; they will prosper who love thee.

Lesson Plan 89

The Book of 1 Samuel

Chapters 10, 11, 12, & 13

Objective: To gain insight on the book of Samuel and the transition between the period of Judges and the monarchy.

Objective Breakdown:

1. Introduction

2. Saul Anoints Saul King of Israel   Chapter 10:1- 8

3. Saul Speaks as a Prophet   Chapter 10:9-16

4. God Confirms His Choice of Saul   Chapter 10:7-27

5. The Ammonites Attacks Jabesh Gilead   Chapter 11:1-3

6. Saul Leads Israel to Victory   Chapter 11:4-11

7. Saul's Coronation in Gilgal   Chapter 11:12-15

8. Saul Asserts His Integrity   Chapter 12:1-5

9. Samuel Calls on Israel to Follow God   Chapter 12:6-18

10. Fear God or Be Swept Away   Chapter 12:19-25

11. Saul Declares War on the Philistines   Chapter 13:1-7

12. Saul Unlawfully Offers a Sacrifice   Chapter 13:8-14

13. Israel Has Few Weapons as Battle Looms   Chapter 13:15-23

Introduction:

Scripture urges parents to raise their children in the ways of the Lord (see Proverbs 22:6; Ephesians 6:4), but it makes no guarantees as to how they will turn out. Sometimes parents of the utmost integrity see their children utterly reject God. Such was the case for Samuel (1 Samuel 8:2-3).

Scripture describes Samuel as a man who seemingly followed the Lord right from the womb (1 Samuel 1:11, 22; 2:8; 3:19). By contrast, his sons, like Eli's sons before them (1 Samuel 2:22-25), turned out to be quite immoral (1 Samuel 8:3). Could Samuel have done anything differently? Who can say? But the fact that he installed the young men as judges in Beersheba (1 Samuel 8:2) raises the question of whether he turned his back on the problems of his sons rather than facing them squarely.

Beersheba was located at the extreme southern end of Israel's territory (see Genesis 21:31). It maybe that in sending his sons there, Samuel was placing them where they could do the least harm. But in the end, their misdeeds caused great harm, as they created an excuse for the elders of Israel to demand a king (1 Samuel 8:4-5). The subsequent selection of Saul was a choice for which God Himself felt sorrow (1 Samuel 15:11).

No one knows how differently things might have turned out had Samuel confronted his sons, and at last resort taken them before the elders (see Deuteronomy 21:18-21). But the legacy of his family is a sober challenge to any parent of a wayward young person to face trouble head-on.

2 Chronicles 7:14

If my people, which are called by my name, shall humble themselves, and pray, and seek my face, and turn from their wicked ways; then will I hear from heaven, and will forgive their sin, and will heal their land.

Psalm 122:6

Pray for the peace of Jerusalem; they will prosper who love thee.

Lesson Plan 90

The Book of 1 Samuel

Chapters 14, 15, & 16

Objective: To gain insight on the book of Samuel and the transition between the period of Judges and the monarchy.

Objective Breakdown:

1. Introduction

2. Saul Declares War on the Philistines   Chapter 13:1-7

3. Saul Unlawfully Offers a Sacrifice   Chapter 13:8-14

4. Israel Has Few Weapons as Battle Looms   Chapter 13:5-23

5. Jonathan Moves on a Philistine Garrison   Chapter 14:1-5

6. Jonathan Kills a Number of Philistines   Chapter 14:6-14

7. The Philistines Flee   Chapter 14:15-23

8. Johnathan Breaks Saul's Rule About Eating   Chapter 14:24-35

9. The People Save Jonathan from Execution   Chapter 14:36-46

10. An Overview of Saul and His Family   Chapter 14:47-52

11. Saul Attacks Amalek but Spare Agag   Chapter 15:1-9

12. Samuel Rebukes Saul   Chapter 15:10-19

13. Saul Excuses Then Admits His Sin   Chapter 15:20-33

14. God Regrets Making Saul King   Chapter 15:34

15. Samuel Anoints David King   Chapter 16:1-13

16. David Becomes a Musician for Saul   Chapter 16:14-23

Introduction:

Saul's military campaigns. Saul's attack on the Amalekites (1 Samuel 15:3-7) was the last of his military victories. By taking King Agag prisoner and keeping the best of the spoils (1 Samuel 15: 8-9), he disobeyed God. He never won another battle.

In his first battle after being proclaimed king, Saul liberated the people of Jabesh Gilead from Ammonite raiders (1 Samuel 11:1-11). A raid on the Philistine garrison at Geba by Saul's son Jonathan touched off war (1 Samuel 13:1-3). The Israelites gathered at Gigal (1 Samuel 13:4), the Philistines at Michmash 1 Samuel 13:5). The battle was joined at nearby pass, where the Philistines were put to flight and the battle shifted to Beth Aven (1 Samuel 14:4-23). Eventually the Philistines were pushed back to Aijalon (1 Samuel 14:31), where the fighting ceased and both sides went home (1 Samuel 14:46).

Saul campaigned successfully against Moab, Ammon, and Edom to the East, the kings of Zoabah in the North, the Philistines in the Southwest, and the Amalekites in the South, until Israel's sovereignty was established (1 Samuel 14:47-48).

Saul's defeated the Amalekites, but disobeyed God by sparing King Agag and failing to destroy all the spoils of war (1 Samuel 15:1-9). Saul's armies engaged the Philistines in the valley of Elah between Azekah and Sochoh (1 Samuel 17:1-3), but could not prevail due to the champion Goliath (1 Samuel 17:4-11) until young David killed him (1 Samuel 17:48-54).

In his final battle, Saul was mortally wounded fighting the Philistines at Mount Gilboa
(1 Samuel 28:4-5; 31:1-3). He then took his life, and his body was disgraced by the enemy
(1 Samuel 31:4, 8-10).

2 Chronicles 7:14

If my people, which are called by my name, shall humble themselves, and pray, and seek my face, and turn from their wicked ways; then will I hear from heaven, and will forgive their sin, and will heal their land.

Psalm 122:6

Pray for the peace of Jerusalem; they will prosper who love thee.

Lesson Plan 91

The Book of 1 Samuel

Chapters 17, 18, & 19

Objective: To gain insight on the book of Samuel and the transition between the period of Judges and the monarchy.

Objective Breakdown:

1. Introduction

2. Goliath Taunts the Israelites   Chapter 17:1-11

3. David Is Sent to is Soldier Brothers   Chapter 17:12-25

4. David Is Eager to Fight Goliath   Chapter 17:26-30

5. Saul's Armour Doesn't Fit David   Chapter 17:31-39

6. David Approaches Goliath with a Sling   Chapter 17:40-47

7. Goliath Is killed   Chapter 17:48-51

8. The Philistine Army Flees   Chapter 17:52-58

9. Jonathan and David Become Friends   Chapter 18:1-4

10. Saul Envies David and Tries to Kill Him   Chapter 18:5-16

11. David Risks His Life to Marry Michel   Chapter 18:17-30

12. Jonathan Intervenes on David's Behalf   Chapter 19:1-7

13. Saul Makes More Attempts on David's Life   Chapter 19:8-17

14. Saul and His Messengers Prophesy   Chapter 19:18-24

Introduction:

Confessions that bring healing. What does it mean to tell God, "I'm sorry" and admit that we have sinned? Samuel's confrontation of Saul about sin that Saul had committed and the responsibilities that he had betrayed (1 Samuel 15:17-31) makes an interesting study in confession. Saul acknowledged his error and described its source; fear of his people rather than of God's commands (1 Samuel 15:24, 30).

Samuel informed Saul that he would lose his kingship because of what he had done (1 Samuel 15:22-31). Here we see an example of sin's long-lasting consequences.

Lesson in Repentance

Job: Learned from his sufferings that he tended toward self-sufficiency, for which he repented. God was pleased and blessed with abundance in the restoration of his property and family (Job 42:1-6).

Moses: Interceded for his people after the incident with the golden calf (Exodus 32:31-35). Although Moses himself was blameless, he appealed to the Lord to forgive the people's sins. God heeded his prayer, but promised to punish the people's rebellion.

Achan: Confessed to filching forbidden spoils of war when confronted by Joshua. Achan was stoned to death, but the Lord turned from His fierce anger toward Israel (Joshua 7:16-26).

David: Admitted his adultery with Bathsheba and the murder of her husband, Uriah, when confronted by Nathan. The child of David and Bathsheba union died after its birth, even though David pleaded with God to heal it. Later, God gave the couple a son, Solomon (2 Samuel 12).

Shimei: Admitted to King David that he had been wrong to curse the king (2 Samuel 16:5-8) during his flight from Absalom. Abishai, an officer David's army, counseled death to the man, but David refused the advice and forgave Shimei for his sin (2 Samuel 19:16-23).

Manasseh: Responded to severe discipline from God for his evil ways by humbling himself before the Lord. After God delivered him, he tried to correct the wrongs he had done but was only partially successful (2 Chronicles 33:10-20).

Ezra: Reacted strongly to the sin of intermarriage with Gentiles committed by many Israelites, by tearing his garments, pulling out his hair, and grieving over their sins for the entire day. Later he confronted the people, challenging them to repent and correct their wrongs, which they did (Ezra 9:1-4; 10:1-44).

Nehemiah: Recognized that the Babylonian exile was the result of his nation's repeated rebelliousness. In response he prayed, fasted, mourned, and repented (Nehemiah 1:4-11). God gave him the opportunity to return to Jerusalem and begin rebuilding the city wall so that His people could live in freedom and security.

As you consider the experiences of these people, what things do you need to confess before God? What areas of your life do you need to carefully examine as to whether you are following God's ways?

Remember, the Lord delights in forgiving repentant sinners (1 John 1:9). Therefore, give Him the gift of your own brokenness and receive the refreshment of His gift of forgiveness and acceptance. Read Psalm 51 for more on what it means to be cleansed by God from sin.

2 Chronicles 7:14

If my people, which are called by my name, shall humble themselves, and pray, and seek my face, and turn from their wicked ways; then will I hear from heaven, and will forgive their sin, and will heal their land.

Psalm 122:6

Pray for the peace of Jerusalem; they will prosper who love thee.

Lesson Plan 92

The Book of 1 Samuel

Chapters 20, 21, 22, & 23

Objective: To gain insight on the book of Samuel and the transition between the period of Judges and the monarchy.

Objective Breakdown:

1. Introduction

2. David Flees from Saul   Chapter 20:1-10

3. Jonathan Plans to Warn David   Chapter 20:11-23

4. Saul Turns Against His Own Son   Chapter 20:24-34

5. Jonathan Says Goodbye to David   Chapter 20:35-42

6. David and His Men Eat Consecrated Bread   Chapter 21:1-6

7. David Flees to Gath in Philistia   Chapter 21:7-15

8. David's Parents Get Protection in Moab   Chapter 22:1-5

9. Doeg the Edomite Betrays Ahimelech   Chapter 22:6-10

10. The Priests Are Slaughtered in Nob   Chapter 22:11-19

11. Abiathar Escapes to David   Chapter 22:20-23

12. David Repels the Philistines in Keilah   Chapter 23:1-5

13. Saul Pursues David but He Escapes   Chapter 23:6-13

14. Jonathan Visits David in the Woods   Chapter 23:14-18

15. Saul Continues His Pursuit   Chapter 23:19-29

Introduction:

Wells. In the ancient Middle East, wells like the one at Sechu (1 Samuel 19:22) were critically important to the life of the cities and towns. Even in favorable locations, water tended to vanish at times during summer months. Without a well to tap the water table or an underground stream, civilization was impossible to maintain.

Many different types of wells are mentioned in the Bible, though English translations lend not to distinguish between dug wells (John 4:11-12) and natural springs (Psalm 84:6), also called living springs (Nehemiah 2:13), and hewn cisterns (Genesis 16:14; 2 Samuel 17:18). Wells in Canaan were usually dug through solid limestone rock, sometimes to a great depth to keep them from running dry in the summer. Jacob's well which still exists, is 75 feet deep and at one time may have been twice that size.

Some wells had a curb or low wall of stone around the top to keep people and animals from falling in. The lip also formed a brace for users to use in letting down their buckets to draw water. Jesus probably sat on a curb of this sort when he talked to the woman at the well in Samaria (John 4:6). If a well was especially large, it was sometimes furnished with descending steps that allowed a person to dip directly from the pool of water (Genesis 24:16).

Because of their strategic importance, the ownership and use of wells tended to become a matter of dispute (Genesis 21:25; Exodus 2:17-19). However, wells also served to bring people together and to remind them of important events in their heritage (Genesis 24:11, 20; John 4:6, 14)

2 Chronicles 7:14

If my people, which are called by my name, shall humble themselves, and pray, and seek my face, and turn from their wicked ways; then will I hear from heaven, and will forgive their sin, and will heal their land.

Psalm 122:6

Pray for the peace of Jerusalem; they will prosper who love thee.

Lesson Plan 93

The Book of 1 Samuel

Chapters 24, 25, 26, & 27

Objective: To gain insight on the book of Samuel and the transition between the period of Judges and the monarchy.

Objective Breakdown:

1. Introduction

2. David Passes Up a Chance to Kill Saul   Chapter 24:1-7

3. David Asserts His Integrity   Chapter 24:8-15

4. Saul Admits He Is at Fault   Chapter 24:16-22

5. Samuel Dies   Chapter 25:1

6. Nabal Refuses to Assist David   Chapter 25:2-13

7. Abigail Comes Out to Visit David   Chapter 25:14-22

8. Abigail Pleads for Her Husband's Life   Chapter 25:23-31

9. David Spares Nabal but God takes Him   Chapter 25:32-38

10. Abigail Becomes David's Wife   Chapter 25:39-44

11. David Spares Saul's Life a Second Time   Chapter 26:1-12

12. Saul Admits His Guilt   Chapter 26:13-25

13. David Swells Among the Philistines   Chapter 27:1-7

14. Raids Against the Southern Lands   Chapter 27:8-12

Introduction:

The value of friendships between men. Many men today have numerous acquaintances but few friends, lots of associates but few companions. As a result, a man can feel lonely, isolated, and misunderstood. Even if he is married to a supportive wife with whom he has good communications, he can feel an emptiness inside, because no one knows his soul "man-to-man."

David and Jonathan shared a rare and valuable friendship. Their bond serves as a model for men today who need and seek healthy relationships with other men.

Perhaps the key, as in any relationship, is trust and loyalty. That was the basis of David and Jonathan's companionship. Why else would a child of royal privilege risk friendship with a rural shepherd boy who was an enemy of the family? Jonathan's family had experienced what today we would call severe dysfunction (1 Samuel 19:1-17). Perhaps insecure and troubled, he was drawn to the commoner David because he recognized him as someone who would be true and faithful.

As the two young men got to know each other, they formalized their commitment to each other. Then they honored that pledge during a time when their relationship was severely tested (1 Samuel 18:1-4; 20:1-4). Know this, "God will never leave you or forsake you and will never separate loved ones who walk in His way and in His Word." (Deuteronomy 31:8).

2 Chronicles 7:14

If my people, which are called by my name, shall humble themselves, and pray, and seek my face, and turn from their wicked ways; then will I hear from heaven, and will forgive their sin, and will heal their land.

Psalm 122:6

Pray for the peace of Jerusalem; they will prosper who love thee.

Lesson Plan 94

The Book of 1 Samuel

Chapters 28, 29, 30, & 31

Objective: To gain insight on the book of Samuel and the transition between the period of Judges and the monarchy.

Objective Breakdown:

1. Introduction

2. The Philistines Gather for War   Chapter 28:1-6

3. Saul Consults a Medium   Chapter 28:7-19

4. Saul Is Terrified by the Prediction   Chapter 28:20-25

5. The Philistines Don't Trust David   Chapter 29:1-11

6. The Amalekites Raid Ziklag   Chapter 30:1-10

7. David Overtakes and Defeats the Raiders Chapter 30:11-20

8. The Division of the Spoils   Chapter 30:21-31

9. Saul and His Sons Die in Battle   Chapter 31:1-13

Introduction:

David passes up the opportunity to kill Saul. David spared Saul's life—twice, once in the cave at En Gedi (1 Samuel 24:1-7) and again in the wilderness of Ziph (1 Samuel 26:2, 7-12). Even though Saul was demented, unfit for office, and bent on destroying David, David refused to take his life because Saul was the Lord's anointed (1 Samuel 24:6).

In fact, David was troubled for having violated even the garment that Saul was wearing (1 Samuel 24:5). It is the similar to the way Americans "pledge allegiance to the flag of the United States…and to the republic for which it stands." To David the robe of Saul represented the king.

David's respect for Saul' position serves as a model for the high respect that God's people today should have for government and its officials, like David, we may not care for the people in office or their actions, but we can at least respect the positions, since government is ordained by God (see Romans 13:1-2).

In fact, all officeholders—whether or not they are Christians or even God-fearing people deserve our respect and prayers (1 Timothy 2:1-2). A government position invested by the prayers of God's people, anointed by God's representative, and confirmed with oath of office invoking God's help—such office is undeniably God-ordained. In a day when disrespect for government is in vogue, Christians have a challenge to adopt a different attitude.

2 Chronicles 7:14

If my people, which are called by my name, shall humble themselves, and pray, and seek my face, and turn from their wicked ways; then will I hear from heaven, and will forgive their sin, and will heal their land.

Psalm 122:6

Pray for the peace of Jerusalem; they will prosper who love thee.

The Book of 2 Samuel

Scripture Focus Chapters 1-24

Objective: To gain insight on the book of 2 Samuel and the reign of David.

Objective Breakdown:

1. Introduction

2. David Learns of Saul's Death   Chapter 1:10

3. The Man Dies Who Said He Killed Saul   Chapter 1:11-16

4. David Laments Saul and Jonathan   Chapter 1:17

5. Judah Accepts David as King   Chapter 2:1-7

6. Abner Makes Ishbosheth King of Israel   Chapter 2:8-11

7. David's Men Overwhelm Ishbosheth's   Chapter 2:12-17

8. Abner Kills Asahel and Retreats   Chapter 2:18-32

9. The Sons Born to David in Hebron   Chapter 3:1-5

10. Abner and Ishbosheth Fall Out   Chapter 3:6-11

11. Abner and David Make Peace   Chapter 3:12-21

12. Joab Avenges Asahel by Killing Abner   Chapter 3:22-30

13. David Mourns Abner   Chapter 3:31-39

14. Ishbosheth Is Assassinated   Chapter 4:1-8

15. David Has the Killers Executed   Chapter 4:9-12

16. David Is Proclaimed King over All Israel   Chapter 5:1-12

17. Children Fathered by David in Jerusalem   Chapter 5:13-16

18. The Philistines Are Beaten and Repelled   Chapter 5:17-29

19. David Attempts to Relocate the Ark   Chapter 6:1-11

20. The Ark Is Brought to Jerusalem   Chapter 6:12-19

Lesson Plan 95

The Book of 2 Samuel

Chapters 1, 2, & 3

Objective: To gain insight on the book of 2 Samuel and the reign of David.

Objective Breakdown:

1. Introduction

2. David Learns of Saul's Death — Chapter 1:10

3. The Man Dies Who Said He Killed Saul — Chapter 1:11-16

4. David Laments Saul and Jonathan — Chapter 1:17

5. Judah Accepts David as King — Chapter 2:1-7

6. Abner Makes Ishbosheth King of Israel — Chapter 2:8-11

7. David's Men Overwhelm Ishbosheth's — Chapter 2:12-17

8. Abner Kills Asahel and Retreats — Chapter 2:18-32

9. The Sons Born to David in Hebron — Chapter 3:1-5

10. Abner and Ishbosheth Fall Out — Chapter 3:6-11

11. Abner and David Make Peace — Chapter 3:12-21

12. Joab Avenges Asahel by Killing Abner — Chapter 3:22-30

13. David Mourns Abner — Chapter 3:31-39

Introduction:

Civil war between north and south. After the death of Saul, David did not immediately ascend to the throne of an united Israelite kingdom. First, he was crowned king of Judah, which he ruled for seven and a half years from Hebron (2 Samuel 2:1-7, 11).

During much of this period, a civil war was fought between David and the heirs of Saul (2 Samuel 3:1). One of these sons, Ishbosheth, (or Esh-Baal, 1 Chronicles 8:33), pieced together a kingdom in the north, aided behind the scenes by Abner, one of Saul's generals (1 Samuel 2:8-9). A great deal of blood was shed determining whether David or Ishbosheth would ultimately rule Israel (1 Samuel 2:12–4:12).

This tragic period in the nation's history reflected the people's earlier insistence on having a king (1Samuel 8: 4-9, 19-22). Had they waited for God to appoint a ruler in His own good time, the heartache of Saul's reign might never have happened and years of civil war after he died could have been avoided

2 Chronicles 7:14

If my people, which are called by my name, shall humble themselves, and pray, and seek my face, and turn from their wicked ways; then will I hear from heaven, and will forgive their sin, and will heal their land.

Psalm 122:6

Pray for the peace of Jerusalem; they will prosper who love thee.

Lesson Plan 96

The Book of 2 Samuel

Chapters 4, 5, 6, & 7

Objective: To gain insight on the Book of 2 Samuel and the reign of David.

Objective Breakdown:

1. Introduction

2. Ishbosheth Is Assassinated   Chapter 4:1-8

3. David Has the Killers Executed   Chapter 4:9-12

4. David Is Proclaimed King Over All Israel   Chapter 5:1-12

5. Children Fathered by David in Jerusalem   Chapter 5:13-16

6. The Philistines Are Beaten and Repelled   Chapter 5:17-29

7. David Attempts to Relocate the Ark   Chapter 6:1-11

8. The Ark Is Brought to Jerusalem   Chapter 6:12-19

9. Michal Is Condemned to Childlessness   Chapter 6:20-23

10. God Makes a Promise to David   Chapter 7:1-17

11.   David Praises the Lord   Chapter 7:18-29

Introduction:

Giving birth to trouble. Many people today have found that success in a career does not necessarily translate into success in personal and family life. David is an illustration of that fact. While the "House of David grew stronger and stronger" his family life was headed for serious trouble (2 Samuel 3:1).

Evidence for that can be found in the list of David's six sons born at Hebron (2 Samuel 3:2-5). Each was born to a different wife, which indicates that David was strengthening his political ties through marriage, a common practice for ancient kings. But in David's case it was a foolish practice.

Not only did David's polygamy violate the Law (Deuteronomy 17:17), it led to enormous problems as he tried to blend his various families together. For example, David's son Amnon violated his half-sister Tamar, then was killed by her avenging brother, Absalom. That led to a bitter estrangement between

Absalom and his father that resulted in the treason and, ultimately, the death of Absalom—all to David's great regret (2 Samuel 13:18).

David's polygamy also set a poor example for his successor, Solomon, who expanded his kingdom while marrying 700 wives and 300 hundred concubines. Just as the Law had predicted, these women turned his heart away from the Lord to idols (1 Kings 11:3). The Lord judged him for that sin by allowing the kingdom to be divided after his death (1 Kings 11:9-13).

David demonstrates the biblical principle that the sins of the parents extend "to the third and fourth generations" (Exodus 20:5). The choices that we make in order to further our professional lives can sometimes do lasting damage to our immediate families and even to our descendants. We may succeed brilliantly in our field, but is it worth it if we wreak havoc on those closest to us?

2 Chronicles 7:14

If my people, which are called by my name, shall humble themselves, and pray, and seek my face, and turn from their wicked ways; then will I hear from heaven, and will forgive their sin, and will heal their land.

Psalm 122:6

Pray for the peace of Jerusalem; they will prosper who love thee.

Lesson Plan 97

The Book of 2 Samuel

Chapters 8, 9, & 10

Objective: To gain insight on the book of 2 Samuel and the reign of David.

Objective Breakdown:

1. Introduction

2. David's Military Victories   Chapter 8:1-8

3. The Kingdom Is Strengthened   Chapter 8:9-18

4. David show Kindness to Mephibosheth   Chapter 9:1-13

5. Ammonites and Syrians War on Israel   Chapter 10:1-8

6. Joab's Men Drive Back the Syrians   Chapter 10:9-19

Introduction:

How will you be remembered? David made a name for himself in the Valley of Salt (2 Samuel 8:13-14), probably the wasteland plain southwest of the Dead Sea. But while his exploits greatly increased his reputation among his own people, they were sowing lasting bitterness elsewhere that would come back to haunt his successor, Solomon.

The "name" that David earned came at the expense of the lives of 18,000 Syrians, who probably were people of Edom. God explicitly commanded His people not to "abhor" the Edomite's, since they were descended from the same ancestor, Jacob (Deuteronomy 23:7-8).

Yet David's General, Joab, carried out a six-month campaign of genocide "until he cut down every male in Edom" (1 Kings 11:15-16). This delighted the Israelites, who had long hated the Edomite's (see Numbers 20:14-21).

However, an Edomite boy named Hadad watched the slaughter before his father's servants escaped with him to Egypt. He never forgot what he had seen. Years later, after David had died and his son Solomon had turned away from the Lord, God allowed Hadad to come back to Palestine, where he became a perennial thorn in Solomon's side (1 Kings 11:14, 19-22).

Thus, the life of Solomon was effected by brutal ethnic policies of David and Joab. The tragic fruit of this legacy raises the question: how will you be remembered by other people, especially your enemies? If you had or are making a name for yourself. What is the basis for that name? Is it being made at someone else's expense?

2 Chronicles 7:14

If my people, which are called by my name, shall humble themselves, and pray, and seek my face, and turn from their wicked ways; then will I hear from heaven, and will forgive their sin, and will heal their land.

Psalm 122:6

Pray for the peace of Jerusalem; they will prosper who love thee.

Lesson Plan 98

The Book of 2 Samuel

Chapters 11, 12, & 13

Objective: To gain insight on the book of 2 Samuel and the reign of David.

Objective Breakdown:

Introduction:

Scandal and cover-up. The account of David's adulterous affair with Bathsheba (2 Samuel 11:2-5) makes a point of the fact that David stayed home in Jerusalem while his armies went to battle. That suggests that the affair occurred because David was neither where he should have been nor doing what he should have been doing.

However, regardless of why David fell into sin, most of the biblical account of it is devoted to the cover-up that David attempted once Bathsheba conceived (2 Samuel 11:6-27). David tried three plans to cover his sin (or so he thought):

Plan A was to make the pregnancy look like the result of normal relationship between Bathsheba and her husband Uriah. But as a man of conscience, Uriah would not allow himself the privilege that was denied the rest of David's troops (2 Samuel 11:6-11). In that way, loyal Uriah put unprincipled David to shame.

Plan B was based on the assumption that drunkenness would lower Uriah's well-guarded principles so that he would sleep with his wife. But again, Uriah resisted the impulse (2 Samuel 11:12-13).

Plan C called for neither coercion nor deception, but outright murder. Uriah was to be sacrificed to the enemy in a way that would make his death appear to be a casualty of war. Then David could respond to the grieving widow by embracing her as his wife (2 Samuel 11:14-27).

David admitted his sins (2 Samuel 12:13) and repented of his wrongdoing, turning to God for forgiveness and the renewal of his spiritual walk (Psalm 51). God forgave him (2 Samuel 12:13), but the child died, Solomon (12:24). Nevertheless, despite his cleansing from the Lord, David was permanently affected by this scandalous episode.

The sins of adultery and murder are grievous offenses before the Lord (Leviticus 20:10; Deuteronomy 5:17-18). But just as hateful in His sight are attempts to cover up one's sins rather than come clean (Psalm 51:17; Proverbs 6:16-19, 1 John1:8-9).

2 Chronicles 7:14

If my people, which are called by my name, shall humble themselves, and pray, and seek my face, and turn from their wicked ways; then will I hear from heaven, and will forgive their sin, and will heal their land.

Psalm 122:6

Pray for the peace of Jerusalem; they will prosper who love thee.

Lesson Plan 99

The Book of 2 Samuel

Chapters 14, 15, & 16

Objective: To gain insight on the book of 2 Samuel and the reign of David.

Objective Breakdown:

Introduction:

Merry and sad with wine. The misuse of fermented beverages has cause grief throughout human history. Absalom's strategy of getting Amnon drunk and then murdering him (2 Samuel 13: 28) was yet another sad tale involving wine. The Bible often reports on the effects of alcohol abuse.

Here are some examples of alcohol abuse in Scripture:

Amnon (2 Samuel 13:28-29) David's oldest son murdered by his half-brother Absalom while drunk.

Ahasuerus (Esther 1:10) drunk at a royal feast, the Persian king commanded Queen Vashti to display herself; when she refused, he had her removed.

Belshazzar (Daniel 5) having entertained a vast number of guests with wine served in golden vessels taken from the temple at Jerusalem, the Babylonian king was frightened when a hand appeared and wrote his fate on the wall; he was killed that very night.

Ben Hadad (1 Kings 20:16) the Syrian ruler hosted 32 kings for a drinking party in his tent before the Israelites attacked.

Elah (1 Kings 6:9) the fourth king of Israel was murdered.

Job (Job 1-5) worried about the constant partying of his children. His concern that his family offspring might have cursed God led him to offer sacrifices on their behalf.

Lot (Genesis 19:32-33) having survived the fire and brimstone that fell on Sodom, he was seduced by his daughters to commit incest while drunk.

Nabal (1 Samuel 25:36-37) the man whose name meant "fool" drank himself into a stupor the night before his wife told him of her conversation with David, which after his heart died within him, and he died ten days later.

Nadab and Abihu (Leviticus 10:1-9) may have been intoxicated when they offered profane fire to the Lord. Afterward, the Lord prohibited the priest from drinking on duty.

Noah (Genesis 9: 21-25) embarrassed his sons in his naked, drunken stupor, then cursed Canaan his descendants.

Uriah (2 Samuel 11:1) was made drunk by David in an attempt to have him sleep with his wife to cover David's of adultery.

Note: The misuse of anything in God's creation is sin, and the misuse of alcohol causes especially serious problems socially, morally, and spiritually.

2 Chronicles 7:14

If my people, which are called by my name, shall humble themselves, and pray, and seek my face, and turn from their wicked ways; then will I hear from heaven, and will forgive their sin, and will heal their land.

Psalm 122:6

Pray for the peace of Jerusalem; they will prosper who love thee.

Lesson 100

The Book of 2 Samuel

Chapters 17, 18, 19, & 20

Objective: To gain insight on the book of 2 Samuel and the reign of David.

Objective Breakdown:

Introduction:

Why Ahimaaz outran the Cushite. A bit off knowledge about the geography near Mahanaim, where David awaited word of the battle with Absalom (2 Samuel 17:27; 18:4-6), helps explain how Ahimaaz arrived before the Cushite messenger (2 Samuel 18:24-32).

The Cushite, probably an Ethiopian (see 2 Chronicles 14:12), was apparently a swift and powerful runner. In fact, he may have been retained in the Army of Joab as an experienced Herald (for foot runner bearing a message). However, he chose to take the direct route from the battlefield to Mahanaim. This took him over terrain, as the city lay in a steep gorge carved out by the Jabbok River.

Ahimaaz was also a renowned runner (2 Samuel 18:27, 36). Perhaps Ahimaaz was more familiar with the terrain, for he chose the way of the plain (2 Samuel 18:23), that is, the smooth riverbed of the Jabbok. He route was less direct but easier to run than that of the Cushite. As a result, Ahimaaz arrived first. Even so, he failed to tell David the sad news of Absalom's death.

The Father's anguish. The tragic account of David's son Absalom is a story of appearance. Apparently, he was the most handsome man in all Israel. His notable feature was his thick, long hair, which he cut annually. Its weight was said to be about 20 shekels, or several pounds (2 Samuel 14; 25-26). As a son of the king, he enjoyed the benefits of the royal family whose empire was on the rise. For example, Hiram of Tyre had built David a palace of Cedar (2 Samuel 5:11; 7:1-2). He was next in line to the throne after his half-brothers Amnon and Chileab. He also must have had a special place in his father's heart, for even after Absalom took Amnon's life, David longed to be with his son (2 Samuel 13:39).

When Amnon violated Absalom's beautiful sister Tamar, Absalom took revenge by luring

Amnon to his country home, where he had his servants kill him after dinner (2 Samuel 13:1-29).

Reinstated after 2 years of exile, Absalom began building a power base among the people, right under the nose of David (2 Samuel 15:1-6). When the time was right, he launched a rebellion to depose his father and rule in his place (2 Samuel 15:7-18). His ultimate act of defiance was to violate his father's concubines, which in effect meant that he had assumed the throne (2 Samuel 16:20-22).

Under the seasoned command of Joab, David's troops severely defeated Absalom's army and, through an odd set of circumstances, brought an end to Absalom's life (2 Samuel 18:6-15). Despite the throne being restored, David's sin with Bathsheba had finally come to its tragic and painful outcome, just as Nathan had predicted (2 Samuel 12:7-12).

2 Chronicles 7:14

If my people, which are called by my name, shall humble themselves, and pray, and seek my face, and turn from their wicked ways; then will I hear from heaven, and will forgive their sin, and will heal their land.

Psalm 122:6

Pray for the peace of Jerusalem; they will prosper who love thee.

Lesson Plan 101

The Book of 2 Samuel

Chapters 21, 22, 23, & 24

Objective: To gain insight on the book of 2 Samuel and the reign of David.

Objective Breakdown:

1. Introduction

2. The Gibeonites Are Avenged   Chapter 21:1-9

3. Saul and Jonathan Are Reburied   Chapter 21:10-14

4. More Philistines Are Killed   Chapter 21:15-22

5. David's Song of Praise   Chapter 22:1-7

6. God's Deliverance   Chapter 22:8-20

7. God's Loyalty to the Righteous   Chapter 22:21-31

8. God Has Provided Victory   Chapter 22:32-46

9. God Is the King's Salvation   Chapter 22:47-51

10. The Last Words of David   Chapter 23:1-7

11. David's Mighty Men   Chapter 23:8-19

12. More Mighty Men   Chapter 23:20-39

13. David Takes a Census of Israel   Chapter 24:1-9

14. David Repents but Must Be Punished   Chapter 24:10-17

15. David Builds an Altar to the Lord   Chapter 24:18-25

Introduction:

A spiritual cause to a natural event. The three famines in the days of David were the result of Saul's violation of the standing peace treaty Israel had with the Gibeonites (2 Samuel 21:1; see Joshua 9:15, 19-21). This suggests two things:

a). Political commitments, such as peace treaties, have spiritual implications. God takes people words— including the words of governments—seriously and expects people to honor their commitments. To break a covenant is a sin against the very character of God, who always remains faithful to His promises.

b). Natural events sometimes have spiritual causes. Famines, floods, diseases, pestilence, and other destructive phenomena of nature can be shown to have natural causes. Nevertheless, Scripture offers many illustrations on the fact that God may sovereignty allow and ordain such events for spiritual reasons.

Songs of Praise and Faith. Singing has always characterized people of faith. For example, when David realized that God had given him peace from his enemies, he composed a song to praise the Lord and celebrate His goodness (2 Samuel 22; Psalm 18). This was a pattern established by numerous Old Testament figures:

Event: Israelis delivered from 400 years of slavery under Pharaoh.

Song: Moses and Miriam lead in a song of celebration (Exodus 15:1-21).

Event: Israel is liberated by Deborah from Canaanite rule.

Song: Deborah and Barak rehearse the victory in song (Judges 5:1-31).

Event: Hannah and Elkanah have a son, Samuel, after years of barrenness.

Song: Hannah rejoices in song (1 Samuel 2:1-10)

Event: Israel defeats their long-standing enemies, the Philistines, under David's leadership.

Song: David sings praises to God (2 Samuel 22:1-55)

Event: The Ark arrives in Jerusalem, signaling Israel's supremacy in Canaan.

Song: David commissions singers to write songs of praise and thanksgiving (1 Chronicles 16:7-36).

Event: Solomon is in love with a Shulamite woman.

Song: He composes a love song to her, the Song of Solomon.

2 Chronicles 7:14

If my people, which are called by my name, shall humble themselves, and pray, and seek my face, and turn from their wicked ways; then will I hear from heaven, and will forgive their sin, and will heal their land.

Psalm 122:6

Pray for the peace of Jerusalem; they will prosper who love thee.

The Book of 1 Kings

Scripture Focus Chapters 1-22

Objective: To gain insight on the Book of 1 Kings as we see David passing from the scene.

Objective Breakdown:

1. Introduction

2. David Grows Old   Chapter 1:1-4

3. Adonijah Seeks His Father's Throne   Chapter 1:5-10

4. Bathsheba Protests to the King   Chapter 1:11-21

5. Nathan Confirms Bathsheba's Warning   Chapter 1:22-27

6. David Affirms Solomon as His Successor   Chapter 1:28-37

7. Adonijah Hears of Solomon's Acclaim   Chapter 1:38-48

8. Adonijah Fears for His Life   Chapter 1:49-53

9. David's Final Instruction   Chapter 2:1-9

10. David Dies   Chapter 2:10-12

11. Adonijah's Request Cost Him His Life   Chapter 2:13-25

12. Abiathar the Priest Is Disposed   Chapter 2:26-27

13. Joab Is Put to Death   Chapter 2:28-35

14. Shimei Breaks a Travel Ban and Dies   Chapter 2:36-46

15. Solomon Asks God for Wisdom   Chapter 3:1-9

16. God Grants Solomon's Request   Chapter 3:10-15

17. Solomon Shows His Wisdom in Judgment   Chapter 3:16-28

18. Solomon's Officials   Chapter 4:1-19

19. Solomon's Reign Prospers   Chapter 4:20-28

20. World Famous Wisdom   Chapter 4:29-34

Lesson Plan 102

The Book of 1 Kings

Chapters 1 & 2

Objective: To gain insight on the Book of 1 Kings as we see David passing from the scene.

Objective Breakdown:

1. Introduction

2. David Grows Old   Chapter 1:1-4

3. Adonijah Seeks His Father's Throne   Chapter 1:5-10

4. Bathsheba Protests to the King   Chapter 1:11-21

5. Nathan Confirms Bathsheba's Warning   Chapter 1:22-27

6. David Affirms Solomon as His Successor   Chapter 1:28-37

7. Adonijah Hears of Solomon's Acclaim   Chapter 1:38-48

8. Adonijah Fears for His Life   Chapter 1:49-53

9. David's Final Instruction   Chapter 2:9

10. David Dies   Chapter 2:10-12

11. Adonijah's Request Cost Him His Life   Chapter 2:13-25

12. Abiathar the Priest Is Disposed   Chapter 2:26-27

13. Joab Is Put to Death   Chapter 2:28-35

14. Shimei Breaks a Travel Ban and Dies   Chapter 2:36-46

Introduction:

None of the Kings quite matched up to David, although at first it appeared that David's son Solomon would surpass him. Solomon building on his father's heritage, distinguished himself by asking the Lord for wisdom rather than great wealth or honor (1 Kings 3:5-14). God rewarded Solomon's by allowing him to construct a magnificent temple at Jerusalem, and to establish the nation as a prominent trading power with a well-organized government and strongly defended borders.

However, despite his great wisdom, Solomon displayed great foolishness by breaking every one of the guidelines prescribed for Israel's kings (See Deuteronomy 17:14-20). The most serious violations of these were his political marriages (See 2 Samuel 3:13-14), through which his heart was turned away from the Lord. As a result, God. allowed the kingdom to be divided in two parts (the northern kingdom and the southern kingdom). The southern kingdom of Judah comprised the tribes of Judah and Benjamin and continued to be ruled by kings of Davis lineage; while the northern kingdom of Israel made up of the remaining ten tribes, and was led by its own succession of kings, several of whom usurped the throne. None of Israel's (northern tribes) is said to have followed the Lord.

2 Chronicles 7:14

If my people, which are called by my name, shall humble themselves, and pray, and seek my face, and turn from their wicked ways; then will I hear from heaven, and will forgive their sin, and will heal their land.

Psalm 122:6

Pray for the peace of Jerusalem; they will prosper who love thee.

Lesson Plan 103

The Book of 1 Kings

Chapters 3, 4, & 5

Objective: To gain insight on the Book of 1 Kings as we see David passing from the scene.

Objective Breakdown:

1. Introduction

2. Solomon Asks God for Wisdom   Chapter 3:1-9

3. God Grants Solomon's Request   Chapter 3:10-15

4. Solomon Shows His Wisdom in Judgment   Chapter 3:16-28

5. Solomon's Officials   Chapter 4:1-19

6. Solomon's Reign Prospers   Chapter 4:20-28

7. World Famous Wisdom   Chapter 4:29-34

8. A Trade Agreement to Build the Temple   Chapter 5:1-12

9. Solomon Raises a Labor Force   Chapter 5:13-18

Introduction:

The gift of an understanding heart. If you were assured that God would grant you your greatest wish, what would you ask for? Money? Health? Happiness? Solomon asked for Wisdom, but it also made a great deal of sense given the circumstances in which Solomon found himself. He was following in the steps of a remarkable man (1 Kings 3:6). He was young and perceived himself to be inexperienced (1 Kings 3:7). He was saddled with the responsibility of leading God's people (1 Kings 3:8), people who had shown themselves on frequent occasions to be stubborn, rebellious, and hard on their leaders (See Numbers 12:3).

The Lord was delighted with his request, as He always is when people show purity of heart (Matthew 5:8). Consequently, God granted him wisdom beyond any measure that Solomon had anticipated (1 Kings 3:12). Then He added gifts that Solomon had not asked for, but that most rulers would want to have: long life, honor, and great wealth (1 Kings 3:13-14).

However, the ability to discern between good and evil is not the same as the ability to do and reject the evil. Despite the gift of wisdom. Solomon did a foolish thing by entering into hundreds of political marriages (1 Kings 11:1-2; see 2 Samuel 3:13-14), violating the Law. His wives turned his heart toward idolatry, and as a result the kingdom was eventually torn in two (1 Kings 11:9-13).

2 Chronicles 7:14

If my people, which are called by my name, shall humble themselves, and pray, and seek my face, and turn from their wicked ways; then will I hear from heaven, and will forgive their sin, and will heal their land.

Psalm 122:6

Pray for the peace of Jerusalem; they will prosper who love thee.

Lesson Plan 104

The Book of 1 Kings

Chapters 6 & 7

Objective: To gain insight on the Book of 1 Kings as we see David passing from the scene.

Objective Breakdown:

1. Introduction

2. The Temple Is Constructed   Chapter 6:1-10

3. The Lord Reaffirms Israel's Covenant   Chapter 6:11-13

4. The Temple Is Overlaid with Gold   Chapter 6:14-22

5. Work on the Temple Is Finished   Chapter 6:23-38

6. Several Palaces Are Constructed   Chapter 7:1-12

7. A Skillful Worker Is Brought from Tyre   Chapter 7:13-26

8. Carts and Lavers of Bronze   Chapter 7:27-39

9. Temple Fixtures and Instruments   Chapter 7:40-51

Introduction:

Spare no expense. Whenever modern-day churches draw up plans and budgets for buildings in which to worship, they face an age-old tension. What is appropriate for a worship center in terms of size, materials, beauty, and expense? For Solomon, there was no limitation as he proposed to build God's temple and spare no expense.

Let's look at the cost of Solomon's temple:

a). It was made of the most precious of building materials, many of them imported: Caesar (1 Kings 5:6), quarried stone (1 Kings 5:15-18), gold (1 Kings 6: 20-22), olive wood (1 Kings 6:23-28, 31-33), cypress (1 Kings 6:34), bronze (1 Kings 7:13-47).

b). Solomon's primary supplier, Hiram, was told to name his price for materials and workers (1 Kings 5:5), in turn Hiram supplied Solomon with as much material as he desired (1 Kings 9:11).

c). The project employed 30,000 labors (1 Kings 6:13), 150,000 stone masons and haulers (1

Kings 6:15), and 3,300 supervisors (1 Kings 6:16).

d). The stone was worked off-site (1 Kings 6:7).

e). Its floors and walls were overlaid with gold (1 Kings 6:20-22).

f). It was furnished with items of finely crafted wood and gold (1 Kings 6:23-35; 7:48-50).

g). So much bronze was used that its weight (and therefore the cost) was not determined (1 Kings 7:45-47).

h). The work continued nonstop for seven years (1 Kings 7:37-38).

Note: The cost of such a venture today would be virtually incalculable.

2 Chronicles 7:14

If my people, which are called by my name, shall humble themselves, and pray, and seek my face, and turn from their wicked ways; then will I hear from heaven, and will forgive their sin, and will heal their land.

Psalm 122:6

Pray for the peace of Jerusalem; they will prosper who love thee.

Lesson Plan 105

The Book of 1 Kings

Chapters 8 & 9

Objective: To gain insight on the Book of 1 Kings as we see David passing from the scene.

Objective Breakdown:

1. Introduction

2. The Ark Is Brought into the Temple   Chapter 8:1-11

3. Solomon Dedicates the Temple   Chapter 8:12-21

4. Solomon's Prayer   Chapter 8:22-30

5. God Is Reminded of His Assurances   Chapter 8:31-40

6. God's Forgiveness Is Solicited   Chapter 8:41-53

7. God Pronounces Blessings   Chapter 8:54-61

8. Dedication Sacrifices Are Offered   Chapter 8:62-66

9. God Renews His Covenant with Solomon   Chapter 9:1-9

10. Solomon Repays Hiram with Cities   Chapter 9:10-14

11. The Work of the Labor Force   Chapter 9:15-25

12. Solomon's Fleet of Ships   Chapter 9:26-28

Introduction:

The cedar trade. The parched and war-torn landscape of the modern-day Lebanon makes it difficult to imagine, but 3000 years ago the area was flourishing with massive cedar trees. The trees were so plentiful that Solomon sent thousands of laborers to cut and transport cedar wood to Jerusalem, where he built numerous structures with it, including his impressive residence, appropriately called the House of the Forest of Lebanon (1 Kings 7:2).

Cedar was also used for the construction of the temple, (1 Kings 5:6-10; 6:9-10; 15-18). It was used again several years later in construction of the second temple, after the Babylonian exile (Ezra 3:7).

Solomon was not the only ruler to import the fragrant, durable, and attractive cedar, as well cypress and fir. Lebanon is known to have traded these woods with Syria, Egypt, and the nations of Mesopotamia.

The forests of Lebanon were decimated by over cutting. Solomon contributed to that, yet even his demand for cedar was exceeded by that of the Babylonian ruler Nebuchadnezzar, according to extra biblical sources and possibly the biblical prophets as well (Habakkuk 2:17). As a result, the ancient cedar forests vanished within a matter of generations, never to be replaced despite the attempts to reforest the land.

2 Chronicles 7:14

If my people, which are called by my name, shall humble themselves, and pray, and seek my face, and turn from their wicked ways; then will I hear from heaven, and will forgive their sin, and will heal their land.

Psalm 122:6

Pray for the peace of Jerusalem; they will prosper who love thee.

Lesson Plan 106

The Book of 1 Kings

Chapters 10, 11, & 12

Objective: To gain insight on the book of 1 Kings as we see David passing from the scene.

Objective Breakdown:

1. Introduction

2. Queen of Sheba Visits Solomon   Chapter 10:1-9

3. Royal Splendor   Chapter 10:10-23

4. Gifts and Imports Flow into Israel   Chapter 10:24-29

5. Solomon's Wives Turn Him Away from God   Chapter 11:1-8

6. God Promises to Punish Solomon   Chapter 11:9-13

7. God Raises Up Adversaries   Chapter 11:14-28

8. Ahijah's Prophecy   Chapter 11:29-40

9. The Death of Solomon   Chapter 11:41-43

10. Rehoboam Rejects Wise Advice   Chapter 12:1-15

11. Rehoboam Reigns Over Judah   Chapter 12:16-24

12. Jeroboam Puts Calves in Bethel and Dan   Chapter 12:25-33

Introduction:

Hiram of Tyre was probably the most valuable ally that David and Solomon had, for he supplied them not only with raw material for their many building projects, but expert craftsmen as well. He also helped launch Israel's ship building industry by providing experienced sailors and ships (1 Kings 9:26-28; 10:11, 22). During the 20 years' period in which Solomon built the Temple and his own palace complex, Israel incurred a trade balance with Phoenica, for which 20 cities along the Galilean-Phoenician border were given to Hiram. However, the cities were later returned when Hiram determined them to be cabal, "good for nothing" (1 Kings 5:1-18; 9:10-14; 2 Chronicles 8:1-2).

Ophir. The exact location and identity of the place called Ophir (1 Kings 9:28) remains a mystery. It is mentioned a number of times in connection with what was apparently was its major export –gold (1 Kings 10:11; 22:48; Job 28:16; Isaiah 13:12).

Several places have been suggested as possible locations of Ophir:

o.   The African lands of Sheba or Punt at the lower end of the Red Sea (modern-day Ethiopia and Somalia).

o.   The southern region of the Arabian Peninsula on the Red Sea (modern-day Yemen).

o.   Southeastern Arabia on the Arabian Sea (modern-day Oman).

o.   A region of northwestern India (just north of modern-day Bombay).

o.   A region of southern Africa (modern-day Zimbabwe).

Wherever Ophir was located, the round trip from Solomon's port at Ezion Geber apparently took three years (1 Kings 10:22). That may mean either three full years or one full year and parts of two other years. Either way the voyage seems to be a lengthy one or as far away as India was not impossible. In fact, trade between the Persian Gulf and India was already established 1,000 years before Solomon. The gold for which Ophir was famous may have originated from Ophir itself or just passed through Ophir. Ophir also exported silver, precious stones, almug trees (possibly sandalwood), ivory, apes, monkeys, or peacocks.

2 Chronicles 7:14

If my people, which are called by my name, shall humble themselves, and pray, and seek my face, and turn from their wicked ways; then will I hear from heaven, and will forgive their sin, and will heal their land.

Psalm 122:6

Pray for the peace of Jerusalem; they will prosper who love thee.

Lesson Plan 107

The Book of 1 Kings

Chapters 13, 14, & 15

Objective: To gain insight on the book of 1 Kings as we see David passing from the scene.

Objective Breakdown:

1. Introduction

2. A Man of God Rebukes Jeroboam   Chapter 13:1-10

3. The Man of God Is Deceived by a Prophet   Chapter 13:11-25

4. The Prophet Buries the Man of God   Chapter 13:26-32

5. Jeroboam Continues in His Evil Way   Chapter 13:33-34

6. The Lord Promises to Judge Jeroboam   Chapter 14:1-16

7. Jeroboam's Reign Comes to an End   Chapter 14:17-20

8. Egypt Attacks Judah   Chapter 14:21-31

9. Abijam Reign Over Judah   Chapter 15:1-8

10. A Treaty with Syria   Chapter 15:9-34

Introduction:

Tax revolt divides the kingdom. Complaints about high taxes are nothing new. In Ancient Israel, the tax burden became so great that the citizens of all, but one tribe revolted, killing the chief tax collector, and forcing King Rehoboam to flee in haste (1 Kings 12:18-19).

Actually, many factors led to the division of the kingdom. But the crisis that touched off rebellion was Rehoboam's decision to add to the people's already high taxes (1 Kings 12:13-14). Under Solomon, heavy taxes were required to pay for his numerous building projects and lavish lifestyle. While Israel's international trade was brisk, and aliens were conscripted for relatively cheap labor, the Israelites themselves lived under a heavy yoke (1 Kings 12:4).

Rehoboam, perhaps intending to outdo his father, rejected the advice of his father's counselors (1 Kings 12:6-8) and raised taxes. As the account makes clear, this was all part of God's plan to judge Solomon and the people for turning to idolatry (1 Kings 11:9-13; 29-39; 12:15). The Kingdom was split, and eventually both parts were carried away into exile.

What can we learn from this incident? Certainly, it illustrates what can happen when government places excessive levies on its people. It also shows what can happen when a nation turns away from the Lord.

Jesus told His followers to give Caesar his due (Matthew 22:17-21), and Paul explicitly urged Christians to pay their taxes (Roman 13:6-7). However, believers can get involved in efforts to make government more responsive to its citizens, more efficient in the use of its revenues, and more responsible in its fiscal policies. By doing so, God's people can help head off the kind of anger, frustration, and injustice that led to Israel's downfall.

2 Chronicles 7:14

If my people, which are called by my name, shall humble themselves, and pray, and seek my face, and turn from their wicked ways; then will I hear from heaven, and will forgive their sin, and will heal their land.

Psalm 122:6

Pray for the peace of Jerusalem; they will prosper who love thee.

Lesson Plan 108

The Book of 1 Kings

Chapters 16, 17, & 18

Objective: To gain insight on the book of 1 Kings as we see David passing from the scene.

Objective Breakdown:

Introduction:

Starting strong ending weak. After spiritual and political decline under Rehoboam and Abijam, the southern kingdom of Judah reversed course under the reformer Asa. His main contribution was a campaign against idolatry that went so far as to banish his grandmother Maachah, who was a notorious worshiper of the Canaanite fertility goddess Asherah (1 Kings 15:11-15).

Asa also strengthened his country's defenses by refortifying its walled cities (2 Chronicles 14:6-7). His military won a decisive victory over Zerah the Ethiopian when the "fear of the Lord" came upon his troops (1 Kings 14:9-15). The Army also took fortified cities and booty during periodic forays against the northern kingdom through the help of Ben Hadad of Syria (1 Kings 15:16-22; 2 Chronicles 16:2-4).

However, this reliance on a foreign government seemed to indicate that Asa no longer felt a need to rely solely on the Lord. He was rebuked by the Prophet Hanani, but instead of listening, he had the seer imprisoned (1 Kings 16:7-10). Toward the end of his life, Asa developed a severe disease in his feet. Yet again he failed to rely on the Lord for healing, and he never recovered (1 Kings 16:12).

2 Chronicles 7:14

If my people, which are called by my name, shall humble themselves, and pray, and seek my face, and turn from their wicked ways; then will I hear from heaven, and will forgive their sin, and will heal their land.

Psalm 122:6

Pray for the peace of Jerusalem; they will prosper who love thee.

Lesson Plan 109

The Book of 1 Kings

Chapters 19, 20, & 21

Objective: To gain insight on the book of 1 Kings as we see David passing from the scene.

Objective Breakdown:

Introduction:

The life of Elijah. Elijah was apparently from the village of Tishbe, south of the Sea of Galilee, he was known as Elijah the Tishbite (1 Kings 17:1). He predicted a drought as God's punishment for idolatry of King Ahab of Israel (1 Kings 17:1, 7; 18:17-18). In his escape from the threats from Queen Jezebel he was miraculously fed by ravens as he rested by the Brook Cherith. (1 Kings 17:2-6). He miraculously provided for a needy widow at Zarephath and raised her son from the dead (1 Kings 17:8-24). He also won a contest with 450 prophets of Baal on Mount Carmel by calling down fire from heaven, which encouraged spiritual revival and ended the drought (1 Kings 18:20-40). He fled to Beersheba and on to Mount Horeb (Sinai) to escape the wrath of Queen Jezebel (1 Kings 19:1-18), after slaying 450 of her prophets on Mount Carmel. He selected Elisha as his successor at Abel Meholah (1 Kings 19:16-21). He then challenged King Ahaziah for sending to the Philistines for divine guidance and predicted that the King would die, which he did (2 Kings 1:2-8, 17).

He set out from Gilgal toward Bethel, when he was taken up into heaven by a whirlwind accompanied by a fiery chariot (2 Kings 2:1-12).

Although, King Ahab called Elijah a "troubler of Israel" it was really King Ahab who was troubling the Northern Kingdom, in that he had forsaken the Lord and turned to idolatry (1 Kings 18:17-18). The tide of wickedness rose to unprecedented heights under the reign of King Ahab (1 Kings 16:30, 33).

One of King Ahab's failures was his decision to marry Jezebel (1 Kings 16:31). By making Ahab her puppet (1 Kings 21:7-8, 25), she introduced the worship of Baal Melqart, protective god of Tyre (1 Kings 16:31-33). She openly opposed the worship of the Lord by massacring His prophets (1 Kings 18:4) and tearing down His altars (1 Kings 19:10, 14).

Yet ironically, Ahab had one shining moment of humility and faith in God. After Jezebel murdered Naboth in order to grab his vineyard for her husband (1 Kings 21:1-16), Elijah prophesied the end of his dynasty (1 Kings 21:21-22). Ahab repented, and the Lord heeded his humility (1 Kings 21:27-29).

2 Chronicles 7:14

If my people, which are called by my name, shall humble themselves, and pray, and seek my face, and turn from their wicked ways; then will I hear from heaven, and will forgive their sin, and will heal their land.

Psalm 122:6

Pray for the peace of Jerusalem; they will prosper who love thee.

Lesson Plan 110

The Book of 1 Kings

Chapter 22

Objective: To gain insight on the book of 1 Kings as we see David passing from the scene.

Objective Breakdown:

1. Introduction

2. Many Prophets Advise War against Syria   Chapter 22:1- 2

3. Micaiah Tries to Warn Ahab   Chapter 22:13-23

4. Micaiah Is Imprisoned   Chapter 22:24-28

5. Ahab Dies in Battle   Chapter 22:29-40

6. Jehoshaphat's Rule Over Judah   Chapter 22:41-50

7. Ahaziah Succeeds His Father Ahab   Chapter 22:51-53

Introduction:

When Elijah was told to stand on the mountain before the Lord (1 Kings 19:11), he was repeating an act performed by Moses centuries earlier (Exodus 19:20). This parallels numerous similarities between the two leaders. For example:

Moses goes to Mount Horeb where he meets with God (Exodus 3:1-6).

Elijah goes to Mount Horeb where he meets with God (1 Kings 19:8-11).

Moses sees God reveal Himself through fire (Exodus 13:21; 19:18; 24:17; Leviticus 10:2; Numbers 11:1; 16:35).

Elijah sees God reveal Himself through fire (1 Kings 18:38; 19:12; 2 Kings 1:10, 12; 22:11).

Moses sees God miraculously provide food (Manna) (Exodus 16).

Elijah sees God miraculously provide food (1 Kings 7:8-16).

Moses reveals God's power through miraculous works (Exodus 7:12).

Elijah reveals God's power through miraculous works (1 Kings 18:30-39).

Moses emphasizes that the Lord is God (Deuteronomy 6:4).

Elijah emphasizes that the Lord is God (1 Kings 18:37-39).

Moses is succeeded by Joshua (whose name means "the Lord is salvation" Deuteronomy 31:7-8; Joshua 1:1-9).

Elijah is succeeded by Elisha (whose name means "God is salvation" 2 Kings 12-14).

Moses' death is surrounded by mystery (Deuteronomy 34:5-6).

Elijah departure is surrounded by mystery (2 Kings 2:11-12).

Moses--the Jordan River parts to begin his successor's ministry (Joshua 3:14-17).

Elijah--the Jordan River parts to begin his successor's ministry (2 Kings 2:13-14).

Moses appears with Jesus at the Transfiguration (Matthew 17:3).

Elijah appears with Jesus at the Transfiguration (Matthew 17:3).

2 Chronicles 7:14

If my people, which are called by my name, shall humble themselves, and pray, and seek my face, and turn from their wicked ways; then will I hear from heaven, and will forgive their sin, and will heal their land.

Psalm 122:6

Pray for the peace of Jerusalem; they will prosper who love thee.

The Book of 2 Kings

Scripture Focus Chapters 1-25

Objective: To gain insight on the book of 2 Kings as we see David passing from the scene and the mantle being passed.

Objective Breakdown:

1. Introduction

2. Elijah Predicts Ahaziah's Death   Chapter 1:1-8

3. Fire Consumes the King's Soldiers   Chapter 1:9-16

4. Ahaziah's Brother Jehoram Succeeds Him   Chapter 1:17-18

5. Elijah Prepares to Depart   Chapter 2:1-6

6. Elijah Ascends in a Fiery Chariot   Chapter 2:7-11

7. Elisha Takes Up the Prophet's Mantle   Chapter 2:12-18

8. Elisha Is Honored and Dishonored   Chapter 2:19-25

9. Three Kings Go to War Against Moab   Chapter 3:1-12

10. Elisha Predicts Victory   Chapter 3:13-20

11. Israel Defeats the Moabites   Chapter 3:21-27

12. God Provides for a Widow   Chapter 4:1-7

13. Elisha Promises a Son to a Barren Woman   Chapter 4:8-17

14. The Woman's Son Dies   Chapter 4:18-28

15. Elisha Restores the Boys Life   Chapter 4:29-37

16. Elisha Removes Poison from a Stew   Chapter 4:38-41

17. Bread Is Multiplied   Chapter 4:42-44

18. Naaman Seeks a Cure for His Leprosy   Chapter 5:1-7

19. Elisha Sends Naaman to the Jordan River   Chapter 5:8-14

20. Naaman Is Determined to Worship the Lord   Chapter 5:15-19

2 Chronicles 7:14

If my people, which are called by my name, shall humble themselves, and pray, and seek my face, and turn from their wicked ways; then will I hear from heaven, and will forgive their sin, and will heal their land.

Psalm 122:6

Pray for the peace of Jerusalem; they will prosper who love thee.

Lesson Plan 111

The Book of 2 Kings

Chapters 1, 2, & 3

Objective: To gain insight on the book of 2 Kings as we see David passing from the scene and the mantle being passed.

Objective Breakdown:

1. Introduction

2. Elijah Predicts Ahaziah's Death   Chapter 1:1-8

3. Fire Consumes the King's Soldiers   Chapter 1:9-16

4. Ahaziah's Brother Jehoram Succeeds Him   Chapter 1:17-18

5. Elijah Prepares to Depart   Chapter 2:1-6

6. Elijah Ascends in a Fiery Chariot   Chapter 2:7-11

7. Elisha Takes Up the Prophet's Mantle   Chapter 2:12-18

8. Elisha Is Honored and Dishonored   Chapter 2:19-25

9. Three Kings Go to War Against Moab   Chapter 3:1-12

10. Elisha Predicts Victory   Chapter 3:13-20

11. Israel Defeats the Moabites   Chapter 3:21-27

Introduction:

Second Kings gives an account of the slow but steady decline of the kingdom of Israel and Judah. A handful of kings in Judah followed the Lord, but overall the two nations became more evil than the Canaanites whom they dispossessed.

Each kingdom had its own kings and its own priests and its own prophets. But one thing they had in common: their governments went from bad to worse with only a few exceptions. The people continued to disregard God even though he sent prophets again and again to set them straight.

Through the years each kingdom became a weakling spiritually and morally. After years of disobedience and struggle, they became sitting ducks for the larger nations around them. Assyria, a nation known for its cruelty in warfare, eventually attacked Israel. Babylon a rich and strong nation to the south, attacked Judah. The Hebrew people were carried away from their country to be slaves and prisoners in a foreign place. The Hebrew people continued to lose their land because they wouldn't listen to God. They wouldn't listen to Him about how to govern their land or how to treat each other. They wouldn't listen to Him about how to worship and who to worship. 2 Kings is their story, and we can learn from their mistakes.

2 Chronicles 7:14

If my people, which are called by my name, shall humble themselves, and pray, and seek my face, and turn from their wicked ways; then will I hear from heaven, and will forgive their sin, and will heal their land.

Psalm 122:6

Pray for the peace of Jerusalem; they will prosper who love thee.

Lesson Plan 112

The Book of 2 Kings

Chapters 4, 5, & 6

Objective: To gain insight on the book of 2 Kings as we see David passing from the scene and the mantle being passed.

Objective Breakdown:

1. Introduction

2. God Provides for a Widow — Chapter 4:1-7

3. Elisha Promises a Son to a Barren Woman — Chapter 4:8-17

4. The Woman's Son Dies — Chapter 4:18-28

5. Elisha Restores the Boys Life — Chapter 4:29-37

6. Elisha Removes Poison from a Stew — Chapter 4:38-41

7. Bread Is Multiplied — Chapter 4:42-44

8. Naaman Seeks a Cure for His Leprosy — Chapter 5:1-7

9. Elisha Sends Naaman to the Jordan River — Chapter 5:8-14

10. Naaman Is Determined to Worship the Lord — Chapter 5:15-19

11. The Servant Gehazi's Greed — Chapter 5:20-27

12. Elisha Causes an Ax Head to Float — Chapter 6:1-7

13. The King of Syria Tries to Get Elisha — Chapter 6:8-15

14. Elisha Reveals the Lord's Army — Chapter 6:16-19

15. Elisha Spares the Syrian Soldiers — Chapter 6:20-23

16. Famine Causes Crisis in Besieged Samaria — Chapter 6:24-31

17. Elisha Predicts Food in the Morning — Chapter 6:32-33

Introduction:

Passing on the mantle. The New Testament urges believers to "make disciples" (Matthew 28:19). Closely making of disciples is the mentoring of leaders. However, neither discipline nor mentoring were invented by the early church. The principle has been around for centuries. Mentoring involves a voluntary investment in others for their growth, development, and success. A number of examples of mentoring can be found in the Old Testament:

Jethro and Moses: Jethro drew alongside his overworked son-in-law and helped him organize leaders over the people of Israel (Exodus Chapter 18);

Moses and Joshua: Moses helped Joshua prepare to assume the leadership of Israel when the people were ready to enter Canaan (Deuteronomy 31:1-8; 34:9);

Deborah and Barak: As a judge over Israel, Deborah challenged Barak to be a commander of the military and encouraged him when he was fearful, as a result, they achieved victory over the Canaanite army (Judges 4:4-16);

Naomi and Ruth: Naomi gave well considered advice to her bereaved minority daughter-in-law to help her avoid a life poverty and discrimination (Ruth 1-4);

Eli and Samuel: Though the priest Eli failed with his own two sons, he helped Samuel developed into a man who could hear God's voice and speak to the nation (1 Samuel 1-3);

Samuel and Saul: Samuel identified Saul as future leader and tried to shape him into a man of principle; even when Saul turned away from the Lord. Samuel challenge Saul on several occasions about his attitude toward the Lord (1 Samuel 9-15);

Samuel and David: Samuel anointed David into leadership and stood by him when Saul was trying to hunt David down (1 Samuel16; 19:18-24);

Mordecai and Esther: A Jew living in Persia. Mordecai mentored his cousin when she found herself in a surprising role as queen, with the opportunity to rescue her people from their hostile enemy, Haman (Esther 1-10).

Is there someone you can serve?

2 Chronicles 7:14

If my people, which are called by my name, shall humble themselves, and pray, and seek my face, and turn from their wicked ways; then will I hear from heaven, and will forgive their sin, and will heal their land.

Psalm 122:6

Pray for the peace of Jerusalem; they will prosper who love thee.

Lesson Plan 113

The Book of 2 Kings

Chapters 7, 8, & 9

Objective: To gain insight on the Book of 2 Kings as we see David passing from the scene and the mantle being passed.

Objective Breakdown:

1. Introduction

2. Elisha Predicts Food in the Morning (continued)   Chapter 7:1-2

3. Lepers Discover the Syrians' Retreat   Chapter 7:3-16

4. The Unbelieving Officer Dies   Chapter 7:17-20

5. The Shunammite's Land Is Restored to Her   Chapter 8:1-6

6. Hazael Murders the Ailing King of Syria   Chapter 8:7-15

7. Jehoram's Wicked Reign in Judah   Chapter 8:16-24

8. Ahaziah Succeeds His Father   Chapter 8:25-29

9. Jehu Is Anointed King of Israel   Chapter 9:1-13

10. Jehu Conspires Against Joram   Chapter 9:14-20

11. Naboth Is Avenged   Chapter 9:21-29

12. The End of Jezebel   Chapter 9:30-37

Introduction:

The Hittites. The Syrian army's fear at the prospect of facing a combined army of Hittites and Egyptians (2 Kings 7:6) was understandable. Camped outside Damascus, the Syrians would have been pinched between the Hittites from the north and the Egyptians from the south. Panic-stricken, the Syrians fled into the night (2 Kings 7:7).

The Hittites of this period were remnant of the empire that dominated northern Canaan between 1800 and 1200 B.C. Their ancestors had migrated from Asia Minor, where they were called Hittites from the name Hatti, another name for Anatolia, the capital of which was Hattusa. In northern Syria they populated cities such as Aleppo, Carchemish, and Hamath.

As the Hittites pushed south over the years, they came into conflict with the Egyptians who tended to use Canaan as a buffer between their country and Mesopotamia. In 1286 B.C., a battle was fought at Kedesh, on the Orontes River. The Hittites waited in hiding until the Egyptians had made their camp, then released their chariots on the unsuspecting Egyptians. The northerners would have won the day had Egyptian reinforcements not arrived from the west, eventually forcing a retreat. Still, the Egyptians suffered heavy losses, and soon a treaty was signed designating the Orontes River as a border between the two powers.

Over the next few decades, relentless attacks by enemies from the west slowly brought the Hittite empire to a close. In Syria, seven-city states remained in a coalition. They were friendly with David and Solomon (2 Samuel 8:9-10; 1 Kings 10:28–11:1). But they came under domination of the Assyrians, and eventually passed into oblivion when their principal cities of Hamath and Carchemish fell (720 and 717 B.C. respectively 2 Kings 18:34; Isaiah 10:9).

The northern Hittites are not to be confused with another group called the Hittites, who live in the Judean Hills near Hebron. These Hittites were descended from Heth, the son of Canaan, and thus were of the tribe of Canaanites. It was a member of this group of Hittites that Abraham purchased the field of Machpelah as a burial ground for his family (Genesis 23:10-20). Years later, Abraham's grandson Esau married two Hittite women, much to the displeasure of his parents (Genesis 26:34-35).

The Hittites of Canaan were among the people to be driven out of the land when Israel entered Canaan under Joshua (Exodus 3:8, 17; Deuteronomy 7:1; Judges 3:5). Centuries later, several Hittites were among David's closest associates and most loyal soldiers (1 Samuel 26:6; 2 Samuel 11:6-11).

2 Chronicles 7:14

If my people, which are called by my name, shall humble themselves, and pray, and seek my face, and turn from their wicked ways; then will I hear from heaven, and will forgive their sin, and will heal their land.

Psalm 122:6

Pray for the peace of Jerusalem; they will prosper who love thee.

Lesson Plan 114

The Book of 2 Kings

Chapters 10, 11, & 12

Objective: To gain insight on the book of 2 Kings as we see David passing from the scene and the mantle being passed.

Objective Breakdown:

1. Introduction

2. Jehu Kills All of the House of Ahab   Chapter 10:1-11

3. Ahab's People in Samaria Are Killed   Chapter 10:12-17

4. Baal Worshipers Are Put to Death   Chapter 10:18-28

5. Jehu's Sins Lead to Loss of Territory   Chapter 10:29-36

6. The Boy Joash (Jehoash) Is Made King of Judah   Chapter 11:1-12

7. Athaliah Is Killed   Chapter 11:13-16

8. Jehoiada the Priest Initiates Reforms   Chapter 11:17-21

9. Jehoash (Joash) Calls for Temple Repairs   Chapter 12:1-8

10. Funds Are Raised for Repairs   Chapter 12:9-16

11. Jehoash (Joash) Pays Tribute to Syria   Chapter 12:17-18

12. Joash (Jehoash) Is Assassinated   Chapter 12:19-20

Introduction:

The life of Elisha. The king of Israel asked Gehazi to tell him all the great things that Elisha had done (2 Kings 8:4). Gehazi mentioned a number of things such as:

a) Turning bad water to wholesome water at Jericho (2 Kings 18:22).

b) Promised King Jehoram of Israel that God would give him and King Jehoshaphat of Judah victory over the Moabites, which happened through miraculous circumstances (2 Kings 3:11-27).

c) Miraculously provided material assistance for a widow of one of the prophets (2 Kings 4:1-7).

d) At Shunem, Elisha predicted that prominent woman who was barren would give birth to a son, which she did (2 Kings 4:8-18; later after the boy fell ill and died, Elisha brought him back to life (2 Kings 4:18-37).

e) At Gilgal, he caused poison to leave a stew (2 Kings 4:38-44).

f) He healed a Syrian general Naaman of Leprosy by having him bathe in the Jordan River (2 Kings 5:1-14).

g) He caused an ax head to float in the Jordan River (2 Kings 6:1-7).

h) Surrounded by Syrian troops, he prayed that his servant might see the armies of the Lord and that the Syrians would be struck blind (2 Kings 6:13-18); led the blinded army of Syrians inside Samaria, where their blindness was removed (2 Kings 6:19-23).

i) Under siege and severe famine in Samaria, predicted correctly that God would remove the attacking Syrians and provide food for all in the city (2 Kings 6:24-7:20).

2 Chronicles 7:14

If my people, which are called by my name, shall humble themselves, and pray, and seek my face, and turn from their wicked ways; then will I hear from heaven, and will forgive their sin, and will heal their land.

Psalm 122:6

Pray for the peace of Jerusalem; they will prosper who love thee.

Lesson Plan 115

The Book of 2 Kings

Chapters 13, 14, & 15

Objective: To gain insight on the book of 2 Kings as we see David passing from the scene and the mantle being passed.

Objective Breakdown:

1. Introduction

2. Jehoahaz Reigns Over Israel   Chapter 13:1-9

3. Jehoash the Son of Jehoahaz Succeeds Him   Chapter 13:10-13

4. Elisha Predicts Three Victories and Dies   Chapter 13:14-21

5. Cities of Israel Are Recaptured   Chapter 13:22-25

6. Amaziah Challenges Jehoash of Israel   Chapter 14:1-10

7. Amaziah Is Defeated in Battle   Chapter 14:11-16

8. Azariah Becomes King of Judah   Chapter 14:17-22

9. Jeroboam II Enlarges Israel   Chapter 14:23-29

10. Azariah of Judah Develops Leprosy   Chapter 15:1-7

12. Zechariah Reigns Six Months in Israel   Chapter 15:8-12

13. Menahem of Israel Pays the Assyrians   Chapter 15:13-22

14. Pekahiah of Israel Is Disposed by Pekah   Chapter 15:23-26

15. Pekah Loses Cities to the Assyrians   Chapter 15:27-31

16. Jotham Succeeds His Father in Judah   Chapter 15:32-38

Introduction:

According to the Law. Amaziah was praised for following the Law's prohibition against executing children for the sins of their fathers (2 Kings 14:6). Thus, he obeyed the Lord...well sort of! Having preserved the lives of murders' children, he turned around and killed 10,000 Edomites and captured one of their cities. Not only might this have been seen as a violation of the spirit of the law against "abhorring" an Edomite (Deuteronomy 23:7), it was the continuation of a long-standing feud between the Israelites and the Edomites.

The roots of the feud went back to Jacob, the ancestor of Israel, and Esau, the ancestor of the Edomites. Down through the centuries Israelites and the Edomites constantly attacked each other, often with little provocation. Each time they did so they were punishing the children of Jacob or Esau for the sins of their respective fathers. Furthermore, Amaziah's attack on Edom bore a grim resemblance to a campaign waged under David's administration. On that occasion, David "made a name for himself" by killing 18,000 Edomites (2 Samuel 8:13-14; 1 Kings 11:15-17). Amaziah apparently also feeling the pride of conquer, threw down his foolish challenge to King Jehoash of Israel, which ended in Amaziah's capture and the sacking of Jerusalem.

2 Chronicles 7:14

If my people, which are called by my name, shall humble themselves, and pray, and seek my face, and turn from their wicked ways; then will I hear from heaven, and will forgive their sin, and will heal their land.

Psalm 122:6

Pray for the peace of Jerusalem; they will prosper who love thee.

Lesson Plan 116

The Book of 2 Kings

Chapters 16, 17, & 18

Objective: To gain insight on the book of 2 Kings as we see David passing from the scene and the mantle being passed.

Objective Breakdown:

1. Introduction

2. Ahaz of Judah Allies with Assyria   Chapter 16:1-9

3. Ahaz Has a New Altar Built in the Temple   Chapter 16:10-20

4. Israel Is Taken into Exile by Assyria   Chapter 17:1-6

5. Israel's History of Sin   Chapter 17:7-18

6. The Evil Legacy of Jeroboam   Chapter 17:19-23

7. Gentiles Resettle Samaria   Chapter 17:24-28

8. The Settlers Worship a Variety of Gods   Chapter 17:29-33

9. The Lord's Commandments Are Forsaken   Chapter 17:34-41

10. God Fearing Hezekiah Reigns over Judah   Chapter 18:1-8

11. The Assyrians Wrest Tribute from Judah   Chapter 18:9-16

12. Rabshakeh Taunts Hezekiah   Chapter 18:17-25

13. Rabshakeh Tries to Convince the People   Chapter 18:26-37

Introduction:

Conspiracy: Access to power. Whether in the workplace, family, or community there seems invariably to rise schemes, methods, and strategies to gain control. The royal court of the Northern Kingdom of Israel, like other centers of power in the ancient Middle East was constantly thrown into chaos by plots, intrigue against the kings. The overthrow of Pekah (2 Kings 15:30) was just one in a long line of coups and coups attempts during the time of the divided kingdom.

Ruler	Event
Rehoam (1 Kings 12:12-20)	He imposed even higher taxes than those levied by his father. Ten tribes rejected his leadership and stoned his chief tax collector
Ben-Hadad (2 Kings 8:7-15)	When the king of Syria lay sick, he sent his representative Hazael to ask the prophet Elisha about his recovery. Hazael returned with encouraging words, but then murdered his master and gained the throne for himself.
Jehu (2 Kings 9:1-29)	After being informed by Elisha that he would become king of Israel, Jehu plotted to overthrow King Joram by killing him at a so-called peace conference.
Jehu (2 Kings 9:30-37)	After assuming the throne, Jehu had old Queen Jezebel thrown from a window to her death, and dogs consumed her body just as Elijah had predicted.
Jehu (2 Kings 10:18:28)	Jehu purged Israel of Baal worship by inviting prophets throughout the land to convene at the temple. After declaring them loyal to Baal, he had his soldiers execute them.
Athaliah (2 Kings 11:1-3, 20-21)	This queen mother destroyed all of her royal heirs after her son died. Her grandson Joah was preserved, and later rose to power and put her to death.
Pekah (2 Kings 15:25-30)	Pekah came to power by assassinating his predecessor. But during Pekah's rule, Assyria plundered more than half of his land, stripping it of its inhabitants. A conspiracy then rose up and Pekah was assassinated.

2 Chronicles 7:14

If my people, which are called by my name, shall humble themselves, and pray, and seek my face, and turn from their wicked ways; then will I hear from heaven, and will forgive their sin, and will heal their land.

Psalm 122:6

Pray for the peace of Jerusalem; they will prosper who love thee.

Lesson Plan 117

The Book of 2 Kings

Chapters 19, 20, 21, & 22

Objective: To gain insight on the book of 2 Kings as we see David passing from the scene and the mantle being passed.

Objective Breakdown:

1. Introduction

2. Isaiah Promises Deliverance from God   Chapter 19:1-7

3. Hezekiah Receives a Derisive Letter   Chapter 19:8-13

4. Hezekiah Turns to the Lord in Prayer   Chapter 19:14-19

5. Isaiah Speaks a Word Against Assyria   Chapter 19:20-34

6. Stricken by God, the Assyrians Withdraw   Chapter 19:35-37

7. Hezekiah Is Healed of a Mortal Illness   Chapter 20:1-11

8. Babylon Sees the Kings Treasures   Chapter 20:12-21

9. Manasseh Turns Away from God   Chapter 21:1-9

10. The Lord Promises Judgment   Chapter 21:10-18

11. Amon's Wicked Reign and Assassination   Chapter 21:19-26

12. Josiah Calls for Temple Repairs   Chapter 22:1-7

13. Hilkiah finds the Book of the Law   Chapter 22:8-13

14. God Promises Personal Peace to Josiah   Chapter 22:14-20

Introduction:

The Assyrians who were they? When Samaria, the capital of the northern kingdom of Israel, finally succumbed to an Assyrian siege in 722 BC. (2 Kings 17:5-6), the Israelites felled into one of the cruelest most feared empires of the ancient world. The atrocities of the Assyrians were legendary. Ancient records indicate that they not only burned cities, but burned children, impaled captives on stakes, beheaded prisoners, or tortured them by chopping off legs and hands. Nevertheless, God used this ruthless superpower to discipline His people because of their stubborn commitment to idolatry and other evils (2 Kings 17:7-12).

The origins and rise to power of the Assyrians…the kingdom of Assyria was located between the Tigris and Euphrates Rivers. Its principal cities were said to be founded by Nimrod (Genesis 10:8-12) between the seventh and ninth centuries B.C. Their rulers dominated the Middle East. Their principal rival was Babylonia which constantly challenged its northern neighbor and finally succeeded in destroying it by 612 B.C.

The end of the Assyrian Kingdom. The capture of Israel occurred as Assyria was reaching the heights of it power. Shalmaneser's successor, Sargon II (722-705 B.C.), defeated the Egyptians in the west and the Elamites in the east. The next king Sennacherib (705-681 B.C.), pushed into Asia Minor and later capture and sacked Babylon.

Nevertheless, the Assyrians days were numbered. The Medes began troubling the Assyria in the east during the seventh century B.C. putting down the uprising diverted attention from the western provinces, and they also began too rebel. In the meantime, the Babylonians were beginning to grow stronger and in 614 B.C. they joined the Medes to capture Assur. Then in 612 B.C., Nineveh itself fell, which fulfilled the prophesies of Nahum and Zephaniah. The last grasp of the Assyrians came at Haran in 609 B.C. Attacked by a determined force of the Babylonians and Scythians and the Assyrian empire was no more.

2 Chronicles 7:14

If my people, which are called by my name, shall humble themselves, and pray, and seek my face, and turn from their wicked ways; then will I hear from heaven, and will forgive their sin, and will heal their land.

Psalm 122:6

Pray for the peace of Jerusalem; they will prosper who love thee.

Lesson Plan 118

The Book of 2 Kings

Chapters 23, 24, & 25

Objective: To gain insight on the book of 2 Kings as we see David passing from the scene and the mantle being passed.

Objective Breakdown:

1. Introduction

2. Josiah Has the Law Read to the People   Chapter 23:1-2

3. Idolatry Is Abolished in Judah   Chapter 23:3-20

4. The People Celebrate Passover   Chapter 23:21-25

5. The Final Days of Josiah   Chapter 23:26-30

6. Jehoahaz and Eliakim Serve Egypt   Chapter 23:31-37

7. The Babylonians Capture Territory   Chapter 24:1-7

8. Jehoiachin Is Taken Captive   Chapter 24:8-16

9. Zedekiah Is Made King Over Judah   Chapter 24:17-20

10. Nebuchadnezzar Takes Jerusalem   Chapter 25:1-7

11. The Temple is Sacked and Burned   Chapter 25:8-17

12. The Priests Are Slaughtered   Chapter 25:18-21

13. Gedaliah Is Made Governor of Judah   Chapter 25:22-26

14. Jehoiachin Is Treated Kindly in Babylon   Chapter 25:27-30

Introduction:

The bright reign of King Hezekiah over Judah of 29 years produced one of the best periods of governments since the time of David. He brought spiritual reforms and carried out extensive renovations and improvements to the nation's defenses.

The history of witchcraft was resorted to by the kings of Israel throughout history (2 Kings 17:17). Even though each king was supposed to write down his own copy of the Law so that he could have it to consult in making decisions (Deuteronomy17:18-20). Many of the kings consulted mediums and soothsayers instead. As a result, God severely judged the nation just as He promised He would (see Deuteronomy 18:9-14).

Jesus said God is a Spirit, and those who worship him must worship in spirit and truth (John 4:24). That means we worship and serve a God whom we cannot see with our eyes but must believe with our hearts. As a result, God is a bit of an abstraction for some people. One way they try to make Him more real, and present is through artifacts that they associate with Him. Yet as understandable as the relics may be, it is a dangerous practice. It can easily tempt people to worship the object rather than the God whom the object is supposed to point to. In essence, the relic becomes a focus of idolatry.

You Reap What you Sow. Moral and spiritual choices have long-term consequences. If we sow seeds of righteousness, we will reap the fruit of righteousness. If we sow the seeds of rebellion and sin, we will ultimately reap bitter harvest.

The Book of 1 and 2 Kings bear witness to this principle. They open on a sad note—the death of King David—yet David's legacy yields lasting benefits for the nation. Under his son Solomon, Israel briefly becomes an empire. Righteousness prevails, and the people live in prosperity.

But having reached the zenith of its history, the nation suddenly turns away from the Lord. The kings revive idolatry. The Law is abandoned, and portions of it eventually lost. The kingdom undergoes a permanent split. The northern kingdom never again follows God. The southern kingdom follows a slow and circuitous road to decline. In the end, both kingdom is overrun by foreigners and taken into Exile— the very consequences that God had warned His people about centuries earlier.

2 Chronicles 7:14

If my people, which are called by my name, shall humble themselves, and pray, and seek my face, and turn from their wicked ways; then will I hear from heaven, and will forgive their sin, and will heal their land.

Psalm 122:6

Pray for the peace of Jerusalem; they will prosper who love thee.

The Book of 1 Chronicles

Scripture Focus Chapters 1-29

Objective: To gain an understanding of the extensive genealogy of the Israelites from Adam to the end of exile in Babylon (538 B.C.).

Objective Breakdown:

1. Introduction

2. From Adam to Noah's Sons   Chapter 1:1-4

3. Descendants of Japheth   Chapter 1:5-7

4. Descendants of Ham   Chapter 1:8-16

5. Descendants of Shem   Chapter 1:17-23

6. From Shem to Abraham's Sons   Chapter 1:24-28

7. The Sons of Ishmael   Chapter 1:29-31

8. Descendants of Abraham's Concubine   Chapter 1:32-33

9. Isaac's Descendants Through Esau   Chapter 1:34-37

10. The Descendants of Seir   Chapter 1:38-42

11. The Kings of the Edomites   Chapter 1:43-54

12. The Twelve Sons of Israel   Chapter 2:1-2

13. From Judah to David   Chapter 2:3-17

14. The Family of Hezron   Chapter 2:18-24

15. The Family of Jerahmeel   Chapter 2:25-33

16. The Family of Sheshan   Chapter 2:34-41

17. The Family of Caleb   Chapter 2:42-55

18. The Family of David   Chapter 3:1-9

19. The Descendants of Solomon   Chapter 3:10-24

20. Descendants of Judah   Chapter 4:1-23

Lesson Plan 119

The Book of 1 Chronicles

Chapters 1 & 2

Objective: To gain an understanding of the extensive genealogy of the Israelites from Adam to the end of the exile in Babylon (538 B.C.)

Objective Breakdown:

1. Introduction

2. From Adam to Noah's Sons   Chapter 1:1-4

3. Descendants of Japheth   Chapter 1:5-7

4. Descendants of Ham   Chapter 1:8-16

5. Descendants of Shem   Chapter 1:17-23

6. From Shem to Abraham's Sons   Chapter 1:24-28

7. The Sons of Ishmael   Chapter 1:29-31

8. Descendants of Abraham's Concubine   Chapter 1:32-33

9. Isaac's Descendants Through Esau   Chapter 1:34-37

10. The Descendants of Seir   Chapter 1:38-42

11. The Kings of the Edomites   Chapter 1:43-54

12. The Twelve Sons of Israel   Chapter 2:1-2

13. From Judah to David   Chapter 2:3-17

14. The Family of Hezron   Chapter 2:18-24

15. The Family of Jerahmeel   Chapter 2:25-33

16. The Family of Sheshan   Chapter 2:34-41

17. The Family of Caleb   Chapter 2:42-55

Introduction:

History is rewritten by every generation, because people need to know where and how they fit into the world. They want to find out where they came from, who their ancestors were, and what events affected them.

The Books of 1 and 2 Chronicles tells the history of Israel from the standpoint of the Jews returning from the Babylonian exile. Imagine the importance of this story to people, many whom had been born during captivity. They were a displaced group seeking to rediscover their roots and reclaim their identity. The Books of 1 and 2 Chronicles help them do that by listing their ancestors and giving an account of their nation, Judah, from the house from the time of David until the decree of Cyprus allowing their return.

Chronicles reminds us that God takes our heritage seriously. We can remember both the triumphs and tragedies of our ancestors as we lift up our past to the Lord of history. In one sense it could be said that the history covered in Chronicles and extends from the beginning of the world to the end of the Babylonian exile as this is the period of the genealogy (1 Chronicles 1-9).

However, the historical narrative of Chronicles begins with the death of Saul in 1011 B.C. (1 Chronicles 10) and ends with the decree of Cyrus allowing the Jews to return to Jerusalem (538 B.C.).

The geography of Chronicles is the same as in the Books of Samuel and Kings—the territory of Israel with occasional references to other parts of the Middle East and Judah being the focal point for most of the action.

2 Chronicles 7:14

If my people, which are called by my name, shall humble themselves, and pray, and seek my face, and turn from their wicked ways; then will I hear from heaven, and will forgive their sin, and will heal their land.

Psalm 122:6

Pray for the peace of Jerusalem; they will prosper who love thee.

Lesson Plan 120

The Book of 1 Chronicles

Chapters 3, 4, & 5

Objective: To gain an understanding of the extensive genealogy of the Israelites from Adam to the end of the exile in Babylon (538 B.C.).

Objective Breakdown:

1. Introduction

2. The Family of David   Chapter 3:1-9

3. The Descendants of Solomon   Chapter 3:10-24

4. Descendants of Judah   Chapter 4:1-23

5. Descendants of Simeon   Chapter 4:24-43

6. Descendants of Reuben   Chapter 5:1-10

7. Descendants of Gad   Chapter 5:11-22

8. Eastern Descendants of Manasseh   Chapter 5:23-26

Introduction:

Records of God's grace. The genealogies of Abraham's sons, Ishmael and Isaac, are more than just a collection of names or an extended family tree. They tell the story of God's work and purposes from generation to generation. As such these genealogies have much to teach us today about our heritage. They remind us to look back with gratitude. Genealogies show us our roots. As the Israelites looked back on their past, they had much for which to praise God. He had chosen them as His people, brought them out of slavery in Egypt, given them a land, and established a kingdom. Through it all He remained faithful to Abraham, Moses, and David.

Look around at our connections. First Chronicles reminds the reader of the kinship between the Edomites and the Israelites—a fact that has importance to this day particularly in a world where ethnicity so often divides. We should look at Scripture which encourages us to see what we have in common.

We should look ahead with faith. The past is often an indication of the future. Because Israel's past showed God's faithfulness to the people, it gives us a basis for trusting God to fulfill His Word among their descendants. Likewise, we today can count on God to honor what He has told us. Every believer is indebted to God's grace for the circumstances that permitted the gospel to be brought to them.

Even though Esau (1 Chronicles 1:35) was the older of Isaac's sons, it was Jacob (called Israel) who inherited Isaac's blessings and family birthright. Nevertheless, Esau's descendants grew into a number of powerful tribes who lived in Edom, the territory south of the Dead Sea (Genesis 36). Over the centuries, the Israelites and Edomites kept up an increasingly violent feud which was exemplified by the slaughter of thousands of Edomite males under David (1 Kings 11:15-16). To understand the roots of this hostility review Genesis 25:27-34.

2 Chronicles 7:14

If my people, which are called by my name, shall humble themselves, and pray, and seek my face, and turn from their wicked ways; then will I hear from heaven, and will forgive their sin, and will heal their land.

Psalm 122:6

Pray for the peace of Jerusalem; they will prosper who love thee.

Lesson Plan 121

The Book of 1 Chronicles

Chapters 6 & 7

Objective: To gain an understanding of the extensive genealogy of the Israelites from Adam to the end of the exile in Babylon (538 B.C.).

Objective Breakdown:

1. Introduction

2. Descendants of Levi   Chapter 6:1-30

3. Musicians in the House of the Lord   Chapter 6:31-48

4. The Family of Aaron   Chapter 6:49-53

5. Levitical Cities   Chapter 6:54-81

6. Descendants of Issachar   Chapter 7:1-5

7. Descendants of Benjamin   Chapter 7:6-12

8. Western Descendants of Manasseh   Chapter 7:13-19

9. Descendants of Ephraim   Chapter 7:20-29

10. Descendants of Asher   Chapter 7:30-40

Introduction:

Turning pain into prayer. Perhaps you feel problems caused by your background or bringing up. Maybe you live with unchangeable circumstances that affect your life in a major way. If so, it's easy to feel like a victim and complain to God. But consider the example of Jabez (11 Chronicles 4:9-10).

In the Books of 1 and 2 Chronicles, many little people of faith loom large, even to the point of overshadowing some of the kings. Jabez was one of these people. He stands out because he was a person of prayer. Jabez's name means pain or misery. His mother bore him in pain, which mean that she had a difficult childbirth or that circumstances in her family were distressing. Whatever the case, Jabez turned pain into prayer, asking God for territorial gain and spiritual blessing. He didn't use his name or background as an excuse with God. Instead of complaining about his lot, he prayed for increased responsibility and an enlarged place in the Promised Land. Jesus told us that we would have tribulation in this life.

If you feel like a victim, you can follow Jabez's example by praying to God. Instead of irresponsibly allowing circumstances of life to overwhelm you, you can begin to take charge of your life by asking God for the power to make changes. God has said in His Word I will never leave you nor forsake you (Deuteronomy 4:31; 31:6; Joshua 1:5; Psalms 94:14; Hebrews 13:5).

2 Chronicles 7:14

If my people, which are called by my name, shall humble themselves, and pray, and seek my face, and turn from their wicked ways; then will I hear from heaven, and will forgive their sin, and will heal their land.

Psalm 122:6

Pray for the peace of Jerusalem; they will prosper who love thee.

Lesson Plan 122

The Book of 1 Chronicles

Chapters 8, 9, & 10

Objective: To gain an understanding of the extensive genealogy of the Israelites from Adam to the end of the exile in Babylon (538 B.C.).

Objective Breakdown:

1. Introduction

2. Descendants of Benjamin   Chapter 8:1-28

3. Saul's Ancestors and Descendants   Chapter 8:29-40

4. Saul's Ancestors and Descendants (cont.)   Chapter 9:1-2

5. Inhabitants of Jerusalem   Chapter 9:3-9

6. Priests at Jerusalem   Chapter 9:10-13

7. Levites at Jerusalem   Chapter 9:14-16

8. Levite Gatekeepers   Chapter 9:17-27

9. Other Levite Responsibilities   Chapter 9:28-34

10. The Family Tree of King Saul   Chapter 9:35-44

11. Saul and His Sons Are Killed   Chapter 10:1-7

12. The Bodies Are Brought to Jabesh   Chapter 10:8-14

Introduction:

Early temple servants. The Nethinim (1 Chronicles 9:2) were a group of temple servants who assisted the Levites. They performed menial chores such as cleaning the temple, carrying water and wood to the altar, and scrubbing utensils used in the sacrificial ceremonies. Nethinim means "those who are given."

Ezra's list of the returnees from captivity mentions the Nethinim in conjunction with the "sons of Solomon's servants" (Ezra 2:43-58). Because the names used are not Hebrew, some have suggested that both groups were Gentiles possibly descendants of the Canaanites or some other group that the Israelites had conquered. David and the leaders of Israel had appointed these groups to serve the Levites

(Ezra 8:20). The Nethinim were not the first group of foreigners to be given service positions among the Israelites. During the conquest of Canaan, Joshua made peace with the men of Gibeon, and they became woodcutters and water carriers (Joshua 9)

Of interest in the descendants of Ephraim, we learn of a daughter by the name of Sheerah. Sheaerah means female relative (I Chronicles 7:24). She was the daughter of Ephraim or his son Beriah. She is best known today for building or rebuilding three cities, the only woman in the Bible said to have done so. The two Beth Horons were located on the mountain pass between the territories of Benjamin and Ephraim, 10 to 12 miles northwest of Jerusalem. Due to their strategic location, they saw much blood shed. The upper city at (2,000 feet) was a fortified citadel, while the lower city (at 1200 feet) was a marketplace. This formed a two-tiered society, not only geographically, but politically as well.

2 Chronicles 7:14

If my people, which are called by my name, shall humble themselves, and pray, and seek my face, and turn from their wicked ways; then will I hear from heaven, and will forgive their sin, and will heal their land.

Psalm 122:6

Pray for the peace of Jerusalem; they will prosper who love thee.

Lesson Plan 123

The Book of 1 Chronicles

Chapters 11, 12, & 13

Objective: To gain an understanding of the extensive genealogy of the Israelites from Adam to the end of the exile in Babylon (538 B.C.).

Objective Breakdown:

1. Introduction

2. David Proclaimed King of Israel   Chapter 11:1-3

3. Jebus Becomes the City of David   Chapter 11:4-9

4. David's Mighty Men   Chapter 11:10-14

5. David Pours Out a Gift of Water   Chapter 11:15-19

6. Abishai's Command   Chapter 11:20-21

7. Benaiah the Warrior   Chapter 11:22-25

8. Other Mighty Men   Chapter 11:26-47

9. David's Troops at Ziklag   Chapter 12:1-7

10. Gadites and Others Join David   Chapter 12:8-18

11. Defections from Manasseh   Chapter 12:19-22

12. David's Forces at Hebron   Chapter 12:23-37

13. A Loyal and Joyful Army   Chapter 12:38-40

14. The Ark of the Covenant Moved   Chapter 13:1-8

15. Uzza Touches the Ark and Dies   Chapter 13:9-14

Introduction:

David's mighty men. David's rise to power was assured from the outset by the promise of God (1 Chronicles 11:10). Nevertheless, the journey from pastures near Bethlehem to the palace in Jerusalem was long and difficult. Along the way, David attracted a growing movement of loyal supporters who helped him attain the throne. Some of the most important of these followers were known as mighty men.

These warriors or champions are celebrated for their military victories (2 Samuel 23; 1 Chronicles 11), many of which were won after David was crowned King of Israel. But the nucleus of these warriors came from humble beginnings. When David was fleeing from Saul, renegades from Israelite society began gathering to the young Bethlehemite. Scripture gives three reasons why they found their way to David: distress, debt, and discontent (1 Samuel 22:2). Having nothing to lose, they sided with David, who was also in trouble with the king.

Saul quickly learned of this band, which at first numbered about 400. Suspicious that his own people might defect, Saul chided his servants, "Will the son of Jesse give every one of you fields and vineyards, and make you all captains?" (1 Samuel 22:7). In fact, the answer to this question is yes. Under David and his successor Solomon, the land prospered exceedingly (2 Samuel 6:19; 7:1; 1 Kings 4:25) and many of David followers became renowned as "mighty men."

2 Chronicles 7:14

If my people, which are called by my name, shall humble themselves, and pray, and seek my face, and turn from their wicked ways; then will I hear from heaven, and will forgive their sin, and will heal their land.

Psalm 122:6

Pray for the peace of Jerusalem; they will prosper who love thee.

Lesson Plan 124

The Book of 1 Chronicles

Chapters 14, 15, 16, & 17

Objective: To gain an understanding of the extensive genealogy of the Israelites from Adam to the end of the exile in Babylon (538 B.C.).

Objective Breakdown:

1. Introduction	
2. Gifts, Wives, and Children	Chapter 14:1-7
3. The Philistines Are Defeated	Chapter 14:8-17
4. Preparation to Retrieve the Ark	Chapter 15:1-15
5. Levites Are Chosen for the Task	Chapter 15:16-24
6. The Ark Is Brought to Jerusalem	Chapter 15:25-29
7. Israel Celebrates the Ark's Return	Chapter 16:1-6
8. David's Psalm of Praise	Chapter 16:7-36
9. Regular Worship at Jerusalem	Chapter 16:37-43
10. God Makes a Covenant with David	Chapter 17:1-15
11. God's Greatness Overwhelms David	Chapter 17:16-22
12. David Praises God in Prayer	Chapter 17:23-27

Introduction:

Understanding the times. People of faith are called to be people of wisdom and discernment. That requires an understanding not only of Scripture, but also of the world in which Scripture must be applied. In ancient Israel, David was blessed to have a group of counselors "who had understanding of the times" and thus could advise him on what the nation should do (1 Chronicles 12:32).

The tribe of Issachar was especially known for such wise men. In fact, tradition holds that representatives from Issachar tended to be the wisest members of the Sanhedrin, the nation's highest ruling body in the days of Jesus (See Stephen's trial and murder at Acts 6:12:32).

No one knows how the counselors went about understanding the times, but it seems reasonable to infer that their job was to perceive the trends, discuss major issues, evaluate information, and consider strategy. Thanks in part to them, David was able to unify the kingdom and establish a growing empire (1 Chronicles 14:2, 17).

Today, God's people still need those who can "understand the times." Our world now faces changes in such magnitude that some have described the situation as nothing short of chaos. For that reason, we need people who can buttress their faith with discernment more than ever. God has not called us to shut down our critical faculties in order to follow every wind of doctrine and promise. Instead, Jesus exhorted his followers to "be wise as serpents and harmless as doves" (Matthew 10:16). That means knowing God and knowing our times.

2 Chronicles 7:14

If my people, which are called by my name, shall humble themselves, and pray, and seek my face, and turn from their wicked ways; then will I hear from heaven, and will forgive their sin, and will heal their land.

Psalm 122:6

Pray for the peace of Jerusalem; they will prosper who love thee.

Lesson Plan 125

The Book of 1 Chronicles

Chapters 18, 19, 20, & 21

Objective: To gain an understanding of the extensive genealogy of the Israelites from Adam to the end of the exile in Babylon (538 B.C.).

Objective Breakdown:

1.   Introduction

2. Further Military Victories   Chapter 18:1-8

3.   The Kingdom Is Firmly Established   Chapter 18:9-17

4. David's Servants Are Humiliated   Chapter 19:1-7

5. Joab Goes to War   Chapter 19:8-15

6. Ammon's Syrian Allies Are Defeated   Chapter 19:16-19

7. The Israelites Take Rabbah   Chapter 20:1-3

8. More Victories Over the Philistines   Chapter 20:4-8

9. David Foolishly Numbers Israel   Chapter 21:1-8

10. God Offers Punishment Options   Chapter 21:9-15

11. David Pleads for Israel   Chapter 21:16-17

12. David Buys Ornan's Threshing Floor   Chapter 21:18-23

13. God Receives David's Burnt Offerings   Chapter 21:24-30

Introduction:

David's triumphs. David enjoyed international acclaim following his rout of the Philistines (1 Chronicles 14:17). The victory was one of numerous victorious military triumphs for example:

He killed Goliath, the champion of the Philistines (1 Samuel 17:1-58).

He defeated the Philistines as one of Saul's commanders (1 Samuel 18:5-7).

He killed 200 Philistines in order to marry Saul's daughter Michal (1 Samuel 18:25-30).

He successfully raided the Geshurites, Girzites, and Amalekites for plundering Ziklag (1 Samuel 30:1-31).

He captured Jerusalem (Jebus) despite the Jebusites boasts (1 Chronicles 11:4-8).

He defeated the Philistines at Baal Perazim (1 Samuel 14:8-12).

He drove back the Philistines from Gibeon as far as Gezer (1 Samuel 14:13-16).

He captured the Philistine city of Gath and its surrounding territory (1 Samuel 18:1).

He defeated Moab (Samuel 18:2).

He defeated the Arameans under Hadadezer, King of Zobah (1 Samuel 18:3-4), and their allies the Syrians (1 Samuel 18:5-8).

He defeated the Edomites (1 Samuel 18:12-13)

He defeated the Ammonites and Syrians (1 Samuel 19:1-19).

2 Chronicles 7:14

If my people, which are called by my name, shall humble themselves, and pray, and seek my face, and turn from their wicked ways; then will I hear from heaven, and will forgive their sin, and will heal their land.

Psalm 122:6

Pray for the peace of Jerusalem; they will prosper who love thee.

Lesson Plan 126

The Book of 1 Chronicles

Chapters 22, 23, 24, 25, & 26

Objective: To gain an understanding of the extensive genealogy of the Israelites from Adam to the end of the exile in Babylon (538 B.C.).

Objective Breakdown:

1. Introduction

2. David Provides for the Temple   Chapter 22:1-5

3. Solomon Is Told to Build the Temple   Chapter 22:6-16

4. Leaders Are to Help Solomon   Chapter 22:17-19

5. David Numbers the Levites   Chapter 23:1-6

6. The Gershonites   Chapter 23:7-11

7. The Kohathites   Chapter 23:12-20

8. The Merarites   Chapter 23:21-23

9. The Duties of the Levites Change   Chapter 23:24-32

10. David Numbers the Priests   Chapter 24:1-6

11. The Organization of Priestly Service   Chapter 24:7-19

12. The Organization of Other Levites   Chapter 24:20-31

13. Musicians and Singers Are Organized   Chapter 25:1-31

14. Gatekeepers Are Organized   Chapter 26:1-19

15. Temple Treasurers Are Organized   Chapter 26:20-28

16. Other Officials   Chapter 26:29-32

Introduction:

The journey of the ark from Sinai to Jerusalem. The ark of the covenant, or the "ark of God" (1

Corinthians 16:1), was the most holy object. The Lord's presence dwelled between the cherubim (or angels) fashioned on top of the ark (1 Corinthians 13:6). Yet the ark underwent a tortuous journey during the years before David finally brought it to Jerusalem.

The ark was constructed in the wilderness probably at Mount Sinai, by the craftsman Bezalel, according to the Lord's instruction and under the supervision of Moses (Exodus 25:10-22; 35:30–36:2; 37:1-9).

The Israelites head toward Canaan, with appointed divisions of the Levites carrying the ark (Numbers 10:17). However, the people's rebellion at Kadesh Barnea results in an additional 40 years of wandering.

The ark carried by priests, lead people across the Jordan River. While the priests stand in the riverbed, the waters were stopped up and the people crossed on dry ground (Joshua 3:14-17).

The ark was carried in a circuit around Jericho for seven days until the walls of the city falls and the city is captured (Joshua 6).

After the conquest, the tabernacle is set up at Shiloh (Joshua 18:1; 1 Samuel 3:3). Possibly the ark is taken for a while to Bethel (Judges 20:26-27).

Eli's sons foolishly carry the ark into battle against the Philistines, who capture it and take it to their own cities (1 Samuel 4:1-11). However, it causes them great distress, and they eventually send it back to the Israelites. (1 Samuel 5:11).

The arch stays for 20 Years at Kirjath Jearim (1 Samuel 7:1-2).

David attempts to bring the ark to Jerusalem but meets with tragedy enroute. The ark is left at Obed-Edom's house for three months (1 Chronicles 13).

David finally brings the ark to Jerusalem, where it is eventually housed in the temple built by Solomon (1 Chronicles 16:1; 2 Chronicles 5:5-14). Years later, the Babylonians capture Jerusalem, destroying the temple (2 Chronicles 36:19). It is not known what became of the ark.

Note: Author believes the original one is in heaven. The one which the Moses instructed Bezalel to make (the earthly ark) was taken to Ethiopia before the Babylonian destruction of the temple and has since been returned from Ethiopia to Israel for the new temple, which is to be constructed in the near future. In any case God knows.

2 Chronicles 7:14

If my people, which are called by my name, shall humble themselves, and pray, and seek my face, and turn from their wicked ways; then will I hear from heaven, and will forgive their sin, and will heal their land.

Pray for the peace of Jerusalem; they will prosper who love thee.

Lesson Plan 127

The Book of 1 Chronicles

Chapters 27, 28, & 29

Objective: To gain an understanding of the extensive genealogy of the Israelites from Adam to the end of the exile in Babylon (538 B.C.).

Objective Breakdown:

1. Introduction

2. Divisions of Israel's Military   Chapter 27:1-15

3. Leaders of the Twelve Tribes   Chapter 27:16-24

4. Civilian Officers   Chapter 27:25-34

5. The Charge to Israel   Chapter 28:1-8

6. The Charge to Solomon   Chapter 28:9-10

7. Detailed Plans for the Temple   Chapter 28:11-21

8. The People Make Donations   Chapter 29:1-9

9. David and the People Bless the Lord   Chapter 29:10-20

10. Solomon Succeeds David   Chapter 29:21-25

11. The Death of David   Chapter 29:6-30

Introduction:

Home at last. When David brought the ark of the covenant to Jerusalem and placed it in the tabernacle, it was a spiritual homecoming that centralized the nation's worship (1 Chronicles 16:37-42). At last, God's presence (as symbolized by the ark) God's chosen people, God's land, and God's appointed king were all, brought together. The Lord and His people were home at last (1 Chronicles 16:43).

David felt restless as he lived in his house of cedar (1 Chronicles 17:1). How could he enjoy a luxurious dwelling when the ark—was housed in a tent. The tabernacle had served well enough as portable worship center during Israel's circuitous journey to the Promised Land. But now David felt it was time to build a permanent house for the Lord.

Perhaps that is what the temple symbolized for David, at least at an emotional level: permanence, security, rest, home. His passion to build a house for the Lord may have something to do with the years he spent as a homeless fugitive running from Saul (1 Samuel 18:31). David eventually came into his kingdom, but it was a long road getting there. In a similar way, the ark had traveled a long a difficult road to Jerusalem. Now David wanted this symbol of God's presence and guidance to be at least as comfortable and secure, as well cared for a he was.

2 Chronicles 7:14

If my people, which are called by my name, shall humble themselves, and pray, and seek my face, and turn from their wicked ways; then will I hear from heaven, and will forgive their sin, and will heal their land.

Psalm 122:6

Pray for the peace of Jerusalem; they will prosper who love thee.

The Book of 2 Chronicles

Scripture Focus Chapters 1-36

Objective: To gain an understanding of how a person can be successful in power, wealth, and prestige (like Solomon), yet lack the true success that comes from knowing and honoring God the way a person should.

Objective Breakdown:

1. Introduction

2. Solomon Leads the People in Worship   Chapter 1:1-6

3. Solomon Requests Wisdom from God   Chapter 1:7-12

4. The King's Wealth   Chapter 1:13-17

5. Solomon Sends to Hiram for Materials   Chapter 2:1-10

6. Hiram's Encouraging Response   Chapter 2:11-16

7. A Census to Conscript Laborers   Chapter 2:17-18

8. Temple Construction Begins   Chapter 3:1-7

9. The Most Holy Place   Chapter 3:8-14

10. Two Main Pillars   Chapter 3:15-17

11. A Bronze Altar, Sea, and Lavers   Chapter 4:1-10

12. Temple Implements   Chapter 4:11-22

13. Temple Implements (cont.)   Chapter 5:1

14. The Ark Is Brought in   Chapter 5:2-10

15. God's Presence Fills the Temple   Chapter 5:11-14

16. Solomon Blesses the People   Chapter 6:1-11

17. The Prayer of Dedication   Chapter 6:12-42

18. Fire Falls from Heaven   Chapter 7:1-3

19. Worship Begins   Chapter 7:4-11

Lesson Plan 128

The Book of 2 Chronicles

Chapters 1, 2, 3, & 4

Objective: To gain an understanding of how a person can be successful in power, wealth, and prestige (like Solomon) yet lack the true success that comes from knowing and honoring God the way a person should.

Objective Breakdown:

1. Introduction

2. Solomon Leads the People in Worship   Chapter 1:1-6

3. Solomon Requests Wisdom from God   Chapter 1:7-12

4. The King's Wealth   Chapter 1:13-17

5. Solomon Sends to Hiram for Materials   Chapter 2:1-10

6. Hiram's Encouraging Response   Chapter 2:11-16

7. A Census to Conscript Laborers   Chapter 2:17-18

8. Temple Construction Begins   Chapter 3:1-7

9. The Most Holy Place   Chapter 3:8-14

10. Two Main Pillars   Chapter 3:15-17

11. A Bronze Altar, Sea, and Lavers   Chapter 4:1-10

12. Temple Implements   Chapter 4:11-22

Introduction:

Solomon: Successful but not satisfied. Thanks to the Lord's help, Solomon apparently became the wealthiest and wisest man of his era (2 Chronicles 1:1). No one, it seems, accumulated or accomplished as much as he did (Ecclesiastes 2:1-9). Yet by his own admission (assuming Solomon wrote Ecclesiastes), his life was far from satisfying (Ecclesiastes 2:1-9), his life was far from satisfying (Ecclesiastes 2:11, 16).

Jesus used Solomon and his splendor as an illustration of how His follower needed to concentrate on trusting, loving, and serving God rather than on material gain or even the problems of day-to-day life (Matthew 6:28-32). Later, Jesus challenged His enemies with the fact that the Queen of Sheba, a Gentile, had shown more faith in coming to Jerusalem to inquire of Solomon than they had shown after seeing His miracles and hearing His teachings (Matthew 12:42).

Stephen (a leader in the early church): In detailing the history of Israel, mentioned Solomon ass one who built a house for God, but praised Solomon's father David as one who found favor with God.... (Acts 7:45-48).

Paul (also a leader in the early church): In reviewing the history of Israel from the Old Testament, mentioned several of the great leaders of Israel, including Samuel, the Judges, Saul, and David but not Solomon (Acts 13:22).

The author of Hebrews listed some of the great models of faith from Israel's history (Hebrews 11) but did not include Solomon. Now Solomon wasn't all bad, but his life shows us that great achievements and success—whether in business, government, academia, or any other field—pale in comparison to being faithful to God. We should focus our priorities on loving and serving our almighty God.

2 Chronicles 7:14

If my people, which are called by my name, shall humble themselves, and pray, and seek my face, and turn from their wicked ways; then will I hear from heaven, and will forgive their sin, and will heal their land.

Psalm 122:6

Pray for the peace of Jerusalem; they will prosper who love thee.

349

Lesson Plan 129

The Book of 2 Chronicles

Chapters 5, 6, 7, & 8

Objective: To gain an understanding of how a person can be successful in power, wealth, and prestige (like Solomon), yet lack the true success that comes from knowing and honoring God the way a person should.

Objective Breakdown:

1. Introduction

2. Temple Implements (cont.)   Chapter 5:1

3. The Ark Is Brought in   Chapter 5:2-10

4. God's Presence Fills the Temple   Chapter 5:11-14

5. Solomon Blesses the People   Chapter 6:1-11

6. The Prayer of Dedication   Chapter 6:12-42

7. Fire Falls from Heaven   Chapter 7:1-3

8. Worship Begins   Chapter 7:4-11

9. God Confirms His Covenant   Chapter 7:12-22

10. Storage Cities   Chapter 8:1-6

11.   Laborers   Chapter 8:7-10

12. Religious Practices   Chapter 8:11-16

13. Shipping   Chapter 8:17-18

Introduction:

God's responses to worship. Scripture assures us that God notices and responds when we worship Him. That worship may be formal and elaborate as the ceremony to dedicate the temple (2 Chronicles 5:11-14), or it may be a simple and spontaneous as the worship of the early church, which often met in people's homes (Acts 2:42; 46-47). What matters is not the setting or the program so much as the content of the worship and the heart attitude of the worshipers (John 4:21-24).

It is interesting to compare the account of temple dedication in 2 Chronicles 5:7 with the account in 1 Kings 8. Second Chronicles provide less detail until it comes to the singers and trumpeters. Then it shows how the musician's harmony in pitch and purpose brought the ceremony to its climax (2 Chronicles 5:13), and how God responded by blessing the occasion and the temple itself with His glory and presence (2 Chronicles 5:14).

The New Testament makes no mention of early Christians engaging in anything like the carefully scripted and rehearsed ritual that the Hebrews practiced. Nevertheless, God responded to the Christians worship with similar assurances of His presence and power (see Acts 4:31).

So, we are encouraged to worship the Lord in whatever ways are appropriate to the circumstances. He invites us to come before His presence with singing (Psalms 100:2) whether that men's painstakingly detailed ceremonies led by professional singers and musicians, or simple prayers and songs of heartfelt praise. Either way, He longs for us to "enter His gates with thanksgiving, and into His courts with praise" (Psalms 100:4). Amen!

2 Chronicles 7:14

If my people, which are called by my name, shall humble themselves, and pray, and seek my face, and turn from their wicked ways; then will I hear from heaven, and will forgive their sin, and will heal their land.

Psalm 122:6

Pray for the peace of Jerusalem; they will prosper who love thee.

Lesson Plan 130

The Book of 2 Chronicles

Chapters 9, 10, 11, & 12

Objective: To gain an understanding of how a person can be successful in power, wealth, and prestige (like Solomon), yet lack the true success that comes from knowing and honoring God the way a person should.

Objective Breakdown:

1. Introduction

2. The Queen of Sheba Visits   Chapter 9:1-8

3. The Two Rulers Exchange Gifts   Chapter 9:9-12

4. Solomon's Royal Revenues   Chapter 9:13-16

5. Unsurpassed Wealth and Wisdom   Chapter 9:17-28

6. The Death of Solomon   Chapter 9:29-31

7. Rehoboam Rejects His Elders' Advice   Chapter 10:1-11

8. The Northern Tribes of Israel Revolt   Chapter 10:12-19

9. Rehoboam Is Told Not to Attack Israel   Chapter 11:1-4

10. Rehoboam Fortifies Judah   Chapter 11:5-12

11. The Levites Come to Judah   Chapter 11:13-17

12. Rehoboam's Family   Chapter 11:18-23

13. Rehoboam Forsakes God, Then Repents   Chapter 12:1-8

14. Egyptians Ransack the Temple   Chapter 12:9-12

15. The Final Years of Rehoboam   Chapter 12:13-16

Introduction:

The attraction of Israel's God. The temple at Jerusalem was intended to be like a magnet, drawing people from all over the world to worship the Lord as did Israel (2 Chronicles 6:32-33). Here are some examples:

a. The Queen of Sheba.... After reviewing Solomon's accomplishments, she praised God

b. The rulers of neighboring kingdoms in Solomon's day....They came to benefit from Solomon's wisdom, which the Lord had given him (2 Chronicles 9:22-24).

c. The Widow of Zarephath....The Phoenician and her son were saved from famine, and her son was raised from the dead because she showed hospitality to Elijah (2 Kings 17:8-24).

d. Naaman....The Syrian general was healed of his leprosy and brought to faith in the Lord because he listened to advice of his wife's Jewish maid and sought out Elisha (2 King 5:1-19).

e. Ebed-Melech....The Ethiopian official under King Zedekiah demonstrated faith in the Lord by intervening on behalf of the prophet Jeremiah, a courageous act for which the Lord spared him at the time of Jerusalem's fall (Jeremiah 38:7-13; 39:15-18).

f. Nebuchadnezzar....Through Daniel and the discipline of the Lord, the Babylonian king learned that heaven rules. As a result, he instituted a reign based on truth, justice, and humility (Daniel 4:34-37).

g. Darius....The Persian ruler concluded that the Lord is the living God after seeing Daniel's deliverance from the lion's den as a result of his steadfast integrity (Daniel 6:24-27).

h. The Wise Men....These men came to worship the new-born baby whom they called King of the Jews, having been drawn by a star they saw in the East (Matthew 2:1-2).

i. Certain Greeks in Jerusalem....This group requested to meet Jesus, perhaps having heard about Him in Galilee (John 12:20-22).

j. The Ethiopian Treasurer....The African official heard and responded to the gospel after traveling to Jerusalem to worship in the temple (Act 8:26-40).

2 Chronicles 7:14

If my people, which are called by my name, shall humble themselves, and pray, and seek my face, and turn from their wicked ways; then will I hear from heaven, and will forgive their sin, and will heal their land.

Psalm 122:6

Pray for the peace of Jerusalem; they will prosper who love thee.

Lesson Plan 131

The Book of 2 Chronicles

Chapters 13, 14, 15, 16, & 17

Objective: To gain an understanding of how a person can be successful in power, wealth, and prestige (like Solomon), yet lack the true success that comes from knowing and honoring God the way a person should.

Objective Breakdown:

1. Introduction

2. Abijah Becomes King Over Judah   Chapter 13:1-3

3. Israel Receives a Warning   Chapter 13:4-12

4. God Gives Abijah Victory Over Israel   Chapter 13:13-22

5. Asa Succeeds Abijah   Chapter 14:1-8

6. Asa Defeats the Ethiopians   Chapter 14:9-15

7. Azariah Urges Asa to Seek the Lord   Chapter 15:1-7

8. Asa Enacts Reforms in Judah   Chapter 15:8-19

9. Syria Helps Asa Against Israel   Chapter 16:1-6

10. Hanani Prophesies Against the Alliance Chapter 16:7-14

11. Jehoshaphat Reigns and Honors God   Chapter 17:1-9

12. Judah Prospers   Chapter 17:10-19

Introduction:

The glory of the Lord. God is a Spirit (John 4:24) and therefore has no body and is invisible to the human eye (John 6:46; Colossians 1:15). How then can God make His presence known? In Old Testament times, He often revealed Himself by showing His "glory" (Hebrews, chabod; 2 Chronicles 7:1).

The glory of the Lord was a term used by the Hebrews to describe the way in which God showed that He was present through visible signs such as thunder, lightning, clouds, or fire (for example Exodus 3:1-6; Exodus 19:16-19; Numbers 12:5, 2 Chronicles 5:13-14). Keeping in mind that the Hebrews were not responding to natural phenomena like calling them God, as some suppose. Rather the invisible God was revealing Himself through means that humans could receive.

When Christ was transfigured, He revealed God in human form. Thus, John could write that the Word became flesh and dwelt among us, and we beheld His glory, the glory of the only begotten of the Father" (John 1:14). And when the Holy Spirit came upon the first believers in the Upper Room, He revealed His presence through tongues of fire and other signs Act 2:1-4).

Two other ways that God reveals His glory are through creation (Psalms 19:1) and through His people (Ephesians 1:12; Colossians 1:27). As believers in Christ, we are the temples of the Holy Spirit, and He wants to fill us with His gory (1 Corinthians 6:19-20).

2 Chronicles 7:14

If my people, which are called by my name, shall humble themselves, and pray, and seek my face, and turn from their wicked ways; then will I hear from heaven, and will forgive their sin, and will heal their land.

Psalm 122:6

Pray for the peace of Jerusalem; they will prosper who love thee.

Lesson Plan 132

The Book of 2 Chronicles

Chapters 18, 19, & 20

Objective: To gain an understanding of how a person can be successful in power, wealth, and prestige (like Solomon), yet lack the true success that comes from knowing and honoring God the way a person should.

Objective Breakdown:

1. Introduction

2. Jehoshaphat's Alliance with Ahab   Chapter 18:1-5

3. God Warns the Kings Through Micaiah   Chapter 18:6-17

4. Micaiah Prophesies Ahab's Downfall   Chapter 18:18-27

5. Ahab Dies in Battle   Chapter 18:28-34

6. Jehoshaphat Appoints Good Judges   Chapter 19:1-11

7. Judah Cries Out for God's Help   Chapter 20:1-13

8. God Assures Judah of Victory   Chapter 20:14-19

9. Judah's Enemies Kill Each Other   Chapter 20:20-24

10. The Spoils Are Gathered   Chapter 20:25-30

11. High Places Are Left Up   Chapter 20:31-34

12. Jehoshaphat Loses His Fleet   Chapter 20:35-37

Introduction:

Heal our nation: 2 Chronicles 7:14. Some 2000 plus years ago, right after Solomon completed the construction of the first Temple. God appeared to Solomon in a night vision. He offered Solomon a "conditional covenant." He told Solomon, "If His people who are called by His name would humble themselves, and pray, and seek His face and turn from their wicked ways, then He would hear from heaven, forgive their sin, and heal their land" (2 Chronicle 7:14).

This Conditional Covenant was given to Solomon right after he had completed the first temple (approximately in 957 B.C.), God simply said if we, His People, would do four things, He would respond by doing three things. The four things in which His people who are called by His name (Christians) are to do:

1. Humble Themselves; 2. Pray; 3. Seek My face; and 4. Turn from Their Wicked Ways. Then, God would do three things: 1. Hear from Heaven; 2. Forgive their Sin; 3. Heal their Land.

Why, we as Christians and children of Abraham haven't embraced this Conditional Covenant is beyond wisdom. Every Pastor and Priest and Teacher should be leading their congregation and their flock, in taking advantage of God's promise, in order that our nation be healed.

2 Chronicles 7:14

If my people, which are called by my name, shall humble themselves, and pray, and seek my face, and turn from their wicked ways; then will I hear from heaven, and will forgive their sin, and will heal their land.

Psalm 122:6

Pray for the peace of Jerusalem; they will prosper who love thee.

Lesson Plan 133

The Book of 2 Chronicles

Chapters 21, 22, & 23

Objective: To gain an understanding of how a person can be successful in power, wealth, and prestige (like Solomon), yet lack the true success that comes from knowing and honoring God the way a person should.

Objective Breakdown:

1.   Introduction

2. Jehoram Kills His Brothers   Chapter 21:1-11

3. A Letter Announces God's Judgment   Chapter 21:12-20

4. The Brief Reign of Ahaziah   Chapter 22:1-9

5. A Future King Is Raised in Secret   Chapter 22:10-12

6. A Faithful Assembly Crowns Joash   Chapter 23:1-11

7. Athaliah Is Deposed   Chapter 23:12-15

8. Jehoiada the Priest Brings Reform   Chapter 23:16-21

Introduction:

Prayers – the best defense. Some people think of prayer as the last resort, an act of desperation to try when all else fails and one is faced with overwhelming odds. But the example of Asa shows that while prayer is the best defense, it is also the best offense, a discipline that should be practiced long before trouble strikes.

Faced with an army more than three times the size of his own 300,000-man force, Asa cried out to God for help. He humbly acknowledged that the Lord, not military might, was his ultimate defense (2 Chronicles 14:11). The Lord responded by defeating the Ethiopians (2 Chronicles 14:12-15).

This incident showed that what matters in battle is not the size of the armies, but trust in the Lord. As always, what counts with God is faith. Yet Asa's trust in God was not just a "foxhole faith," motivated by fear, He was able to pray as he did, because he had been praying, worshiping, and honoring the Lord for years (2 Chronicles 14:3-7). In fact, his reign had reversed many of the sins initiated by his great-grandfather Solomon.

Less than two decades earlier, Solomon's successor Rehoboam had been defeated by Egyptian forces, which included Ethiopians. The invaders from the south overran Judah and captured Jerusalem with far fewer military resources (2 Chronicles 12:1-12) than the army which Asa saw crushed. This emphasis the point that when people of God made worship and prayer their first priority, God was faithful to take care of them. But when they turned away from the Lord and made other things such as wealth and prestige their priority, then the Lord allowed them to fail.

So, it is with spiritual warfare today. God wants to see whether we respond in faith when circumstances overwhelm us. But He is also interested in the quality of our faith before tragedy strikes, when thing s are not going well. Either way in calm or crisis we need to pray to the Lord in faith (1 John 5:4).

2 Chronicles 7:14

If my people, which are called by my name, shall humble themselves, and pray, and seek my face, and turn from their wicked ways; then will I hear from heaven, and will forgive their sin, and will heal their land.

Psalm 122:6

Pray for the peace of Jerusalem; they will prosper who love thee.

Lesson Plan 134

The Book of 2 Chronicles

Chapters 24, 25, 26, & 27

Objective: To gain an understanding of how a person can be successful in power, wealth, and prestige (like Solomon), yet lack the true success that comes from knowing and honoring God the way a person should.

Objective Breakdown:

1.   Introduction

2.   Joash Undertakes Temple Repairs   Chapter 24:1-14

3.   Judah's Leaders Turn Away from God   Chapter 24:15-22

4.   Joash Is Assassinated   Chapter 24:23-27

5.   Amaziah Becomes King of Judah   Chapter 25:1-4

6.   Amaziah Prepares for War   Chapter 25:5-10

7.   The Slaughter of the Edomites   Chapter 25:11-16

8.   Israel Battles and Captures Amaziah   Chapter 25:17-28

9.   Uzziah Reigns in Judah   Chapter 26:1-8

10. Strong Defenses Are Set Up   Chapter 26:9-15

11. Uzziah Turns from God and Dies a Leper   Chapter 26:16-23

12. King Jotham Builds Extensively   Chapter 27:1-9

Introduction:

The Ethiopians: The Ethiopians that attacked Judah (2 Chronicles 12:9-10) were from an ancient African nation just to the south of Egypt, in a region sometime called Nubia or Cush. This land was known for its rivers, the Blue Nile and White Nile (Isaiah 18:1), its Papyrus boats (Isaiah 18:2), and its topaz gems (Job 28:19). The people were known for their black skin (Jeremiah 13:23), their tallness and smooth skin (Isaiah18:2), and their fierceness in battle (Jeremiah 46:9).

The Ethiopians were descended from Noah's son Ham (Genesis 10:6; 1 Chronicles 1:8-10), as were the

Egyptians (called Mizraim). These two nations were closely connected throughout their histories, and the biblical writers often mention the two together (i.e., Isaiah 20:3-5; Ezekiel 30:4-5). Ethiopia was generally controlled by the Egyptians until after the time of David (about 1000 B.C.). During this period the Ethiopians often served as hired soldiers for the Egyptian army and others (2 Samuel 18:21-32; 2 Chronicles 12:3).

The Ethiopians attained their greatest strength during the time of Hezekiah (about 700 B.C.), when Egypt was suffering from internal disunity and political instability. An Ethiopian dynasty ruled Egypt or 60 years during this period, but an invasion by the Assyrian kings Esarhaddon and Ashurbanipal eventually brought its power to an end (Isaiah 20:2-6). Later the prophets Ezekiel (Ezekiel 30:4-10) and Jeremiah (Jeremiah 46:9-10; 13-14) predicted that Ethiopia and Egypt would be attacked by the king of Babylon, and the prophet Isaiah foretold a Persian conquest of the territory (Esther 1:1; 8-9; Isaiah 43:3). Yet in the midst of these judgments, the Lord promised that someday people of His would return to the Holy Land from Ethiopia (Isaiah 11:11).

2 Chronicles 7:14

If my people, which are called by my name, shall humble themselves, and pray, and seek my face, and turn from their wicked ways; then will I hear from heaven, and will forgive their sin, and will heal their land.

Psalm 122:6

Pray for the peace of Jerusalem; they will prosper who love thee.

Lesson Plan 135

The Book of 2 Chronicles

Chapters 28, 29, 30, & 31

Objective: To gain an understanding of how a person can be successful in power, wealth, and prestige (like Solomon), yet lack the true success that comes from knowing and honoring God the way a person should.

Objective Breakdown:

1.   Introduction

2. Wicked King Ahaz Suffers Defeat   Chapter 28:1-8

4. Israel Returns Its Judean Captives   Chapter 28:9-15

4. Judah Declines Further Under Ahaz   Chapter 28:16-27

5. Hezekiah Begins His Reforms   Chapter 29:1-11

6. Levites Cleanse the Temple   Chapter 29:12-19

7. Sacrifices and Praises Are Offered   Chapter 29:20-30

8. Many Offerings Are Brought   Chapter 29:31-36

9. All Are Invited to Celebrate Passover   Chapter 30:1-9

10. Some Scoff, but Many Come to Jerusalem   Chapter 30:10-20

11. The Feast Days Are Extended   Chapter 30:21-27

13. The People Go Out and Destroy Idols   Chapter 31:1-3

14. Support for the Priests and Levites   Chapter 31:4-10

15. Priests and Levites Are Reorganized   Chapter 31:11-21

Introduction:

God fearing judges. In many Western countries today, political leaders can have influence on the ethical and moral fiber of their countries through judges they appoint and the judicial policies they support and enforce. In a similar way, King Jehoshaphat brought reform to Judah by appointing judges and other legal officials and declaring specific policies to guide them (Chronicles 19:5-7).

Judges were to take the job seriously (2 Chronicles 19:6). Again and again, Jehoshaphat urged his legal officials to pay attention to what they were doing. They were accountable to God (2 Chronicles 19:6). As king, Jehoshaphat was responsible for the legal system both he and the judges were responsible to God from which all power and authority originates. They needed to serve in fear of Him (2 Chronicles 19:7), faithfully and with a loyal heart (2 Chronicles 19:9).

Judicial character is a mirror to God's character (2 Chronicles 19:7), so judges need to judge with purity and equity. In everyday terms they need to avoid partiality and or taking bribes. The Judges' role is to warn and educate as well as decide cases (2 Chronicles 19:10). There was a preventative aspect to Jehoshaphat's concept of the judiciary. He expected judges to use the disputes as teachable moments to instruct the people in the law and to warn them about violating God's commandments. If they (judges) failed to do so, they would be guilty before the Lord if the people fell into sin.

Would Jehoshaphat's reforms work today? They would serve as a broad outline of the godly basis on which true justice is founded. The answer is yes!

2 Chronicles 7:14

If my people, which are called by my name, shall humble themselves, and pray, and seek my face, and turn from their wicked ways; then will I hear from heaven, and will forgive their sin, and will heal their land.

Psalm 122:6

Pray for the peace of Jerusalem; they will prosper who love thee.

Lesson Plan 136

The Book of 2 Chronicles

Chapters 32, 33, & 34

Objective: To gain an understanding of how a person can be successful in power, wealth, and prestige (like Solomon), yet lack the true success that comes from knowing and honoring God the way a person should.

Objective Breakdown:

1.   Introduction

2. The Assyrians Attack Judah   Chapter 32:1-8

3. Jerusalem Is Besieged   Chapter 32:9-19

4. The Lord Saves the City   Chapter 32:20-23

5. The Final Days of Hezekiah   Chapter 32:24-33

6. The Disobedience of King Manasseh   Chapter 33:1-9

7. Manasseh Is Punished and Repents   Chapter 33:10-13

8. Manasseh Strengthens Jerusalem   Chapter 33:14-20

9. The Brief and Evil Reign of Amon   Chapter 33:21-25

10. Josiah Turns Judah Back to God   Chapter 34:1-7

11. The Temple Is Repaired   Chapter 34:8-13

12. The Book of the Law Is Found   Chapter 34:14-21

13. Huldah Prophesies Jerusalem's Fall   Chapter 34:22-28

14. Josiah Renews the Covenant   Chapter 34:29-33

Introduction:

The indispensable value of a spiritual mentor. Quite often, the difference between success and failure in a person's career is determined by whether that person has been guided and nurtured by a mentor. The same can be true in spiritual matters. The extent in which a person matures spiritually and stays that way is often determined by the presence of a spiritual mentor.

King Joah is a case in point, as long as the godly priest Jehoiada was around to guide young Joash, the king ruled well and brought spiritual renewal to the land (2 Chronicles 23:16–24:16). But after Jehoiada died, Joash turned to wickedness, allowing idolatry creep back in (2 Chronicles 24:17-18), and even killing Zechariah, the son of his mentor Jehoiada (2 Chronicles 24:22). Joash eventually suffered military defeat and was murdered by his own servants (2 Chronicles 24:23-25). A tragic ending to what started out as a good reign. Joash's apostasy reminds us that leaders today need spiritual mentors and religious guidance if they are to stay on course. If you're a person in position of authority, who are you looking for godly wisdom and counsel?

Demographers today classify roughly one seventh of the world's population as Christian. However, church leaders are quick to point out that many adherents of Christianity, particularly in the west can only be classified as nominal Christians because they are Christians in name only. The attend church sporadically and show little if any spiritual commitment.

The faith of Amaziah of Judah was nominal. He generally followed the Lord, but not whole- heartedly (2 Chronicles 25:2). Apparently, he practiced the law, but probably did so more out of tradition than out of heart felt commitment to the Lord. So, it is not surprising to learn that Amaziah took ethical shortcuts when it was convenient. For example, he spared the lives of Israelite children of murderers, in accordance with the law (2 Chronicles 25:3-4) but then he killed 10,000 innocent Edomites (2 Chronicles 25:11-12; 2 Kings 14:7-10).

Amaziah's legacy is a sobering reminder that nominal faith is almost as bad as no faith at all. A person can lead a fine, upstanding life, yet have little or no relationship with God. If the main point of life is to know, love, and serve God, then following a noble religious tradition is of little value and dangerously self-deceiving.

2 Chronicles 7:14

If my people, which are called by my name, shall humble themselves, and pray, and seek my face, and turn from their wicked ways; then will I hear from heaven, and will forgive their sin, and will heal their land.

Psalm 122:6

Pray for the peace of Jerusalem; they will prosper who love thee.

Lesson Plan 137

The Book of 2 Chronicles

Chapters 35 & 36

Objective: To gain an understanding of how a person can be successful in power, wealth, and prestige (like Solomon), yet lack the true success that comes from knowing and honoring God the way a person should.

Objective Breakdown:

1.   Introduction

2. Preparations for Passover   Chapter 35:1-9

3. The Passover Is Celebrated   Chapter 35:10-19

4. Josiah Is Fatally Wounded in Battle   Chapter 35:20-27

5. The Egyptians Depose Jehoahaz   Chapter 36:1-4

6. Jehoiakim Becomes King   Chapter 36:5-8

7. Jehoiachin Reigns Briefly   Chapter 36:9-10

8. Judah Is Taken into Captivity   Chapter 36:11-21

9. Cyrus Orders the Temple Rebuilt   Chapter 36:22-23

Introduction:

Obeying begins by listening. He English word "obey" (2 Chronicles 30:12) comes from the Latin word meaning "to hear." Thus, the old proverb is literary true: to hear is to obey. As exasperated parent ask a child who comes late to the dinner table, "Why didn't you come when I called you?" The child responds, "I didn't hear you until the third time!" Thus, we see that obedience involves an informed choice.

Do you know how to obey (listen to) God? It helps if you allow your familiarity with God's interests and values to grow through some regular form of Bible reading. As you read God's Word ask yourself what is God telling me to do as a result of His Word.

Many believers today pray for revival, but one of the conditions for revival is unity among believers. If God's people are divided in what they believe or contradictory in what they say, it can be very difficult for unbelievers to take the gospel seriously.

During Hezekiah's reign in Judah, spiritual revival came about largely because the Lord gave the people "singleness of heart" to obey His commandments, as given through the leaders (2 Chronicles 30:12). This newfound unity to obey God and honor the covenant contrasted sharply with the disunity that marked the Israelites since the days of Rehoboam (2 Chronicles 10:1-19). Hezekiah invited the survivors of the northern kingdom to rejoin their brothers and sisters in the South (2 Chronicles 30:6-9). Most of the northerners resisted this call, but a few responded (2 Chronicles 30:10-11).

One reason why the people were again able to follow God wholeheartedly was that Hezekiah was doing so. Scripture attest that in everything he did, Hezekiah honored the Lord "with his whole heart" (2 Chronicles 31:21). This is what we need to do and be committed in singleness of heart giving honor and praise to our Lord Jesus Christ, the Holy Spirit and the Father Almighty Amen!!

2 Chronicles 7:14

If my people, which are called by my name, shall humble themselves, and pray, and seek my face, and turn from their wicked ways; then will I hear from heaven, and will forgive their sin, and will heal their land.

Psalm 122:6

Pray for the peace of Jerusalem; they will prosper who love thee.

The Book of Ezra

Scripture Focus Chapters 1-10

Objective: To gain some insight that in the Middle East, the Persians were more humane and benevolent toward those they had defeated when compared to the ancient Assyrians and Babylonians.

Objective Breakdown:

1. Introduction
2. The Proclamation of Cyrus   Chapter 1:1-4
3. Materials Are Donated for the Temple   Chapter 1:5-11
4. A Census of the Returnees   Chapter 2:1-35
5. Priests, Levites, and Other Officials   Chapter 2:36-58
6. Some Cannot Trace Their Lineage   Chapter 2:59-63
7. The Assembly Returns to Judah   Chapter 2:64-70
8. Worship Is Restored at a New Altar   Chapter 3:1-7
9. The Foundation of the Temple Is Laid   Chapter 3:8-13
10. Adversaries Oppose the Construction   Chapter 4:1-6
11. Accusations Are Sent to Artaxerxes   Chapter 4:7-16
12. Artaxerxes Orders the Work Halted   Chapter 4:17-24
13. Zerubbabel Resumes the Project   Chapter 5:1-6
14. The Governor Complains to Darius   Chapter 5:7-17
15. Darius Finds the Decree of Cyrus   Chapter 6:1-5
16. The Governor Is Told to Help the Jews   Chapter 6:6-12
17. The Temple Is Finished and Dedicated   Chapter 6:13-18
18. The Passover Is Kept   Chapter 6:19-22
19. The Scribe Ezra Returns to Jerusalem   Chapter 7:1-10
20. The Letter of Commission and Credit   Chapter 7:11-26

Lesson Plan 138

The Book of Ezra

Chapters 1 & 2

Objective: To gain insight on the marvelous design and promise God had for His people, the Jewish nation.

Objective Breakdown:

1. Introduction

2. The Proclamation of Cyrus   Chapter 1:1-4

3. Materials Are Donated for the Temple   Chapter 1:5-11

4. A Census of the Returnees   Chapter 2:1-35

5. Priests, Levites, and Other Officials   Chapter 2:36-58

6. Some Cannot Trace Their Lineage   Chapter 2:59-63

7. The Assembly Returns to Judah   Chapter 2:64-70

Ezra was a godly man marked by strong trust in the Lord, moral integrity, and grief over sin. He was a contemporary of Nehemiah (Nehemiah 8:1-9; 12:36) who arrived in Jerusalem in 444 B.C. Tradition holds that Ezra was the founder of the Great Synagogue where the canon of Old Testament was settled. Another tradition says that he collected the biblical books into a unit and that he originated the synagogue form of worship.

Ezra wrote this book probably between 457 B.C. (the events of Ezra 7-10) and 444 B.C. (Nehemiah's arrival in Jerusalem). During the period of time covered by the Book of Ezra, Gautama Buddha is in India (560-480 B.C.), Confucius is in China (551-479 B.C.), and Socrates is in Greece (470-399 B.C.).

The following table shows a chronological relationship of the books of Ezra, Nehemiah, and Esther:

First Return	Not Applicable	Second Return	Third Return
538-515 B.C.	483-473 B.C.	457 B.C.	444-425 B.C.
Zerubbabel	Esther	Ezra	Nehemiah

Ezra 1-6	Book of Esther	Ezra 7-10	Book of Nehemiah
49,897	Israelites	1,754 Israelites	

These books fit against the background of these Persian kings:

Cyrus	(550-530 B.C.)	20 years
Cambyses	(530-522 B.C.)	8 years
Smerdis	(522 B.C.)	1 year
Darius I	(521-486 B.C.)	35 years
Ahasuerus	(486-464 B.C.)	22 years
Artaxerxes	(464-423 B.C.)	41 years
Darius II	(423-404 B.C.)	19 years

The Book of Ezra continues the story of where 2 Chronicles ends and shows how God's promise to bring His people back to their land is fulfilled (Jeremiah 29:10-14): "For thus saith the Lord, that after seventy years be accomplished at Babylon I will visit you, and perform my good word toward you, in causing you to return to this place. For I know the thoughts that I think toward you, saith the Lord, thoughts of peace, and not of evil, to give you an expected end. Then shall ye call upon me, and ye shall go and pray unto me, and I will hearken unto you. And ye shall seek me, and find me, when ye shall search for me with all your heart. And I will be found of you, saith the Lord: and I will turn away your captivity, and I will gather you from all the nations, and from all the places whither I have driven you, saith the Lord; and I will bring you again into the place whence I caused you to be carried away captive."

Ezra relates the story of the first two returns from Babylon, the first led by Zerubbabel and the second led decades later by Ezra. Its two divisions are the restoration of the temple (chapters 1–6) and the reformation of the people (chapters 7-10), and they are separated by a fifty-eight-year gap during which the story of Esther takes place.

Out of a population of perhaps 2 or 3 million only 49, 897 choose to take advantage of this offer. Only the most committed are willing to leave a life of relative comfort in Babylon, endure a trek of nine hundred miles, and face further hardships by rebuilding a destroyed temple and city. Zerubbabel, a "prince" of Judah (a direct descendant of King David), leads the faithful remnant back to Jerusalem. Those who return are from the tribes of Judah, Benjamin, and Levi; but it is evident that representatives from the other ten tribes eventually return as well. The ten "lost tribes" are not entirely lost.

2 Chronicles 7:14

If my people, which are called by my name, shall humble themselves, and pray, and seek my face, and turn from their wicked ways; then will I hear from heaven, and will forgive their sin, and will heal their land.

Psalm 122:6

Pray for the peace of Jerusalem; they will prosper who love thee.

Every evening at 9:00 pm Eastern Time (8:00 pm Central) (6:00 pm Pacific), stop whatever you are doing and spend one-minute praying for the safety of the United States, our troops, our citizens, and for a return to a Godly nation. If you know anyone else who would like to participate, please pass this along.

Read Ephesians 4:29-32 daily

Let no corrupt communication proceed out of your mouth, but that which is good to the use of edifying, that it may minister grace unto the hearers.

And grieve not the Holy Spirit of God, whereby ye are sealed unto the day of redemption.

Let all bitterness, and wrath, and anger, and clamor, and evil speaking, be put away from you, with all malice.

And be ye kind one to another, tenderhearted, forgiving one another, even as God for Christ's sake hath forgiven you.

Lesson Plan 139

The Book of Ezra

Chapters 3, 4, 5, & 6

Objective: To gain insight on the marvelous design and promise God had for His people, the Jewish nation.

Objective Breakdown:

1. Introduction

2. Worship Is Restored at a New Temple   Chapter 3:1-7

3. The Foundation of the Temple Is Laid   Chapter 3:8-13

4. Adversaries Oppose the Construction   Chapter 4:1-6

5. Accusations Are Sent to Artaxerxes   Chapter 4:7-16

6. Artaxerxes Orders the Work Halted   Chapter 4:17-24

7. Zerubbabel Resumes the Project   Chapter 5:1-6

8. The Governor Complains to Darius   Chapter 5:7-17

9. Darius Finds the Decree of Cyrus   Chapter 6:1-5

10. The Governor Is Told to Help the Jews   Chapter 6:6-12

11. The Temple Is Finished and Dedicated   Chapter 6:13-18

12. The Passover Is Kept   Chapter 6:19-22

Introduction:

Ezra was a godly man marked by strong trust in the Lord, moral integrity, and grief over sin. He was a contemporary of Nehemiah (Nehemiah 8:1-9; 12:36) who arrived in Jerusalem in 444 B.C. Tradition holds that Ezra was the founder of the Great Synagogue where the canon of Old Testament was settled. Another tradition says that he collected the biblical books into a unit and that he originated the synagogue form of worship.

Ezra wrote this book probably between 457 B.C. (The events of Ezra 7-10) and 444 B.C. (Nehemiah's arrival in Jerusalem). During the period of time covered by the Book of Ezra, Gautama Buddha is in

India (560-480B.C.), Confucius is in China (551-479 B.C.), and Socrates is in Greece (470-399 B.C.).

The following table shows a chronological relationship of the books of Ezra, Nehemiah, and Esther:

First Return	Not Applicable	Second Return	Third Return
538-515 B.C.	483-473 B.C.	457 B.C.	444-425 B.C.
Zerubbabel	Esther	Ezra	Nehemiah
Ezra 1-6	Book of Esther	Ezra 7-10	Book of Nehemiah
49,897	Israelites	1,754	Israelites

These books fit against the background of these Persian kings:

Cyrus	(550-530 B.C.)	20 years
Cambyses	(530-522 B.C.)	8 years
Smerdis	(522 B.C.)	1 year
Darius I	(521-486 B.C.)	35 years
Ahasuerus	(486-464 B.C.)	22 years
Artaxerxes	(464-423 B.C.)	41 years
Darius II	(423-404 B.C.)	19 years

The Book of Ezra continues the story of where 2 Chronicles ends and shows how God's promise to bring His people back to their land is fulfilled (Jeremiah 29:10-14): "For thus saith the Lord, that after seventy years be accomplished at Babylon I will visit you, and perform my good word toward you, in causing you to return to this place. For I know the thoughts that I think toward you, saith the Lord, thoughts of peace, and not of evil, to give you an expected end. Then shall ye call upon me, and ye shall go and pray unto me, and I will hearken unto you. And ye shall seek me, and find me, when ye shall search for me with all your heart. And I will be found of you, saith the Lord: and I will turn away your captivity, and I will gather you from all the nations, and from all the places whither I have driven you, saith the Lord; and I will bring you again into the place whence I caused you to be carried away captive."

Ezra relates the story of the first two returns from Babylon, the first led by Zerubbabel and the second led decades later by Ezra. Its two divisions are the restoration of the temple (chapters 1–6) and the reformation of the people (chapters 7-10), and they are separated by a fifty-eight year gap during which the story of Esther takes place.

Out of a population of perhaps 2 or 3 million only 49,897 choose to take advantage of this offer. Only the most committed are willing to leave a life of relative comfort in Babylon, endure a trek of nine hundred miles, and face further hardships by rebuilding a destroyed temple and city. Zerubbabel, a "prince" of Judah (a direct descendant of King David), leads the faithful remnant back to Jerusalem. Those who return are from the tribes of Judah, Benjamin, and Levi; but it is evident that representatives from the other ten tribes eventually return as well. The ten "lost tribes" are not entirely lost.

Read Ephesians 4: 29-32 daily

Let no corrupt communication proceed out of your mouth, but that which is good to the use of edifying, that it may minister grace unto the hearers. And grieve not the Holy Spirit of God, whereby ye are sealed unto the day of redemption. Let all bitterness, and wrath, and anger, and clamor, and evil speaking, be put away from you, with all malice: And be ye kind one to another, tenderhearted, forgiving one another, even as God for Christ's sake hath forgiven you.

2 Chronicles 7:14

If my people, which are called by my name, shall humble themselves, and pray, and seek my face, and turn from their wicked ways; then will I hear from heaven, and will forgive their sin, and will heal their land.

Psalm 122:6

Pray for the peace of Jerusalem; they will prosper who love thee.

Lesson Plan 140

The Book of Ezra

Chapters 7, 8, 9, & 10

Objective: To gain insight on the marvelous design and promise God had for His people, the Jewish nation.

Objective Breakdown:

1. Introduction

2. The Scribe Ezra Returns to Jerusalem   Chapter 7:1-10

3. A Letter of Commission and Credit   Chapter 7:11-26

4. Ezra Declares His Encouragement   Chapter 7:27-28

5. Genealogy of the Returnees   Chapter 8:1-14

6. Ezra Finds Levites to Accompany Him   Chapter 8:15-20

7. Ezra Puts His Trust in God   Chapter 8:21-23

8. Valuables Are Entrusted to the Priests   Chapter 8:24-30

9. The Journey from Babylon to Jerusalem   Chapter 8:31-36

10. Ezra Learns of marriages with Pagans   Chapter 9:1-4

11. Ezra Asks God's Forgiveness   Chapter 9:5-15

12. The People Agree to Submit to Ezra   Chapter 10:1-6

13. Ezra Commands Divorce of Pagan Wives   Chapter 10:7-17

14. A List of Men Who Had Married Pagan Wives   Chapter 10:18-44

Introduction:

Persians. The kingdom of Persia that Cyrus II oversaw (Ezra 1:8) was on its way to becoming a powerful empire that flourished between 539 and 331 B.C. Cyrus' rise to power began with his ascension to the throne in 559 B.C. He secured the empire's future through a cunning victory over Babylon (539 B.C.).

In contrast to previous rulers in the Middle east, Cyprus was humane and benevolent toward whom he defeated. One of the most politically popular policies was to allow vassal states to retain their own religions, and to receive back their idols which the Babylonians had seized. For the Jews, this policy meant a return to their homeland following their long period of captivity (2 Chronicles 36:22-23; Ezra 1:1-4).

Cyrus governed his growing empire through a system of provinces, called satrapies, ruled by governors who answered directly to him. Under his leadership, the Persians developed road, cities, postal systems, and legal codes.

Cyprus's son and successor, Cambyses II (530-522 B.C.) added Egypt to the Persian Empire. The next ruler Darius I (521-486 B.C.) defeated nine kings to claim all 23 Persian satrapies. That brought a vast territory nearly 3000 miles long and 500 to 1500 miles wide under Persian control.

After Darius, Xerxes I (called Ahasuerus; Esther Chapter 1:1) ruled Persia (486-465 B.C.). The book of Esther tells how a Jewish woman named Esther became queen in the seventh year of his reign, a position in which she was able to save her people from genocide. Under Artaxerxes I Longimanus (464-424 B.C.), two of three returns of the Jews from captivity occurred. The third return in 444 B.C. is described in the Book of Nehemiah led by Nehemiah in 444 B.C. for the purpose of rebuilding the Jerusalem walls.

2 Chronicles 7:14

If my people, which are called by my name, shall humble themselves, and pray, and seek my face, and turn from their wicked ways; then will I hear from heaven, and will forgive their sin, and will heal their land.

Psalm 122:6

Pray for the peace of Jerusalem; they will prosper who love thee.

The Book of Nehemiah

Scripture Focus Chapters 1-13

Objective: To get an understanding of how Nehemiah who was strategically positioned in the Persian royal court, used his connections to accomplish great things on behalf of the Lord.

Objective Breakdown:

1. Introduction

2. Nehemiah Hears of Jerusalem's Distress   Chapter 1:1-4

3. Nehemiah Cries Out to God   Chapter 1:5-11

4. Nehemiah's Request of the King   Chapter 2:1-6

5. Artaxerxes Commissions Nehemiah   Chapter 2:7-10

6. A Nighttime Tour of Jerusalem   Chapter 2:11-16

7. "Come and Let Us Build the Wall"   Chapter 2:17-20

8. Workers and Their Stations on the Wall   Chapter 3:1-32

9. The Work Continues Amid Opposition   Chapter 4:1-9

10. Nehemiah Sets Defenses Against Attack   Chapter 4:10-23

11. A Problem of Usury Is Resolved   Chapter 5:1-13

12. Nehemiah Sets a Good Example   Chapter 5:14-19

13. More Opposition to the Project   Chapter 6:1-9

14. An Informer Against Nehemiah Is Hired   Chapter 6:10-14

15. The Wall Is Finished   Chapter 6:15-19

16. Nehemiah Appoints Leaders   Chapter 7:1-3

17. A Record of Ezra's Census Is Found   Chapter 7:4-38

18. Priests, Levites, and Other Officials   Chapter 7:39-60

19. Some Cannot Trace Their Lineage   Chapter 7:61-65

20. The Assembly Returns to the Cities   Chapter 7:66-73

Lesson Plan 141

The Book of Nehemiah

Chapters 1, 2, 3, 4, & 5

Objective: To get an understanding of how Nehemiah who was strategically positioned in the Persian royal court, used his connections to accomplish great things on behalf of the Lord.

Objective Breakdown:

1. Introduction

2. Nehemiah Hears of Jerusalem's Distress   Chapter 1:1-4

3. Nehemiah Cries Out to God   Chapter 1:5-11

4. Nehemiah's Request of the King   Chapter 2:1-6

5. Artaxerxes Commissions Nehemiah   Chapter 2:7-10

6. A Nighttime Tour of Jerusalem   Chapter 2:11-16

7. "Come and Let Us Build the Wall"   Chapter 2:17-20

8. Workers and Their Stations on the Wall   Chapter 3:1-32

9. The Work Continues Amid Opposition   Chapter 4:1-9

10. Nehemiah Sets Defenses Against Attack   Chapter 4:10-23

11. A Problem of Usury Is Resolved   Chapter 5:1-13

12. Nehemiah Sets a Good Example   Chapter 5:14-19

Introduction:

Nehemiah's prayer: a model to follow. Nehemiah's prayer (Nehemiah1:4-11) offers several important lessons for believers today concerning the discipline of prayer:

(1) Nehemiah's first response was to turn to God in prayer. Prayer was not something that Nehemiah engaged in after he had exhausted all other alternatives. He did mot approach it as a last-ditch effort with the attitude, "what have I got to lose?" Instead, his response to the news of trouble back home was too fast and pray (Nehemiah 1:4).

(2) Nehemiah recognized God's sovereignty. He realized that he Lord has the first and primary claim over all nations and peoples, whether they were Israelites or Persians. He saw himself and his people as being in the hands of God, dependent on His Grace.

(3) Nehemiah identified with his people. He used the pronoun "we" in his prayer. Rather than blame others he uses the corporate responsibility for his people's sin.

(4) Nehemiah recognized the whole of God's promises and commandments. In praying to God. It is easy to focus on what one wants from God, but ignore what God asks and expects from His people. Nehemiah knew what the Scripture said about the Lord's covenant with Israel, and he accepted the responsibilities of the covenant, not just the privileges.

Note: Lord God of Heaven and Earth, please give we your children, a strong disciplined and healthy prayer life, in order that we can give you honor and praise and defeat the darts and temptations of the evil one and his associate demonic angels. Thank you, Lord. Amen!

2 Chronicles 7:14

If my people, which are called by my name, shall humble themselves, and pray, and seek my face, and turn from their wicked ways; then will I hear from heaven, and will forgive their sin, and will heal their land.

Psalm 122:6

Pray for the peace of Jerusalem; they will prosper who love thee.

Lesson Plan 142

The Book of Nehemiah

Chapters 6, 7, & 8

Objective: To get an understanding of how Nehemiah who was strategically positioned in the Persian royal court, used his connections to accomplish great things on behalf of the Lord.

Objective Breakdown:

1. Introduction

2. More Opposition to the Project   Chapter 6:1-9

3. An Informer Against Nehemiah Is Hired   Chapter 6:10-14

4. The Wall is Finished   Chapter 6:15-19

5. Nehemiah Appoints Leaders   Chapter 7:1-3

6. A Record of Ezra's Census Is Found   Chapter 7:4-38

7. Priests, Levites, and Other Officials   Chapter 7:39-60

8. Some Cannot Trace Their Lineage   Chapter 7:61-65

9. The Assembly Returns to the Cities   Chapter 7:66-73

10. Ezra Reads the Book of the Law   Chapter 8:1-6

11. The People Celebrate   Chapter 8:7-12

12. The Feast of Tabernacles Is Kept   Chapter 8:13-18

Introduction:

Nehemiah the cupbearer. God often places his people in strategic positions in order to accomplish his purposes. To bring about the reconstruction of the wall at Jerusalem, God used Nehemiah, a man who perhaps closest to and most trusted by the Persian King Artaxerxes I.

As the King's cupbearer Nehemiah 1:11, Nehemiah held one of the most important assignments a courtier could have in the ancient world. Cupbearers tasted a ruler's food in order to taste its safety and endure against poisoning, whether intentional or accidental. In the Assyrian, Babylonian, and Persian courts, which were notorious for political intrigue and assassination, the cup bearer carried enormous responsibility.

Usually foreigners, cupbearers often became trusted confidants of the rulers they served. Given the nature of their position, they enjoyed unusual political privilege and prestige. It was in the ruler's self-interest to keep his tasters happy, so their requests were listened to carefully and their wishes frequently granted.

This situation worked to Jeremiah's advantage. Unburdening himself to the king about the situation at Jerusalem, he requested and received a leave of absence and letters of authority to go and rebuild the city (Nehemiah 2:3-8). Later, when his adversaries at Jerusalem threatened to falsely accuse him of rebellion (Nehemiah 6:5-9), Nehemiah must have been comforted by the fact of his close association with Artaxerxes and trust that his years of service had earned.

Where has God placed you in order to accomplish His purposes? What position and responsibility do you hold to bring about good? Like Nehemiah are you in prayer about what God is doing in your world? And are you prayerfully considering ways to leverage your influence to bring about His will? Let's hope we are.

Note: Lord God of Heaven and Earth please give we your children, a strong disciplined and healthy prayer life, in order that we can give you honor and praise and defeat the darts and temptations of the evil one and his associate demonic angels. Thank you, Lord. Amen!

2 Chronicles 7:14

If my people, which are called by my name, shall humble themselves, and pray, and seek my face, and turn from their wicked ways; then will I hear from heaven, and will forgive their sin, and will heal their land.

Psalm 122:6

Pray for the peace of Jerusalem; they will prosper who love thee.

Lesson Plan 143

The Book of Nehemiah

Chapters 9, 10, & 11

Objective: To get an understanding of how Nehemiah who was strategically positioned in the Persian royal court, used his connections to accomplish great things on behalf of the Lord.

Objective Breakdown:

Introduction:

Why start with the wall? The city of Jerusalem to which Nehemiah returned was in gross disrepair. Its temple had been restored by Ezra, but little else was functioning effectively. The wall was broken down, the gates were burned, the roads were cluttered with debris, and most of the homes and building stood vacant. It must have been depressing place to visit, let alone live.

The project of rebuilding was achievable. Restoring the city's many systems of commerce and public life required complex long-term processes. By contrast, the wall could be rebuilt in a mere 53 days (Nehemiah 6:15). Thus, Nehemiah provided a means of success to a people who had experienced nothing but defeat for decades.

The task was something in which everyone could participate. The physical labor of rebuilding the wall did not require highly technical or intellectual skills. A few carpenters and masons were needed but most of the work required nothing more complicated than lifting stones and clearing a path. Thus, everyone could get involved. As a result, the task brought them together the entire community.

Rebuilding the wall had both practical and symbolic value of restoring the security to the city. For too long, Jerusalem had been open to the domination of strongmen such as Sanballat, Tobiah, and their cronies (Nehemiah 4:1,7; 6:1). By closing up the walls, Nehemiah was improving the safety of the citizens. He was also serving notice that the Israelites were back, putting thugs and thieves out of business.

Note: Lord God of Heaven and Earth, please give we your children, a strong disciplined and healthy prayer life, in order that we can give you honor and praise and defeat the darts and temptations of the evil one and his associate demonic angels. Thank you, Lord. Amen!

2 Chronicles 7:14

If my people, which are called by my name, shall humble themselves, and pray, and seek my face, and turn from their wicked ways; then will I hear from heaven, and will forgive their sin, and will heal their land.

Psalm 122:6

Pray for the peace of Jerusalem; they will prosper who love thee.

Lesson Plan 144

The Book of Nehemiah

Chapters 12 & 13

Objective: To get an understanding of how Nehemiah who was strategically positioned in the Persian royal court, used his connections to accomplish great things on behalf of the Lord.

Objective Breakdown:

Introduction:

Who is Sanballat? He was probably the governor of Samaria during Nehemiah's time. He was in strident opposition to the rebuilding of the wall by Nehemiah, employing such tactics as ridicule, mockery, rumors, lies and letters to the king.

Sanballat (Nehemiah 4:1, 7; 6:1) is called the Horonite (Nehemiah 2:10) that he came from Beth Horon, 12 miles northwest of Jerusalem. He was descended from either a family of Israelites that may had been left behind when the northern kingdom was captured by Assyria in 722 B.C. or a racially mixed Samaritans that resulted from Assyria's resettlement of the area (2 Kings 17:24).

Tobiah the Ammonite (2 Kings 4:3, 7; 6:1) is referred to as an official literally servant which may mean that he was appointed but the Persian government or Sanballat's deputy. In any case they were both in opposition to the construction of the wall by Nehemiah.

How do you revitalize dead or dying urban neighborhoods that have many abandoned houses and buildings, few if any businesses, and an infrastructure that lying in ruin? Nehemiah came up with a novel solution for the problems in Jerusalem: let the outlying suburbs donate one-tenth of their people to move into the city (Nehemiah 11:1-2). In effect, the districts surrounding Jerusalem, tithe people for the purpose of community development.

Nehemiah's recruitment program for the re population of Jerusalem involved casting lots to determine who would relocate (Nehemiah 11:2). Those who were selected were blessed.

Note: Lord God of Heaven and Earth, please give we your children, a strong disciplined and healthy prayer life, in order that we can give you honor and praise and defeat the darts and temptations of the evil one and his associate demonic angels. Thank you, Lord. Amen!

2 Chronicles 7:14

If my people, which are called by my name, shall humble themselves, and pray, and seek my face, and turn from their wicked ways; then will I hear from heaven, and will forgive their sin, and will heal their land.

Psalm 122:6

Pray for the peace of Jerusalem; they will prosper who love thee.

The Book of Esther

Scripture Focus Chapters 1-10

Objective: To learn of a young Jewish woman in Persia (Esther), who becomes the Queen of Persia, and saves her people (the Jews) from annihilation.

Objective Breakdown:

Lesson Plan 145

The Book of Esther

Chapters 1, 2, & 3

Objective: To learn of a young Jewish Woman in Persia (Esther) who becomes Queen of Persia and saves her people (the Jews) from annihilation.

Objective Breakdown:

1. Introduction

2. King Ahasuerus Holds a Feast   Chapter 1:1-9

3. Vashti Refuses to Parade Her Beauty   Chapter 1:10-15

4. Vashti Is Deposed by Royal Decree   Chapter 1:16-22

5. Esther Prepares to Meet the King   Chapter 2:1-11

6. Ahasuerus Makes Esther His Queen   Chapter 2:12-18

7. Mordecai Reveals a Conspiracy   Chapter 2:19-23

8. Haman Is Promoted   Chapter 3:1-6

9. Haman Is Permitted to Destroy the Jews   Chapter 3:7-11

10. A Decree of Mass Execution Is Sent   Chapter 3:12-15

Introduction:

Esther is the only book of the bible that does not mention or allude to God. In that sense, it is the "secular" book of Scripture, for that reason, the meaning of Esther has been debated for centuries. Some has been denied that it should be regarded as God's Word. Others have defended its inspiration, but then ignored it. Some early Christians allegorized it. Interestingly, many Christians in Iran, the modern-day successor to ancient Persia, where story took place take a very literal view.

Questions about the interpretation of Esther will probably continue, but two lines of thought are worth considering. First, even though God's name does not appear in the book, God's purposes do. A theological high point occurs in the narrative when Mordecai informs his young cousin (Esther) about a genocidal plot against the Jews. He warns her that she is mistaken if she thinks she can escape death simply because she has been queen.

Then Mordecai challenges Esther to act. He seems unaffected if she chooses not to: "If you remain completely silent at this time, relief and deliverance will arise for the Jews from another place," He confidently says (Esther 4:14), in what is taken as a quiet display of faith in God's protection. Then he adds, "Yet who knows whether you have come to the kingdom for such a time as this?"

Apparently, Esther concurred, because she asked Mordecai to have all the Jews fast for three days clearly an act of religious devotion. (See the Value of fasting at 1 Chronicles 10:12). After Haman's plot is exposed and he is executed, the tables are turned, and the Jews are allowed to destroy their enemies. At first, they kill more than 500 men (Esther 9:1-10). Then Esther asks for a second day of vengeance, and they kill 75,300 (Esther 9:15-17).

2 Chronicles 7:14

If my people, which are called by my name, shall humble themselves, and pray, and seek my face, and turn from their wicked ways; then will I hear from heaven, and will forgive their sin, and will heal their land.

Psalm 122:6

Pray for the peace of Jerusalem; they will prosper who love thee.

Lesson Plan 146

The Book of Esther

Chapters 4, 5, 6, & 7

Objective: To learn of a young Jewish woman in Persia (Esther) who becomes Queen of Persia and saves her people (the Jews) from annihilation.

Objective Breakdown:

1. Introduction

2. Mordecai Mourns and Esther Hears of It   Chapter 4:1-9

3. Esther Agrees to Speak to the King   Chapter 4:10-17

4. The King Grants Audience to Esther   Chapter 5:1-8

5. Haman Prepares a Gallows for Mordecai   Chapter 5:9-14

6. The King Decides to Honor Mordecai   Chapter 6:1-10

7. Haman Is Humiliated and Dejected   Chapter 6:11-14

8. Esther Intercedes for Her People   Chapter 7:1-4

9. Haman Is Hanged on His Own Gallows   Chapter 7:5-10

Introduction:

Every man king of his own castle. Fear of woman learning to exert themselves is nothing new, as the account of Esther shows. Queen Vashti's refusal to parade her beauty at her husband's men only, week-long drinking-fest (Esther 1:5-12) was officially interpreted as nothing less than an act of rebellion against male authority (Esther 1:16-17). As a result, the King Ahasuerus fired off a decree intended to reinforce the mastery of every male in the empire over women in his household (Esther 1:22).

It would be perilous to try and judge ancient cultures and customs against modern understandings of gender issues. Nevertheless, it seems clear that some of the men of Persia felt threatened by Queen Vashti's self-will. Perhaps they felt social chaos that might result if women refused to comply with their husbands' wishes, no matter how disregarding those wishes might be.

Many men today display similar fears about assertive and independent women. The Book of Esther can help by showing the value of a women with strong character. Vashti's successor, Esther, also showed assertiveness by not waiting to be called by Ahasuerus, but entering into his presence on her own initiative, at the risk of her life (Esther 4:11;5:1-3). As a result, she saved her people the Jews from genocide.

Esther is hardly the Bible's last word on the subject of authority in female and male relationships (See Ephesians 5:21-29 and James 4:7). In any case Esther encourages women to speak their minds and assert their wills to combat evil and promote good.

2 Chronicles 7:14

If my people, which are called by my name, shall humble themselves, and pray, and seek my face, and turn from their wicked ways; then will I hear from heaven, and will forgive their sin, and will heal their land.

Psalm 122:6

Pray for the peace of Jerusalem; they will prosper who love thee.

Lesson Plan 147

The Book of Esther

Chapters 8, 9, & 10

Objective: To learn of a young Jewish woman in Persia (Esther) who becomes Queen of Persia and saves her people (the Jews) from annihilation.

Objective Breakdown:

1. Introduction

2. Esther Pleads Again for Her People   Chapter 8:1-6

3. Ahasuerus Revokes Haman's Decree   Chapter 8:7-10

4. The Jews Are Permitted to Retaliate   Chapter 8:11-17

5. The Jews Defeat Their Enemies   Chapter 9:1-10

6. Haman's Ten Sons Are Hanged   Chapter 9:11-17

7. A Celebration Is Held   Chapter 9:18-25

8. The Feast of Purim Is Decreed   Chapter 9:26-32

9. Mordecai Is Promoted   Chapter 10:1-3

Introduction:

New acquaintances—old enemies. Sin involves more than just personal misdeeds. It can extend into family histories and become incorporated into public policy and cultural systems. The enmity between Haman and Mordecai (Esther 3:2-6) showed that principal at work. At first glance, the hostility between the two men appears to be a simple case of disrespect on Mordecai's part (Esther 3:2) possibly for religious reasons, although the text does not say so, and racial prejudice on Haman's part (Esther 3:6).

The Book of Esther stresses that haman was the son of Hammedatha the Agagite (Esther 3:1, 10; 8:3, 5; 9:24). Tradition holds that the Agagites, were descendants of Agag, the Amalekite king whom Saul, Israel's first king had failed to kill, disobeying the Lord's instruction (1 Samuel 15). The Amalekites stood under permanent judgment of God for attacking the Israelites during their journey from Egypt to Canaan (Exodus 17:8-13; Deuteronomy 25:17-19).

Now with Haman's rise to power, the Amalekites were in a sense threatening once again to destroy God's people. But this time, the Lord used Mordecai to frustrate the plan. Ironically, Mordecai was descended from Kish (Esther 2:5) the same family of Benjamites from which Saul had come (1 Samuel (9:1). Thus, in the end, Mordecai carried out what Saul had failed to accomplish (Esther 7:10; 9:4-5; 13-15).

2 Chronicles 7:14

If my people, which are called by my name, shall humble themselves, and pray, and seek my face, and turn from their wicked ways; then will I hear from heaven, and will forgive their sin, and will heal their land.

Psalm 122:6

Pray for the peace of Jerusalem; they will prosper who love thee.

The Book of Job

Scripture Focus Chapters 1-42

Objective: To gain insight on how Job dealt with the fundamental questions of evil, suffering, justice, the meaning of life, the value of life and how human beings can understand God's ways.

Objective Breakdown:

1. Introduction

2. Job and His Family Prosper   Chapter 1:1-5

3. Satan Questions Job's Character   Chapter 1:6-12

4. Job Loses His Children and Possessions   Chapter 1:13-19

5. Job Humbles Himself Before the Lord   Chapter 1:20-22

6. Satan Slurs Job's Character Again   Chapter 2:1-6

7. Satan Strikes Job with Boils   Chapter 2:7-10

8. Job's Three Friends Come to Comfort Him   Chapter 2:11-13

9. Job Curses the Day of His Birth   Chapter 3:1-10

10. Job Longs for Death to End His Misery   Chapter 3:11-26

11. Eliphaz Wonders What Has Befallen Job   Chapter 4:1-11

12. Can Anyone Be Pure Before God?   Chapter 4:12-21

13. Eliphaz Would Seek God for Protection   Chapter 5:1-16

14. Job Should Respect God's Correction   Chapter 5:17-27

15. Job Replies in Agony   Chapter 6:1-13

16. More Kindness is in Order from a Friend   Chapter 6:14-23

17. Job Asks Where He Has Gone Wrong   Chapter 6:24-30

18. Job Bemoans the Weariness of Life   Chapter 7:1-10

19. Job Wants to Be Left Alone or Pardoned   Chapter 7:11-21

20. Bildad: Job Should Repent Before God   Chapter 8:1-18

Lesson Plan 148

The Book of Job

Chapters 1, 2, & 3

Objective: To gain insight on how Job dealt with the fundamental questions of evil, suffering, justice, the meaning of life, the value of life and how human beings can understand God's ways.

Objective Breakdown:

1. Introduction

2. Job and His Family Prosper   Chapter 1:1-5

3. Satan Questions Job's Character   Chapter 1:6-12

4. Job Loses His Children and Possessions   Chapter 1:13-19

5. Job Humbles Himself Before the Lord   Chapter 1:20-22

6. Satan Slurs Job's Character Again   Chapter 2:1-6

7. Satan Strikes Job with Boils   Chapter 2:7-10

8. Job's Three Friends Come to Comfort Him   Chapter 2:11-13

9. Job Curses the Day of His Birth   Chapter 3:1-10

10. Job Longs for Death to End His Misery   Chapter 3:11-26

Introduction:

Blaming Satan: A common view today is that Satan (Job 1:6) is not a real person, but just a mythological way ancient people had of explaining evil and suffering. However, the Book of Job does not support that view, nor does the rest of the Bible.

Notice particularly how Satan figures in this book. He appears in the first two chapters, but then completely drops out of the narrative. Most of the rest of the book contains a discussion between Job's and his four friends as they try to make sense of Job's trials. But nothing is heard directly from or about Satan again. The speakers propose numerous suggestions and insights concerning suffering, but they never resort to blaming Satan or even to mention him.

These important implications for believers today, especially given that we live in a society with an increasing secular worldview. On the one hand, the Book of Job shows us that Satan does exists and does influence what happens to individuals. In other words, we live in a universe where the supernatural affects day to day life. We cannot dismiss the Bible's teaching about angels and demons as nothing but myths from the past.

Yet on the other hand, the Book of Job cautions us against just blaming Satan for the troubles we face. Job and his friends disagree on the exact cause of Job's sufferings, but they agree that people are morally responsible for the choices they make. Their focus is not so much on Satan as their adversary as it is on God as their Judge (Job 5:8, 17; 8:3-6; 9:1-3; 11:5-6).

2 Chronicles 7:14

If my people, which are called by my name, shall humble themselves, and pray, and seek my face, and turn from their wicked ways; then will I hear from heaven, and will forgive their sin, and will heal their land.

Psalm 122:6

Pray for the peace of Jerusalem; they will prosper who love thee.

Lesson Plan 149

The Book of Job

Chapters 4, 5, & 6

Objective: To gain insight on how Job dealt with the fundamental questions of evil, suffering, justice, the meaning of life, the value of life and how human beings can understand God's ways.

Objective Breakdown: Land of Uz

1. Introduction

2. Eliphaz Wonders What Has Befallen Job   Chapter 4:1-11

3. Can Anyone Be Pure Before God?   Chapter 4:12-21

4. Eliphaz Would Seek God for Protection   Chapter 5:1-16

5. Job Should Respect God's Correction   Chapter 5:17-27

6. Job Replies in Agony   Chapter 6:1-13

7. More Kindness is in Order from a Friend   Chapter 6:14-23

8. Job Asks Where He Has Gone Wrong   Chapter 6:24-30

Introduction:

No one knows the exact location of Job's homeland, the land of Uz (Job 1:1). However, the Bible states or suggest several things about Uz:

a. It was located in the East (Job 1:3). This probably means somewhere East of the Jordan river.

b. Job's friend came from Teman (Job 2:11), known to be in Edom (See Genesis 36:8; Jeremiah 49:20).

c. Teman was the grandson of Esau (Genesis 36:11), and the region of Teman was probably named for him. It seems appropriate that Eliphaz was a Temanite, for apparently the Temanites had a reputation for wisdom (Jeremiah 49:7).

d. Uz was accessible to Sabean raiders (Job 1:15). The Sabeans were inhabitants of Sheba,   probably in the mountainous region of southwest Arabia (now Yemen).

e. Uz was also accessible to Chaldean raiders (Job 1:17). Chaldea was the small territory of southern Babylon bordering the head of the Persian Gulf between the Arabian Desert and the Euphrates delta.

f.   Jeremiah named Uz in a list of kingdoms and peoples including Judah, Egypt, Philistia, Edom, Moab, Ammon, Tyre, Sidon, and others (Jeremiah 25:17-26).

g.   The book of Lamentations seems to indicate that Edom and Uz were nearly the same (Lamentations 4:21). The parallelism of the Hebrew poetry used at the introduction to Job provides perhaps the strongest indication that Edom and Uz were one and the same or close to it.

2 Chronicles 7:14

If my people, which are called by my name, shall humble themselves, and pray, and seek my face, and turn from their wicked ways; then will I hear from heaven, and will forgive their sin, and will heal their land.

Psalm 122:6

Pray for the peace of Jerusalem; they will prosper who love thee.

Lesson Plan 150

The Book of Job

Chapters 7, 8, & 9

Objective: To gain insight on how Job dealt with the fundamental questions of evil, suffering, justice, the meaning of life, the value of life and how human beings can understand God's ways.

Objective Breakdown: Land of Uz

1. Introduction

2. Job Bemoans the Weariness of Life	Chapter 7:1-10
3. Job Wants to Be Left Alone or Pardoned	Chapter 7:11-21
4. Bildad: Job Should Repent Before God	Chapter 8:1-18
5. God Would Not Cast Away the Blameless	Chapter 8:19-22
6. Job: Who Can Be Righteous Before God?	Chapter 9:1-13
7. If God Isn't Behind This Then Who?	Chapter 9:14-24
8. Job Has No Way to Make His Case	Chapter 9:25-33

Introduction:

Sudden Calamity: Almost by definition, disaster usually strikes suddenly and without warning. Even though people know that earthquakes, famine, accidents, and deaths are bound to occur, they are still shocked when they do.

The tragedies that claimed Job's possessions and family (Job 1:13-17) came suddenly and without warning. In hindsight, we can guess that Job surely knew of the ever-present risks under which he and his family lived: bands of Sabean raiders (Job 1:15), lightning (the "fire of God," Job 1:16), bands of Chaldeans on the prowl for fresh camels (Job 11:17), and windstorms (Job 1:19). Yet even though he must have known that sooner or later he would confront dangers like these. Job was still thunderstruck when news of their concurrence reached him (Job 1:20).

In this way Job and his family were like most people, then and now: conscious of the risks, but living out their lives in day-to-day routines. Then when calamity strikes, their world is turned upside down. Jesus warned that at the end of the ages would be similar. People would be going about their routines—

eating and drinking, marrying, and giving in marriage—forgetful of the fact the Lord is returning, no one knows when (Matthew 24:38, 42). Jesus has urged us as His followers to be "ready" by faithfully going about the responsibilities that He has entrusted to us (Mathew 24:44-46).

2 Chronicles 7:14

If my people, which are called by my name, shall humble themselves, and pray, and seek my face, and turn from their wicked ways; then will I hear from heaven, and will forgive their sin, and will heal their land.

Psalm 122:6

Pray for the peace of Jerusalem; they will prosper who love thee.

Lesson Plan 151

The Book of Job

Chapters 10, 11, & 12

Objective: To gain insight on how Job dealt with the fundamental questions of evil, suffering, justice, the meaning of life, the value of life and how human beings can understand God's ways.

Objective Breakdown: Land of Uz

1. Introduction

2. Job Pleads His Humanity   Chapter 10:1-7

3. God Is Job's Maker and Knows Him   Chapter 10:8-17

4. Why Did God Let Job Be Born?   Chapter 10:18-22

5. Zophar Challenges Job   Chapter 11:1-9

6. Job Should Make a Clean Confession   Chapter 11:10-20

7. Job Feels Mocked by His Friends   Chapter 12:1-6

8. The Sovereign God Must Have Done This   Chapter 12:7-25

Introduction:

The sons of God. The term "sons of God" (Job 2:1; compare Job 1:6; 38:7) refers here to the angels, heavenly beings who are superior to humans in power and intelligence (see Matthew 8: 28-34). According to the Book of Job these beings would periodically present themselves before God, though we know little about the gatherings.

It may seem strange to find Satan mentioned as one of the "sons of God." Elsewhere Scripture describes him as an angel who was cast out of heaven for rebelling against God (see Luke 11:14). Now he seeks to undermine the cause of righteousness in the world. In fact, the name Satan means "Adversary."

The Hebrew word for "son" bar, can refer not only to an immediate male offspring, but also to a member of an entire class or category. For example, the Old Testament speaks of the "sons of Israel" (Exodus 28:9) to refer to the descendants of Israel (Jacob), the Israelites. Likewise, the sons of Asaph (1 Chronicles 25:1) refers to temple musicians descended from Asaph, King David's principal musician.

In Job, the term "sons of God" is a descriptive term meaning "from or made by God," in a sense angel, fallen or not, are spirits and inhabit the supernatural realm.

2 Chronicles 7:14

If my people, which are called by my name, shall humble themselves, and pray, and seek my face, and turn from their wicked ways; then will I hear from heaven, and will forgive their sin, and will heal their land.

Psalm 122:6

Pray for the peace of Jerusalem; they will prosper who love thee.

Lesson Plan 152

The Book of Job

Chapters 13, 14, & 15

Objective: To gain insight on how Job dealt with the fundamental questions of evil, suffering, justice, the meaning of life, the value of life and how human beings can understand God's ways.

Objective Breakdown:

1. Introduction

2. Job Condemns His Friends' Advice   Chapter 13:1-12

3. Job Calls on God Not to Abandon Him   Chapter 13:13-27

4. The Mortality of a Man   Chapter 13:28

5. The Mortality of a Man (cont.)   Chapter 14:1-6

6. Death Ends a Man's Life on Earth   Chapter 14:7-12

7. Job Looks Forward to His Death   Chapter 14:13-22

8. Eliphaz: Job's Own Words Condemn Him   Chapter 15:1-6

9. Human Words Cannot Be Trusted   Chapter 15:7-16

10. Trouble Comes to the Wicked   Chapter 15:17-26

11. The Wealth of the Rich Is Temporary   Chapter 15:27-35

Introduction:

Satan can go only so far. Given all the evil and suffering in the world, some people argue that God must not exist, or that if He does exist, He must not be in control. But the Book of Job affirms that not only does God exist, He sets the limit on evil. For example, he told Satan that although he was allowed to touch Job's body, he could not take his life (Job 2:6). Earlier God limited Satan's destructive power to Job's possessions (Job 1:12).

God's sovereignty is a comforting thought as we contend with an increasing chaotic world. God may allow evil in His world, but He will allow it only so far before He cuts it back. Ultimately, He will do away with all sin and evil and those who promote it, handing over the rule of His perfect creation to His

Son, Jesus Christ (1 Corinthians 15:24-28; Philippians 2:9-11).

When Adam and Eve disobeyed God and thereby allowed sin to enter the world, God immediately responded by placing limits on the evil. He refused to let it go unchecked. There can be no question that evil and pain pose a massive problem to faith in and obedience toward God. Theology offers no knock down solution, but the Bible (God's Word) does give us ground to stand on as we try to live in a world where suffering is real.

2 Chronicles 7:14

If my people, which are called by my name, shall humble themselves, and pray, and seek my face, and turn from their wicked ways; then will I hear from heaven, and will forgive their sin, and will heal their land.

Psalm 122:6

Pray for the peace of Jerusalem; they will prosper who love thee.

Lesson Plan 153

The Book of Job

Chapters 16, 17, & 18

Objective: To gain insight on how Job dealt with the fundamental questions of evil, suffering, justice, the meaning of life, the value of life and how human beings can understand God's ways.

Objective Breakdown:

1. Introduction

2. Job: I Am Delivered to the Ungodly   Chapter 16:1-17

3. Job Begs for a Just Hearing   Chapter 16:18-22

4. Job Begs for a Just Hearing (cont.)   Chapter 17:1-9

5. Job Feels Completely Hopeless   Chapter 17:10-16

6. Bildad Responds Angrily to Job   Chapter 18:1-4

7. Such Is the End of the Sinful   Chapter 18:5-21

Introduction:

Little security in Job's world. Job doesn't explain what "the thing I greatly feared" was (Job 3:25). but there was little security in the world in which he lived. The dangers were many:

a. diseases that struck livestock and people;

b. famine, drought, and crop failure;

c. destructive pests such as locusts and worms, and predators such as lions and wolves;

d. weather-related calamities such as thunderstorms and tornadoes and lighting, floods, hail, windstorms and tornadoes;

f. bandits, raiders, and foreign invaders; and

g. stillbirths and death to women due to complications in labor.

Job had lost his wealth, family, and health due to a number of these perils. The suddenness and enormity of his downfall is a reminder that the people of ancient world lived on the edge, never far from complete ruin.

There was little they could do to protect themselves. For example, the catastrophic loss of Job's wealth points to the fact that there were no banks. Most of Job's wealth were on hoof in the fields, extremely vulnerable to danger and loss.

One way that ancient people tried to protect their valuables was to bury them in the ground beneath their tents or houses.

2 Chronicles 7:14

If my people, which are called by my name, shall humble themselves, and pray, and seek my face, and turn from their wicked ways; then will I hear from heaven, and will forgive their sin, and will heal their land.

Psalm 122:6

Pray for the peace of Jerusalem; they will prosper who love thee.

Lesson Plan 154

The Book of Job

Chapters 19, 20, & 21

Objective: To gain insight on how Job dealt with the fundamental questions of evil, suffering, justice, the meaning of life, the value of life and how human beings can understand God's ways.

Objective Breakdown:

1. Introduction

2. Job Feels Tormented by His Friends   Chapter 19:1-12

3. All Have Forsaken Job   Chapter 19:13-22

4. Job Still Hopes for Redemption   Chapter 19:23-29

5. Zophar: A Hypocrite's Joy Is Fleeting   Chapter 20:1-11

6. A Man's Wickedness Will Overtake Him   Chapter 20:12-29

7. Job: Why Do the Wicked Prosper?   Chapter 21:1-16

8. The Wicked Are Blessed in This World   Chapter 21:17-26

9. A Day of Doom Awaits the Wicked   Chapter 21:27-34

Introduction:

Why? Faced with sudden tragedy, such as the loss of health, wealth, or a loved one, the natural question to ask is: Why? Why did this happen? Why did this happen to me? Why now?

Job struggled with questions of why as he tried to make sense of the sufferings (Job 7:20-21). So did Jesus' disciples when they came upon a man who had been born blind. "Who sinned?"they asked Jesus. "This man or his parents?" (John 9:1-2). They were asking why in the sense of causality: What was the reason for his blindness? They assumed somehow sin must have been involved.

Yet on another level, the disciples were asking why in in a sense of purpose: What was the significance for the man's blindness? In reply, Jesus borrowed an answer from Job. He assured the disciples that through the man's blindness, the glorious works of God would be made evident (John 9:3-5). Then, He fulfilled that claim by healing the man both on a physical and spiritual level.

Job, too, eventually realized the awesome glory and grace of God as a result of His sufferings (Job 42:1-6). That should offer some comfort to those of us today who face seemingly senseless tragedy. The pain is real and must not be denied. But someday we will see the glory of God, even in the things that we suffer. We have the assurance of Job and Jesus on that. And if Jesus said it, you can take it to the bank.

2 Chronicles 7:14

If my people, which are called by my name, shall humble themselves, and pray, and seek my face, and turn from their wicked ways; then will I hear from heaven, and will forgive their sin, and will heal their land.

Psalm 122:6

Pray for the peace of Jerusalem; they will prosper who love thee.

Lesson Plan 155

The Book of Job

Chapters 22, 23, & 24

Objective: To gain insight on how Job dealt with the fundamental questions of evil, suffering, justice, the meaning of life, the value of life and how human beings can understand God's ways.

Objective Breakdown:

1. Introduction

2. Eliphaz Accuses Job of Wickedness   Chapter 22:1-11

3. God Sees and Knows Everything   Chapter 22:12-20

4. Eliphaz Urges Job to Return to God   Chapter 22:21-30

5. Job Seeks God but Cannot Find Him   Chapter 23:1-12

6. Job Is Terrified by God   Chapter 23:13-17

7. God Seems Not to Notice Wickedness   Chapter 24:1-12

8. Criminals Count on Not Being Detected   Chapter 24:13-21

9. The Righteous Are Soon Taken Away   Chapter 24:22-25

Introduction:

Learning to pray for your family. Our families can be a source of both joy and sorrow in our lives. Job saw his children as great blessing and was overwhelmed with grief when they were suddenly and tragically taken away. In the midst of his despair, he cried out to God, wishing that he had never been born (Job 10:18-22).

Do you use prayer to talk to God about the tragedies and triumphs of your family life? Do you pray about long-term concerns as well? The Bible give us numerous examples of people who prayed about their families. Their prayers tend to be honest expressions about belonging to community where love and sin exist. By considering their prayers, you can gain insight into how to pray constructively about family situation. Below are some examples of praying for their families:

a. Abraham prayed about his and Sarah's lack of child, grieving that he had no heir (Genesis 15:1-6).

b. Abraham's servant prayed for help in finding a wife for Isaac (Genesis 24:12-14).

c. Isaac Prayed about Rebekah barrenness (Genesis 25:21).

d. Jacob prayed in preparation for meeting in estranged brother Esau, whom he had not seen in many years (Genesis 32:9-12).

e. Moses prayed for God's mercy on his brother Aaron after the incident with the golden calf (Deuteronomy 9:20).

f. Hannah prayed for a son and promised to give him back to God if He would end her barrenness (1 Samuel 1:9-20).

g. David prayed that God would spare the life of his infant son born to Bathsheba (2 Samuel 12:15-16).

h. David prayed for his son Solomon, that God would grant him a faithful heart to lead Israel and build the temple (1 Chronicles 29:16-19).

Do you pray for your family? Do you let God hear your deepest feelings and hopes for them? God longs for you to express yourself to Him for them.

2 Chronicles 7:14

If my people, which are called by my name, shall humble themselves, and pray, and seek my face, and turn from their wicked ways; then will I hear from heaven, and will forgive their sin, and will heal their land.

Psalm 122:6

Pray for the peace of Jerusalem; they will prosper who love thee.

Lesson Plan 156

The Book of Job

Chapters 25, 26, 27, & 28

Objective: To gain insight on how Job dealt with the fundamental questions of evil, suffering, justice, the meaning of life, the value of life and how human beings can understand God's ways.

Objective Breakdown:

1. Introduction

2. Bildad: No One Is Righteous Before God   Chapter 25:1-6

3. Job: How Could Anyone Know God's Mind?   Chapter 26:1-14

4. Job Affirms His Righteousness   Chapter 27:1-12

5. The Destiny of the Wicked   Chapter 27:13-23

6. People Search the Earth for Riches   Chapter 28:1-11

7. No Amount of Searching Reveals Wisdom   Chapter 28:12-19

8. The Fear of the Lord Is Wisdom   Chapter 28:20-28

Introduction:

Is there life after death? Throughout history people have wondered whether this life is all there is. Is there a heaven or hell? Or does it all end here? Job asked that same questions as he contemplated his sufferings (Job 14:14). He believed that death would end his pain (Job 14:13); but would it also end his existence? Elsewhere Job described death as the "way of no return" (Job 16:22) and the "king of terrors" (Job 18:14). At times it appears that Job did not have a particularly positive outlook as he faced the end of life.

Yet even in readings bout Job's prospective on death, it is important to remember that he was working from a smaller knowledge base than God's people have today. He probably had no written portion of Scripture, and he was unfamiliar with the work of Jesus to deliver people from sin and death (Romans 6:23; 1 Corinthians 15:20-28).

Yet even with these important truths, Job had a certain confidence that he would see God after death. In fact, his strong declaration of faith, beginning with the words, "I know that my Redeemer lives" (Job

19:25-27), has provided hope for people for generations.

Whatever questions about death may have lingered from the days of Job, Jesus answered them when he declared, "He who believes in Me, though he may die, he shall live" (John 11:25). For that reason, Jesus' followers can celebrate even in the midst of grief and mourning over loss of friends and loved ones. Jesus has promised eternal life to believers, free from all tears, sorrow, and pain (Revelation 21:4) that is why when it comes to death, Christians are a people of hope.

2 Chronicles 7:14

If my people, which are called by my name, shall humble themselves, and pray, and seek my face, and turn from their wicked ways; then will I hear from heaven, and will forgive their sin, and will heal their land.

Psalm 122:6

Pray for the peace of Jerusalem; they will prosper who love thee.

Lesson Plan 157

The Book of Job

Chapters 29, 30, & 31

Objective: To gain insight on how Job dealt with the fundamental questions of evil, suffering, justice, the meaning of life, the value of life and how human beings can understand God's ways.

Objective Breakdown:

1. Introduction

2. Job Longs for the Old Days   Chapter 29:1-6

3. Job Once Had the Respect of His Peers   Chapter 29:7-17

4. Job Reflects on How Good Life Was   Chapter 29:18-25

5. Now Vile Men Mock and Persecute Job   Chapter 30:1-15

6. Job Lives in Misery and Affliction   Chapter 30:16-31

7. Job Maintains His Purity   Chapter 31:1-12

8. Job Says He Has Not Abused Others   Chapter 31:13-23

9. Job Has Not Honored Wealth, But God   Chapter 31:24-40

Introduction:

An inventory of evil. One of the best ways to assess the integrity of someone's' heart is to look at that person's treatment of the poor and disadvantaged. Job recognized that principle. He knew God takes a special interest in downcast. In fact, Job was distressed because he knew of evils against the poor that were going unpunished.

Job mentioned what some of those evils were. His list provides a useful inventory by which anyone can self-evaluate character:

(1) Do you cheat in business or steal other people's possessions (Job 24:2)?

(2) Do you take away the resources of the powerless and drive them into needless debt (Job 24:3)?

(3) Do you abuse the poor and force them out of your way (Job 24:4)?

(4) Do you cause the poor to lose work, so that they must fend for themselves as best they can to find food, clothing, and shelter (Job 24:5-8)?

(5) Do you lock powerless people into situations and systems that bleed them but benefit you (Job 24:9-10)?

(6) Do you live lavishly, even as people nearby dying for lack of basic resources (Job 24:11- 12)?

Job had been an extremely wealthy man (Job 1:3), so he probably knew many people who practiced these evils. As we read Job's six-point inventory of evil, how do we score? We need to learn of the ways that God wants us to go and walks in those ways. "His ways."

2 Chronicles 7:14

If my people, which are called by my name, shall humble themselves, and pray, and seek my face, and turn from their wicked ways; then will I hear from heaven, and will forgive their sin, and will heal their land.

Psalm 122:6

Pray for the peace of Jerusalem; they will prosper who love thee.

Lesson Plan 158

The Book of Job

Chapters 32, 33, & 34

Objective: To gain insight on how Job dealt with the fundamental questions of evil, suffering, justice, the meaning of life, the value of life and how human beings can understand God's ways.

Objective Breakdown:

1. Introduction

2. Elihu Declares His Wrath   Chapter 32:1-14

3. Elihu Is Bursting with Things to Say   Chapter 32:15-22

4. Elihu Refutes Job's Innocence   Chapter 33:1-18

5. God Will Heed the Prayer of Repentance   Chapter 33:19-33

6. Elihu Reviews Job's Complaint   Chapter 34:1-9

7. God Cannot Do Evil   Chapter 34:10-15

8. God Is Just and Impartial   Chapter 34:16-20

9. God Sees and Repays Everything   Chapter 34:21-30

10. Elihu Rebukes Job's Statements   Chapter 34:31-37

Introduction:

Naked before God. It is easy to forget that ultimately, we will stand naked before God (Job 1:20-21; 26:6). We can surround ourselves with clothing, houses cars, and other possessions that hide our true condition. Yet in the end all of that will slip away, and then we must consider: what will we have left?

The author of Ecclesiastes faced that issue. Like Job, he was one of the wealthiest and wisest men who ever lived. Yet after taking his kingdom to the height of its prosperity, he wrote, 'he wrote, as a person came from his mother's womb, naked shall he return" (Ecclesiastes 5:15). An Arab proverb offers a similar perspective: "There are no pockets in a burial shroud."

So, we cannot rely on our possessions when we stand before God, what will we present? At least Job had his integrity and righteousness (Job 27:2-6). How much of that will we have when we stand before

God? Ultimately, our standing must be determined by Christ's work on our behalf (Philippians 3:9). Nevertheless, God will evaluate our character and how we lived our lives—either to His glory or to our shame (1 Corinthians 3:9-15; 2 Corinthians 5:1-11).

2 Chronicles 7:14

If my people, which are called by my name, shall humble themselves, and pray, and seek my face, and turn from their wicked ways; then will I hear from heaven, and will forgive their sin, and will heal their land.

Psalm 122:6

Pray for the peace of Jerusalem; they will prosper who love thee.

Lesson Plan 159

The Book of Job

Chapters 35, 36, 37, & 38

Objective: To gain insight on how Job dealt with the fundamental questions of evil, suffering, justice, the meaning of life, the value of life and how human beings can understand God's ways.

Objective Breakdown:

1. Introduction

2. Elihu Says Job Is Being Self-Righteous   Chapter 35:1-8

3. Job Has Uttered Empty Talk Against God   Chapter 35:9-16

4. Elihu Proclaims God's Goodness   Chapter 36:1-15

5. Elihu Thinks Job Is Being Judged   Chapter 36:16-21

6. The Power and Greatness of God   Chapter 36:22-33

7. The Creator Oversees the Earth   Chapter 37:1-13

8. Consider the Works of God   Chapter 37:14-24

9. God the Creator Himself Questions Job   Chapter 38:1-11

10. God Made Dawn, Sea, and Snow   Chapter 38:12-24

11. Rain, Stars, and Weather Are from God   Chapter 38:25-33

12. God Takes Care of Animals   Chapter 38:34-41

Introduction:

A new set of friends. Pain is a great leveler. Whether one is high and mighty or lowly and unknown, physical and emotional suffering attack without discrimination, treating one the same as another. Job discovered that truth, and in the process found a whole new set of friends—the poor (Job 31:13-29).

Before his troubles, Job had been a champion of the poor (see Job 29:12-17). But his wealth and position of importance in the community had probably distanced him from the pain. Not unlike many government officials and well to do citizens today, he was aware of their plight, but never experienced it himself.

The series of disasters struck, and overnight Job was reduced to poverty. As a result, the poor were no longer a class of people that needed help, but fellow suffers with whom Job was in the same boat. He began to identify with slaves who feared unjust treatment from their masters (Job 31:13). He now understood what widows and orphans felt when they were forced to go without food, clothing and shelter while watching others living in luxury (Job 31:16-21; see and compare Job 24:2-12).

In the end Job discovered a new sense of equality as a result of his downfall: "Did not He who made me in the womb make them?" He asked rhetorically (Job 31:15). He realized that people are basically the same. Possessions and positions have nothing to do with their fundamental humanity.

Perhaps one reason that Job was able to come to that conclusion had to do with the Near Eastern culture in which he lived. Modern Westerners tend to interpret Job's situation as a case study in personal suffering. To them, the key issue to resolve would be, "Why is this happening to me?"

Job's experience challenges Bible readers today to consider what it would take for us to befriend the friendless and seek justice for the powerless.

2 Chronicles 7:14

If my people, which are called by my name, shall humble themselves, and pray, and seek my face, and turn from their wicked ways; then will I hear from heaven, and will forgive their sin, and will heal their land.

Psalm 122:6

Pray for the peace of Jerusalem; they will prosper who love thee.

Lesson Plan 160

The Book of Job

Chapters 39, 40, 41, & 42

Objective: To gain insight on how Job dealt with the fundamental questions of evil, suffering, justice, the meaning of life, the value of life and how human beings can understand God's ways.

Objective Breakdown:

1. Introduction

2. God Takes Care of Animals (cont.)   Chapter 39:1-12

3. God Allocates Wisdom and Abilities   Chapter 39:13-30

4. Job Is Silenced Before God   Chapter 40:1-5

5. God Exposes Job's Limited Viewpoint   Chapter 40:6-14

6. God Made the Mighty Behemoth   Chapter 40:15-24

7. God Made the Fierce Leviathan   Chapter 41:1-34

8. Job Confesses His Ignorance   Chapter 42:1-6

9. Job Offers Sacrifices for His Friends   Chapter 42:7-11

10. God Restores Job's Family and Fortune   Chapter 42:12-17

Introduction:

Leviathan. No one knows the identity of the creature that Scripture calls Leviathan (Job 41:1). The name comes from a Hebrew word which means "twisted" and a handful of biblical descriptions suggest a serpent like creature living in water. Thus, some have suggested that Leviathan refers to the whale or the crocodile. Leviathan is mentioned five times in Scripture.

Job 3:8. Leviathan is to be aroused in a way that upsets the stars and the planets. Many believe that Job was referring to the popular idea in the ancient world that a great dragon cause eclipses by devouring or wrapping its coils around the sun.

Job 41. The second description of the Leviathan in Job is quite lengthy and seems to match the characteristics of the crocodile (for example, (Job 41:13, 15).

Psalm 74:14. Leviathan seems to be used symbolically to refer to Pharaoh who was destroyed in the crossing of the Red Sea (Exodus 14:26-29).

Psalm 104:26. The Psalmist praises God for His works by looking at the creatures of the sea (probably the Mediterranean).

Isaiah 27:1. Given the poetic and prophetic language of this portion of Isaiah, Leviathan is probably used metaphorically. Some believe that it indicates Assyria, and that the fleeing serpent refers to the Tigris, with its swift current, while the twisted serpent refers to the more slowly moving Euphrates. Leviathan is described as a reptile, though the term can be translated other ways. Ezekiel used similar language to describe God's judgment on Pharaoh of Egypt (Ezekiel 29:3-5).

2 Chronicles 7:14

If my people, which are called by my name, shall humble themselves, and pray, and seek my face, and turn from their wicked ways; then will I hear from heaven, and will forgive their sin, and will heal their land.

Psalm 122:6

Pray for the peace of Jerusalem; they will prosper who love thee.

The Book of Psalms

Scripture Focus Psalms 1-150

Objective: To gain insight on the Book of Psalms which reflects the international scope of God's activity and involvement with all His people.

Introduction

The Book of Psalms was written by many people over centuries of time. One of the earliest of the Psalmist was Moses who probably composed Psalm 90 during the Exodus. Seventy-three of the Psalms are preceded by the phrase "of David" supporting that he was one of the most prolific of the writers of thee Psalms. Two other group of Psalmist were composed of professional guilds of musicians, the Sons of Asaph (see 1 Chronicles 25:2) and the Sons of Korah. A number of Psalms are of unknown origin.

Each Psalm must be dated individually, or as a part of a group. For example, those composed by David would have produced between 1040 and 971 B.C. Likewise, the two Psalms attributed to Solomon (Psalms 27), assuming that he wrote them, would be dated between 971 and 931 B.C. But the writing of the Psalms was not limited to the period of the monarchy, it reaches back to the time of Moses (around 1400 B.C.) an extends to the period of Exile (mid-fifth century B.C.).

In fact, some believe that the collection of Psalms as we know it did not take final shape until the time of Ezra, when it became the "hymnbook of the second temple."

Because Psalms were produced from such a wide variety of backgrounds, the geography of the Book of Psalms covers the entire world as it would have been known to the ancient Israelite.

Objective Breakdown:

Psalms 1-41

1.	Two Responses to God	Psalm 1:1-6
2.	Vain Nations Challenge the Messiah	Psalm 2:1-12
3.	The Lord Protects His People	Psalm 3:1-8
4.	Relying and Resting on God	Psalm 4:1-8
5.	The Wicked and the Righteous Compared	Psalm 5:1-12
6.	A Cry for God to Hear and Heal	Psalm 6:1-10
7.	David Prays for Vindication	Psalm 7:1-17

Psalms 42-72

Synopsis of the Psalms

PSALMS 1

Synopsis: - The holiness and happiness of a godly man. (1-3)

The sinfulness and misery of a wicked man, The ground and reason of both. (4-6)

PSALMS 2

Synopsis: - Threatening's against the enemies of Christ's kingdom. (1-6)

Promise to Christ as the Head of this kingdom. (7-9)

Counsel to all, to espouse its interests. (10-12)

PSALMS 3

Synopsis: - David complains to God of his enemies, and confides in God. (1-3)

He triumphs over his fears, and gives God the glory, and takes to himself the comfort. (4-8)

PSALMS 4

Synopsis: - The children of men proved, and the happiness of godly people. (1-5)

God's favor is happiness. (6-8)

PSALMS 5

Synopsis: - God will certainly hear prayer: David gives to God the glory, and takes to himself the comfort. (1-6) He prayed for himself, that God would guide him, and for all the Lord's people, that God would give them joy, and keep them safe. (7-12)

PSALMS 6

Synopsis: - The psalmist deprecates God's wrath, and begs for the return of his favor. (1-7)

He assures himself of an answer of peace. (8-10)

PSALMS 7

Synopsis: - The psalmist prays to God to plead his case, and judge for him. (1-9)

He expresses confidence in God, and will give him the glory of his deliverance. (10-17)

PSALMS 8

Synopsis: - God is to be glorified, for making known himself to us. (1,2)

And for making even the heavenly bodies useful to man, thereby placing him but little lower than the angels. (3-9)

PSALMS 9

Synopsis: - David praises God for protecting his people. (1-10)

And for cause to praise him. (11-20)

PSALMS 10

Synopsis: - The psalmist complains of the wickedness of the wicked. (1-11)

He prays to God to appear for the relief of his people. (12-18)

PSALMS 11

Synopsis: - David's struggle with, and triumph over a strong temptation to distrust God, and betake himself to indirect means for his own safety, in a time of danger.

PSALMS 12

Synopsis: - The psalmist begs help of God, because there were none among men whom he durst trust.

PSALMS 13

Synopsis: - The psalmist complains that God had long withdrawn. He earnestly prays for comfort. He assures himself of an answer of peace.

PSALMS 14

Synopsis: - A description of the depravity of human nature, and the deplorable corruption of a great part of mankind.

PSALMS 15

Synopsis - The way to heaven, if we would be happy, we must be holy. We are encouraged to walk in that way.

PSALMS 16

Synopsis: - This psalm begins with expressions of devotion, which may be applied to Christ; but ends with such confidence of a resurrection, as must be applied to Christ, and to him only.

PSALMS 17

Synopsis: - David's integrity. (1-7)

The character of his enemies. His hope of happiness. (8-15)

PSALMS 18

Synopsis: - David rejoices in the deliverances God wrought for him. (1-19)

He takes the comfort of his integrity, which God had cleared up. (20-28)

He gives to God the glory of all his mighty deeds. (29-50)

PSALMS 19

Synopsis: - The glory of God's works. (1-6)

His holiness and grace as shown in his word. (7-10)

Prayer for the benefit of them. (11-14)

PSALMS 20

Synopsis: - This psalm is a prayer for the kings of Israel, but with relation to Christ.

PSALMS 21

Synopsis: - Thanksgiving for victory. (1-6)

Confidence of further success. (7-13)

PSALMS 22

Synopsis: - Complaints of discouragement. (1-10)

With prayer for deliverance. (11-21)

Praises for mercies and redemption. (22-31)

PSALMS 23

Synopsis: - Confidence in God's grace and care.

PSALMS 24

Synopsis: - Concerning the kingdom of Christ, and the subjects of that kingdom. (7-10) Concerning the King of that kingdom. (1-6)

PSALMS 25

Synopsis: - David, in this psalm, appeals to God touching his integrity.

PSALMS 26

Synopsis: - The psalmist's faith. (1-6)

His desire toward God, and expectation from him. (7-14)

PSALMS 27

Synopsis: - A prayer in distress. (1-5)

Thanksgiving for deliverance. (6-9)

PSALMS 28

Synopsis: - Exhortation to give glory to God.

PSALMS 29

Synopsis: - Praise to God for deliverance. (1-5)

Others encouraged by his example. (6-12)

PSALMS 29

Synopsis: - Praise to God for deliverance. (1-5)

Others encouraged by his example. (6-12)

PSALMS 30

Synopsis: - Confidence in God. (1-8)

Prayer in trouble. (9-18)

Praise for God's goodness. (19-24)

PSALMS 31

Synopsis: - The happiness of a pardoned sinner. (1-2)

The misery that went before, and the comfort that followed the confession of sins. (3-7)

Sinners instructed, believers encouraged. (8-11)

PSALMS 32

Synopsis: - God to be praised. (1-11)

His people encouraged by his power. (12-22)

PSALMS 33

Synopsis: - David praises God, and encourages to trust him. (1-10)

He exhorts to fear. (11-22)

PSALMS 34

Synopsis: - David prays for safety. (1-10)

He complains of his enemies. (11-16)

Calls upon God to support him. (17-28)

PSALMS 35

Synopsis: - The bad state of the wicked. (1-4)

The goodness of God. (5-12)

PSALMS 36

Synopsis: - David persuades to patience and confidence in God, by the state of the godly and of the wicked.

PSALMS 37

Synopsis: - God's displeasure at sin. (1-11)

The psalmist's sufferings and prayers. (12-22)

PSALMS 38

Synopsis: - David meditates on man's frailty. (1-6)

He applies for pardon and deliverance. (7-13)

PSALMS 39

Synopsis: - Confidence for deliverance. (1-5)

Christ's work of redemption. (6-10)

Prayer for mercy and grace. (11-17)

PSALMS 40

Synopsis: - God's care for his people. (1-4)

The treachery of David's enemies. (5-13)

PSALMS 41

Synopsis: - The conflict in the soul of a believer.

PSALMS 42

Synopsis: - David endeavors to still his spirit, with hope and confidence in God.

PSALMS 43

Synopsis: - A petition for succor and relief.

PSALMS 44

Synopsis: - This psalm is a prophecy of Messiah the Prince, and points to him as a Bridegroom espousing the church to himself, and as a King ruling in it, and for it.

PSALMS 45

Synopsis: - Confidence in God. (1-5)

An exhortation to behold it. (6-11)

PSALMS 46

Synopsis: - The people exhorted to praise God.

PSALMS 47

Synopsis: - The glories of the church of Christ.

PSALMS 48

Synopsis: - A call for attention. (1-5)

Folly of worldlings. (6-14)

Against fear of death. (15-20)

PSALMS 49

Synopsis: - The glory of God. (1-6)

Sacrifices to be changed for prayers. (7-15)

Obedience required. (16-23)

PSALMS 50

Synopsis: - The psalmist prays for mercy, humbly confessing and lamenting his sins. (1-6)

He pleads for pardon, that he may promote the glory of God and the conversion of sinners. (7-15)

God is pleased with a contrite heart, a prayer for the prosperity of Zion. (16-19)

PSALMS 51

Synopsis: - The enemies of the truth and the church described their destruction. (1-5)

The righteous rejoice. (6-9)

PSALMS 52

Synopsis: - The corruption of man by nature.

PSALMS 53

Synopsis: - David complains of the malice of his enemies. (1-3)

Assurance of the Divine favour and protection. (4-7)

PSALMS 54

Synopsis: - Prayer to God to manifest his favor. (1-8)

The great wickedness and treachery of his enemies. (9-15)

He is sure that God would in due time appear for him. (16-23)

PSALMS 55

Synopsis: - David seeks mercy from God, amidst the malice of his enemies. (1-7)

He rests his faith on God's promises, and declares his obligation to praise him for mercies. (8-13)

PSALMS 56

Synopsis: - David begins with prayer and complaint. (1-6)

He concludes with joy and praise. (7-11)

PSALMS 57

Synopsis: - Wicked judges described and reproved. (1-5)

A prayer that they may be disabled, and their ruin predicted. (6-11)

PSALMS 58

Synopsis: - David prays for deliverance from his enemies. (1-7)

He foresees their destruction. (8-17)

PSALMS 59

Synopsis: - David prays for the deliverance of Israel from their enemies. (1-5)

He entreats God to carry on and complete their victories. (6-12)

PSALMS 60

Synopsis: - David seeks God upon former experience. (1-4)

He vows to serve God. (5-8)

PSALMS 61

Synopsis: - David's confidence in God. (1-7)

No trust to be put in worldly things. (8-12)

PSALMS 62

Synopsis: - David's desire toward God. (1,2)

His satisfaction in God. (3-6)

His dependence upon God, and assurance of safety. (7-11)

PSALMS 63

Synopsis: - Prayer for deliverance. (1-6)

The destruction of the wicked, encouragement to the righteous. (7-10)

PSALMS 64

Synopsis: - God is to be praised in the kingdom of grace. (1-5)

In the kingdom of providence. (6-13)

PSALMS 65

Synopsis: - Praise for God's sovereign power in the creation. (1-7)

For his favour to his church. (8-12). And the psalmist's praise for his experience of God's goodness. (13-20)

PSALMS 66

Synopsis: - A prayer for the enlargement of Christ's kingdom.

PSALMS 67

Synopsis: - A prayer-- The greatness and goodness of God. (1-6)

The wonderful works God wrought for his people. (7-14)

The presence of God in his church. (15-21)

The victories of Christ. (22-28)

Enlargement of the church. (29-31)

The glory and grace of God. (32-35)

PSALMS 68

Synopsis: - David complains of great distress. (1-12)

And begs for succor. (13-21)

He declares the judgments of God. (22-29)

He concludes with joy and praise. (30-36)

PSALMS 69

Synopsis: - The speedy destruction of the wicked, and the preservation of the godly.

PSALMS 70

Synopsis: - Prayers that God would deliver and save. (1-13)

Believing praises. (14-24)

PSALMS 71

Synopsis: - David begins with a prayer for Solomon. (1)

He passes into a prophecy of the glories of his reign, and of Christ's kingdom. (2-17)

Praise to God. (18-20)

PSALMS 72

Synopsis: - The psalmist's temptation. (1-14)

How he gained a victory over it. (15-20). How he profited by it. (21-28)

PSALMS 73

Synopsis: - The desolation of the sanctuary. 12-17. Pleas for encouraging faith. 18-23. Petitions for deliverance.

PSALMS 74

Synopsis: - The psalmist declares his resolution of executing judgment. (1-5)

He rebukes the wicked, and concludes with resolutions to praise God. (6-10)

PSALMS 75

Synopsis: - The psalmist speaks of God's power. (1-6)

All have to fear and to trust in him. (7-12)

PSALMS 76

Synopsis: - The psalmist's troubles and temptation. (1-10)

He encourages himself by the remembrance of God's help of his people. (11-20)

PSALMS 77

Synopsis: - Attention called for. (1-8)

The history of Israel. (9-39)

Their settlement in Canaan. (40-55)

The mercies of God to Israel contrasted with their ingratitude. (56-72)

PSALMS 78

Synopsis: - The deplorable condition of the people of God. (1-5)

A petition for relief. (6-13)

PSALMS 79

Synopsis: - The psalmist complains of the miseries of the church. (1-7)

Its former prosperity and present desolation. (8-16)

A prayer for mercy. (17-19)

PSALMS 80

Synopsis: - God is praised for what he has done for his people. (1-7)

Their obligations to him. (8-16)

PSALMS 81

Synopsis: - An exhortation to judges. (1-5)

The doom of evil rulers. (6-8)

PSALMS 82

Synopsis: - The designs of the enemies of Israel. (1-8)

Earnest prayer for their defeat. (9-18)

PSALMS 83

Synopsis: - The psalmist expresses his affection to the ordinances of God. (1-7)

His desire towards the God of the ordinances. (8-12)

PSALMS 84

Synopsis: - Prayers for the continuance of former mercies. (1-7)

Trust in God's goodness. (8-13)

PSALMS 85

Synopsis: - The psalmist pleads his earnestness, and the mercy of God, as reasons why his prayer should be heard. (1-7)

He renews his requests for help and comfort. (8-17)

PSALMS 86

Synopsis: - The glory of the church. (1-3)

It is filled with the Divine blessing. (4-7)

PSALMS 87

Synopsis: - The psalmist pours out his soul to God in lamentation. (1-9)

He wrestles by faith, in his prayer to God for comfort. (10-18)

PSALMS 88

Synopsis: - God's mercy and truth, and his covenant. (1-4)

The glory and perfection of God. (5-14)

The happiness of those in communion with him. (15-18)

God's covenant with David, as a type of Christ. (19-37)

A calamitous state lamented, Prayer for redress. (38-52)

PSALMS 89

Synopsis: - The eternity of God, the frailty of man. (1-6)

Submission to Divine chastisements. (7-11)

Prayer for mercy and grace. (12-17)

PSALMS 90

Synopsis: - The safety of those who have God for their refuge. (1-8)

Their favour with Him. (9-16)

PSALMS 91

Synopsis: - Praise is the business of the Sabbath. (1-6)

The wicked shall perish, but God's people shall be exalted. (7-15)

PSALMS 92

Synopsis: - The majesty, power, and holiness of Christ's kingdom.

PSALMS 93

Synopsis: - The danger and folly of persecutors. (1-11)

Comfort and peace to the persecuted. (12-23)

PSALMS 94

Synopsis: - An exhortation to praise God. (1-7)

A warning not to tempt Him. (7-11)

PSALMS 95

Synopsis: - A call to all people to praise God. (1-9)

God's government and judgment. (10-13)

PSALMS 96

Synopsis: - The Lord Jesus reigns in power that cannot be resisted. (1-7)

His care of his people, and his provision for them. (8-12)

PSALMS 97

Synopsis: - The glory of the Redeemer. (1-3)

The joy of the Redeemer. (4-9)

PSALMS 98

Synopsis: - The happy government God's people are under. (1-5)

Its happy administration. (6-9)

PSALMS 99

Synopsis: - An exhortation to praise God, and rejoice in him.

PSALMS 100

Synopsis: - David's vow and profession of godliness.

PSALMS 101

Synopsis: - A sorrowful complaint of great afflictions. (1-11)

Encouragement by expecting the performances of God's promises to his church. (12-22)

The unchangeableness of God. (23-28)

PSALMS 102

Synopsis: - An exhortation to bless God for his mercy. (1-5)

And to the church and to all men. (6-14)

For the constancy of his mercy. (15-18)

For the government of the world. (19-22)

PSALMS 103

Synopsis: - God's majesty in the heavens, the creation of the sea, and the dry land. (1-9)

His provision for all creatures. (10-18)

The regular course of day and night, and God's sovereign power over all the creatures. (19-30)

A resolution to continue praising God. (31-35)

PSALMS 104

Synopsis: - A solemn call to praise and serve the Lord. (1-7)

His gracious dealings with Israel. (8-23)

Their deliverance from Egypt, and their settlement in Canaan. (24-45)

PSALMS 105

Synopsis: - The happiness of God's people. (1-5)

Israel's sins. (6-12)

Their provocations. (13-33)

Their rebellions in Canaan. (34-46)

Prayer for more complete deliverance. (47,48)

PSALMS 106

Synopsis: - God's providential care of the children of men in distresses, in banishment, and dispersion. (1-9)

In captivity. (10-16)

In sickness. (17-22)

Danger at sea. (23-32)

God's hand is to be seen by his own people. (33-43)

PSALMS 107

Synopsis: - We may usefully select passages from different psalms, as here, Psalms 56 and 60, to help our devotions, and enliven our gratitude. When the heart is firm in faith and love, the tongue, being employed in grateful praises, is our glory. Every gift of the Lord honours and profits the possessor, as it is employed in God's service and to his glory. Believers may pray with assured faith and hope, for all the blessings of salvation, which are secured to them by the faithful promise and covenant of God. Then let them expect from him help in every trouble, and victory in every conflict. Whatever we do, whatever we gain, God must have all the glory. Lord, visit all our souls with this salvation, with this favour which thou bearest to thy chosen people.

PSALMS 108

Synopsis: - David complains of his enemies. (1-5)

He prophesies their destruction. (6-20)

Prayers and praises. (21-31)

PSALMS 109

Synopsis: - Christ's kingdom.

PSALMS 110

Synopsis: - The Lord is to be praised for his works.

PSALMS 111

Synopsis: - The blessedness of the righteous.

PSALMS 112

Synopsis: - An exhortation to praise God.

PSALMS 113

Synopsis: - An exhortation to fear God.

PSALMS 114

Synopsis: - Glory to be ascribed to God. (1-8)

By trusting in Him and praising Him. (9-18)

PSALMS 115

Synopsis: - The psalmist declares his love to the Lord. (1-9)

His desire to be thankful. (10-19)

PSALMS 116

Synopsis: - All people called upon to praise God.

PSALMS 117

Synopsis: - It is good to trust in the Lord. (1-18)

The coming of Christ in his kingdom. (19-29)

PSALMS 118

Synopsis: - The general scope and design of this psalm is to magnify the Divine law, and make it honorable. There are ten words by which Divine revelation is called in this psalm, and each expresses what God expects from us, and what we may expect from him. 1. God's law; this is enacted by him as our Sovereign. 2. His way; this is the rule of his providence. 3. His testimonies; they are solemnly declared to the world. 4. His commandments; given with authority. 5. His precepts; not left as indifferent matters to us. 6. His word, or saying; it is the declaration of his mind. 7. His judgments; framed in infinite wisdom. 8. His righteousness; it is the rule and standard of what is right. 9. His statutes; they are always binding. 10. His truth or faithfulness; it is eternal truth; it shall endure forever verses 1-8. This psalm may be considered as the statement of a believer's experience. As far as our views, desires, and affections agree with what is here expressed, they come from the influences of the Holy Spirit, and no further. The pardoning mercy of God in Christ is the only source of a sinner's happiness. And those are most happy, who are preserved most free from the defilement of sin, who simply believe God's testimonies, and depend on his promises. If the heart be divided between him and the world, it is evil. But the saints carefully avoid all sin; they are conscious of much evil that clogs them in the ways of God, but not of that wickedness which draws them out of those ways. The tempter would make men think they are at them out of those ways. The tempter would make men think they are at liberty to follow the word of God or not, as they please. But the desire and prayer of a good man agree with the will and command of God. If a man expects by obedience in one thing to purchase indulgence for disobedience in others, his hypocrisy will be detected; if he is not ashamed in this world, everlasting shame will be his portion.

The psalmist coveted to learn the laws of God, to give God the glory. And believers see that if God forsakes them, the temper will be too hard for them 9-16. To original corruption all have added actual sin. The ruin of the young is either living by no rule at all, or choosing false rules: let them walk by Scripture rules. To doubt of our own wisdom and strength, and to depend upon God, proves the purpose of holiness is sincere. God's word is treasure worth laying up, and there is no laying it up safe but in our hearts, that we may oppose God's precepts to the dominion of sin, his promises to its allurements, and his threatening to its violence. Let this be our plea with Him to teach us his statutes, that, being partakers of his holiness, we may also partake of his blessedness. And those whose hearts are fed with the bread of life, should with their lips feed many. In the way of God's commandments there is the unsearchable riches of Christ. But we do not meditate on God's precepts to good purpose, unless our good thoughts produce good works. I will not only think of thy statutes, but do them with delight. And it will be well to try the sincerity of our obedience by tracing the spring of it; the reality of our love by cheerfulness in appointed duties.

17-24 If God deals in strict justice with us, we all perish. We ought to spend our lives in his service; we shall find true life in keeping his word. Those that would see the wondrous things of God's law and gospel, must beg him to give them understanding, by the light of his Spirit. Believers feel themselves strangers on earth; they fear missing their way, and losing comfort by erring from God's commandments. Every sanctified soul hungers after the word of God, as food which there is no living without. There is something of pride at the bottom of every willful sin. God can silence lying lips; reproach and contempt may humble and do us good, and then they shall be removed. Do we find the weight of the cross is above that we are able to bear? He that bore it for us will enable us to bear it; upheld by him we cannot sink. It is sad when those who should protect the innocent, are their betrayers. The psalmist went on in duty, and he found comfort in the word of God. The comforts of the word of God are most pleasant to a gracious soul, when other comforts are made bitter; and those that would have God's testimonies to be their delight, must be advised by them. May the Lord direct us in exercising repentance of sin, and faith in Christ.

25-32 While the souls of the children of this world cleave to the earth as their portion, the children of light are greatly burdened, because of the remains of carnal affections in their hearts. It is unspeakable comfort to a gracious soul, to think with what tenderness all its complaints are received by a gracious God. We can talk of the wonders of redeeming love, when we understand the way of God's precepts, and walk in that way. The penitent melts in sorrow for sin: even the patient spirit may melt in the sense of affliction, it is then its interest to pour out its soul before God. The way of lying means all false ways

449

by which men deceive themselves and others, or are deceived by Satan and his instruments. Those who know and love the law of the Lord, desire to know it more, and love it better. The way of serious godliness is the way of truth; the only true way to happiness: we must always have actual regard to it. Those who stick to the word of God, may in faith expect and pray for acceptance with God. Lord, never leave me to do that by which I shall shame myself, and do not thou reject my services. Those that are going to heaven, should still press forward. God, by his Spirit, enlarges the hearts of his people when he gives them wisdom. The believer prays to be set free from sin.

33-40 Teach me thy statutes, not the mere words, but the way of applying them to myself. God, by his Spirit, gives a right understanding. But the Spirit of revelation in the word will not suffice unless we have the Spirit of wisdom in the heart. God puts his Spirit within us, causing us to walk in his statutes. The sin here prayed against is covetousness. Those that would have the love of God rooted in them, must get the love of the world rooted out; for the friendship of the world is enmity with God. Quicken me in thy way; to redeem time, and to do every duty with liveliness of spirit. Beholding vanity deadens us, and slackens our pace; a traveler must not stand gazing upon every object that presents itself to his view. The promises of God's word greatly relate to the preservation of the true believer. When Satan has drawn a child of God into worldly compliances, he will reproach him with the falls into which he led him. Victory must come from the cross of Christ. When we enjoy the sweetness of God's precepts, it will make us long for more acquaintance with them. And where God has wrought to will, he will work to do.

41-48 Lord, I have by faith thy mercies in view; let me by prayer prevail to obtain them. And when the salvation of the saints is completed, it will plainly appear that it was not in vain to trust in God's word. We need to pray that we may never be afraid or ashamed to own God's truths and ways before men. And the psalmist resolves to keep God's law, in a constant course of obedience, without backsliding. The service of sin is slavery; the service of God is liberty. There is no full happiness, or perfect liberty, but in keeping God's law. We must never be ashamed or afraid to own our religion. The more delight we take in the service of God, the nearer we come to perfection. Not only consent to his law as good, but take pleasure in it as good for us. Let me put forth all the strength I have, to do it. Something of this mind of Christ is in every true disciple.

49-56 Those that make God's promises their portion, may with humble boldness make them their plea. He that by his Spirit works faith in us, will work for us. The word of God speaks comfort in affliction. If, through grace, it makes us holy, there is enough in it to make us easy, in all conditions. Let us be certain we have the Divine law for what we believe, and then let not scoffers prevail upon us to decline from it. God's judgments of old comfort and encourage us, for he is still the same. Sin is horrible in the eyes of all that are sanctified. Ere long the believer will be absent from the body, and present with the Lord. In the meantime, the statutes of the Lord supply subjects for grateful praise. In the season of affliction, and in the silent hours of the night, he remembers the name of the Lord, and is stirred up to keep the law. All who have made religion the first thing, will own that they have been unspeakable gainers by it.

57-64 True believers take the Lord for the portion of their inheritance, and nothing less will satisfy them. The psalmist prayed with his whole heart, knowing how to value the blessing he prayed for: he desired the mercy promised, and depended on the promise for it. He turned from by-paths and returned to God's testimonies. He delayed not. It behooves sinners to hasten to escape; and the believer will be equally in haste to glorify God. No care or grief should take away God's word out of our minds, or hinder the comfort it bestows. There is no situation on earth in which a believer has not cause to be thankful. Let us feel ashamed that others are more willing to keep from sleep to spend the time in sinful pleasures, than we are to praise God. And we should be more earnest in prayer, that our hearts may be filled with his mercy, grace, and peace.

65-72 However God has dealt with us, he has dealt with us better than we deserve; and all in love, and for our good. Many have knowledge, but little judgment; those who have both, are fortified against the snares of Satan, and furnished for the service of God. We are most apt to wander from God when we are easy in the world. We should leave our concerns to the disposal of God, seeing we know not what is good for us. Lord, thou art our bountiful Benefactor; incline our hearts to faith and obedience. The psalmist will go on in his duty with constancy and resolution. The proud are full of the world, and its wealth and pleasures; these make them senseless, secure, and stupid. God visits his people with affliction, that they may learn his statutes. Not only God's promises, but even his law, his precepts, though hard to ungodly men, are desirable, and profitable, because they lead us with safety and delight unto eternal life.

73-80 God made us to serve him and enjoy him; but by sin we have made ourselves unfit to serve him, and to enjoy him. We ought, therefore, continually to beseech him, by his Holy Spirit, to give us understanding. The comforts some have in God, should be matter of joy to others.

PSALMS 119

Synopsis: - The general scope and design of this psalm is to magnify the Divine law and make it honorable. There are ten words by which Divine revelation is called in this psalm, and each expresses what God expects from us, and what we may expect from him. 1. God's law; this is enacted by him as our Sovereign. 2. His way; this is the rule of his providence. 3. His testimonies; they are solemnly declared to the world. 4. His commandments; given with authority. 5. His precepts; not left as indifferent matters to us. 6. His word, or saying; it is the declaration of his mind. 7. His judgments; framed in infinite wisdom. 8. His righteousness; it is the rule and standard of what is right. 9. His statutes; they are always binding. 10. His truth or faithfulness; it is eternal truth; it shall endure forever. Verse 1-8 This psalm may be considered as the statement of a believer's experience. As far as our views, desires, and affections agree with what is here expressed, they come from the influences of the Holy Spirit, and no further. The pardoning mercy of God in Christ is the only source of a sinner's happiness. And those are most happy, who are preserved most free from the defilement of sin, who simply believe God's testimonies, and depend on his promises. If the heart be divided between him and the world, it is evil. But the saints carefully avoid all sin; they are conscious of much evil that clogs them in the ways of God, but not of that wickedness which draws them out of those ways. The tempter would make men think they are at them out of those ways. The tempter would make men think they are at liberty to follow the word of God or not, as they please. But the desire and prayer of a good man agree with the will and command of God. If a man expects by obedience in one thing to purchase indulgence for disobedience in others, his hypocrisy will be detected; if he is not ashamed in this world, everlasting shame will be his portion.

The psalmist coveted to learn the laws of God, to give God the glory. And believers see that if God forsakes them, the temper will be too hard for them. 9-16 To original corruption all have added actual sin. The ruin of the young is either living by no rule at all or choosing false rules: let them walk by Scripture rules. To doubt of our own wisdom and strength, and to depend upon God, proves the purpose of holiness is sincere. God's word is treasure worth laying up, and there is no laying it up safe but, in our hearts, that we may oppose God's precepts to the dominion of sin, his promises to its allurements, and his threatening to its violence. Let this be our plea with Him to teach us his statutes, that, being partakers of his holiness, we may also partake of his blessedness. And those whose hearts are fed with the bread of life, should with their lips feed many. In the way of God's commandments there is the unsearchable riches of Christ. But we do not meditate on God's precepts to good purpose, unless our good thoughts produce good works. I will not only think of thy statutes but do them with delight. And it will be well to try the sincerity of our obedience by tracing the spring of it, the reality of our love by cheerfulness in appointed duties.

17-24 If God deals in strict justice with us, we all perish. We ought to spend our lives in his service; we shall find true life in keeping his word. Those that would see the wondrous things of God's law and gospel, must beg him to give them understanding, by the light of his Spirit. Believers feel themselves strangers on earth; they fear missing their way, and losing comfort by erring from God's commandments. Every sanctified soul hungers after the word of God, as food which there is no living without. There is something of pride at the bottom of every willful sin. God can silence lying lips; reproach and contempt may humble and do us good, and then they shall be removed. Do we find the weight of the cross is above that we are able to bear? He that bore it for us will enable us to bear it; upheld by him we cannot sink. It is sad when those who should protect the innocent, are their betrayers. The psalmist went on in duty, and he found comfort in the word of God. The comforts of the word of God are most pleasant to a gracious soul, when other comforts are made bitter; and those that would have God's testimonies to be their delight, must be advised by them. May the Lord direct us in exercising repentance of sin, and faith in Christ.

25-32 While the souls of the children of this world cleave to the earth as their portion, the children of light are greatly burdened, because of the remains of carnal affections in their hearts. It is unspeakable comfort to a gracious soul, to think with what tenderness all its complaints are received by a gracious God. We can talk of the wonders of redeeming love, when we understand the way of God's precepts, and walk in that way. The penitent melts in sorrow for sin: even the patient spirit may melt in the sense of affliction, it is then its interest to pour out its soul before God. The way of lying means all false ways by which men deceive themselves and others or are deceived by Satan and his instruments. Those who know and love the law of the Lord, desire to know it more, and love it better. The way of serious godliness is the way of truth; the only true way to happiness: we must always have actual regard to it. Those who stick to the word of God, may in faith expect and pray for acceptance with God. Lord, never leave me to do that by which I shall shame myself, and do not thou reject my services. Those that are going to heaven, should still press forward. God, by his Spirit, enlarges the hearts of his people when he gives them wisdom. The believer prays to be set free from sin.

33-40 Teach me thy statutes, not the mere words, but the way of applying them to myself. God, by his Spirit, gives a right understanding. But the Spirit of revelation in the word will not suffice unless we have the Spirit of wisdom in the heart. God puts his Spirit within us, causing us to walk in his statutes. The sin here prayed against is covetousness. Those that would have the love of God rooted in them, must get the love of the world rooted out; for the friendship of the world is enmity with God. Quicken me in thy way; to redeem time, and to do every duty with liveliness of spirit. Beholding vanity deadens us and slackens our pace; a traveler must not stand gazing upon every object that presents itself to his view. The promises of God's word greatly relate to the preservation of the true believer. When Satan has drawn a child of God into worldly compliance, he will reproach him with the falls into which he led him. Victory must come from the cross of Christ. When we enjoy the sweetness of God's precepts, it will make us long for more acquaintance with them. And where God has wrought to will, he will work to do.

41-48 Lord, I have by faith thy mercies in view; let me by prayer prevail to obtain them. And when the salvation of the saints is completed, it will plainly appear that it was not in vain to trust in God's word. We need to pray that we may never be afraid or ashamed to own God's truths and ways before men. And the psalmist resolves to keep God's law, in a constant course of obedience, without backsliding. The service of sin is slavery; the service of God is liberty. There is no full happiness, or perfect liberty, but in keeping God's law. We must never be ashamed or afraid to own our religion. The more delight we take in the service of God, the nearer we come to perfection. Not only consent to his law as good, but take pleasure in it as good for us. Let me put forth all the strength I have, to do it. Something of this mind of Christ is in every true disciple.

49-56 Those that make God's promises their portion, may with humble boldness make them their plea. He that by his Spirit works faith in us, will work for us. The word of God speaks comfort in affliction. If, through grace, it makes us holy, there is enough in it to make us easy, in all conditions. Let us be certain we have the Divine law for what we believe, and then let not scoffers prevail upon us to decline from it. God's judgments of old comfort and encourage us, for he is still the same. Sin is horrible in the eyes of all that are sanctified. Ere long the believer will be absent from the body, and present with the Lord. In the meantime, the statutes of the Lord supply subjects for grateful praise. In the season of affliction, and in the silent hours of the night, he remembers the name of the Lord, and is stirred up to keep the law. All who have made religion the first thing, will own that they have been unspeakable gainers by it.

57-64 True believers take the Lord for the portion of their inheritance, and nothing less will satisfy them. The psalmist prayed with his whole heart, knowing how to value the blessing he prayed for: he desired the mercy promised, and depended on the promise for it. He turned from by-paths and returned to God's testimonies. He delayed not. It behooves sinners to hasten to escape; and the believer will be equally in haste to glorify God. No care or grief should take away God's word out of our minds or hinder the comfort it bestows. There is no situation on earth in which a believer has not cause to be thankful. Let us feel ashamed that others are more willing to keep from sleep to spend the time in sinful pleasures, than we are to praise God. And we should be more earnest in prayer, that our hearts may be filled with his mercy, grace, and peace.

65-72 However God has dealt with us, he has dealt with us better than we deserve; and all in love, and for our good. Many have knowledge, but little judgment; those who have both, are fortified against the snares of Satan, and furnished for the service of God. We are most apt to wander from God when we are easy in the world. We should leave our concerns to the disposal of God, seeing we know not what is good for us. Lord, thou art our bountiful Benefactor; incline our hearts to faith and obedience. The psalmist will go on in his duty with constancy and resolution. The proud are full of the world, and its wealth and pleasures; these make them senseless, secure, and stupid. God visits his people with affliction, that they may learn his statutes. Not only God's promises, but even his law, his precepts, though hard to ungodly men, are desirable, and profitable, because they lead us with safety and delight unto eternal life.

73-80 God made us to serve him and enjoy him; but by sin we have made ourselves unfit to serve him, and to enjoy him. We ought, therefore, continually to beseech him, by his Holy Spirit, to give us understanding. The comforts some have in God, should be matter of joy to others. But it is easy to own, that God's judgments are right, until it comes to be our own case. All supports under affliction must come from mercy and compassion. The mercies of God are tender mercies, the mercies of a father, the compassion of a mother to her son. They come to us when we are not able to go to them. Causeless reproach does not hurt and should not move us. The psalmist could go on in the way of his duty and find comfort in it. He valued the good will of saints and was desirous to keep up his communion with them. Soundness of heart signifies sincerity in dependence on God, and devotedness to him.

81-88 The psalmist sought deliverance from his sins, his foes, and his fears. Hope deferred made him faint; his eyes failed by looking out for this expected salvation. But when the eyes fail, yet faith must not. The convictions and commands of his law. When trouble is near, God is near. He is never far to seek. All his commandments are truth. And God's promises will be performed. All that ever trusted in God have found him faithful.

153-160 The closer we cleave to the word of God, both as our rule and as our stay, the more assurance we have of deliverance. Christ is the Advocate of his people, their Redeemer. Those who were quickened by his Spirit and grace, when they were dead in trespasses and sins, often need to have the work of grace revived in them, according to the word of promise. The wicked not only do not God's statutes, but they do not even seek them. They flatter themselves that they are going to heaven; but the longer they persist in sin, the further it is from them. God's mercies are tender; they are a fountain that can never be exhausted. The psalmist begs for God's reviving, quickening grace. A man, steady in the way of his duty, though he may have many enemies, needs to fear none. Those that hate sin truly, hate it as sin, as a transgression of the law of God, and a breaking of his word. Our obedience is only pleasing to God, and pleasant to ourselves, when it comes from a principle of love. All, in every age, who receive God's word in faith and love, find every saying in it faithful.

161-168 Those whose hearts stand in awe of God's word, will rather endure the wrath of man, than break the law of God. By the word of God, we are unspeakable gainers. Every man hates to have a lie told him, but we should more hate telling a lie; by the latter we give an affront to God. The more we see the beauty of truth, the more we shall see the hateful deformity of a lie. We are to praise God even for afflictions; through grace we get good from them. Those that love the world have great vexation, for it does not answer what they expect; those that love God's word have great peace, for it outdoes what they expect. Those in whom this holy love reigns, will not perplex themselves with needless scruples, or take offense at their brethren. A good hope of salvation will engage the heart in doing the commandments. And our love to the word of God must subdue our lusts and root out carnal affections: we must make heart work of it, or we make nothing of it. We must keep the commandments of God by obedience to them, and his promises by reliance on them. God's eye is on us at all times; this should make us very careful to keep his commandments.

169-176 The psalmist desired grace and strength to lift up his prayers, and that the Lord would receive and notice them. He desired to know more of God in Christ; to know more of the doctrines of the word, and the duties of religion. He had a deep sense of unworthiness, and holy fear that his prayer should not come before God; Lord, what I pray for is, what thou hast promised. We have learned nothing to purpose if we have not learned to praise God. We should always make the word of God the rule of our discourse, so as never to transgress it by sinful speaking, or sinful silence. His own hands are not sufficient, nor can any creature lend him help; therefore, he looks up to God, that the hand that had made him may help him. He had made religion his deliberate choice. There is an eternal salvation all the saints long for, and therefore they pray that God would help their way to it. Let thy judgments help me; let all ordinances and all providences, (both are God's judgments,) further me in glorifying God; let them help me for that work. He often looks back with shame and gratitude to his lost estate. He still prays for the tender care of Him who purchased his flock with his own blood, that he may receive from him the gift of eternal life. Seek me, that is, find me; for God never seeks in vain. Turn me, and I shall be turned. Let this psalm be a touchstone by which to try our hearts, and our lives. Do our hearts, cleansed in Christ's blood, make these prayers, resolutions, and confessions our own? Is God's word the standard of our faith, and the law of our practice? Do we use it as pleas with Christ for what we need? Happy those who live in such delightful exercises.

PSALMS 120

Synopsis: - The psalmist prays to God to deliver him from false and malicious tongues. (5-7)

He complains of wicked neighbors.

PSALMS 121

Synopsis: - The safety of the godly.

PSALMS 122

Synopsis: - Esteem for Jerusalem. (1-5)

Concern for its welfare. (6-9)

PSALMS 123

Synopsis: - Confidence in God under contempt.

PSALMS 124

Synopsis: - The deliverance of the church. (1-5)

Thankfulness for the deliverance. (6-8)

PSALMS 125

Synopsis: - The security of the righteous. (1-3)

Prayer for them, the ruin of the wicked. (4, 5)

PSALMS 126

Synopsis: - Those returned out of captivity are to be thankful. (1-3)

Those yet in captivity are encouraged. (4-6)

PSALMS 127

Synopsis: - The value of the Divine blessing.

PSALMS 128

Synopsis: - The blessings of those who fear God.

PSALMS 129

Synopsis: - Thankfulness for former deliverances. (1-4)

A believing prospect of the destruction of the enemies of Zion. (5-8)

PSALMS 130

Synopsis: - The psalmist's hope in prayer. (1-4)

His patience in hope. (5-8)

PSALMS 131

Synopsis: - The psalmist's humility. Believers encouraged to trust in God.

PSALMS 132

Synopsis: - David's care for the ark. (1-10)

The promises of God. (11-18)

PSALMS 133

Synopsis: - The excellency of brotherly love.

PSALMS 134

Synopsis: - An exhortation to bless the Lord.

PSALMS 135

Synopsis: - God to be praised for his mercy. (1-4)

For his power and judgments. (5-14)

The vanity of idols. (15-21)

PSALMS 136

Synopsis: - God to be praised as the Creator of the world. (1-9)

As Israel's God and Saviour. (10-22)

For his blessings to all. (23-26)

PSALMS 137

Synopsis: - The Jews bewail their captivity. (1-4)

Their affection for Jerusalem. (5-9)

PSALMS 138

Synopsis: - The psalmist praises God for answering prayer. (1-5)

The Lord's dealing with the humble and the proud. (6-8)

PSALMS 139

Synopsis: - God knows all things. (1-6)

He is everywhere present. (7-16)

The psalmist's hatred to sin, and desire to be led aright. (17-24)

PSALMS 140

Synopsis: - David encourages himself in God. (1-7)

He prays for and prophesies the destruction of his persecutors. (8-13)

PSALMS 141

Synopsis: - David prays for God's acceptance and assistance. (1-4)

That God would appear for his rescue. (5-10)

PSALMS 142

Synopsis: - David's comfort in prayer.

PSALMS 143

Synopsis: - David complains of his enemies and distresses. (1-6)

He prays for comfort, guidance, and deliverance. (7-12)

PSALMS 144

Synopsis: - David acknowledges the great goodness of God and prays for help. (1-8)

He prays for the prosperity of his kingdom. (9-15)

PSALMS 145

Synopsis: - David extols the power, goodness, and mercy of the Lord. (1-9)

The glory of God's kingdom, and his care of those that love him. (10-21)

PSALMS 146

Synopsis: - Why we should not trust in men. (1-4)

Why we should trust in God. (5-10)

PSALMS 147

Synopsis: - The people of God are exhorted to praise him for his mercies and care. (1-11)

For the salvation and prosperity of the church. (12-20)

PSALMS 148

Synopsis: - The creatures placed in the upper world called on to praise the Lord. (1-6)

Also, the creatures of this lower world, especially his own people. (7-14)

PSALMS 149

Synopsis: - Joy to all the people of God. (1-5)

Terror to their enemies. (6-9)

PSALMS 150

Synopsis: - A psalm of praise.

Lesson Plan 161

The Book of Psalms

Psalms 1-41

Objective: To gain insight on the Book of Psalms which reflects the international scope of God's activity and involvement with all His people.

Objective Breakdown:

1. Introduction

2. Two Responses to God   Psalm 1:1-6

3. Vain Nations Challenge the Messiah   Psalm 2:1-12

4. The Lord Protects His People   Psalm 3:1-8

5. Relying and Resting on God   Psalm 4:1-8

6. The Wicked and the Righteous Compared   Psalm 5:1-12

7. A Cry for God to Hear and Heal   Psalm 6:1-10

8. David Prays for Vindication   Psalm 7:1-17

9. God's Glory in Creation   Psalm 8:1-9

10. Judgment and Justice from the Lord   Psalm 9:1-20

11. How Long Will the Wicked Prosper?   Psalm 10:1-18

12. Protection in Time of Crisis   Psalm 11:1-7

13. The Man of God Confronts Moral Decay   Psalm 12:1-8

14. God Has Not Forgotten   Psalm 13:1-6

15. The Folly of Unbelief and Sin   Psalm 14:1-7

16. Integrity in Daily Living   Psalm 15:1-5

17. A Life Centered on the Lord   Psalm 16:1-11

18. A Prayer for Vindication   Psalm 17:1-15

Introduction:

The Book of Psalms was written by many people over centuries of time. One of the earliest of the

Psalmist was Moses who probably composed Psalm 90 during the Exodus. Seventy-three of the Psalms are preceded by the phrase "of David" supporting that he was one of the most prolific of the writers of thee Psalms. Two other group of Psalmist were composed of professional guilds of musicians, the Sons of Asaph (see 1 Chronicles 25:2) and the Sons of Korah. A number of Psalms are of unknown origin.

Each Psalm must be dated individually, or as a part of a group. For example, those composed by David would have produced between 1040 and 971 B.C. Likewise, the two Psalms attributed to Solomon (Psalms 27), assuming that he wrote them, would be dated between 971 and 931 B.C. But the writing of the Psalms was not limited to the period of the monarchy, it reaches back to the time of Moses (around 1400 B.C.) an extends to the period of Exile (mid-fifth century B.C.).

In fact, some believe that the collection of Psalms as we know it did not take final shape until the time of Ezra, when it became the "hymnbook of the second temple."

Because Psalms were produced from such a wide variety of backgrounds, the geography of the Book of Psalms covers the entire world as it would have been known to the ancient Israelite.

2 Chronicles 7:14

If my people, which are called by my name, shall humble themselves, and pray, and seek my face, and turn from their wicked ways; then will I hear from heaven, and will forgive their sin, and will heal their land.

Psalm 122:6

Pray for the peace of Jerusalem; they will prosper who love thee.

Lesson Plan 162

Book of Psalms

Psalms 42-72

Objective: To gain insight on the Book of Psalms which reflects the international scope of God's activity and involvement with all His people.

Objective Breakdown:

1. Introduction

2.	Thirsting for God	Psalm 42:1-11
3.	Longing for a Time of Worship	Psalm 43:1-5
4.	Crying to God in the Midst of Defeat	Psalm 44:1-26
5.	An Anthem for the King's Wedding	Psalm 45:1-17
6.	God Is the Refuge of His People	Psalm 46:1-11
7.	Praise to God the King	Psalm 47:1-9
8.	Praise for God Who Dwells in the City	Psalm 48:1-14
9.	Death Comes to Everyone	Psalm 49:1-20
10.	God Is the Righteous Judge	Psalm 50:1-23
11.	Confession and Prayer for Restoration	Psalm 51:1-19
12.	God Shall Destroy the Wicked	Psalm 52:1-9
13	The Folly of Ignoring God	Psalm 53:1-6
14.	Betrayal Prompts a Plea for Help	Psalm 54:1-7
15.	The Treachery of Friends	Psalm 55:1-23
16.	Trusting God Among the Philistines	Psalm 56:1-13
17.	God Gives Protection from Enemies	Psalm 57:1-11
18.	A Call for God to Judge Wicked Judges	Psalm 58:1-11

Introduction:

People are notorious for setting up divisions between themselves and establishing rules and customs to decide who is in and who is out. Thus, we have tensions, hostilities, and exclusions between nations, races, ethnic groups, income groups, age groups, and on and on.

But God's divisions are different. God divides the world into two categories of people; the righteous and ungodly (Psalms 1:6), those who obey Him, and those who disobey Him. What God pays attention to is whether people seek and follow His ways. Because of Christ, we know that obedience to God includes trusting in the cross of Christ for salvation (John 3:15-16; Acts 2:36-39). Those who reject this provision are choosing eternal death.

No one is excluded from coming to God. The door is open to all (John 6:37), and the key to the door is faith in Christ. The nature of sin is to defy God, and the strong tendency of people in power is to stay in power by any means possible—even if it means defying God to do so. Thus, rulers of the world often conspire together against the Lord (Psalm 2:1-2). But what these leaders fail to realize is that the Lord's Anointed is King and Lord over all the nations of the world, including their own. God has given Him the nations as an inheritance (Psalm 2:8).

God is sovereign even over nations that rage against Him. The psalmist realized that his own country was just a part of God's international reign. Do we understand the same truth about our own nations and governments?

2 Chronicles 7:14

If my people, which are called by my name, shall humble themselves, and pray, and seek my face, and turn from their wicked ways; then will I hear from heaven, and will forgive their sin, and will heal their land.

Psalm 122:6

Pray for the peace of Jerusalem; they will prosper who love thee.

Lesson Plan 163

Book of Psalms

Psalms 73-89

Objective: To gain insight on the Book of Psalms which reflects the international scope of God's activity and involvement with all His people.

Objective Breakdown:

1. Introduction

2. The Prospects of the Good and the Evil   Psalm 73:1-28

3. A Plea for God to Defend His Honor   Psalm 74:1-23

4. God Will Pour Out His Wrath   Psalm 75:1-10

5. God Has Victory Over His Enemies   Psalm 76:1-12

6. A Sleepless Night   Psalm 77:1-20

7. God and Israel: A History   Psalm 78:1-72

8. A Captive Begs for Deliverance   Psalm 79:1-13

9. A Prayer for Israel's Restoration   Psalm 80:1-19

10. Israel Is Urged to Follow God   Psalm 81:1-16

11. God Is the Judge of Judges   Psalm 82:1-8

12. A Plea Against an Unholy Alliance   Psalm 83:1-18

13. The Joy of Dwelling with God   Psalm 84:1-12

14. A Prayer for Revival and Restoration   Psalm 85:1-13

15. An Adoration of God   Psalm 86:1-17

16. Zion the Spiritual Center   Psalm 87:1-7

17. The Problem of Suffering   Psalm 88:1-18

18. God's Covenant with David   Psalm 89:1-52

Introduction:

No authority except from God. Psalm 2 is sending a similar message to that of Romans chapter 13, which affirms the institution of government by asserting that "there is no authority except from God" (Romans 13:1). Psalm 2 describes how far-reaching are the implications of this truth that by showing that even the raging nations and rebellious kings who reigns must answer to God, the great King who reigns from Jerusalem through His appointed servant (Psalm 2:1-6).

All government power is derived and delegated power. Ultimately it comes from God. Human governments are visible institutions and political agents that are accountable to and limited by Him.

This encourages political leaders to bow their knee in humble worship of the Lord and to serve Him with fear (Psalm 2:10-11). In the spirit of this psalm, they can show respect to God who placed them in authority and stands ready to help them govern with goodness and justice.

2 Chronicles 7:14

If my people, which are called by my name, shall humble themselves, and pray, and seek my face, and turn from their wicked ways; then will I hear from heaven, and will forgive their sin, and will heal their land.

Psalm 122:6

Pray for the peace of Jerusalem; they will prosper who love thee.

Lesson Plan 164

Book of Psalms

Psalms 90-106

Objective: To gain insight on the Book of Psalms which reflects the international scope of God's activity and involvement with all His people.

Objective Breakdown:

1. Introduction

2. Man Is Frail and God Is Eternal   Psalm 90:1-17

3. Finding a Refuge in God   Psalm 91:1-16

4. The Righteous Know God and Praise Him   Psalm 92:1-15

5. The Majesty of God   Psalm 93:1-5

6. God Will Stand Up for the Righteous   Psalm 94:1-23

7. Security from God   Psalm 95:1-11

8. The God of Every Nation   Psalm 96:1-13

9. The God of the Heavens and the Earth   Psalm 97:1-12

10. A Worldwide Song of Praise   Psalm 98:1-9

11. Worshiping God on His Holy Hill   Psalm 99:1-9

12. A Pageant of Praise   Psalm 100:1-5

13. A Commitment to a Holy Lifestyle   Psalm 101:1-8

14. Remembering God in a Troubled Time   Psalm 102:1-28

15. Blessing God for His Many Benefits   Psalm 103:1-22

16. Praise for God the Creator   Psalm 104:1-35

17. God Can and Will Keep His Promises   Psalm 105:1-45

18. The Mighty God Has Mercy   Psalm 106:1-48

Introduction:

The righteous rebuke to the nations. However, nations might justify and judge their actions, the ultimate judge of their conduct is God. His righteousness, which flows from their His very character is the final standard against which right and wrong are measured (Psalm 9:3-8). This righteous Judge rebuked the nations of David's day for failing to do what David had done in Psalm 8 -acknowledge God (Psalm 8:1,9).

The Kingdom of Israel quickly rose to a place of prominence and power under David and his successor Solomon. This window of opportunity opened during the period in which no one empire dominated the Middle East (1000 B.C.). Egypt was in decline, and Assyria had not yet become a major power. The two Israelite kings seize the moment by strengthening Israel's defenses, expanding its borders, increasing its trade, and storing up enormous wealth (2 Chronicles 9:26).

Meanwhile, many of Israel's neighbors continued to ignore God and govern with wickedness. Instead of ruling their people with justice and compassion, they often oppressed them. They often attacked other nations without provocation, destroying innocent people (Psalm 9:6). But God responded by destroying the destroyers. He pledged not to forget the needy and helpless, and avenged the injustices they had suffered by blotting out the wicked (Psalm 9:7-18).

The same righteous God sits in judgment on the world today. He watches what nations do and will not leave their sins unpunished. Nations and their leaders are still accountable to the Lord for their programs and policies. This fact should kindle a healthy fear of the Lord and a humble recognition that human leaders are only mortal (Psalm 9:20).

2 Chronicles 7:14

If my people, which are called by my name, shall humble themselves, and pray, and seek my face, and turn from their wicked ways; then will I hear from heaven, and will forgive their sin, and will heal their land.

Psalm 122:6

Pray for the peace of Jerusalem; they will prosper who love thee.

Lesson Plan 165

Book of Psalms

Psalms 107-150

Objective: To gain insight on the Book of Psalms which reflects the international scope of God's activity and involvement with all His people.

Objective Breakdown:

1. Introduction

2. Praise for God's Willingness to Help   Psalm 107:1-43

3. Looking Forward to God's Support   Psalm 108:1-13

4. A Plea for Judgment on Persecutors   Psalm 109:1-31

5. Messiah the King Comes to Judge   Psalm 110:1-7

6. Praising God for His Great Works   Psalm 111:1-10

7. The Fear of the Lord Brings Blessings   Psalm 112:1-10

8. God on High Sees the Lowly   Psalm 113:1-9

9. The Earth Responds to the Exodus   Psalm 114:1-8

10. Israel's God Is the One True God   Psalm 115:1-18

11. A Psalm of Grateful Worship   Psalm 116:1-19

12. The World Is Called to Praise God   Psalm 117:1-2

13. Trust in the Lord's Mercy   Psalm 118:1-29

14. They Who Honor God's Word Are Blessed   Psalm 119:1-176

15. Crying Out to God in Distress   Psalm 120:1-7

16. Help from the Lord   Psalm 121:1-8

17. A Prayer for the Peace of Jerusalem   Psalm 122:1-9

18. Looking for God   Psalm 123:1-4

Introduction:

You are unique. A fundamental truth of Scripture is that God has created people in His image (Genesis 1:26-28). Not only humanity in general, but every individual, including you (Psalm 33:15). The same God whose mind and power that fashioned the stars, the seas, the animals, and all other human beings has carefully, intentionally, and individually crafted you. You are not just a collection of molecules thrown together by random chance. The Lord of the universe has called you into being.

The truth has profound implications:

(a) You are unique. Even though you share many things in common with other people, you are essentially one of a kind. No one else has been given the same exactly the same makeup as God has given you. Your face, your fingerprints, your voice, your genetic makeups are matched by no one else. Likewise, God has handcrafted you with your personality, your unique set of talents and motivations, and your special "bent" in life. This leads to the fact that that:

(b) You have a unique purpose. Not only has God made you, He has designed you for a special reason. He has crafted you to carry out a unique purpose and mission in life—what the New Testament calls your "good works" (Ephesians 2:10). God had intended that your life would be aimed toward these special ends before He created you. For that reason, ultimate meaning in life comes from discovering and carrying out this unique purpose.

(c) You have a responsibility to your Creator. God created you both to live with Him and to live for Him. Ultimately you belong to Him (Romans 14:7-8). Therefore, your life needs to center on Him. The great tragedy of many people is that they have turned their backs on the Creator and lived their lives unto themselves. But all will give an account to the Lord for how they have lived their lives. He will ask whether or not they have used what He has given them to honor Him and fulfill His purposes.

2 Chronicles 7:14

If my people, which are called by my name, shall humble themselves, and pray, and seek my face, and turn from their wicked ways; then will I hear from heaven, and will forgive their sin, and will heal their land.

Psalm 122:6

Pray for the peace of Jerusalem; they will prosper who love thee.

The Book of Proverbs

Scripture Focus Chapters 1-31

Objective: To gain insight on the book of Proverbs which reflects good counsel for everyone who wants to honor God in their life.

Objective Breakdown:

1. Introduction

2. The Purpose of Proverbs — Chapter 1:1-7

3. Do Not Be Enticed by Sinners — Chapter 1:8-19

4. Seek Wisdom or Be Destroyed — Chapter 1:20-33

5. Wisdom Will Bring Understanding — Chapter 2:1-9

6. Wisdom Will Protect from Evil — Chapter 2:10-22

7. "Lean Not on Your Own Understanding" — Chapter 3:1-12

8. Benefits of Wisdom — Chapter 3:13-26

9. Be Kind to Your Neighbors — Chapter 3:27-35

10. A Father's Instruction — Chapter 4:1-9

11. Two Paths, Two Outcomes — Chapter 4:10-19

12. Practice Self-Control — Chapter 4:20-27

13. Shun Sexual Immorality — Chapter 5:1-14

14. Seek Love from Your Own Spouse — Chapter 5:15-23

15. Don't Make Unwise Promises — Chapter 6:1-5

16. The Folly of Laziness — Chapter 6:6-15

17. Seven Abominations — Chapter 6:16-19

18. Stay Away from the Seductress — Chapter 6:20-29

19. Adultery Is Self-Destruction — Chapter 6:30-35

20. A Crafty Harlot Lures a Young Man — Chapter 7:1-20

2 Chronicles 7:14

If my people, which are called by my name, shall humble themselves, and pray, and seek my face, and turn from their wicked ways; then will I hear from heaven, and will forgive their sin, and will heal their land.

Psalm 122:6

Pray for the peace of Jerusalem; they will prosper who love thee.

Lesson Plan 166

The Book of Proverbs

Chapters 1, 2, & 3

Objective: To gain insight on the book of Proverbs which reflects good counsel for everyone who wants to honor God in his life.

Objective Breakdown:

1. Introduction

2. The Purpose of Proverbs   Chapter 1:1-7

3. Do Not Be Enticed by Sinners   Chapter 1:8-19

4. Seek Wisdom or Be Destroyed   Chapter 1:20-33

5. Wisdom Will Bring Understanding   Chapter 2:1-9

6. Wisdom Will Protect from Evil   Chapter 2:10-22

7. "Lean Not on Your Own Understanding"   Chapter 3:1-12

8. Benefits of Wisdom   Chapter 3:13-26

9. Be Kind to Your Neighbors   Chapter 3:27-35

Introduction:

Wisdom. The purpose of Proverbs is straight forward "to know Wisdom" (Proverbs 1:2). It is common to conceive of wisdom as either an advanced form of knowledge or learning, or else are sense of deep understanding and insight. This view of wisdom has a touch of the mystical about it, as if those who possess it had in some way tapped into profound, enigmatic truths from ages past.

However, there is no mystery about wisdom talked about in Proverbs, nor is it necessarily limited to a privileged few. The wisdom which Proverbs mention more than 40 times and that Ecclesiastes mentions 27 times is the Hebrew chokmah, which means something like "the skill of living." This wisdom is practical, not esoteric. It means that person knows how to live in a responsible, productive, and prosperous way.

From the standpoint, the wisdom of Proverbs has a lot in common with what we might call common sense, or even "street smarts." It is an understanding of the way the world works. That is why Proverbs deals with so many day-to-day issues of life, especially those involving moral choices and other decisions that affect the future.

The Book of Proverbs stresses the need for counsel for every person who wants to honor God in life. Yes! The wisdom of Proverbs has benefits for everyone—even those who do not believe in God.

2 Chronicles 7:14

If my people, which are called by my name, shall humble themselves, and pray, and seek my face, and turn from their wicked ways; then will I hear from heaven, and will forgive their sin, and will heal their land.

Psalm 122:6

Pray for the peace of Jerusalem; they will prosper who love thee.

Lesson Plan 167

The Book of Proverbs

Chapters 4, 5, & 6

Objective: To gain insight on the book of Proverbs which reflects good counsel for everyone who wants to honor God in his life.

Objective Breakdown:

1. Introduction

2. A Father's Instruction   Chapter 4:1-9

3. Two Paths, Two Outcomes   Chapter 4:10-19

4. Practice Self-Control   Chapter 4:20-27

5. Shun Sexual Immorality   Chapter 5:1-14

6. Seek Love from Your Own Spouse   Chapter 5:15-23

7. Don't Make Unwise Promises   Chapter 6:1-5

8. The Folly of Laziness   Chapter 6:6-15

9. Seven Abominations   Chapter 6:16-19

10. Stay Away from the Seductress   Chapter 6:20-29

11. Adultery Is Self-Destruction   Chapter 6:30-35

Introduction:

Wisdom from a father to his son. Many of the Proverbs were originally addressed to young men as wisdom from fathers to their sons (Proverbs 1:8; 2:1; 3:1; 11, 21; 4:1). This reflects the nature of the ancient Hebrew culture, in which sons were expected to inherit leadership of the family and the nation.

These youths are warned about the many of the traps that commonly ensnare young men:

     o. Sexual temptation (Proverbs 5:15-20; 7:1-27);

     o. Foolishness (Proverbs 12:15-16);

     o. Ill-gotten gain (Proverbs 10:2; 13:11);

o. Verbal abuse (Proverbs 13:2-3; 15:1);

o. Strong drink (Proverbs 31:4);

o. Pride or selfish ambition (Proverbs 16:1-9).

However, the fact that the book has a masculine tone should not lead us to think that woman is excluded from either the giving or the receiving of Proverbs' teaching. The book repeatedly urges youth to pay attention to the instruction of their mothers (Proverbs 1:8; 6:20; 10:1; 30:7). Likewise, the principles and warnings of the book apply just as much to young women as they do to young men—particularly in our own culture, where both sexes engage in many of the same activities.

2 Chronicles 7:14

If my people, which are called by my name, shall humble themselves, and pray, and seek my face, and turn from their wicked ways; then will I hear from heaven, and will forgive their sin, and will heal their land.

Psalm 122:6

Pray for the peace of Jerusalem; they will prosper who love thee.

Lesson Plan 168

The Book of Proverbs

Chapters 7, 8, 9, & 10

Objective: To gain insight on the book of Proverbs which reflects good counsel for everyone who wants to honor God in his life.

Objective Breakdown:

1. Introduction

2. A Crafty Harlot Lures a Young Man   Chapter 7:1-20

3. He Who Is Seduced Is Ruined   Chapter 7:21-27

4. Wisdom Cries Out for a Hearing   Chapter 8:1-11

5. Wisdom Prospers Those Who Love Her   Chapter 8:12-21

6. Wisdom Has Been from Everlasting   Chapter 8:22-31

7. Blessed Is the One Who Gains Wisdom   Chapter 8:32-36

8. The House of Wisdom   Chapter 9:1-12

9. The House of Foolishness   Chapter 9:13-18

10. Solomon on Wisdom and Foolishness   Chapter 10:1-32

Introduction:

Honoring God with your whole paycheck. Most Christians are well aware of their responsibility to financially support the work of the church. However, once they have fulfilled that obligation, many have assumed that the rest of their income is theirs to use as they please. But God is as interested in what we as believers do with the money we keep as He is with the money we give away. It is from that prospective that Scripture exhorts us to honor the Lord with our possessions (Proverbs 3:9-10).

The ancient Israelites gave God the "first fruits," the first born of the flocks and the first crops gathered at harvest time. These were dedicated to God by formally presenting them at the temple on the Day of Pentecost (Numbers 28:26). Giving to God the first and best of one harvest indicated a recognition that everything belonged to Him.

Included among possessions that the Israelites owned were the means of production—land, animals, tools, mills, looms, potter's wheels, carts, boats, and the likes. Therefore, honoring the Lord with one's possessions went far beyond a weekly or monthly check in the offering basket or a year end contribution to a charity in essence, it meant that all of one's work was to be dedicated to God.

According to Proverbs, the outcome of such a lifestyle would be prosperity (Proverbs 3:10). It is tempting for modern day Christians to read as a promise of financial gain in exchange for obedience to God. However, the Proverbs are not so much promises to be claimed as they are observations about the way life tends to work. For the most part, people prosper as they honor God in their work and with their income derived from their work.

2 Chronicles 7:14

If my people, which are called by my name, shall humble themselves, and pray, and seek my face, and turn from their wicked ways; then will I hear from heaven, and will forgive their sin, and will heal their land.

Psalm 122:6

Pray for the peace of Jerusalem; they will prosper who love thee.

Lesson Plan 169

The Book of Proverbs

Chapters 11, 12, 13, & 14

Objective: To gain insight on the book of Proverbs which reflects good counsel for everyone who wants to honor God in his life.

Objective Breakdown:

1. Introduction

2. Wickedness Leads to Death   Chapter 11:1-20

3. Blessing Comes to the Righteous   Chapter 11:21-31

4. The Wise and Righteous Are Blessed   Chapter 12:1-28

5. Honesty and Hard Work Pay Off   Chapter 13:1-25

6. Wisdom and Foolishness Compared   Chapter 14:1-35

Introduction:

Many of us are so busy that we never take time to consider where we are going—or why. Yet we humans are the only creatures that God created with the capacity for self-reflection. We can think about ourselves, evaluate our lives, and make changes in light of what we see. Proverbs encourages us to stay on the path of wisdom, to be careful not to stray "to right or to the left" (Proverbs 4:25-27).

To invest in the future of another person is a praiseworthy activity. God especially calls parent to invest in the lives of their children (Proverbs 1:8; 4:1), but others also play a vital role. Teachers, coaches, and other adults can have a lasting influence in the development of young people (Proverbs 4:11-13).

One of the most fundamental and far-reaching truths of Scripture is that God is the Creator of the universe (Proverbs 3:19-20). Solomon realized the significance of this truth and affirmed it early in Proverbs in order to emphasize that true wisdom is not of human origin but comes from the Lord who made all things.

An important implication of God being the Creator is that He is King over all peoples of the world. In wisdom He has brought every person into existence. Therefore, everyone owes ultimate allegiance to the Lord, an allegiance that transcends family, tribal, ethnic, and national claims. It is not that these are unimportant. But wisdom says that each of us needs to fear the Lord first and foremost (Proverbs 1:7).

Anyone can follow God's ways, and everyone is accountable to the Creator. Is that the wisdom you are pursuing?

2 Chronicles 7:14

If my people, which are called by my name, shall humble themselves, and pray, and seek my face, and turn from their wicked ways; then will I hear from heaven, and will forgive their sin, and will heal their land.

Psalm 122:6

Pray for the peace of Jerusalem; they will prosper who love thee.

Lesson Plan 170

The Book of Proverbs

Chapters 15, 16, 17, & 18

Objective: To gain insight on the book of Proverbs which reflects good counsel for everyone who wants to honor God in his life.

Objective Breakdown:

1. Introduction

2. Wisdom in Speech   Chapter 15:1-12

3. Happiness in Life   Chapter 15:13-20

4. The Blessing of Good Advice   Chapter 15:21-33

5. The Obedient Heart   Chapter 16:1-33

6. The Actions of Wisdom and Foolishness   Chapter 17:1-28

7. Foolishness Is Shown by Words   Chapter 18:1-24

Introduction:

Co-signing for loans. A common policy among lending institutions today is to require people with risky credit to have someone co-sign their loan. The co-signer must be able to make good on the note if the principal borrower defaults on repayment. In effect the risk in the transaction is being transferred from the lender to the co-signer. However, Proverbs warns would-be co-signers that the risks are too great to accept, even for a friend (17:18).

We are accountable both to God (Matthew 25:14-30) and to our families and heirs (Proverbs 13:22) for how we manage our property. We are to use our resources to the glory of God and for the benefits of others (1 Peter 4:10) not risk them unnecessarily.

Co-signing lessens the incentive for the principal borrower to pay back the loan, and thus may encourage irresponsibility. Are there circumstances under which co-signing a note is permissible? Scripture does not flatly prohibit suretyship. In fact, it offers several examples which indicate that guaranteeing a loan can be form of service to others, and even a testimony of love and the self-sacrificial spirit that lies at the heart of the Gospel.

The patriarch Judah volunteered to be "collateral" lot his younger half-brother Benjamin (Genesis 43:8-9). Joseph was overwhelmed by this willingness of Judah to place himself at risk (Genesis 44:32; 45:11). Judah was demonstrating the kind self-sacrifice that Jesus later urged His followers to practice: "Greater love has no one than this, than to lay down one's life for his friends (John 15:13).

2 Chronicles 7:14

If my people, which are called by my name, shall humble themselves, and pray, and seek my face, and turn from their wicked ways; then will I hear from heaven, and will forgive their sin, and will heal their land.

Psalm 122:6

Pray for the peace of Jerusalem; they will prosper who love thee.

Lesson Plan 171

The Book of Proverbs

Chapters 19, 20, 21, & 22

Objective: To gain insight on the book of Proverbs which reflects good counsel for everyone who wants to honor God in his life.

Objective Breakdown:

1. Introduction

2. Wickedness Will Have Its Results   Chapter 19:1-29

3. Integrity and Corruption Contrasted   Chapter 20:1-30

4. Ethical and Unethical Actions   Chapter 21:1-31

5. Advice for Moral Living   Chapter 22:1-16

6. The Words of the Wise   Chapter 22:17-29

Introduction:

The basis of government. Political parties often formulate a platform to let voters know what their fundamental belief ad values are, and where their candidates stand on issues. But what is the underlying "platform" or basis for the institution of government itself? Scripture teaches that government ultimately derives from God's wisdom (Proverbs 8:15-16).

For some, this truth may be hard to adept in light of widespread disillusionment with government today, the decisions of political leaders and government officials around the world sometimes look most unwise. Yet that does not change the fact that God established rule and authority, and that all leaders will ultimately answer to Him for their leadership (Proverbs 2:1 and Romans 13:2). And as evil and foolish as governments sometimes are, the world be in anarchy without them.

Proverbs challenges governments leaders to fulfill their roles with godly wisdom. They can start by fearing the Lord (Proverbs 1:7; 2:1-9). Then they can be wise about who they listen to and how they make decisions (Proverbs 24:6). If the wisdom of God placed leaders in power, then it makes sense for them to wield power according to the wisdom of God. The book of Proverbs is good place to start acquiring wisdom.

Proverbs personifies wisdom as a companion and associate of the Lord when He created the heavens and the earth. Wisdom as both a craftsman and delightful colleague in enjoyable, even playful work (Proverbs 8: 30-31). It is easy to see wisdom's mastery as a worker. Every aspect of creation reveals infinite insight and genius (Proverbs 8:27-30 and 104:24).

2 Chronicles 7:14

If my people, which are called by my name, shall humble themselves, and pray, and seek my face, and turn from their wicked ways; then will I hear from heaven, and will forgive their sin, and will heal their land.

Psalm 122:6

Pray for the peace of Jerusalem; they will prosper who love thee.

Lesson Plan 172

The Book of Proverbs

Chapters 23, 24, 25, 26, & 27

Objective: To gain insight on the book of Proverbs which reflects good counsel for everyone who wants to honor God in his life.

Objective Breakdown:

1. Introduction

2. Advice to Promote Wisdom   Chapter 23:1-28

3. A Warning About Alcohol Abuse   Chapter 23:29-35

4. Avoid Evil and Seek Wisdom   Chapter 24:1-22

5. More Sayings of the Wise   Chapter 24:23-34

6. Behavior in Public Life   Chapter 25:1-28

7. Warnings About the Foolish and Lazy   Chapter 26:1-28

8. Wisdom for Living   Chapter 27:1-27

Introduction:

The dangerous tongue. Has your tongue ever gotten you into trouble? Perhaps you have said something that you wish you had not. Or perhaps you have been on the receiving end of a biting or thoughtless comment and have felt wounded or slandered. If so, then you can appreciate the great damage that can come from an uncontrolled tongue (Proverbs 10:18-21). Hatred, slander, and wickedness thrive because of words we speak.

Jesus' brother James recognized this destructive pattern in the early church. He realized how easy it is to blurt out comments without weighing the consequences. He warned the early church about lack of restraint when it comes to the tongue:

He urged them to be quick to listen but slow to speak (James 1:19).

He cautioned them not to think of themselves as religious if they could not control what they said (James 1:26).

He told them not to claim to have faith unless their deeds matched their words (James 2:14-24).

He warned them that the tongue boasts great things despite it being tiny (James 3:5).

He warned them that the tongue is a "world of iniquity" (James 3:6), "an unruly evil, full of deadly poison" (James 3:8), and a fountain of grumbling (James 5:9).

He pointed out that speech can be a blessing or cursing, like a spring of that gives fresh or bitter water or a fig tree that bears olives or a grape vine that bears figs (James 3:10-12).

He noted that some were using speech as a means of maligning one another (James 4:11).

He challenged believers about making oaths and promises that were inconsistent (James 5:12).

2 Chronicles 7:14

If my people, which are called by my name, shall humble themselves, and pray, and seek my face, and turn from their wicked ways; then will I hear from heaven, and will forgive their sin, and will heal their land.

Psalm 122:6

Pray for the peace of Jerusalem; they will prosper who love thee.

Lesson Plan 173

The Book of Proverbs

Chapters 28, 29, 30, & 31

Objective: To gain insight on the Book of Proverbs which reflects good counsel for everyone who wants to honor God in his life.

Objective Breakdown:

1. Introduction

2. Forsake Evil and Follow Righteousness   Chapter 28:1-28

3. How to Tell the Wise from the Foolish   Chapter 29:1-27

4. The Reflections of Agur   Chapter 30:1-33

5. The Words of King Lemuel   Chapter 31:1-9

6. The Virtuous Woman   Chapter 31:10-31

Introduction:

Respect for the poor. Sometimes people dismiss the poor by misapplying Jesus' remarks that "you have the poor with you always" (Mark 14:7). This can be a smug way of disavowing responsibility to help or even care about the plight of poor people. The rationalization is, "they 'll always be around, and there is nothing I can do about it, so why even try?"

The Book of Proverbs declares that God so identifies with the poor that to mock the poor is to insult God (Proverbs 17:5). Consider the ways that we may be mocking the poor: by laughing at their condition; by jumping to conclusions about why they are poor; by taunting them with words; by training our eyes to look upon them as if they were invisible; or even adopting the pious attitude, "There by the grace of God go I."

Jesus words about the inevitability of there being poor people can also be read as a call to His followers to serve the poor after He was gone. His other statements would certainly support that. By serving the poor, we are continually serving Jesus. But if we close our eyes and ears to their plight, then God warns that we will not be noticed when we fall on hard times (Proverbs 21:13).

Have you ever struggled with yourself about whether you should give spare change to a homeless person? On the one hand you don't want to be heartless. On the other hand, you don't want to encourage what may be irresponsible behavior or feed someone's possible addiction to drugs or alcohol. What should you do? Scripture does not make a decision for us, but it does show a shaft of light on the issue. In some unspecified way, whatever charity we show to the poor will be repaid, not necessarily by the poor but by the Lord (Proverbs 19:17). Somehow the Lord assumes the debt.

2 Chronicles 7:14

If my people, which are called by my name, shall humble themselves, and pray, and seek my face, and turn from their wicked ways; then will I hear from heaven, and will forgive their sin, and will heal their land.

Psalm 122:6

Pray for the peace of Jerusalem; they will prosper who love thee.

The Book of Ecclesiastes

Scripture Focus Chapters 1-12

Objective: To gain insight on the book of Ecclesiastes which reflects good counsel for everyone who wants to honor God in their life.

Objective Breakdown:

1. Introduction

2. All Is Vanity   Chapter 1:1-11

3. "I Set My Heart to Know Wisdom"   Chapter 1:12-18

4. The King Tests Pleasure   Chapter 2:1-9

5. Pleasure Is Found Wanting   Chapter 2:10-17

6. Wealth Must Go to Another Someday   Chapter 2:18-26

7. Life Has Its Times and Seasons   Chapter 3:1-15

8. The Problem of Evil in the World   Chapter 3:16-22

9. The Tears of the Oppressed   Chapter 4:1-6

10. The Problem of Human Isolation   Chapter 4:7-16

11. False Vows and Oppression   Chapter 5:1-9

12. Bad Investments and Loss of Wealth   Chapter 5:10-20

13. Not Everyone Can Enjoy Life   Chapter 6:1-9

14. Humanity Is Limited   Chapter 6:10-12

15. Consideration of What Is Good   Chapter 7:1-14

16. The Limitations of Good   Chapter 7:15-29

17. The Limitations of Good (cont.)   Chapter 8:1

18. "Keep the King's Commandment"   Chapter 8:2-8

19. The Fear of God Brings Well-Being   Chapter 8:9-17

20. Knowledge of the Future Escapes Us   Chapter 9:1-8

Lesson Plan 174

The Book of Ecclesiastes

Chapters 1, 2, & 3

Objective: To grasp the wisdom and understanding that are reflected within the book of Ecclesiastes.

Objective Breakdown:

1. Introduction

2. All is Vanity   Chapter 1:1-11

3. "I set my Heart to Know Wisdom"   Chapter 1:12-18

4. The King Tests Pleasure   Chapter 2:1-9

5. Pleasure is Found Wanting   Chapter 2:10-17

6. Wealth Must Go to Another Someday   Chapter 2:18-26

7. Life Has its Times and Seasons   Chapter 3:1-15

8. The Problem of Evil in the World   Chapter 3:16-22

Introduction:

Ecclesiastes says that it is the work of "the Preacher, the son of David, king in Jerusalem" (Ecclesiastes 1:1). This and the description of the author's luxurious and at times even reckless lifestyle (Ecclesiastes 2:1-16) point to Solomon as the source for this book. If so, Ecclesiastes would have been written sometime in the later part of Solomon's life, perhaps around 920 B.C.

Life with–and–without God (Ecclesiastes 1:13-14). In many ways, Ecclesiastes spells out the significance of what happened in the Garden of Eden. When we take an honest look at life, we have to acknowledge the ultimate futility of life without God.

The message of Ecclesiastes may be sobering, but it remains relevant for Christians for Christians today. It helps to temper our expectations for life here and now. God will surely make us all that He created us to be in Christ (Philippians 1:6), but as long as we are on this side of heaven, we will groan as Paul put it, along with the rest of creation, waiting for the Lord to free us from the curse (Romans 8:21-22).

The book provides one answer to life which is the foundation of wisdom: "Fear God and keep His commandments" (Ecclesiastes 12:13). And "there is nothing new under the sun" (Ecclesiastes 1:9); and "to everything there is a season, a time for every purpose under heaven" (Ecclesiastes 3:1).

2 Chronicles 7:14

If my people, which are called by my name, shall humble themselves, and pray, and seek my face, and turn from their wicked ways; then will I hear from heaven, and will forgive their sin, and will heal their land.

Psalm 122:6

Pray for the peace of Jerusalem; they will prosper who love thee.

Lesson Plan 175

The Book of Ecclesiastes

Chapters 4, 5, 6, & 7

Objective: To gain insight on the Book of Ecclesiastes which reflects good counsel for everyone who wants to honor God in their life.

Objective Breakdown:

1. Introduction

2. The Tears of the Oppressed   Chapter 4:1-6

3. The Problem of Human Isolation   Chapter 4:7-16

4. False Vows and Oppression   Chapter 5:1-9

5. Bad Investments and Loss of Wealth   Chapter 5:10-20

6. Not Everyone Can Enjoy Life   Chapter 6:1-9

7. Humanity Is Limited   Chapter 6:10-12

8. Consideration of What Is Good   Chapter 7:1-14

9. The Limitations of Good   Chapter 7:15-29

Introduction: Which is Better?

They say that sometimes good is the enemy of the best, yet making a choice is not always easy. Wisdom is better than much wealth; it is more profitable (Proverbs 3:13–14; 8:11). Fearing the Lord is to be preferred over great treasure associated with trouble (Proverbs 15:16). A simple meal with love is better than a feast with hatred (Proverb 15:17).

Associating with the humble is better than getting wealthy with the proud (Proverbs 16:19).

Self-control is better than getting to rule your own city (Proverbs 16:32).

It is better to be poor and honest than rich and crooked (Proverbs 19:22; 22:1; 28:6).

An open rebuke is to be preferred over love that is never expressed (Proverbs 27:5).

Solomon devoted much time of his life to the acquisition of great riches. "Whatever my eyes desired

I did not keep from them," he said, "this nothing but *vanity* and grasping for the wind" (Ecclesiastes 2:10-11).

Do you own possessions, or do they own you? Consider how many things you have that you could just as easily live without.

Self-Assessment:

1. Do you have specific possession that you would never consider giving away to anyone?

2. How do you define success?

3. Do you have any friends who you would consider poor? If not, why not?

4. How do you measure self-fulfillment? How do you know you are happy?

2 Chronicles 7:14

If my people, which are called by my name, shall humble themselves, and pray, and seek my face, and turn from their wicked ways; then will I hear from heaven, and will forgive their sin, and will heal their land.

Psalm 122:6

Pray for the peace of Jerusalem; they will prosper who love thee.

Lesson Plan 176

The Book of Ecclesiastes

Chapters 8, 9, 10, 11, 12

Objective: To gain insight on the book of Ecclesiastes which reflects good counsel for everyone who wants to honor God in their life.

Objective Breakdown:

1. Introduction

2. The Limitations of Good (cont.)   Chapter 8:1

3. "Keep the King's Commandment"   Chapter 8:2-8

4. The Fear of God Brings Well-Being   Chapter 8:9-17

5. Knowledge of the Future Escapes Us   Chapter 9:1-8

6. Enjoy Family and Work   Chapter 9:9-15

7. Proverbs of the Preacher   Chapter 9:16-18

8. Proverbs of the Preacher (cont.)   Chapter 10:1-20

9. God's Ways Cannot Be Fathomed   Chapter 11:1-6

10. Youth and Old Age   Chapter 11:7-10

11. Youth and Old Age (cont.)   Chapter 12:1-7

12. Conclusion: All Is Vanity – Fear God   Chapter 12:8-14

Introduction:

Biblical Truths for Spiritual Transformation

a. We are to fulfill each day's God-given obligations, for we may not have tomorrow.

b. When we act responsibly before God and experience disappointing or even disastrous results, we are still to continue living as God wants.

c. Regardless of the uncertainties inherent in most enterprises, we are to act responsibly before God, trusting Him to accomplish through us what He purposes.

The Way of Godly Wisdom ultimately leads to...without God.

Learning	Cynicism (1:7-8)
Greatness	Sorrow (1:16-18)
Pleasure	Disappointment (2:1-2)
Labor	Hatred of life (2:17)
Philosophy	Emptiness (3:1-9)
Eternity	A lack of fulfillment (3:11)
Life	Depression (4:2-3)
Religion	Meaningless (5:7)
Wealth	Trouble (5:12)
Existence	Frustration (6:12)
Wisdom	Despair (11:1-8)

The beginning of wisdom is the fear of God (Proverbs 1:7; Ecclesiastes 12:13), a deep respect for and commitment to the ways and words of God. Godly fear ultimately leads to fulfillment.

Wisdom for our souls

Ephesians 4:29-32

29. Let no corrupt communication proceed out of your mouth, but that which is good to the use of edifying, that it may minister grace unto the hearers.

30. And grieve not the holy spirit of God, whereby ye are sealed unto the day of redemption.

31. Let all bitterness, and wrath, and anger, and clamour, and evil speaking, be put away from you, with all malice:

32. And be ye kind one to another, tenderhearted, forgiving one another, even as God for Christ's sake hath forgiven you.

2 Chronicles 7:14

If my people, which are called by my name, shall humble themselves, and pray, and seek my face, and turn from their wicked ways; then will I hear from heaven, and will forgive their sin, and will heal their land.

Pray for the peace of Jerusalem; they will prosper who love thee.

Lesson Plan 177

The Book of Song of Solomon

Scripture Focus Chapters 1-8

Objective: To gain insight on the book of Song of Solomon which takes us back to the ideal of love as God intended. It celebrates the romance of Solomon and his young bride Shulamite (Song 6:13).

Objective Breakdown:

1. Introduction

2. The Bride Desires to Be with the King   Chapter 1:1-7

3. The Bride Has the King's Approval   Chapter 1:8-17

4. The Bride Has the King's Approval (cont.)   Chapter 2:1-3

5. The King Brings His Bride Home   Chapter 2:4-7

6. The Bride Says She Belongs to the King   Chapter 2:8-17

7. The Bride Searches for Her Beloved   Chapter 3:1-5

8. The Wedding Procession   Chapter 3:6-11

9. The Beauty of the Bride   Chapter 4:1-8

10. The Longing of the King   Chapter 4:9-16

11. The Longing of the King (cont.)   Chapter 5:1

12. Suddenly the Royal Groom Is Gone   Chapter 5:2-9

13. Why the King Is So Special   Chapter 5:10-16

14. The Bride's Faith in the King's Love   Chapter 6:1-3

15. The Bride's Beauty Is Praised   Chapter 6:4-9

16. The Bride Returns   Chapter 6:10-13

17. Adoration for the Beautiful Bride   Chapter 7:1-9

18. The Bride Longs for the King   Chapter 7:10-13

2 Chronicles 7:14

If my people, which are called by my name, shall humble themselves, and pray, and seek my face, and turn from their wicked ways; then will I hear from heaven, and will forgive their sin, and will heal their land.

Psalm 122:6

Pray for the peace of Jerusalem; they will prosper who love thee.

Lesson Plan 178

The Book of Song of Solomon

Chapters 1, 2, & 3

Objective: To gain insight on the book of Song of Solomon which takes us back to the ideal of love as God intended. It celebrates the romance of Solomon and his young bride Shulamite (Song 6:13).

Objective Breakdown:

1. Introduction

2. The Bride Desires to be with the King	Chapter 1:1-7
3. The Bride Has the King's Approval	Chapter 1:8-17
4. The Bride Has the King's Approval (cont.)	Chapter 2:1-3
5. The King Brings His Bride Home	Chapter 2:4-7
6. The Bride Says She Belongs to the King	Chapter 2:8-17
7. The Bride Searches for Her Beloved	Chapter 3:1-5
8. The Wedding Procession	Chapter 3:6-11

Introduction:

If we take the Song of Solomon at face value, we find a delightful love poem that portrays the pure and powerful affection that a wedded couple feel for each other. Why would that sort of literature be included in Scripture? Because sinful people can easily forget what genuine love can look like. In thinking about this book, we need to remember that God created male and female, and that originally the first couple were "both naked" and were not ashamed (Genesis 2:25). Sex was God's idea. It was not until Adam and Eve disobedience that sexuality was tainted by shame and the potential for abuse (Genesis 3:8-13, 21).

The Song of Solomon takes us back to the ideal of love as God intended. It celebrates the romance of Solomon and his young bride, only identified as the Shulamite (Song 6:13). The Song of Solomon is not the only passage of Scripture to address the virtues of love. The love chapter 1 Corinthians 13, describes unfailing love which Christians are to live. Ephesians 5:25-33 discusses the love that men ought to show toward wives—the kind of sacrificial love that Christ has for the Church. Indeed, as Christians we can see in the Song of Solomon's a wonderful parallel between Solomon's love for his bride and Christ's love for the Church.

2 Chronicles 7:14

If my people, which are called by my name, shall humble themselves, and pray, and seek my face, and turn from their wicked ways; then will I hear from heaven, and will forgive their sin, and will heal their land.

Psalm 122:6

Pray for the peace of Jerusalem; they will prosper who love thee.

Lesson Plan 179

The Book of Song of Solomon

Chapters 4, 5, 6, 7, & 8

Objective: To gain insight on the book of Song of Solomon which takes us back to the ideal of Love as God intended. It celebrates the romance of Solomon and his young bride Shulamite (Song 6:13).

Objective Breakdown:

1. Introduction

2. The Beauty of the Bride   Chapter 4:1-8

3. The Longing of the King   Chapter 4:9-16

4. The Longing of the King (cont.)   Chapter 5:1

5. Suddenly the Royal Groom Is Gone   Chapter 5:2-9

6. Why the King Is So Special   Chapter 5:10-16

7. The Bride's Faith in the King's Love   Chapter 6:1-3

8. The Bride's Beauty Is Praised   Chapter 6:4-9

9. The Bride Returns   Chapter 6:10-13

10. Adoration for the Beautiful Bride   Chapter 7:1-9

11. The Bride Longs for the King   Chapter 7:10-13

12. The Bride Longs for the King (cont.)   Chapter 8:1-2

13. Joy in Love Renewed   Chapter 8:3-14

Introduction:

Couples in love. Solomon and his wife show all of the affection associated with being in love (Song 2:16). There is one of a number of stories about romantic love told in the Bible. Here are a few:

Isaac and Rebekah...A father seeks and finds a wife for his son, and the young couple love each other deeply.

Jacob and Rachel...Jacob labors 14 years for his father-in-law in order to gain Rachel as his

505

wife.

Boaz and Ruth…Legal technicalities bring together a Moabite widow and a wealthy landowner of Bethlehem, and through them a king is descended.

Elkanah and Hannah…A woman is loved by her husband despite being childless, and God eventually blesses her with birth of a son, who becomes a mighty judge over Israel.

David and Michal…Genuine love is manipulated by a jealous king, but instead of ridding himself of his nemesis the ruler gains a son-in law.

Solomon and the Shulamite…The commitments and delight of two lovers are told in a beautiful poem.

Hosea and Gomer…God calls the prophet Hosea to seek out his adulterous spouse and restore the relationship despite what she has done.

Christ and the Church…Having won His bride's salvation from sin, Christ loves and serves her as His own body, thereby setting an example for husbands everywhere.

Love should command a healthy blend of commitment, service, passion, and joy in our lives.

2 Chronicles 7:14

If my people, which are called by my name, shall humble themselves, and pray, and seek my face, and turn from their wicked ways; then will I hear from heaven, and will forgive their sin, and will heal their land.

Psalm 122:6

Pray for the peace of Jerusalem; they will prosper who love thee.

The Book of Isaiah

Scripture Focus Chapters 1-66

Objective: To gain an understanding and insight on the book of Isaiah which provides us with a strategic concept of God's intentions for the world.

Objective Breakdown:

1. Introduction

2. God's People Have Rebelled   Chapter 1:1-9

3. Hypocritical Worship Is Condemned   Chapter 1:10-20

4. God Will Punish the Faithless   Chapter 1:21-31

5. Zion Established in the Latter Days   Chapter 2:1-9

6. Hiding from the Terror of God   Chapter 2:10-22

7. Judah Will Be Plundered   Chapter 3:1-7

8. Jerusalem Is Likened to Sodom   Chapter 3:8-15

9. Zion's Haughty Women Will Be Shamed   Chapter 3:16-26

10. Zion's Haughty Women Will Be Shamed (cont.)   Chapter 4:1-2

11. Purity and Peace Will Follow Judgment   Chapter 4:3-6

12. The Parable of the Vineyard   Chapter 5:1-7

13. Woe to Oppressors and Drunkards   Chapter 5:8-23

14. Invaders Stand Ready to Be Used by God   Chapter 5:24-30

15. A Vision of the Lord   Chapter 6:1-7

16. Isaiah Is Called to Be a Prophet   Chapter 6:8-13

17. God Sends Reassurance to Ahaz   Chapter 7:1-9

18. A Sign: A Virgin Shall Conceive   Chapter 7:10-17

19. Assyria Will Be God's Hired Razor   Chapter 7:18-25

20. Assyria Will Overpower Damascus   Chapter 8:1-10

Lesson Plan 180

The Book of Isaiah

Chapters 1 & 2

Objective: To give us an understanding of God's strategic plan for the world and for His chosen people.

Objective Breakdown:

1. Introduction

2. God's People Have Rebelled   Chapter 1:1-9

3. Hypocritical Worship Is Condemned   Chapter 1:10-20

4. God Will Punish the Faithless   Chapter 1:21-31

5. Zion Established in the Latter Days   Chapter 2:1-9

6. Hiding from the Terror of God   Chapter 2:10-22

Introduction:

The meaning of the name of Isaiah means "Salvation of Jehovah." Isaiah was a man of the city. He was an aristocrat and a man of culture and always seemed at home in the king's court. He grew up in a day of influence and prosperity. His ministry was about fifty years (750 B.C. to 700 B.C.) and in the city of Jerusalem, his city. He did not dress as an aristocrat, he walked around in a garment of hair cloth like Elijah calling the people to repentance. Isaiah was a great speaker and a perfectionist with words. His speech was from the Lord.

Isaiah was married and had two sons. His first son was named Shear-Jashub (Isaiah 7:3), which means "a remnant shall return." His second son has the longest name in the Bible, Mahershalal-hash-baz, which means "speed the spoil," meaning a speedy doom for Judah's enemies.

Isaiah was called the Messianic Prophet because he was so thoroughly imbued with the idea that his nation was to be a Messianic Nation to the world; that is a nation through which one day a great and wonderful blessing would come from God to all nations. He continually spoke of the day when that great and wonderful work would be done.

Isaiah was a prophetic of the southern Kingdom, Judah, at the time the Northern Kingdom, Israel, was destroyed by the Assyrians. He lived in the reigns of Uzziah, Jotham, Ahaz and Hezekiah. His call was in the year of Uzziah's death, but some of his visions may have been earlier (see Isaiah Chapter 6:1).

According to Jewish tradition, he was slain by Manasseh.

Isaiah prophesied during the reign of 5 kings of Judah (Uzziah, Jotham, Ahaz, Hezekiah, and Manasseh). He is the Messianic prophet. Only the Psalms have more material about Christ than the Book of Isaiah.

While Isaiah was yet a young man (734 B.C.) Assyria carried away all of Northern Israel. Thirteen years later (721 B.C.), Samaria fell and the rest of Israel was carried away. Then a few years later the Assyrians came on into Judah, destroyed 46 walled cities and carried away 200,000 captives. Finally, in (701 B.C.), when Isaiah was an old man, the Assyrians were stopped before the walls of Jerusalem by an angel of God. Thus, Isaiah's whole life was spent under the shadow of threatening Assyrian power and except for Jerusalem, he witnessed the ruin of the entire nation of Israel.

Tradition in the Talmud, which was accepted by the early Church Fathers, states that Isaiah resisted Manasseh's idolatrous decrees and was fasten between two planks and sawn asunder, thus suffering a most horrible death.

2 Chronicles 7:14

If my people, which are called by my name, shall humble themselves, and pray, and seek my face, and turn from their wicked ways; then will I hear from heaven, and will forgive their sin, and will heal their land.

Psalm 122:6

Pray for the peace of Jerusalem; they will prosper who love thee.

Lesson Plan 181

The Book of Isaiah

Chapters 3, 4, & 5

Objective: To give us an understanding of God's strategic plan for the world and for His chosen people.

Objective Breakdown:

1. Introduction

2. Judah Will Be Punished   Chapter 3:1-7

3. Jerusalem is likened to Sodom   Chapter 3:8-15

4. Zion's haughty Women Will Be Shamed   Chapter 3:16-26

5. Purity and Peace Will Follow Judgment Chapter 4:1-6

6. The Parable of the Vineyard   Chapter 5:1-7

7. Woe to Oppressors and Drunkards   Chapter 5:8-23

8. Invaders Stand Ready to be Used by God Chapter 5:24-30

Introduction:

Chapters 2, 3, and 4 are a pre-vision of the Christian age. The book of Isaiah is generally regarded as one of the six greatest in the Bible. The others are: Romans, John, the Psalms, Genesis and Revelation.

God will not allow evil and wickedness to go on forever—neither in a person, a city, nor society at large. He may tolerate disobedience for a while, but sooner or later He will root it out. That is what He did with His people in Judah. Their sins of idolatry, hypocritical worship, and injustice toward the poor, eventually brought destruction on their land. Isaiah described this devastation from the perspective of the women who would survive.

The prophet Isaiah notes their behavior before the fall of the city: proud, seductive, extravagant, self-assured (Isaiah 3:16). But after the men had been slaughtered (Isaiah 3:1-3, 25) and the city gates burned with fire and its walls torn down (Isaiah 3:26), these haughty women would be brought low. Their beauty would be disfigured, and their pride turned to shame (Isaiah 3:17). God would allow the invaders (the Babylonians) to strip them of their expensive jewelry and fine clothing (Isaiah 3:17-23) and leave them childless widows (Isaiah 4:1).

Hundreds of years before the fall of Jerusalem (586 B.C.), Isaiah painted this grim scene of what women of Jerusalem would face after the battle. He described with devastating accuracy the kinds of dishonor to which the Babylonians routinely subjected their captives (Isaiah 3:24).

Yet the vision ended on a note of perspective and hope. The destruction of Jerusalem would not be without purpose. God use it to purify His people from sin (Isaiah 4:4). Then once the evil had been removed, He would raise up people who would enjoy His presence and protection (Isaiah 4:5-6). Many see this promise as the foreshadowing and emergence of the church in the New Testament.

2 Chronicles 7:14

If my people, which are called by my name, shall humble themselves, and pray, and seek my face, and turn from their wicked ways; then will I hear from heaven, and will forgive their sin, and will heal their land.

Psalm 122:6

Pray for the peace of Jerusalem; they will prosper who love thee.

Lesson Plan 182

The Book of Isaiah

Chapters 6, 7, & 8

Objective: To give us an understanding of God's strategic plan for the world and for His chosen people.

Objective Breakdown:

1. Introduction

2. Vision of the Lord   Chapter 6:1-7

3. Isaiah Is Called to be a Prophet   Chapter 6:8-13

4. God Sends Reassurance to Ahaz   Chapter 7:1-9

5. A Sign a Virgin Shall Conceive   Chapter 7:10-17

6. Assyria Will Be God's Hired Razor   Chapter 7:18-25

7. Assyria Will Overpower Damascus   Chapter 8:1-10

8. The People Should Turn Only to God   Chapter 8:11-21

Introduction

At the time of King Uzziah's death (Chapter 6:1), Judah was enjoying prosperity that it had not known since the days of Solomon. The king had followed the Lord during most of his reign, even though he committed a grievous sin during his later years (2 Chronicles 26:16-23).

During the last ten years of Uzziah's life, his son Jotham had ruled in his place. Jotham excelled in honoring the Lord and the prosperity continued (2 Chronicles 27:1-6). But Scripture tells us that despite the two kings' godly leadership, "still the people acted corruptly" (2 Chronicles 27:2). Isaiah describes some of their evil ways (Isaiah 2:1-3:26).

For a while God continued to bless Judah. But as soon as Jotham died and his son Ahaz came to power, the nation turned completely away from the Lord. (2 Kings 16:3-4; 2 Chronicles 28:19). They forgot God's goodness and willfully turned a deaf ear to His pleas for repentance. As a result, the nation would soon reap the consequences of moral and spiritual decline (Isaiah 6:11-12).

King Ahaz practiced idolatry that included child sacrifice (2 Kings 16:3-4), and he actively encouraged moral decline among his people (2 Chronicles 28:19). As a result, the Lord allowed Judah's neighbors to seize much of its territory:

Pekah of Israel and Rezin of Damascus formed an alliance and attacked Judah, killing 120,000 men, and carrying away as captives hundreds of thousands of others. Then they besieged the city of Jerusalem in an attempt to install their own king, but they were unable to take the city (2 Kings 16:5; 2 Chronicles 28:5-8; Isaiah 7:6), just as Isaiah had prophesied (Isaiah 7:7-9).

Rezin captured Elath, Judah's port on the Red Sea (2 Kings 16:5). This enabled the Edomites to attack Judah from the South and carry away captives (2 Chronicles 28:17).

The Philistines invaded the lowlands west of Jerusalem, capturing numerous cities and villages (2 Chronicles 28:18).

Despite these defeats, Ahaz refused to turn back to the Lord. Instead, he appealed for help from the Assyrians. He emptied out the treasuries of the temple and palace and sent what money he had to King Tilgath-Pilser III (2 Kings 16:7-8; 2 Chronicles 28:21). The Assyrian king Tilgath-Pilser responded by capturing Damascus and killing Rezin, king of Syria (2 Kings 16:9). But this only brought Judah under greater Assyrian control.

Observing these events, Isaiah warned Ahaz that his reliance on Tilgath-Pilser was an affront to God that would lead to his downfall (Isaiah 7:10-8:22).

2 Chronicles 7:14

If my people, which are called by my name, shall humble themselves, and pray, and seek my face, and turn from their wicked ways; then will I hear from heaven, and will forgive their sin, and will heal their land.

Psalm 122:6

Pray for the peace of Jerusalem; they will prosper who love thee.

Lesson Plan 183

The Book of Isaiah

Chapters 9, 10, & 11

Objective: To give us an understanding of God's strategic plan for the world and for His chosen people.

Objective Breakdown:

1. Introduction

2. The Prince of Peace Will Be Born   Isaiah 9:1-7

3. Israel will be Devoured   Isaiah 9:8-17

4. Israelites Will Fight Each Other   Isaiah 9:18-21

5. Woe to the Oppressors of the Poor   Isaiah 10:1-4

6. Woe to Assyria   Isaiah 10:5-11

7. God Will Punish Assyria's King   Isaiah 10:12-19

8. A Remnant of Israel Will Return   Isaiah 10:20-23

9. Assyria's Path of Invasion is Traced   Isaiah 10:24-34

10. A Rod from the Stem of Jesse   Isaiah 11:1-5

11. The Peaceable Kingdom   Isaiah 11:6-10

12. God Will Reassemble His People   Isaiah 11:11-16

Introduction:

The district of Galilee, located in the hill country of Zebulun and Naphtali, was inhabited by a mixed population of Israelites and heathen. Galilee was situated on a major trade route, which brought foreigners to the area. Thus, it came to be frowned upon as Galilee of the Gentiles" (Isaiah 9:1).

Yet God promised to send a "great light" on these "people who walked in darkness" (9:2). Who is this light who came for both Gentiles and Israelites? According to the Gospel of Matthew, it was Jesus Christ: "When Jesus heard that John had been put in prison, He departed to Galilee.... that it might be fulfilled which was spoken by Isaiah" (Matthew 4:12-17).

Isaiah's reference to the Midianites, (Isaiah 9:4) recalled the seven years of oppression that Israel endured under the Midianites (Judge 6), descendants of Abraham through the son of his concubine, Keturah. The Midianites attacked the Israelites each year at harvest time, destroying the crops and leaving the people without sustenance. The danger and violence became so severe that the Israelites finally built caves and strongholds in the mountains in order to hide whenever the Midianites attacked.

Finally, God raised up Gideon to lead a small band of warriors against the invaders. Through miraculous means the Lord delivered His people from the scourge of the Midianites.

In a similar way, Isaiah foresaw that God would deliver Judah from the Assyrians, who ruthlessly oppressed the kingdoms of the eastern Mediterranean. And in fact, the Assyrians were eventually turned back from besieging Jerusalem through a miracle that no one but Isaiah anticipated (Isaiah 37:36-37)..

2 Chronicles 7:14

If my people, which are called by my name, shall humble themselves, and pray, and seek my face, and turn from their wicked ways; then will I hear from heaven, and will forgive their sin, and will heal their land.

Psalm 122:6

Pray for the peace of Jerusalem; they will prosper who love thee.

Lesson Plan 184

The Book of Isaiah

Chapters 12 &13

Objective: To give us an understanding of God's strategic plan for the world and for His chosen people.

Objective Breakdown:

1. Introduction

2. Two Songs of Praise   Chapter 12:1-6

3. A Prophecy Against Babylon   Chapter 13:1-8

4. The World Will Be Punished for Evil   Chapter 13:9-16

5. God Will Stir Up the Medes   Chapter 13:17-22

Introduction:

Isaiah's name means "Salvation of Jehovah." Little is known of Isaiah background. We are told in Isaiah 1 that he was the son of Amoz. Traditions tells us that Amoz was the brother to King Amaziah, who was the brother to Uzziah, the king. In that event Isaiah was first cousin of King Uzziah.

Isaiah was a man of the city. He lived all his life in the city. His ministry and labor were in the city. His ministry of over 50 years, from750 B.C. to about 700 B.C. was in the city. His city was Jerusalem. Isaiah was an aristocrat. He was a man of culture and always seemed at home in the Kings court. He grew up in a day of influence and prosperity. King Uzziah of Judah and Jereboam II of Israel (Northern Kingdom), brought the people to the highest heights of prosperity. With prosperity came vice. The history and the Book of Isaiah read like the lives of some Americans who have grown up knowing nothing but wealth and plenty.

Isaiah was great speaker and a perfectionist with the words of the Lord. He spoke as a prophet of Judah, Israel, as well as to the Gentile nations.

Critics of Christianity sometimes point to God's Wrath as a contradiction in His supposedly loving character. "How can you say God is a God of love when the Old Testament says that He is going to strike the earth with the rod of His mouth?" they scornfully ask. To that I would say if you think the Old Testament is rough wait till you see Revelation in the New Testament. God's wrath is based on His righteous character (Isaiah 11:5). When He judges people and nations it is because wrongs need to be righted. His wrath is against evil and wickedness. And God's anger results in a righteous outcome.... peace (Isaiah 6-9).

2 Chronicles 7:14

If my people, which are called by my name, shall humble themselves, and pray, and seek my face, and turn from their wicked ways; then will I hear from heaven, and will forgive their sin, and will heal their land.

Psalm 122:6

Pray for the peace of Jerusalem; they will prosper who love thee.

Lesson Plan 185

The Book of Isaiah

Chapters 14, 15, 16, & 17

Objective: To give us an understanding of God's strategic plan for the world and for His chosen people.

Objective Breakdown:

1. Introduction

2. A Song of Triumph over Babylon   Chapter 14:1-8

3. The Fall of Lucifer   Chapter 14:9-17

4. Babylon Will Be Utterly Wiped-Out   Chapter 14:18-23

5. Assyria Will Be Broken   Chapter 14:24-27

6. A Prophecy Against Philistia   Chapter 14:28-32

7. A Prophecy Against Moab   Chapter 15:1-9

8. Moab's Pride will be Brought Low   Chapter 16:1-7

9. Silence in Moab's Vineyards   Chapter 16:8-14

10. A Prophecy Against Syria and Israel   Chapter 17:1-8

11. Destruction in City and Field   Chapter 17:9-14

Introduction:

God said that judgment would come upon Moab "within three years." For centuries Moab, east of the Dead Sea, had been an enemy of Israel. In Israel's wilderness wanderings, Moabite women seduced Israel's men (Numbers 31:15-17). In the time of Judges Israel was oppressed by Moab for 18 years (Judges 3:12-14). Saul fought Moab (1 Samuel 14:47) and David defeated Moab (2 Samuel 8:2,12). Solomon was influenced by his wives to build an altar to Moab's god Chemosh (1 King 11:7-8). Mesha, Moab's king, had to pay tribute to Ahab, king of Israel (2 Kings 3:5-27). The destruction of Moab described in Isaiah chapters 15 & 16 caused the Moabites, under Assyrian attack to flee south to Edom.

Lament over Moab, Chapter 15:1-4. The names of several Moabite cities and towns are mentioned by Isaiah. Ar and Kir had been destroyed before Isaiah recorded this oracle. These unlocated towns may have been near the southern end of the Dead Sea. Dibon (modern day Dhiban)) was one of Moab's main cities. Nebo, not to be confused with Mount Nebo, is either present-day Khirbet Ayn Musa or Khirbet el Mukkayet. Medweba is modern-day Madaba.

Shaving one's head (Job 1:20) Jeremiah 47:5; Ezekiel 7:18, Amos 8:10; Micah 1:16) and cutting one's beard were signs of humiliation (Isaiah 7:20; Jeremiah 48:37). Isaiah exposed the pride and conceit of Moab.

The people of Moab should have realized their impotence before the Assyrians and turned to God through neighbor Israel, but they refused to do so. As a result of their pride, confident that they did not need God, the fruitfulness and productivity of their land would be stopped by the invading Assyrian army and by the drought which would accompany the invasion. It would and did wipe out Moab's chances of survival.

2 Chronicles 7:14

If my people, which are called by my name, shall humble themselves, and pray, and seek my face, and turn from their wicked ways; then will I hear from heaven, and will forgive their sin, and will heal their land.

Psalm 122:6

Pray for the peace of Jerusalem; they will prosper who love thee.

Lesson Plan 186

The Book of Isaiah

Chapters 18, 19, 20, & 21

Objective: To give us an understanding of God's strategic plan for the world and for his chosen people.

Objective Breakdown:

1. Introduction

2. A Prophecy Against Ethiopia   Isaiah 18:1:7

3. A Prophecy Against Egypt   Isaiah 19:1-15

4. Someday Egypt will Serve the Lord   Isaiah 19:16-25

5. Ashdod's Fall Warns Egypt and Ethiopia   Isaiah 20:1-6

6. The Medes will Conquer Babylon   Isaiah 21:1-10

7. Prophecies Against Edom and Arabia   Isaiah 21:11-17

Introduction:

No one knows exactly when Isaiah declared his "burden" against Egypt, or when the civil war and take over that he predicted (Isaiah 19:2-4) was fulfilled. But in Isaiah's day, Egypt was in serious decline. In fact, the city of Thebes, which the Egyptians considered holy, was the site of violent strife— "Egyptians against Egyptians." In spite of these problems, Hosea, the last of the kings of the northern kingdom of Israel (732-722 B.C.), allied with so, King of Egypt against the Assyrians (725 B.C.; 2 Kings 17:4). This proved to be his undoing. When the Assyrians King Shalmaneser found out about the pact he sent his armies against Samaria. No Egyptians came to the city's aid, and it fell in 722 B.C.

Two years later, Egypt itself was conquered by the Ethiopians. This was the first time in a thousand years that Egypt had come under foreign control. But the Ethiopian dominance was short lived. The Assyrians invaded, demolished Thebes so badly that the prophet Nahum used the carnage as an illustration of what would ultimately befall Nineveh (Nahum 3:8-10).

Spiritual superhighway. Developed nations are currently building an "information superhighway" to link societies together through interactive computer technology. In Isaiah's time, Judah was flanked by two empires. To the north and east lay Assyria, a fierce, ambitious nation that dominated the Near East. To the south and west was Egypt, the ancient nemesis of the Israelites, but by then an aging superpower

526

that was collapsing in upon itself through civil war and political strife.

Isaiah had predicted the eventual demise of Egypt (Isaiah 19:1-15) and Assyria (Isaiah 10:5-12). Yet the prophet offered a word of hope even on the midst of God's judgment. "In that day" the Lord would bring into existence a highway of commerce and peace extending from Egypt to Assyria, passing through a revived Israel. Egyptians and Assyrians would join Israelites to worship God together. When will this spiritual highway come about? Its completion still lies in the future, but one can say that portion have already being constructed. Recall Pentecost.

2 Chronicles 7:14

If my people, which are called by my name, shall humble themselves, and pray, and seek my face, and turn from their wicked ways; then will I hear from heaven, and will forgive their sin, and will heal their land.

Psalm 122:6

Pray for the peace of Jerusalem; they will prosper who love thee.

Lesson Plan 187

The Book of Isaiah

Chapters 22, 23, & 24

Objective: To give us an understanding of God's strategic plan for the world and for his chosen people.

Objective Breakdown:

1. Introduction

2. Jerusalem's Fall Is Foreseen   Chapter 22:1-11

3. Merrymaking Instead of Mourning   Chapter 22:12-14

4. Shebna's Inappropriate Tomb   Chapter 22:15-24

5. A Prophecy Against Tyre   Chapter 23:1-18

6. The Earth's Impending Judgment   Chapter 24:1-13

7. The Lord's Name Will Be Vindicated   Chapter 24:14-23

Introduction:

The sounds of modern warfare include loud explosions, jet aircraft, helicopters, etc. In Isaiah's day the noise of ancient warfare was primarily the sounds of human beings crying out either in victory or defeat. The din of battle can be heard in Isaiah's vivid description of the fall of Jerusalem: shouting from the roof tops (Isaiah 22:1); the thud of arrows shot by armies of skilled archers (Isaiah 22:2-3); the moaning and weeping of captives (Isaiah 22:3-4); the pounding of battering rams on city gates and walls (Isaiah 22:5); the clamoring for help that never comes (Isaiah 22:5); the thundering of chariots and the neighing of horses

(Isaiah 22:6-7) and the collapse of houses in order to furnish building materials for fortifying the walls (Isaiah 22:10).

Ecclesiastes says that there is a "time to weep and a time to laugh, a time to mourn and a time to dance" (Ecclesiastes 3:4). It is crucial that we know which time is which. Apparently, the people of Jerusalem failed to recognize that God had called them to weeping and mourning instead of gladness (Isaiah 22:12-14). From God's perspective there was little for His people to celebrate especially in the last days of the southern kingdom.

For example, even as the armies of Babylon were coming against Jerusalem, King Zedekiah (597-587 B.C.) and his people completely turned away from the Lord. The king "stiffened his neck and hardened his heart" against God (2 Chronicles 36:13). The king ignored the words of Jeremiah the prophet (2 Chronicles 36:12) and the people likewise mocked and scoffed at the prophets and despised their words (2 Chronicles 36:16). Zedekiah reneged on a sworn oath by rebelling against the Babylonians (2 Chronicles 36:13). The chief priests and the people practiced the idolatrous abominations of pagan nations, even to the extent of defiling the temple (2 Chronicles 36:14).

In short, the people went about their lives as if God did not matter. When they should have been repenting of sin and calling on the Lord for help. They held parties, violated God's ways, and took a fatalistic attitude toward life: "Let us eat and drink for tomorrow we die!" What "time" is it for us? Are we frittering away precious time on trivialities?

2 Chronicles 7:14

If my people, which are called by my name, shall humble themselves, and pray, and seek my face, and turn from their wicked ways; then will I hear from heaven, and will forgive their sin, and will heal their land.

Psalm 122:6

Pray for the peace of Jerusalem; they will prosper who love thee.

Lesson Plan 188

The Book of Isaiah

Chapters 25, 26, & 27

Objective: To give us an understanding of God's strategic plan for the world and for His chosen people.

Objective Breakdown:

1. Introduction

2. God Is Praised for Coming Restoration   Isaiah 25:1-12

3. Perfect Peace for the City   Isaiah 26:1-15

4   Birth Pangs of Renewal   Isaiah 26:16-21

5. Israel Shall Blossom and Bud   Isaiah 27:1-6

6. God Will take Away His People's Sin   Isaiah 27:7-13

Introduction:

Chapter 25 Synopsis: A song of praise (1-5). A declaration of the gospel blessings (Verses 6-8). The destruction of the enemies of Christ's church (Verses 9-12). However, this might show the deliverance of the Jews out of captivity, it looked further, to the praises that should be offered up to God for Christ's victories over our spiritual enemies, and the comforts he has provided for all believers (Verses 1-5). True faith simply credits the Lord's testimony and relies on his truth to perform his promises. As God weakens the strong who are proud and secure, so he strengthens the weak that are humble, and stay themselves upon him. God protects his people in all weathers. The Lord shelters those who trust in him from the insolence of oppressors. Their insolence is but the noise of strangers; it is like the heat of the sun scorching in the middle of the day; but where is it when the sun is set? The Lord ever was, and ever will be, the Refuge of distressed believers. Having provided them a shelter, he teaches them to flee unto it.

The abolition of death. Here Isaiah has transported himself beyond the crash of worlds, into the age of the new heavens and new earth and put into the mouth of the redeemed a song of praise to God for His wonderful works. Most wonderful of all is the destruction of death (Isaiah 25:8), and the wiping away of all tears.

Chapter 26 Synopsis: The Divine mercies encourage to confidence in God. (Verses 1-4); His judgments.

(Verses 5-11); His people exhorted to wait upon Him. (Verses 12-19) Deliverance promised. (Verses 20, 21)

Verses 1-4 "That day," seems to mean when the New Testament Babylon shall be leveled with the ground. The unchangeable promise and covenant of the Lord are the walls of the church of God. The gates of this city shall be open. Let sinners then be encouraged to join to the Lord. Thou wilt keep him in peace; in perfect peace, inward peace, outward peace, peace with God, peace of conscience, peace at all times, in all events. Trust in the Lord for that peace, that portion, which will be forever. Whatever we trust to the world for, it will last only for a moment; but those who trust in God shall not only find in him, but shall receive from him, strength that will carry them to that blessedness which is forever. Let us then acknowledge him in all our ways and rely on him in all trials.

Verses 5-11 The way of the just is evenness, a steady course of obedience and holy conversation. And it is their happiness that God makes their way plain and easy. **Verses 20, 21** When dangers threaten, it is good to retire and lie hid; when we commend ourselves to God to hide us, he will hide us either under heaven or in heaven. Thus, we shall be safe and happy in the midst of tribulations. It is but for a short time, as it were for a little moment; when over, it will seem as nothing. God's place is the mercy-seat; there he delights to be: when he punishes, he comes out of his place, for he has no pleasure in the death of sinners. But there is hardly any truth more frequently repeated in Scripture, than God's determined purpose to punish the workers of iniquity. Let us keep close to the Lord, and separate from the world; and let us seek comfort in secret prayer. A day of vengeance is coming on the world, and before it comes we are to expect tribulation and suffering. But because the Christian looks for these things, shall he be restless and dismayed? No, let him repose himself in his God. Abiding in him, the believer is safe. And let us wait patiently the fulfilling of God's promises.

Chapter 27 Synopsis: God's care over his people (1-5). A promise of their recall to Divine favor (6-13). **Verses 1-5** The Lord Jesus with His strong sword, the virtue of His death, and the preaching of His gospel does and will destroy him that had the power of death, that is, the devil, that old serpent. The world is a fruitless, worthless wideness; but the church is a vineyard, a place that has great care taken of it, and from which precious fruits are gathered. God will keep it in the night of affliction and persecution, and in the day of peace and prosperity, the temptations of which are not less dangerous. God also takes care of the fruitfulness of this vineyard. We need the continual watering of Divine Grace; if these be at any time withdrawn, we wither, and come to nothing. Though God sometimes contends with his people, yet he graciously waits to be reconciled unto them. It is true, when he finds briers and thorns instead of vines, and they are set in array against him, he will tread them down and burn them. Here is a summary of the doctrine of the gospel, with which the church is to be watered every moment.

Verses 6-13 In the days of the gospel, the latter days, the gospel church shall be more firmly fixed than the Jewish church and shall spread further. May our souls be continually watered and kept, that we may abound in the fruits of the Spirit, in all goodness, righteousness, and truth. The Jews yet are kept a separate and a numerous people; they have not been rooted out as those who slew them. The condition of that nation, through so many ages, forms a certain proof of the Divine origin of the Scriptures. **Verses 12, 13,** seem to predict the restoration of the Jews after the Babylon captivity, and their recovery from their present dispersion. This is further applicable to the preaching of the gospel, by which sinners are gathered into the Grace of God; the gospel proclaims the acceptable year of the Lord. Those gathered by the sounding of the gospel trumpet, are brought into worship God, and added to the church; and the last trumpet will gather the saints together.

2 Chronicles 7:14

If my people, which are called by my name, shall humble themselves, and pray, and seek my face, and turn from their wicked ways; then will I hear from heaven, and will forgive their sin, and will heal their land.

Psalm 122:6

Pray for the peace of Jerusalem; they will prosper who love thee.

Lesson Plan 189

The Book of Isaiah

Chapters 28 & 29

Objective: To give us an understanding of God's strategic plan for the world and for His chosen people.

Objective Breakdown:

1. Introduction

2. A Prophecy Against Israel   Isaiah 28:1-8

3. The Scornful Refuse to Hear God's Word   Isaiah 28:9-15

4. God's Cornerstone in Zion   Isaiah 28:16-22

5. God will Crush Israel Like Grain   Isaiah 28:23-29

6. The Siege of Jerusalem is Described   Isaiah 29:1-4

7. Vast Armies Will Surround the City   Isaiah 29:5-10

8. Pious Words and Hypocritical Actions   Isaiah 29:11-24

Introduction:

In about 701 B.C. the Assyrian King Sennacherib sent forces to quell numerous uprisings among kingdoms in the western empire. First, they attacked the Phoenicians, deposing the king of Tyre. Then they moved South along the coast to the Philistine city-states of Ashkelon and Ekron, which had openly rebelled after the death of Sargon II (705 B.C.), Sennacherib's predecessor. Finally, the Assyrians turned east to attempt to capture Judah.

As Sennacherib's armies bore down on Jerusalem, King Hezekiah considered how he would defend his capital. He made extensive preparations (2 Chronicles 32:3-6, 30). But were they adequate to withstand the full force of the Assyrian might?

One option open to Hezekiah was to appeal for help from the Egyptians. But Isaiah's counsel was to reject such an alliance (Isaiah 30:1-5). To pursue it would show a lack of faith in the Lord to deliver His people. In fact, the Law prohibited the Israelites from allying themselves with the Egyptians or even importing armaments from them (Deuteronomy 17:16).

Apparently, Hezekiah heeded Isaiah's word. When Sennacherib's general taunted him and demanded a surrender, he asked the prophet to pray and ask God for help. Isaiah did so, and the Lord responded by delivering the city (2 Kings18:13-19:37; 2 Chronicles 32:1-21).

This contrasted sharply with the actions of Hoshea, the last of Israel's kings. Faced with a situation similar to Hezekiah's, Hoshea had appealed for help from So, king of Egypt. Before long, the Assyrians had overrun Israel, destroyed its capital of Samaria, and deported its inhabitants (2 Kings 17:1-18).

2 Chronicles 7:14

If my people, which are called by my name, shall humble themselves, and pray, and seek my face, and turn from their wicked ways; then will I hear from heaven, and will forgive their sin, and will heal their land.

Psalm 122:6

Pray for the peace of Jerusalem; they will prosper who love thee.

Lesson Plan 190

The Book of Isaiah

Chapters 30, 31, & 32

Objective: To give us an understanding of God's strategic plan for the world and for His chosen people.

Objective Breakdown:

1. Introduction

2. The Folly of Trusting in Egypt   Isaiah 30:1-5

3. Egypt's Help Will Be Worthless   Isaiah 30:6-14

4. The People Are Urged to Trust God   Isaiah 30:15-22

5. The Benefits of Faith and Faithfulness   Isaiah 30:23-26

6. God Will Punish His Enemies   Isaiah 30:27-33

7. God Should Be Trusted, Not Egypt   Isaiah 31:1-5

8. Assyria Will Fall by a Divine Sword   Isaiah 31:6-9

9. A Reign of Righteousness   Isaiah 32:1-8

10. A Warning to Jerusalem's Women   Isaiah 32:9-15

11. A Promise of Peace for God's People   Isaiah 32:16-20

Introduction:

Justice in the wilderness. Perhaps like many people you think of the countryside as gentle, quiet refuge from the complications of urban life. However, in Bible times, rural area was generally places without law and order, where everyone "did what was right in his own eyes" (Judges 21:25). It was the city that tended to offer peace and protection.

For that reason, Isaiah's vision of justice in the wilderness was a remarkable promise. The key to transformation was the presence of the Holy Spirit (Isaiah 32:15). However, the Holy Spirit would not impose God's peace on unwilling people. Rather peace would be the fruit of seeds sown in righteousness (Isaiah 32:17).

The Lord challenged the complacent women of Judah to wail for the woeful consequence that would befall their corrupt, escapist society (Isaiah 32:9-13). However, God promised to intervene. The city would be secure, not because of its walls, but because the Holy Spirit would defend it. Whether or not you live in an urban area, Isaiah's vision of God's peace is instructive. As you sow the seeds of righteousness in your community, you give the Holy Spirit an opportunity to bring blessings on you and your neighbors. Those "seeds" may involve feeding the hungry, shutting down a business based on immorality, or simply praying for civic leaders. Whatever the action you take, know that the Holy Spirit can multiply your efforts many times. "The fruit of righteousness is sown in peace by those who make peace" (James 3:18).

Security comes from honoring the Lord!!

2 Chronicles 7:14

If my people, which are called by my name, shall humble themselves, and pray, and seek my face, and turn from their wicked ways; then will I hear from heaven, and will forgive their sin, and will heal their land.

Psalm 122:6

Pray for the peace of Jerusalem; they will prosper who love thee.

Lesson Plan 191

The Book of Isaiah

Chapters 33, 34, & 35

Objective: To give us an understanding of God's strategic plan for the world and for His chosen people.

Objective Breakdown:

1. Introduction

2. A Plea for God's Grace   Isaiah 33:1-9

3. God Will Rise in Judgment   Isaiah 33:10-16

4. The Lord Will Rule in Zion   Isaiah 33:17-27

5. Judgment on the Nations   Isaiah 34:1-7

6. The Day of the Lord's Vengeance   Isaiah 34:8-17

7. The Highway of Holiness   Isaiah 35:1-10

Introduction:

God will impose justice on a corrupt society. He warns that his judgment will fall like a plague of devouring locust (Isaiah 33:3-4), disrupting the business-as-usual complacency of His people (Isaiah 33:7-8). He will assert Himself among those who have assumed that He either does not care about their wrongdoings or is too weak to act (Isaiah 33:10-13).

Yet in the midst of judgment, there is hope for the righteous. As in some of the psalms, which contain questions and answers regarding conditions for admittance to worship (for example, Psalm 15:1-5), Isaiah describes those who will escape punishment and dwell with the Lord in safety (Isaiah 33:15). They are those who:

o live lives of righteous behavior;

o speak only what is right and true;

o makes it plain that their integrity cannot be bought with a bribe;

o won't even listen to suggestions for eliminating competitors and opponents by resorting to violence; and o won't tolerate evil in their presence.

The comfort of this passage is that those who pursue godly character will be eligible to enjoy the Lord's protection (Isaiah 33:16). He will make lives secure when He comes to reside and rule over Jerusalem. He will fill the city with justice and righteousness. Little wonder, then, that the refugees from the rural areas will seek refuge there (Isaiah 33:20).

Why not spend some time this evening to reflect on your life—where it has come from, where it is, and where it is going. Do we need to make some changes? Remember, that security comes from honoring God.

2 Chronicles 7:14

If my people, which are called by my name, shall humble themselves, and pray, and seek my face, and turn from their wicked ways; then will I hear from heaven, and will forgive their sin, and will heal their land.

Psalm 122:6

Pray for the peace of Jerusalem; they will prosper who love thee.

Every Day Should be the National Day of Prayer.

Lesson Plan 192

The Book of Isaiah

Chapters 36, 37, & 38

Objective: To give us an understanding of God's strategic plan for the world and for His chosen people.

Objective Breakdown:

1. Introduction

2. The Assyrians Besiege Jerusalem   Isaiah 36:1-3

3. The Rabshakeh Makes a Defiant Offer   Isaiah 36:4-10

4. Hezekiah Is Spoken Against   Isaiah 36:11-22

5. Isaiah Promises Deliverance from God   Isaiah 37:1-7

6. Hezekiah Prays to the Lord   Isaiah 37:8-20

7. God's Word Against Assyria   Isaiah 37:21-35

8. The Stricken Assyrians Withdraw   Isaiah 37:36-38

9. Hezekiah is Healed of a Deadly Disease   Isaiah 38:1-8

10. Hezekiah Song of Praise   Isaiah 38:9-21

Introduction:

The sounds of modern warfare include loud explosions, jet aircraft, helicopters, etc. In Isaiah's day the noise of ancient warfare was primarily the sounds of human beings crying out either in victory or defeat. The din of battle can be heard in Isaiah's vivid description of the fall of Jerusalem: shouting from the roof tops (Isaiah 22:1); the thud of arrows shot by armies of skilled archers (Isaiah 22:2-3); the moaning and weeping of captives (Isaiah 22:3-4); the pounding of battering rams on city gates and walls (Isaiah 22:5); the clamoring for help that never comes (Isaiah 22: 5); the thundering of chariots and the neighing of horses (Isaiah 22: 6-7) and the collapse of houses in order to furnish building materials for fortifying the walls (Isaiah 22:10).

Ecclesiastes says that there is a "time to weep and a time to laugh, a time to mourn and a time to dance" (Ecclesiastes 3:4). It is crucial that we know which time is which. Apparently, the people of Jerusalem failed to recognize that God had called them to weeping and mourning instead of gladness (Isaiah 22:12-

14). From God's perspective there was little for His people to celebrate especially in the last days of the Southern Kingdom.

For example, even as the armies of Babylon were coming against Jerusalem, King Zedekiah (597-587 B.C.) and his people completely turned away from the Lord. The king "stiffened his neck and hardened his heart" against God (2 Chronicles 36:13). The king ignored the words of Jeremiah the prophet (2 Chronicles 36:12) and the people likewise mocked and scoffed at the prophets and despised their words (2 Chronicles 36:16). Zedekiah reneged on a sworn oath by rebelling against the Babylonians (2 Chronicles 36:13). The chief priests and the people practiced the idolatrous abominations of pagan nations, even to the extent of defiling the temple (2 Chronicles 36:14).

In short, the people went about their lives as if God did not matter. When they should have been repenting of sin and calling on the Lord for help. They held parties, violated God's ways, and took a fatalistic attitude toward life: "Let us eat and drink for tomorrow we die!"

What "time" is it for us? Are we frittering away precious time on trivialities?

The 10 periods of pagan persecutions. These pagan (Roman) persecutions are different that the persecutions from the Church within (which started approximately one thousand years later). Below are the Pagan/Roman Persecutions:

First Persecution, Under Nero, A.D. 67

*Second Persecution, Under Domitian, A.D. 81

Third Persecution, Under Trajan, A.D. 108

Fourth Persecution, Under Marcus Aurelius Antoninus, A.D. 162

Fifth Persecution, Commencing with Severus, A.D. 192

Sixth Persecution, Under Maximus, A.D. 235

Seventh Persecution, Under Decius, A.D. 249

Eight Persecution, Under Valerian, A.D. 257

Ninth Persecution, Under Aurelian, A. D. 274

Tenth Persecution, Under Diocletian, A.D. 303

*Nicodemus, a benevolent Christian of some distinction, suffered at Rome during the rage of Domitian's persecution. Domitian commanded that all lineage of David be put to death. St. John was boiled in oil, and afterward banished to Patmos.

2 Chronicles 7:14

If my people, which are called by my name, shall humble themselves, and pray, and seek my face, and turn from their wicked ways; then will I hear from heaven, and will forgive their sin, and will heal their land.

Psalm 122:6

Pray for the peace of Jerusalem; they will prosper who love thee.

Every Day Should be the National Day of Prayer.

Lesson Plan 193

The Book of Isaiah

Chapters 39, 40, 41, & 42

Objective: To give us an understanding of God's strategic plan for the world and for His chosen people.

Objective Breakdown:

1. Survey of the Book of Isaiah

2. Babylonians See the Royal Treasures   Chapter 39:1-8

2. Comfort Because of Israel's Deliverance   Chapter 40:1-11

3. Comfort Because of God's Character   Chapter 40:12-31

4. Comfort Because of God's Greatness   Chapter 41:1-29

5. Comfort Because of God's Servant   Chapter 42:1-25

Survey of the Book of Isaiah:

The Book of Isaiah can be broken down into **three** major areas:

Chapters 1-35 are prophecies of **Condemnation**.

Chapters 36-39 are **Historical parenthesis** and

Chapters 40-66 are **Prophecies of Comfort**.

Time frame of Isaiah's ministry is from 740 to 680 B.C.

Condemnation: His first message of condemnation is aimed at his own countrymen in Judah (chapters 1-12). Chapter 1 is a capsulized message of the entire book. Judah is riddled with moral and spiritual disease. The people are neglecting God as they bow to ritualism and selfishness. But God graciously invites them (Jewish people) to repent and return to Him, because this is their only hope of avoiding judgment. Isaiah's call to proclaim God's message is found in chapter 6, and this is followed by the chapters (7-12) referring repeatedly to the Messiah and anticipating the blessings of His future reign. In chapters 13-23, Isaiah focuses on the oracles (prophetic declarations) of surrounding nations. The eleven nations are Babylon, Assyria, Philistia, Moab, Damascus (Syria), Ethiopia, Egypt, Babylon (again), Edom, Arabia, Jerusalem (Judah), and Tyre. Isaiah's little apocalypse chapters 24-27 depicts universal tribulation followed by the blessings of the kingdom. Chapters 28-33 pronounces six woes on Israel and

Judah for specific sins. Isaiah's prophetic condemnation closes with a general picture of international devastation that will proceed a universal blessing in chapters 34-35.

Historical Parenthesis chapters 36-39 looks back to the Assyrian invasion of Judah in 701 B.C. and anticipates the coming Babylon invasion of Judah. Judah escapes captivity by Assyria (chapters 36 & 37), but they will not escape from the hands of Babylon (chapter 38 and 39).

Prophecies of Comfort (chapters 40-66). Having pronounced Judah's divine condemnation, Isaiah comforts them with God's promises of hope and restoration. The basis for this hope is the sovereignty and majesty of God (40-48). Of the 216 verses in these nine chapters, 115 speak of God's greatness and power. The Creator is contrasted with idols, the creations of men. His sovereign character is Judah's assurance of future restoration. Babylon will indeed carry them off; but Babylon will finally be judged and destroyed and God's people will be released from captivity. Chapters 49-57 concentrate on the coming Messiah who will be their Savior and suffering Servant. This exalted One will pay for their iniquities and usher in a kingdom of peace and righteousness throughout the earth. All who acknowledge their sins and trust in Him will be delivered (58-66). In the day Jerusalem will be rebuilt, Israel's borders will be enlarged, and the Messiah will reign in Zion. God's people will confess their sins and His enemies will be judged. Peace, prosperity, and justice will prevail, and God will make all things new.

2 Chronicles 7:14

If my people, which are called by my name, shall humble themselves, and pray, and seek my face, and turn from their wicked ways; then will I hear from heaven, and will forgive their sin, and will heal their land.

Psalm 122:6

Pray for the peace of Jerusalem; they will prosper who love thee.

Words for Comfort of the Soul

Ephesians 4:29, Let no corrupt word proceed out of your mouth, but what is good for necessary edification, that it may impart grace to the hearers.

Ephesians 4:30, Do not grieve the Holy Spirit of God, by whom you were sealed for the day of redemption.

Ephesians 4:31, Let all bitterness, wrath, anger, clamor, and evil speaking be put away from you, with all malice.

Ephesians 4:32, Be kind to another, tenderhearted, forgiving one another, even as God in Christ forgave you.

Philippians 4:6, Be anxious for nothing, but in everything by prayer and supplication, with thanksgiving, let your requests be made known to God; and the peace of God, which surpasses all understanding, will guard your hearts and minds through Christ Jesus.

Lesson Plan 194

The Book of Isaiah

Chapters 43, 44, & 45

Objective: To give us an understanding of God's strategic plan for the world and for His chosen people.

Objective Breakdown:

1. Introduction

2. Through the Water and Fire   Chapter 43:1-7

3. Israel Will Be God Witness   Chapter 43:8-13

4. God Will Bring the Babylonians   Chapter 43:14-28

5. There Is No Other God   Chapter 44:1-8

6. The Making of Idols   Chapter 44:9-17

7. God Will Confound Idolaters   Chapter 44:18-22

8. The Lord Alone Deserves Glory   Chapter 44:23-28

9. Cyrus, a Leader Anointed by God   Chapter 45:1-13

10. Do Not Argue with the Sovereign God   Chapter 45:14-17

11. I Am God, and There Is No Other   Chapter 45:18-25

Introduction:

Some Bible readers assume that the Holy Spirits' activity in Scripture is limited to the New Testament. But actually, the Holy Spirit is just as active in the Old Testament. There is no clearer statement of the intimate inter-working of the triune God—Father, Son, and Holy Spirit—especially of the Spirits' powerful role, which can be found in Isaiah's prophecy of the Servant of the Lord (Isaiah 42:1-9).

The passage summarizes the redeeming work of all three Persons of the Trinity in the salvation of the lost. Thus, it ties together in remarkable harmony both the Old Testament and New Testament understandings of God's grace. It also sheds light on our understanding of the Holy Spirit:

The Spirit participated in creation (Genesis 1:2; Job 26:13; Isaiah 32:15).

The Spirit gives life to humanity and other creatures (Psalm 104:29-30). It is interesting that when Genesis says "breath" is the same word translated elsewhere as "spirit."

The Spirit strives with sinners (Genesis 6:3), which is perhaps related to His work in convicting people of sin (John 16:8-11).

The Spirit came upon certain judges, warriors, and prophets in a way that gave them extraordinary power: for example, Joshua (Numbers 27:18), Othniel (Judges 3:10), Gideon (Judges 6:34), Samson (Judges 13:25; 14:6) and Saul (1 Samuel 10:9-10).

However, the Spirit later departed from Saul because of disobedience (Samuel 16:14).

The Spirit inspired holiness in Old Testament believers (Psalm 143:10).

And Scripture promised that someday God would put His Spirit in His people in a way that would cause them to live according to His statues (Ezekiel 36:27).

1. Behold my servant, (Jesus) whom I uphold; mine elect, in whom my soul delighteth; I have put my Spirit upon him: he shall bring forth judgment to the Gentiles.

2. He shall not cry, nor lift up, nor cause his voice to be heard in the street.

3. A bruised reed shall he not break, and the smoking flax shall He not quench: He shall bring forth judgment unto truth.

4. He shall not fail nor be discouraged, till He have set judgment in the earth: and the isles shall wait for His law.

5. Thus saith God the Lord (Father), He that created the heavens, and stretched them out; He that spread forth the earth, and that which cometh out of it; He that giveth breath (Spirit) unto the people upon it, and Spirit to them that walk therein:

6. I the Lord have called thee in righteousness, and will hold thine hand, and will keep thee, and give thee for a covenant of the people, for a light of the Gentiles;

7. To open the blind eyes, to bring out the prisoners from the prison, and them that sit in darkness out of the prison house.

8. I am the Lord: that is my name: and my glory will I not give to another, neither my praise to graven images.

9. Behold, the former things are come to pass, and new things do I declare: before they spring forth I tell you of them. The Spirit was there at creation; the Spirit gives life to humanity and other creatures; the Spirit strives with sinners in convicting them; the Spirit inspired holiness in the Old Testament believers. There are numerous places in Scripture where the Holy Spirit was active in the Old Testament.

2 Chronicles 7:14

If my people, which are called by my name, shall humble themselves, and pray, and seek my face, and turn from their wicked ways; then will I hear from heaven, and will forgive their sin, and will heal their land.

Psalm 122:6

Pray for the peace of Jerusalem; they will prosper who love thee.

Lesson Plan 195

The Book of Isaiah

Chapters 46, 47, & 48

Objective: To give us an understanding of God's strategic plan for the world and for His chosen people.

Objective Breakdown:

1. Introduction

2. God Will Show His Superiority to Idols   Isaiah 46:1-4

3. Idols and God Contrasted   Isaiah 46:5-13

4. Babylon Will Be Humiliated   Isaiah 47:1-9

5. Enchantments Will Fail   Isaiah 47:10-15

6. Prophecy Shows That the Lord Is God   Isaiah 48:1-11

7. God Will Free His People from Babylon   Isaiah 48:12-22

Introduction:

Perhaps you think of idols as objects of wood, stone, or metal worshiped by ancient civilizations or primitive peoples. You would be accurate. But from the Bible's point of view, idolatry fundamentally involves allowing anything or anyone to stand in the place of God.

The ancient Babylonians fashioned many idols for both public and private worship (Isaiah 46:6-7), the Lord ridiculed this practice, for the gods of Babylon were impotent: they had to hand carried, as they could not move on their own, they were mute and they were powerless.

The Lord will not allow those who practice idolatry to go unpunished. Consider His Judgment on the Babylonians (Isaiah 47:10-15). Is there any reason why He would not pour out just as much wrath on Idolaters today? He still hates idolatry (Deuteronomy 7:25-26):

25. The graven images of their gods shall ye burn with fire: thou shalt not desire the silver or gold that is on them, nor take it unto thee, lest thou be snared therein: for it is an abomination to the Lord thy God. 26. Neither shalt thou bring an abomination into thine house, lest thou be a cursed thing like it: but thou shalt utterly detest it, and thou shalt utterly abhor it; for it is a cursed thing.

The First and Second commandment are still there (Exodus 20:2-7). And the Lord is still who He declared Himself to be to the ancients: "I am God, and there is no other; I am God, and there is none like Me" (Isaiah 46:9).

Exodus 20:2. I am the Lord thy God, which have brought thee out of the land of Egypt, out of the house of bondage. 3. Thou shalt have no other gods before me. 4. Thou shalt not make unto thee any graven image, or any likeness of anything that is in heaven above, or that is in the earth beneath, or that is in the water under the earth. 5. Thou shalt not bow down thyself to them, nor serve them: for I the Lord thy God am a jealous God, visiting the iniquity of the fathers upon the children unto the third and fourth generation of them that hate me; 6. And showing mercy unto thousands of them that love me, and keep my commandments. 7. Thou shalt not take the name of the Lord thy God in vain; for the Lord will not hold him guiltless that taketh his name in vain.

2 Chronicles 7:14

If my people, which are called by my name, shall humble themselves, and pray, and seek my face, and turn from their wicked ways; then will I hear from heaven, and will forgive their sin, and will heal their land.

Psalm 122:6

Pray for the peace of Jerusalem; they will prosper who love thee.

Lesson Plan 196

The Book of Isaiah

Chapters 49, 50, & 51

Objective: To give us an understanding of God's strategic plan for the world and for His chosen people.

Objective Breakdown:

1. Introduction

2. God's Servant Is Called from the Womb   Isaiah 49:1-7

3. God's People Come Back from Exile   Isaiah 49:8-13

4. God Can Never Forget His People   Isaiah 49:14-21

5. Nations Will Serve God's People   Isaiah 49:22-26

6. The Servant Redeems Sinners   Isaiah 50:1-6

7. The Servant Overcomes Adversity   Isaiah 50:7-11

8. An Appeal to Pursue Righteousness   Isaiah 51:1-8

9. A Prayer for God's Help   Isaiah 51:9-11

10. The Lord's Reply   Isaiah 51:12-20

11. The Afflicter Will Be Afflicted   Isaiah 51:21-23

Introduction:

The purpose of prophecy. Perhaps you think of prophecy as mainly to do with predictions about the future. That is understandable, since prophets in Bible times sometimes told what would happen in the future (for example Isaiah 7:14-17; 45:1-7; Jeremiah 28:12-17). However, the purpose of prophecy goes beyond merely informing people about things to come. There are at least two additional reasons why God spoke through Old Testament prophets:

(1) To show that God is God. A god who cannot reveal himself to human beings is unlikely to command much respect. But through prophecies, the Lord made Himself known in compelling ways. For example, He demonstrated His omniscience by revealing to the Israelites what would happen in the future, something no pagan idol could do (Isaiah 48:5). He also demonstrated His power through the prophets

in a way which left no doubt about who He is (1 Kings 18:36-39).

(2) To proclaim God's Word. Closely related to God's revelation of Himself through prophecy is His communication of truth He wants people to know. Prophecy is often referred to as the "Word of the Lord" (Isaiah 1:10; 28:14; 38:4); in fact, it is often prefaced by the words, "thus says the Lord God." Thus, prophecy is revelation from God. It brings to light things that would otherwise remain unexpressed.

The point of these revelation is not to merely to inform, but to declare what is true, and then tell people how they should live in light of what is true. Sometimes prophecy helps to warn people about consequences of their actions, sometimes it encourages them when circumstances appear to be desperate. But whatever its effect on people, the purpose of prophecy is to proclaim God and His Word.

2 Chronicles 7:14

If my people, which are called by my name, shall humble themselves, and pray, and seek my face, and turn from their wicked ways; then will I hear from heaven, and will forgive their sin, and will heal their land.

Psalm 122:6

Pray for the peace of Jerusalem; they will prosper who love thee.

Lesson Plan 197

The Book of Isaiah

Chapters 52, 53, & 54

Objective: To give us an understanding of God's strategic plan for the world and for His chosen people.

Objective Breakdown:

1. Jerusalem Will Be Set Free   Isaiah 52:1-6

2. Good News God Reigns   Isaiah 52:7-12

3. God's Servant's Face Will Be Marred   Isaiah 52:13-15

4. He was Wounded for Our Transgressions   Isaiah 53:1-6

5. The Suffering Servant   Isaiah 53:7-12

6. The Lord Will Marry His People   Isaiah 54:1-8

7. God's Merciful Covenant   Isaiah 54:9-17

Death by Crucifixion: Isaiah 53 vividly portrays the suffering of Jesus Christ. The climax of Christ's suffering was His crucifixion when He was "led as a Lamb to the slaughter (Isaiah 53:7). Medical Experts who have studied crucifixion report that it was designed to maximize the victim's pain.

A man who was to be crucified was usually exhausted from mistreatment by the time he reached the site of the execution. After the victim was placed on the planks of wood that formed the cross, heavy spikes were driven through his wrists in a way that allowed his arms some flexibility and movements.

His feet were then crossed, and a nail was driven through his arches. When the cross was raised up and dropped into place, the weight of his body on the spikes caused excruciating, fiery pain to shoot through his upper body, if he attempted to ease this pain by pushing upward on his feet, the agony shifted to his lower body.

Eventually the arms tired, and throbbing cramps developed in his muscles. These made it increasingly difficult for the victim to push himself upward to breathe, resulting in a buildup of carbon dioxide in the lungs and bloodstream in a way, this was a blessing because it dulled the cramps somewhat, enabling him to push himself upward again for breaths of air.

This cycle of agonizing cramps and partial asphyxiation went on for hours. The rough wood of the cross rubbing against the man's back tore away tissue. The chest cavity started filling with serum and began to press on the heart, causing the organ to struggle to pump ever-thickening blood through the body. Shock and the chill of death began to set in. Finally, the condemned man gave up, and welcomed death as an end to his suffering.

Jesus did it for you when He was "wounded for our transgressions" and "bruised for our iniquities" (Isaiah 53:5). He took on Himself the "chastisement," or punishment, that we deserved for our sins so that we would not have to bear it. He did not want to suffer, but He submitted to suffering because of His great love for us. Hundreds of years (approximately 700 years) before Jesus came, Isaiah described in remarkable detail how the Messiah, would suffer on behalf of others.

2 Chronicles 7:14

If my people, which are called by my name, shall humble themselves, and pray, and seek my face, and turn from their wicked ways; then will I hear from heaven, and will forgive their sin, and will heal their land.

Psalm 122:6

Pray for the peace of Jerusalem; they will prosper who love thee.

Lesson Plan 198

The Book of Isaiah

Chapters 55, 56, & 57

Objective: To give us an understanding of God's strategic plan for the world and for His chosen people.

Objective Breakdown:

1. Introduction

2. Seek God While He May Be Found   Isaiah 55:1-7

3. Creation Shall Break Forth in Praise   Isaiah 55:8-13

4. Keep Justice and Do Righteousness   Isaiah 56:1-8

5. Derelict Watchmen   Isaiah 56:9-12

6. The Adultery of God's People   Isaiah 57:1-10

7. No Peace for the Wicked   Isaiah 57:11-21

Introduction:

An invitation to life. If you listen carefully to public discourse today, you hear the recurring theme that modern society is in moral and spiritual decline. Having heaped upon incredible affluence, Western Civilization is believed by many to have lost its soul. This makes the message of Isaiah, as timely as ever. To those who "spend money for what is not bread" and wages for "what does not satisfy" (Isaiah 55:2), the Lord offers a compelling invitation: "Come to Me...and your soul shall live" (Isaiah 55:3).

This marvelous call of God is extended to the whole world. He invites nations who do not even know of Israel to come to Him. Anyone who is thirsty can drink of His waters of grace (Isaiah 5:1, 5).

This same invitation is still in effect today. In the Book of Revelation, the Lord says: "I will give of the fountain of water of life freely to him who thirsts...And let him who thirsts come. Whoever desires, let him take the water of life freely" (Revelation 21:6; 22:7).

Have you personally responded to God's gift of life through faith in Jesus Christ?

Are you dying of thirst? The Lord invites you to come and drink!

2 Chronicles 7:14

If my people, which are called by my name, shall humble themselves, and pray, and seek my face, and turn from their wicked ways; then will I hear from heaven, and will forgive their sin, and will heal their land.

Psalm 122:6

Pray for the peace of Jerusalem; they will prosper who love thee.

Read Ephesians 4:29-32 Daily

29. Let no corrupt communication proceed out of your mouth, but that which is good to the use of edifying, that it may minister grace unto the hearers.

30. And grieve not the Holy Spirit of God, whereby ye are sealed unto the day of redemption.

31. Let all bitterness, and wrath, and anger, and clamour, and evil speaking, be put away from you, with all malice:

32. And be ye kind one to another, tenderhearted, forgiving one another, even as God for Christ's sake hath forgiven you.

2 Chronicles 7:14

If my people, which are called by my name, shall humble themselves, and pray, and seek my face, and turn from their wicked ways; then will I hear from heaven, and will forgive their sin, and will heal their land.

Psalm 122:6

Pray for the peace of Jerusalem; they will prosper who love thee.

Lesson Plan 199

The Book of Isaiah

Chapters 58, 59, & 60

Objective: To give us an understanding of God's strategic plan for the world and for His chosen people.

Objective Breakdown:

1. Introduction

2. Hypocritical Worshipers   Isaiah 58:1-5

3. The Lord Describes True Worship   Isaiah 58:6-14

4. A Society Devoted to Wickedness   Isaiah 59:1-8

5. Sin Separates People from God   Isaiah 59:9-15

6. God Intervenes to Redeem Sinners   Isaiah 59:16-21

7. The Nations Come to Worship   Isaiah 60:1-7

8. All Will Honor God in His City   Isaiah 60:8-16

9. Peace Praise and Everlasting Light   Isaiah 60:17-22

Introduction:

Do you worry about society? Do you feel as if God had turned His back on your country? Do you sometimes feel as if prayers for the nation were going unheard? The people of Isaiah's day experienced that. As they faced a dark and dangerous world, they looked for God's guidance, but did not find it. They hoped that God would take up their cause and defend them, but help did not come (Isaiah 59:9-10). What was wrong?

Isaiah pointed out that the problem was not with God but with the people: their own sins were separating them from the Lord (Isaiah 59:1-2,12). These failures were not occasional lapses of morality, but a nationwide, cultural acceptance of sinful ways. As Isaiah describes it (Isaiah 59:3-8), they were given as a society to: violence and bloodshed; lies and deception; absence of justice or truth; and entrenched patterns of sin and evil that replicated themselves with every passing generation.

Overall, the Godly qualities that should have characterized God's people—justice, righteousness, truth, and equity–were held back and thwarted (Isaiah 59:14). As a result, the Lord was displayed. Rather than standing with His people in troubles, He would stand against them (Isaiah 59:15-18). So, where sin is widespread, institutionalized, and culturally sanctioned, we can expect God to eventually bring judgment.

2 Chronicles 7:14

If my people, which are called by my name, shall humble themselves, and pray, and seek my face, and turn from their wicked ways; then will I hear from heaven, and will forgive their sin, and will heal their land.

Psalm 122:6

Pray for the peace of Jerusalem; they will prosper who love thee.

Read Ephesians 4:29-32 Daily

29. Let no corrupt communication proceed out of your mouth, but that which is good to the use of edifying, that it may minister grace unto the hearers.

30. And grieve not the Holy Spirit of God, whereby ye are sealed unto the day of redemption.

31. Let all bitterness, and wrath, and anger, and clamor, and evil speaking, be put away from you, with all malice:

32. And be ye kind one to another, tenderhearted, forgiving one another, even as God for Christ's sake hath forgiven you.

Romans Road to Salvation

3:23   For all have sinned, and come short of the glory of God;

6:23   For the wages of sin is death; but the gift of God is eternal life through Jesus Christ our Lord.

5:8   But God commended his love toward us, in that, while we were yet sinners, Christ died for us.

10:9   That if thou shalt confess with thy mouth the Lord Jesus, and shalt believe in thine heart that God hath raised him from the dead, thou shalt be saved.

10:10 For with the heart man believeth unto righteousness; and with the mouth confession   is made unto salvation.

10:13 For whosoever shall call upon the name of the Lord shall be saved.

Critical Scriptures

John Chapter 3

3. Jesus answered and said unto him, Verily, verily, I say unto thee, except a man be born again, he cannot see the kingdom of God.

4. Nicodemus saith unto him, how can a man be born when he is old? can he enter the second time into his mother's womb, and be born?

5. Jesus answered, Verily, verily, I say unto thee, except a man be born of water and of the Spirit, he cannot enter into the kingdom of God.

6. That which is born of the flesh is flesh; and that which is born of the Spirit is Spirit.

7. Marvel not that I said unto thee, Ye must be born again.

John 14:6 Jesus saith unto him, I am the way, the truth, and the life and no man cometh unto the Father, but by me.

John 14:7 If ye had known me, ye should have known my Father also: and from henceforth ye know him, and have seen him.

Lesson Plan 200

The Book of Isaiah

Chapters 61 & 62

Objective: To give us an understanding of God's strategic plan for the world and for His chosen people.

Objective Breakdown:

1. Introduction

2. The Spirit of the Lord Is on His Son — Isaiah 61:1-3

3. A Time of Rebuilding and Renewal — Isaiah 61:4-11

4. God Will Rejoice as a Bridegroom — Isaiah 62:1-5

5. Salvation Is Coming to Zion — Isaiah 62:6-12

Introduction:

Isaiah was married and had two sons. His first son was named Shear-Jashub (Isaiah 7:3), which means "a remnant shall return." His second son has the longest name in the Bible, Maher shalal-hash-baz, which means "speed the spoil," meaning a speedy doom for Judah's enemies.

Isaiah, was called the Messianic Prophet because he was so thoroughly imbued with the idea that his nation was to be a Messianic Nation to the world; that is a nation through which one day a great and wonderful blessing would come from God to all nations. He continually spoke of the day when that great and wonderful work would be done.

Isaiah was a prophetic of the Southern Kingdom, Judah, at the time the Northern Kingdom, Israel, was destroyed by the Assyrians. He lived in the reigns of Uzziah, Jotham, Ahaz and Hezekiah. His call was in the year of Uzziah's death, but some of his visions may have been earlier (See Isaiah Chapter 6:1). He was slain, according to Jewish tradition by Manasseh.

Isaiah prophesied during the reign of 5 kings of Judah (Uzziah, Jotham, Ahaz, Hezekiah, and Manasseh). He is the Messianic prophet. Only the Psalms have more material about Christ than the Book of Isaiah.

While Isaiah was yet a young man (734 B.C.) Assyria carried away all of Northern Israel. Thirteen years later (721 B.C.), Samaria fell and the rest of Israel was carried away. Then a few years later the Assyrians came on into Judah, destroyed 46 walled cities and carried away 200,000 captives. Finally, in 701 B.C., when Isaiah was an old man, the Assyrians were stopped before the walls of Jerusalem by an angel of

God. Thus, Isaiah's whole life was spent under the shadow of threatening Assyrian power and except for Jerusalem, he witnessed the ruin of the entire nation of Israel.

Tradition in the Talmud, which was accepted by the early Church Fathers, states that Isaiah resisted Manasseh's idolatrous decrees and was fasten between two planks and sawn asunder, thus suffering a most horrible death.

2 Chronicles 7:14

If my people, which are called by my name, shall humble themselves, and pray, and seek my face, and turn from their wicked ways; then will I hear from heaven, and will forgive their sin, and will heal their land.

Psalm 122:6

Pray for the peace of Jerusalem; they will prosper who love thee.

Lesson Plan 201

The Book of Isaiah

Chapters 63, 64, 65, & 66

Objective: To give us an understanding of God's strategic plan for the world and for His chosen people.

Objective Breakdown:

1.	God Will Tread the Grapes of His Wrath	Isaiah 63:1-6
2.	The Loving Kindness of God Will Prevail	Isaiah 63:7-14
3.	An Appeal for Divine Mercy	Isaiah 63:15-19
4.	A Plea for God to Assert Himself	Isaiah 64:1-5
5.	A Confession of Sin	Isaiah 64:6-12
6.	A Rebellious People Turn from God	Isaiah 65:1-7
7.	God Will Preserve Some of His People	Isaiah 65:8-12
8.	Only God's Servants Will Prosper	Isaiah 65:13-16
9.	A New Heaven and a New Earth	Isaiah 65:17-25
10.	God Will Regard the Contrite	Isaiah 66:1-5
11.	Zion Will Bring Forth Her Children	Isaiah 66:6-11
12.	Peace for Some and Fury for Others	Isaiah 66:12-17
13.	The World Will Come to Worship	Isaiah 66:18-24

Introduction:

Imagine a world without sin. No problem is too great to be solved. No one goes without food. Everyone's needs are met. People live in peace and prosperity. Justice reigns. There is no crime. Death is unknown.

Down through history, various groups have grasped at that utopian ideal. None has succeeded. Yet the dream lives on, and for good reason, that was God's original intention for His creation. He made a perfect world and placed humankind in it with a mandate to "be fruitful and multiply" (Genesis 1:28). Likewise, He has promised to someday restore His creation to its original purpose and perfection (Revelation 21:1-

4).

In the meantime, humanity must live with the memory of what Eden was and the hope of what the new creation will be. God helps people keep alive that vision of life with Him–which sometimes seems more like a dream–by offering occasional glimpses of it:

Genesis describes what Eden was like (Genesis. 1:1-2:25). The account tells of a world that was "very good" as God determines "good" (Genesis 1:31).

In the Law, God promises to bless His people Israel with a land of peace and prosperity if they uphold His commandments (Leviticus 26:3). Life in the Promised Land would not be a return to Eden, but it would have much of the same character. For example, God promised to make the people "fruitful" and help them "multiply."

In the Psalms, the world as it is, even in its fallen condition, is full of the "possessions" of the Lord. He has not left it to fend for itself. He maintains the earth and its creatures and rejoices in His works (Psalms 104:24-30).

Isaiah foresees new heavens and a new earth. There will be no more weeping or, by implication, sin, or death. God's people will build houses in a renewed Jerusalem and will do meaningful, satisfying work (Isaiah 65:17-23).

Paul also looks forward to the day when creation will be set free from its "futility," a day when God's people will finally be "delivered from the bondage of corruption" (Romans 8:19-25).

God's people live in hope. They base their lives on the promise that God's original design and purpose will not be crushed under the terrible load of sin, rebellion, and condemnation. Instead, because of Christ, they look forward to the day when they will enter a new world to live with God forever.

2 Chronicles 7:14

If my people, which are called by my name, shall humble themselves, and pray, and seek my face, and turn from their wicked ways; then will I hear from heaven, and will forgive their sin, and will heal their land.

Psalm 122:6

Pray for the peace of Jerusalem; they will prosper who love thee.

The Book of Jeremiah

Scripture Focus Chapters 1-52

Objective: To gain insight on the Book of Jeremiah which gives us prophecies during the reign of five kings of Judah: Josiah, Jehoahaz, Jehoiakim, Jeoiachin, and Zedekiah.

Objective Breakdown:

1. Introduction

2. The Call of Jeremiah   Chapter 1:1-10

3. God Tells Jeremiah to Arise and Speak   Chapter 1:11-19

4. Judah Has Forgotten the Lord   Chapter 2:1-8

5. The People Have Sought Help from Egypt   Chapter 2:9-19

6. Judah Worships Idols   Chapter 2:20-30

7. The Sin of Judah Is Apparent   Chapter 2:31-37

8. Spiritual Adultery   Chapter 3:1-5

9. Judah Has Seen Her Backsliding Sister   Chapter 3:6-15

10. Repentance and Reconciliation   Chapter 3:16-25

11. Circumcised Hearts   Chapter 4:1-4

12. The Lord Will Allow an Invasion   Chapter 4:5-13

13. A Plea for Repentance   Chapter 4:14-22

14. A Vision of Chaos and Desolation   Chapter 4:23-31

15. Not a Righteous Soul in Jerusalem   Chapter 5:1-9

16. The Invaders Receive Permission   Chapter 5:10-19

17. The Reasons for God's Judgment   Chapter 5:20-31

18. Jeremiah Predicts a Siege   Chapter 6:1-8

19. Everyone Will Be Judged   Chapter 6:9-15

20. The People Have Refused to Obey   Chapter 6:16-20

2 Chronicles 7:14

If my people, which are called by my name, shall humble themselves, and pray, and seek my face, and turn from their wicked ways; then will I hear from heaven, and will forgive their sin, and will heal their land.

Psalm 122:6

Pray for the peace of Jerusalem; they will prosper who love thee.

Lesson Plan 202

The Book of Jeremiah

Chapters 1 & 2

Objective: To give us insight on the Book of Jeremiah which contain the prophecies that were given during the lowest point in the history of Judah—the beginning of the Babylonian exile.

Objective Breakdown:

1. Introduction

2. The Call of Jeremiah   Chapter 1:1-10

3. God tells Jeremiah to Rise and Speak   Chapter 1:11-19

4. Judah Has Forgotten the Lord   Chapter 2:1-8

5. The People Have Sought Help from Egypt   Chapter 2:9-19

6. Judah Worships Idols   Chapter 2:20-30

5. The Sin of Judah Is Apparent   Chapter 2:31-37

Introduction:

God first spoke to Jeremiah in the thirteenth year of the reign of King Josiah (626 B.C.). Jeremiah referred to himself as a youth at the time of his call (chapter 1:1-6) which suggests that he may have been in his teens or possibly in his early twenties.

Jeremiah probably grew up during the evil reigns of Manasseh (686-642 B.C.) and Amon, his son (642-640 B.C.). Manasseh distinguished himself by leading Judah into more wickedness than was practiced by any of the people whom the Israelites dispossessed when they entered Canaan (2 Kings 21:9,11).

His son Amon continued that legacy during his brief reign. The sins of the two kings included:

1) Rebuilding the idolatrous "high places" (Deuteronomy 12:2) that Manasseh's father Hezekiah   had removed (2 Kings 21:3);

2) Reviving Baal worship; initiating worship of Assyrian gods (2 Kings 21:3);

3) Building pagan altars in the temple of the Lord itself (2 Kings 21:4-5);

4) Practicing child sacrifice (2 Kings 21-6);

5) Using various occult practices, including soothsaying, witchcraft, and mediums (2 Kings 21:6; Deuteronomy 18:9-14);

6) Erecting an Asherah pole in the temple of the Lord (2 kings 21:7-8; Deuteronomy 32:39); and

7) Shedding so much innocent blood that Jerusalem was said to be filled with it from one end to the other (2 Kings 21:16).

For these sins, God promised to judge Judah with a devastating calamity (2 Kings 21:12), wiping out Jerusalem as one wipes food from a dish (2 Kings 21:13). So, when Jeremiah was born, the people's fate had already been forecast. Indeed, the prophet was called from the womb to proclaim God's impending judgment (Jeremiah 1:5, 9-10). Despite the impressive reforms of Josiah (2 Kings 23), Judah would go into exile, and this was the bitter word that Jeremiah was called to deliver to his people.

Genesis 12:3. I will bless those who bless you, and I will curse him who curses you.

2 Chronicles 7:14

If my people, which are called by my name, shall humble themselves, and pray, and seek my face, and turn from their wicked ways; then will I hear from heaven, and will forgive their sin, and will heal their land.

Psalm 122:6

Pray for the peace of Jerusalem; they will prosper who love thee.

Lesson Plan 203

The Book of Jeremiah

Chapters 3 & 4

Objective: To give us insight on the Book of Jeremiah which contain the prophecies that were given during the lowest point in the history of Judah—the beginning of the Babylonian exile.

Objective Breakdown:

1. Introduction

2. Spiritual Adultery   Chapter 3:1-5

3. Judah Has Seen Her Backsliding Sister   Chapter 3:6-15

4. Repentance and Reconciliation   Chapter 3:16-25

5. Circumcised Hearts   Chapter 4:1-4

6. The Lord Will Allow an Invasion   Chapter 4:5-13

7. A Plea for Repentance   Chapter 4:14-22

8. A Vision of Chaos and Desolation   Chapter 4:23-31

Introduction:

Jeremiah's third chapter is a call for the nation of Judah to turn away from idols. In verses 9-13, the people are described as:

- o Committing spiritual harlotry and adultery;

- o Being treacherous;

- o Backsliding;

- o Transgressing against the Lord; and

- o Disobeying the Lord's voice.

Yet in spite of these sins, God extended an invitation to the nation to be reconciled to Him, and to find mercy and healing. The way back was through confession of and repentance from sin, and a wholehearted return to the Lord (Jeremiah 3:13, 22).

In the middle of this call to repent, the Lord also revealed His heart for the other nations of the world. First Israel would return to Him, then all nations would be gathered around His name at Jerusalem (Jeremiah 3:17). People from all over the world would serve Him rather than following the "dictates of their evil hearts.

God offer of hope and salvation still extends to everyone on earth. As before, his primary strategy for drawing nations to Himself is through His people. In light of Judah's history, believers today do well to consider whether their sins may be drawing others away from the Lord.

2 Chronicles 7:14

If my people, which are called by my name, shall humble themselves, and pray, and seek my face, and turn from their wicked ways; then will I hear from heaven, and will forgive their sin, and will heal their land.

Psalm 122:6

Pray for the peace of Jerusalem; they will prosper who love thee.

Lesson Plan 204

The Book of Jeremiah

Chapters 5 & 6

Objective: To give us insight on the Book of Jeremiah which contain the prophecies that were given during the lowest point in the history of Judah—the beginning of the Babylonian exile.

Objective Breakdown:

1. Introduction

2. Not a Righteous Soul in Jerusalem   Chapter 5:1-9

3. The Invaders Receive Permission   Chapter 5:10-19

4. The Reasons for God's Judgment   Chapter 5:20-31

5. Jeremiah Predicts a Siege   Chapter 6:1-8

6. Everyone Will Be Judged   Chapter 6:9-15

7. The People Refused to Obey   Chapter 6:16-20

8   The Invaders Are Described   Chapter 6:21-30

Introduction:

It takes only one to save the city. The prophets frequently compared Jerusalem to the ancient city of Sodom. God destroyed Sodom for its persistent wickedness and rebellion against Him. However, the Lord would have spared the city if Abraham could have found even ten righteous people living there. Apparently, he could not (Genesis 18:32-33; 19:24-25).

How many righteous people would have spared Jerusalem from a similar judgment? Only one, according to Jeremiah (Jeremiah 5:1). But the prophet search in vain for that one. First, he went to the poor, but quickly discovered that they were ignorant of justice and truth (Jeremiah 5:4). Then he went to the "great men," the leaders, because they could read the law, which had been rediscovered by Josiah (2 Kings 22:8-23:3). Yet he found every single one of them to be guilty of departing from God's ways (Jeremiah 5:5).

So, Jerusalem was bound for judgment. It had become so degenerate that God would have settled for even one righteous person rather than ten.

By this standard, how would you evaluate the cities of today? Are they morally better or worse than Sodom? How do they compare with Jerusalem? If Jeremiah were to search in your city today for one righteous person, would he find one? Would that person be you? If not, what changes do the people of your city need to make?

2 Chronicles 7:14

If my people, which are called by my name, shall humble themselves, and pray, and seek my face, and turn from their wicked ways; then will I hear from heaven, and will forgive their sin, and will heal their land.

Psalm 122:6

Pray for the peace of Jerusalem; they will prosper who love thee.

Lesson Plan 205

The Book of Jeremiah

Chapters 7 & 8

Objective: To give us insight on the Book of Jeremiah which contain the prophecies that were given during the lowest point in the history of Judah—the beginning of the Babylonian exile.

Objective Breakdown:

1. Introduction

2. God Sends His Prophet to the Temple   Chapter 7:1-11

3. The Example of Shiloh   Chapter 7:12-20

4. A History of Ignoring God   Chapter 7:21-26

5. God Will Cut Off His People   Chapter 7:27-24

6. There Will Be Nowhere to Bury the Dead   Chapter 8:1-3

7. The People Refuse to Listen   Chapter 8:4-13

8. There Will Be No Help from the Lord   Chapter 8:14-22

Introduction:

A sobering object lesson: Shiloh was a sobering object lesson for Judah. Once a center of Israel's religious life and site of the tabernacle (see 1 Samuel 1:3), Shiloh lay in ruins in Jeremiah's day, and its people had been taken captivity by the Assyrians. Why? Because the northern kingdom of Israel had turned away from the Lord to idols. Jeremiah warned that the same outcome awaited the people of Jerusalem–and for the same reason (Jeremiah 7:12-15).

Jeremiah's message of judgment must have sounded incredible. Jerusalem was the site of the temple, the magnificent house of worship that David had envisioned and Solomon had built to the glory of God (see 2 Chronicles 5:1). How could God allow His temple and its city to be destroyed? Yet if anyone doubted Jeremiah's warning, all they had to do was travel a little more than 20 miles north to Shiloh.

Apparently, few people heeded the prophet's word, because Jerusalem fell to the Babylonians within a few short years. The temple was burned and most of the people were either killed or deported.

This tragic outcome challenges us to consider whether idols exist in our own lives today?

We don't bow down to images of wood or stone, but if we allow anything to take the place of God, then we are practicing idolatry (see Isaiah 46:5-10, and Jeremiah 10:1-10). This can happen in our work, in our relationships, and, like the people of ancient Judah, even in our houses of worship. In that case, God may take away the thing that we hold dear in order to redirect our attention and affection to where they belong–on Him. The first Commandment is still in effect: "You shall have no other gods before Me" (Exodus 20:3).

2 Chronicles 7:14

If my people, which are called by my name, shall humble themselves, and pray, and seek my face, and turn from their wicked ways; then will I hear from heaven, and will forgive their sin, and will heal their land.

Psalm 122:6

Pray for the peace of Jerusalem; they will prosper who love thee.

Lesson Plan 206

The Book of Jeremiah

Chapters 9 & 10

Objective: To give us insight on the Book of Jeremiah which contain the prophecies that were given during the lowest point in the history of Judah—the beginning of the Babylonian exile.

Objective Breakdown:

1. Introduction

2. Jeremiah's Sorrow   Chapter 9:1-6

3. Judah Will Be Refined by fire   Chapter 9:7-16

4. A Time of Death and Mourning   Chapter 9:17-26

5. The Futility of Idols   Chapter 10:1-10

6. Idols and Idolaters Will Be Destroyed   Chapter 10:11-17

7. A Lamentation for the Land   Chapter 10:18-25

Introduction:

A false sense of security. It is a normal human tendency to flee from danger by running to places of safety. However, real peace and security do not come from gates, guards, or guns. Ultimately, they come from God.

The people of Jeremiah's day lived in an increasingly dangerous world. The Assyrian Empire was in decline, creating political instability in the Middle East. Seizing the opportunity, the Egyptians began to stage offensive campaigns from the South. Meanwhile, Babylon was emerging as a new superpower.

Yet in the midst of these dangerous signs, false prophets in Judah comforted the Israelites with words of peace (Jeremiah 8:11). The citizens took comfort in their walled cities, assuming that these defenses would be a safe heaven against a hostile force (Jeremiah 8:14). But they were merely denying their true condition. The gravest danger the residents of Judah faced was one that they had created themselves, and one that they brought with them into their cities: they had turned their backs on God (Jeremiah 8:5, 8:12).

In our day, many people have sought refuge from urban crime by moving to the suburbs. In fact, some new developments have taken a step back toward the days of walled cities by building gated communities. Such attempts to curb violent crime are understandable, but evil is not so easily excluded (Jeremiah 8:15). It cannot be controlled by merely controlling the environment. Ultimately, evil is a matter of dealing with sin, whether personal or institutional, and that means repentance and turning toward the Lord (Jeremiah 25:4-7; 35:15; Matthew 11:28).

What are you trusting in for peace and security? There's nothing wrong with wanting to protect yourself and your family from harm. But inner peace cannot come from shutting out evils from the outside; it also takes rooting out evils from the inside.

2 Chronicles 7:14

If my people, which are called by my name, shall humble themselves, and pray, and seek my face, and turn from their wicked ways; then will I hear from heaven, and will forgive their sin, and will heal their land.

Psalm 122:6

Pray for the peace of Jerusalem; they will prosper who love thee.

Lesson Plan 207

The Book of Jeremiah

Chapters 11, 12, & 13

Objective: To give us insight on the Book of Jeremiah which contain the prophecies that were given during the lowest point in the history of Judah—the beginning of the Babylonian exile.

Objective Breakdown:

1. Introduction

2. God Urges a Return to the Covenant   Chapter 11:1-8

3. Judgment on Covenant Breakers   Chapter 11:9-14

4. The Wrath of God Is Certain   Chapter 11:15-23

5. Why Do the Wicked Prosper   Chapter 12:1-4

6. The People Are Abandoned to Judgment   Chapter 12:5-13

7. God Will Eventually Show Compassion   Chapter 12:14-17

8. The Illustration of the Ruined Sash   Chapter 13:1-11

9. God Will Destroy His Drunken People   Chapter 13:12-19

10. The Faithless Flock Will Be Scattered   Chapter 13:20-27

Introduction:

Sin is sin. Jeremiah presents a sobering message, to the people of his day as well as the people of today: God is against all sin. His judgment of wrath falls on the sin of all individuals and nations, without exception (Jeremiah 9:25-26). It doesn't matter whether one is a Jew (circumcised) or Gentile (uncircumcised). No group is exempt. No one has special privileges. As Paul put it, the wrath of God is revealed from Heaven against all ungodliness and unrighteousness of men (Romans 1:18). All have sinned and stand under God's judgment (Romans 3:10-18, 23).

God leaves no room for bargaining. He says that God will punish Egypt, Judah, Edom, Ammon, Moab, and every other nation, even those living in the farthest corners of the earth. That includes all the nations that ever existed or will exist. Apparently, God sees no difference between the sins of Judah and the sins of Egypt, the sins of ancient culture or the sins of modern culture. Sin is sin. There are no good sins. The sins of one people are as evil as the sins of another.

This is the bad news which makes the good news of Christ's work on the Cross very good news indeed. Yet even the bad news shows that God is an even handed in His Judgment on all, but He also offers life to all. No one can hide from the all-seeing eye of the Lord. But no one needs to lose out on His salvation, unless that person rejects God's provision, Christ.

2 Chronicles 7:14

If my people, which are called by my name, shall humble themselves, and pray, and seek my face, and turn from their wicked ways; then will I hear from heaven, and will forgive their sin, and will heal their land.

Psalm 122:6

Pray for the peace of Jerusalem; they will prosper who love thee.

Lesson Plan 208

The Book of Jeremiah

Chapters 14, 15, & 16

Objective: To give us insight on the Book of Jeremiah which contain the prophecies that were given during the lowest point in the history of Judah—the beginning of the Babylonian exile.

Objective Breakdown:

1. Introduction

2. A Prophecy Concerning Droughts   Chapter 14:1-10

3. Jeremiah Complains About False Prophets   Chapter 14:11-16

4. Utter Desolation Is Coming   Chapter 14:17-22

5. Jerusalem Will Pay for Manasseh's Sins   Chapter 15:1-9

6. Jeremiah's Dejection   Chapter 15:10-21

7. Jeremiah Is Told to Remain Unmarried   Chapter 16:1-9

8. The Judeans Are Worse Than Their Ancestors   Chapter 16:10-21

Introduction:

The waste of fine material. The meaning of Jeremiah's parable of the ruined sash (Jeremiah 13-11) is itself-evident: just as the sash was ruined, so the pride of God's people had ruined them in terms of fulfilling God's purpose. Their evil ways had made them "profitable for nothing" (Jeremiah 13:10).

The linen sash was especially appropriate as a symbol for proud Judah. Linen was a costly material (Isaiah 3:23), often imported from Egypt (Proverbs 7:16). The Israelites generally reserved its use for making exquisite furnishing, such as those in the tabernacle (Exodus 26:1, 31, 36), and fine garments, such as worn by the priest (Exodus 28:39) or a favorite person (Esther 8:15; Ezekiel 16:10, 13).

The Lord cautioned Jeremiah to avoid letting his linen sash get wet (Jeremiah 13:1). To do so would have cause waste of fine material. Yet later, God instructed the prophet to hide the sash along the Euphrates River (Jeremiah 13:4) so that the waters could rot the belt over time. This made it into a powerful image of what Judah looked like—a people intended for worthy noble purposes, but now worthless and rotten because of sinful pride.

The days of powder and dust. If ever there were a testimony to the fact that God keeps His word, it would be the droughts that came on Judah in the days of Jeremiah (Jeremiah 14:1). Hundreds of years earlier, God had promised that if His people followed Him, He would bless their land with abundance. But if they turned away from Him, disobeying His laws and worshiping other gods, he would turn the annual rain to "powder and dust" (Leviticus 26:18-19; Deuteronomy 28:1-24). Judah surpassed Israel in its idolatry and wickedness, so the Lord kept His promise by sending a series of droughts. Jeremiah pleaded for mercy, but God told him that it was too late; He had given His people over to judgment (Jeremiah 14:11-12).

2 Chronicles 7:14

If my people, which are called by my name, shall humble themselves, and pray, and seek my face, and turn from their wicked ways; then will I hear from heaven, and will forgive their sin, and will heal their land.

Psalm 122:6

Pray for the peace of Jerusalem; they will prosper who love thee.

Lesson Plan 209

The Book of Jeremiah

Chapters 17, 18, & 19

Objective: To give us insight on the Book of Jeremiah which contain the prophecies that were given during the lowest point in the history of Judah—the beginning of the Babylonian exile.

Introduction:

False forecasting. When modern day weather forecasters miss a forecast, and it rains rather than shines, or snows a blizzard rather than turning out clear and cold, the public outcry is often severe, especially if property or lives have been placed at risk as a result of the inaccurate information.

Imagine though if the forecasters knowingly lie about the weather! That is what God charged the false prophets of Judah with doing (Jeremiah 14:14), only their forecast was not about the weather, but about political and spiritual matters. Rather than listening for a word from the Lord these charlatans resorted to divination, attempting to tell the future through such means as astrology or examining the entrails or ritually slaughtered animals. Scripture strongly denounces this practice, along with other forms of the occult arts.

The persecuted prophets. Throughout his ministry Jeremiah had to endure intense persecution because of his stand for the Lord (Jeremiah 15:15). In this he was not alone. Another prophet named Urijah also spoke out against the wicked policies and practices of the leaders in Jerusalem. For this he was sentenced to die, but fled to Egypt. However, King Jehoiakim was able to have him extradited back to the city, whereupon he was put to death (Jeremiah 26:20-23).

Later the leaders turned on Jeremiah, launching a campaign of verbal attacks against him and plotting ways to destroy him (Jeremiah 18:18). Eventually they put him on trial for speaking against Jerusalem, a charge which they demanded the death penalty (Jeremiah 26:10-11). Fortunately, an official named Ahikam intervened and was able to spare the prophet's life (Jeremiah 26:24).

Nevertheless, Jeremiah was imprisoned for his message. Yet eventually he was vindicated when his prediction that Jehoiakim would not die peacefully in Jerusalem (Jeremiah 22:18-19) came to pass about 598 B.C. (2 Chronicles 36:5-6).

2 Chronicles 7:14

If my people, which are called by my name, shall humble themselves, and pray, and seek my face, and turn from their wicked ways; then will I hear from heaven, and will forgive their sin, and will heal their land.

Psalm 122:6

Pray for the peace of Jerusalem; they will prosper who love thee.

Lesson Plan 210

The Book of Jeremiah

Chapters 20, 21, & 22

Objective: To give us insight on the Book of Jeremiah which contain the prophecies that were given during the lowest point in the history of Judah—the beginning of the Babylonian exile.

Objective Breakdown:

1. Introduction

2. Pashhur Abuses Jeremiah.   Chapter 20:1-6

3. Jeremiah's Prayer and Sorrow   Chapter 20:7-18

4. God Himself Will Fight Zedekiah   Chapter 21:1-10

5. A Message to the house of David   Chapter 21:11-14

5. An Appeal for Justice   Chapter 22:1-9

6. A Message Concerning Jehoahaz   Chapter 22:10-12

7. A Message Concerning Jehoiackim   Chapter 22:13-23

8. Jehoiachin Will Be Cast Out   Chapter 22:24-30

Introduction:

The "dead" for whom Jeremiah was told not to weep (Jeremiah 22:10) may have been king Josiah, Judah's boy king who grew up to lead a nationwide reform. Josiah died in battle against Pharaoh Necho of Egypt. Necho was advancing North to help the Assyrians defend themselves against the Babylonians when Josiah brought his army against him. Josiah may have seen Necho's trespass through Canaan as a challenge to Judah's sovereignty.

Whatever Josiah's reasoning the Egyptian king warned him against attacking. He insisted that God had summoned him to aid the struggling Assyrians. But Josiah ignored Necho's advice and joined battle. As a result, he was mortally wounded by Egyptian archers (2 Chronicles 35:20-24).

This was a grievous loss for Judah. In the first place, it brought to an end the spiritual vitality that had been revived under Josiah. Moreover, it signaled the beginning of the end for the nation. Even before Josiah was born, God had promised that judgment was coming (2 Kings 21:10-15). He reaffirmed that intention when Josiah asked for a word from the Lord, though He promised to delay the end until Josiah's death (2 Kings 22:15-22).

Now the final days of the kingdom were at hand. Ironically, Josiah's attack on the Egyptians had delayed them from arriving in time to help the Assyrians, and as a result the Babylonians became masters of the Middle East in about 598 B.C., Nebuchadnezzar captured Jerusalem and deported most of its leadership. In about 587 B.C., he returned to destroy the city and carry off the survivors into exile. Josiah was the last of the God-fearing kings of Judah.

2 Chronicles 7:14

If my people, which are called by my name, shall humble themselves, and pray, and seek my face, and turn from their wicked ways; then will I hear from heaven, and will forgive their sin, and will heal their land.

Psalm 122:6

Pray for the peace of Jerusalem; they will prosper who love thee.

Lesson Plan 211

The Book of Jeremiah

Chapters 23, 24, & 25

Objective: To give us insight on the Book of Jeremiah which contain the prophecies that were given during the lowest point in the history of Judah—the beginning of the Babylonian exile.

Objective Breakdown:

1. Introduction

Introduction:

The cup of fury. One of the most sobering chapters in the Bible is Jeremiah 25. It describes the "wine cup of fury" that the Lord was going to force the nations of Jeremiah's day to drink (Jeremiah 25:15-16, 27-29). The reasons God's scathing judgment is clear: He is the Creator and sovereign Lord, who revealed Himself to and through His people, the Israelites, and through His prophets such as Jeremiah. Yet the entire world of that day—Judah included—had turned away from Him to worship and serve false gods.

The situation was similar to that described by Paul in the opening of Romans: "Although they knew God, they did not glorify Him as God....but became futile in their thoughts and changed the glory of the incorruptible God into an image made like corruptible man and birds and four-footed animals and creeping things" (Romans 1:21-23). Every nation was deeply committed to idolatry, and stood under imminent judgment (Jeremiah 25:8-26):

(1) Judah was among the worse. Therefore, God's wrath would begin with Babylon's destruction of Judah (Jeremiah 25:8-11).

(2) Eventually God would punish Babylon for its own sins (Jeremiah 25:12-14). Then the Lord's wrath would spread to all nations (Jeremiah 25:19-26).

(3) Egypt, Uz, and Philistia in the southwest;

(4) Edom, Moab, and Ammon in the southeast;

(5) Tyre, Sidon, and the coastlands in the northwest;

(6) Dedan, Tema, Buz, and other nations in the farthest corners of the earth;

(7) Arabia and the desert peoples, and Zimri, Elam, and Media in the east; and

(8) All kings of the north, and all the kingdoms on the face of the earth.

The terror of God's wrath upon sin, particularly the sin of idolatry is worldwide in its scope. No one is excluded. This sobering truth is repeated again and again in the Bible, all the way to the end (Revelation Chapters 6-18).

2 Chronicles 7:14

If my people, which are called by my name, shall humble themselves, and pray, and seek my face, and turn from their wicked ways; then will I hear from heaven, and will forgive their sin, and will heal their land.

Psalm 122:6

Pray for the peace of Jerusalem; they will prosper who love thee.

Lesson Plan 212

The Book of Jeremiah

Chapters 26, 27, & 28

Objective: To give us insight on the Book of Jeremiah which contain the prophecies that were given during the lowest point in the history of Judah—the beginning of the Babylonian exile.

Objective Breakdown:

1. Introduction

2. Jeremiah's appeal at the Temple   Chapter 26:1-9

3. The Leaders Demand Jeremiah's Death   Chapter 26:10-19

4. Urijah's Execution   Chapter 26:20-24

5. The Illustration of Bonds and Yokes   Chapter 27:1-11

6. Jeremiah's Urges Submission to Babylon   Chapter 27:12-22

7. A False Prophecy Against Hananiah   Chapter 28:1-9

8. Jeremiah Predicts Hananiah's Death   Chapter 28:10-17

Introduction:

"Nebuchadnezzar, my servant." Who is the most dangerous world leader you can think of? Who would you say is the greatest threat to world peace and stability today? Whoever it is, you probably cannot regard that person with greater suspicion and disdain than the people of Judah had for Nebuchadnezzar of Babylon.

Yet God described this pagan king as His own "servant" (Jeremiah 27:6; compare 25:9). That had to be unimaginable for the people of Jeremiah's day. To them, Nebuchadnezzar was a great evil. He ruled ruthless superpower that was poised to overrun their land and destroy their cities. How could he possibly be God's servant?

Interestingly, the description of Nebuchadnezzar sounds a lot like the description of Cyrus, the Persian king, given through Isaiah: "My shepherd" and His anointed" (Isaiah 44:28-45:1).

Both of these rulers had power over vast territories in the ancient Middle East. Their decisions determined much of what happened in history at that time. From a human perspective they were in charge.

590

But the prophecies of Isaiah and Jeremiah show that ultimately they (Nebuchadnezzar & Cyrus) were not in control of the final outcomes. Whether they knew it or not, they were only finite human beings placed in position of authority by the hand of God. As such they were God's servants, God's agents. God is the King of all kings—then and now. If that is so, what does it say about the leaders of the world today?

2 Chronicles 7:14

If my people, which are called by my name, shall humble themselves, and pray, and seek my face, and turn from their wicked ways; then will I hear from heaven, and will forgive their sin, and will heal their land.

Psalm 122:6

Pray for the peace of Jerusalem; they will prosper who love thee.

Lesson Plan 213

The Book of Jeremiah

Chapters 29, 30, & 31

Objective: To give us insight on the Book of Jeremiah which contain the prophecies that were given during the lowest point in the history of Judah–the beginning of the Babylonian exile.

Objective Breakdown:

1. Introduction

2. Jeremiah Writes to Captives   Chapter 29:1-9

3. Seventy Years of Exile   Chapter 29:10-20

4. God Will Punish the False Prophets   Chapter 29:21-29

5. The Time of Jacob's Trouble   Chapter 30:1-7

6. God Says He Will Save Israel   Chapter 30:8-11

7. Incurable Malady   Chapter 30:12-17

8. God Will Renew Israel   Chapter 30:18-24

9. The Remnant of Israel   Chapter 31:1-9

10. Mourning Will Turn to Joy   Chapter 31:10-17

11. The Lord Will Create a New Thing   Chapter 31:18-22

12. God Will Build and Plant   Chapter 31:23-30

13. A New Covenant   Chapter 31:31-40

Introduction:

Seeking the peace of the city. Christians live with the future hope in the return of Christ and eternity with Him. In the meantime, we are visitors or "sojourners" on earth (1 Peter 2:11). What should our attitude be toward this less-than-perfect world? We can gain some insight into our situation from the Lord's instructions to the captives of Judah living in Babylon (Jeremiah 29:4-7).

The Babylonians came against Judah in 605 B.C., and again in 599-597 B.C. In both cases they carried off the best and brightest of the nation's leaders (2 Kings 24:14-16; Jeremiah 27:20; 29:2; Daniel 1:1-6). These exiles were settled on the Chebar River (Ezekiel 1:1), possibly a canal of the Euphrates on the eastern side of Babylon.

Shortly after the second deportation, a false prophet named Hananiah announced to Zedekiah and the remaining people in Jerusalem that the captives would be returned within two years (Jeremiah 28:1-4). Apparently, the prophets in Babylon were saying the same thing (Jeremiah 29:8-9). But Jeremiah denounced this claim (Jeremiah 28:15-16), and Hananiah died in the seventh month of the same year (Jeremiah 28:17).

Jeremiah then sent a letter to the exiles in Babylon to tell them to expect 70 years of Babylonian captivity (Jeremiah 29:1, 10), not two. The message opened with a remarkable statement: God has caused the exiles to be carried away to Babylon (Jeremiah 29:4). Ultimately their plight was not merely the result of Nebuchadnezzar policies, but God's purposes. They (exiles) were people sent to fulfill a mission. Jeremiah told the people to put down roots, to build, plant gardens marry and have children (Jeremiah 29:5-6), because they weren't going anywhere for 70 years.

2 Chronicles 7:14

If my people, which are called by my name, shall humble themselves, and pray, and seek my face, and turn from their wicked ways; then will I hear from heaven, and will forgive their sin, and will heal their land.

Psalm 122:6

Pray for the peace of Jerusalem; they will prosper who love thee.

Lesson Plan 214

The Book of Jeremiah

Chapter 32

Objective: To give us insight on the Book of Jeremiah which contain the prophecies that were given during the lowest point in the history of Judah—the beginning of the Babylonian exile.

Objective Breakdown:

1. Introduction

2. Zedekiah Puts Jeremiah in Prison   Chapter 32:1-5

3. Jeremiah Buys His Cousin's Field   Chapter 32:6-15

4. Jeremiah's Prays to the Lord   Chapter 32:16-25

5. The Fall of Jerusalem Is Certain   Chapter 32:26-35

6. The Lord Will Bring Back His People   Chapter 32:36-44

Introduction:

Written on their hearts. Knowing God mean, in part, having a personal relationship with Him, thanks to Christ's work on the Cross. Yet centuries before Christ came, Scripture was describing what that sense of personal intimacy with God would be like. The Lord privileged Jeremiah with a vision of this "new covenant" (Jeremiah 31:31), or way of relating to people, that Jesus would initiate. God intends that the hope expressed in Jeremiah 31 would be the experience of every genuine believer. The Lord promised that:

o God's children would know Him, not just know about Him (Jeremiah 31:34)

o God Himself would be their teacher (Jeremiah 31:31), as He (God) became Jesus' teacher (John 5:19; 8:28; 12:49; 14:10)

o His teaching would go beyond a mere collection of moral precepts, and even beyond an external code of ethics, to the inscription of His word (His "law") on the hearts of His children, where it would shape their identity and behavior (Jeremiah 31:33).

The New Testament further reveals that the words that God has promised to write on the hearts of His people are written by the Holy Spirit (2 Corinthians 3:1-3), who empowers them to live in a manner that reflect the very character of God. This profound truth of God's new covenant is so significant that Jeremiah 31 is quoted three times in the New Testament (John 6:45; Hebrews 8:10; 10:16-17).

Are you experiencing the close, personal knowledge of the Lord referred to by Jeremiah? If not, is it possible that in fact you have never come to know Him by placing faith in what Jesus did for you? If not, you can establish a personal relationship with God right now by calling out to Him, confessing your own sinfulness, and thanking Him for the forgiveness He extends to you as a result of Jesus' work on the Cross.

2 Chronicles 7:14

If my people, which are called by my name, shall humble themselves, and pray, and seek my face, and turn from their wicked ways; then will I hear from heaven, and will forgive their sin, and will heal their land.

Psalm 122:6

Pray for the peace of Jerusalem; they will prosper who love thee.

Lesson Plan 215

The Book of Jeremiah

Chapters 33, 34, & 35

Objective: To give us insight on the Book of Jeremiah which contain the prophecies that were given during the lowest point in the history of Judah—the beginning of the Babylonian exile.

Objective Breakdown:

1. Introduction

2. The Ruins of Jerusalem Will Be Rebuilt   Chapter 33:1-9

3. God Reaffirms His Covenant with David   Chapter 33:10-16

4. The Lord Our Righteousness   Chapter 33:17-26

5. Zedekiah Gets a Warning and a Promise   Chapter 34:1-7

6. Slaves Are Freed, Then Taken Back   Chapter 34:8-16

7. God Denounces the Slaveholders   Chapter 34:17-22

8. The Obedient Rechabites   Chapter 35:1-11

9. While Will Not Others Obey   Chapter 35:12-19

Introduction:

Jerusalem from desolation to joy. Jerusalem the holy city, was destroyed by Babylonians in 587 B.C. but Jeremiah envisioned a restoration of the city and a return to joy and prosperity (Jeremiah 32:42-44; 33:10-11). This prophecy was partially fulfilled when Zerubbabel, Ezra and later Nehemiah led exiles back to rebuild, beginning with the temple and the city walls.

However, Jerusalem's joy would come about ultimately as a result of a new covenant (Jeremiah 31:31), which would be initiated at the coming of Christ (Hebrews 8:6-13).

That new covenant would provide a lasting basis for hope and joy, knowing God. God withdrew from Jerusalem for a while in order to judge His people for violating their covenant with Him (Jerusalem 32:28-42). But under the new covenant, His people would know Him personally, with the result that the city of desolation would become a city of joy.

"Everybody's doing it." People sometimes excuses or justify their immoral behavior with the attitude that "everybody's doing it." But that notion is false. Not everyone is doing it. Not everyone is giving way to popular opinion. Some people maintain their moral convictions—even those which are not based on specific biblical teachings.

Jeremiah shows us an example. The wicked people of Judah were faithless when it came to keeping the covenant, so God gave them a case study in loyalty. He told Jeremiah, to offer wine to a group of people called the Rechabites (Jeremiah 35:2), a family descended from Jonadab son of Rechab (Jeremiah 35:6). The Rechabites refused Jeremiah's offer (as God knew they would), based a centuries-old tradition established by their ancestor.

2 Chronicles 7:14

If my people, which are called by my name, shall humble themselves, and pray, and seek my face, and turn from their wicked ways; then will I hear from heaven, and will forgive their sin, and will heal their land.

Psalm 122:6

Pray for the peace of Jerusalem; they will prosper who love thee.

Lesson Plan 216

The Book of Jeremiah

Chapters 36 & 37

Objective: To give us insight on the Book of Jeremiah which contain the prophecies that were given during the lowest point in the history of Judah—the beginning of the Babylonian exile.

Objective Breakdown:

1. Introduction

2. Baruch Reads Jeremiah's Scroll   Chapter 36:1-8

3. A Fast Is Proclaimed   Chapter 36:9-15

4. The King Burns the Scroll   Chapter 36:16-26

5. God Promises to Punish Jehoiakim   Chapter 36:27-32

6. A Warning Not to Put Hope in Egypt   Chapter 37:1-10

7. Jeremiah Is Charged with Defecting   Chapter 37:11-21

Introduction:

Jerusalem was partly destroyed in 606 B.C.; further devastated in 597 B.C.; finally burned and desolated in 586 B.C. Jeremiah lived through these terrible years, the close of the monarchy, the death and agony of a nation. Jeremiah during this period cried out that if the nation would repent God would save them from Babylon.

As Assyria had been the background of Isaiah's ministry, so Babylon was the background of Jeremiah's ministry.

The internal situation was that the Northern Kingdom had fallen (721 B.C.), and much of Judah. Judah had suffered reverse after reverse, till Jerusalem alone was left. Still Judah ignored the continued warnings of the prophets and grew harder and harder in their idolatry and wickedness. The hour of doom was ahead.

The international situation there was a three-cornered contest for world supremacy at play: Assyria, Babylon, and Egypt. For 300 hundred years Assyria, in the North Euphrates valley with Nineveh as its capital, had ruled the world; but now Assyria was growing weak. Babylon in the Southern Euphrates valley was becoming powerful. Egypt, in the Nile valley, which 1000 years earlier had been a world power and had declined, was again becoming ambitious. Babylon became the leading power about the middle of Jeremiah's ministry. It broke the power of Assyria (607 B.C.); and two years later crushed Egypt, in the battle of Carchemish (605 B.C.); and for 70 years ruled the world, the same 70 years as Jews captivity.

Contemporary Prophets

Jeremiah, was one of the leading prophets that God had clustered around the destruction of Jerusalem.

Ezekiel, a fellow priest somewhat younger than Jeremiah was preaching in Babylon the same things that Jeremiah was preaching in Jerusalem (taken to Babylon 597 B.C.).

Daniel, man of royal blood taken to Babylon in 607 B.C.

Habakkuk and Zephaniah, helping Jeremiah in Jerusalem.

Nahum, at the same time was predicting the Fall of Nineveh.

Obadiah, at the same time was predicting the Ruin of Edom.

2 Chronicles 7:14

If my people, which are called by my name, shall humble themselves, and pray, and seek my face, and turn from their wicked ways; then will I hear from heaven, and will forgive their sin, and will heal their land.

Psalm 122:6

Pray for the peace of Jerusalem; they will prosper who love thee.

Lesson Plan 217

The Book of Jeremiah

Chapters 38 & 39

Objective: To give us insight on the Book of Jeremiah which contain the prophecies that were given during the lowest point in the history of Judah—the beginning of the Babylonian exile.

Objective Breakdown:

1. Introduction

2. Jeremiah Is Imprisoned in a Cistern   Chapter 38:1-13

3. Zedekiah Meets Privately with Jeremiah   Chapter 38:14-16

4. Jeremiah Urges the King to Surrender   Chapter 38:17-28

5. Jerusalem Falls and the King Is Taken   Chapter 39:1-10

6. A Promise to Ebed-Melech the Ethiopian   Chapter 39:11-18

Introduction:

Jeremiah—a traitor? The complaint that the princes of Judah brought against Jeremiah (Jeremiah 38:4) was nothing less than a charge of treason. If the prophet were found guilty, their request for the death penalty would have been justified.

The case against Jeremiah was considerably strengthened by a damaging piece of evidence, albeit a circumstantial one. Around 589 B.C. the Babylonians besieged Jerusalem in response to a rebellious alliance of which King Zedekiah was a part. However, the siege was temporarily lifted when Babylonians heard rumors of an approaching army of Egyptians (Jeremiah 37:5).

During the lull in the fighting, Jeremiah made the mistake of traveling North toward his hometown in Benjamin to take care of personal business. This must have been the route that the Babylonians had taken, for when Jeremiah arrived in Benjamin, he was arrested and charged with attempting to defect to the Babylonians. He was returned to Jerusalem and imprisoned (Jeremiah 37:11-15).

When the siege resumed, Jeremiah continued to urge surrender rather than resistance (Jeremiah 38:1-3). So, in addition to defection, Jeremiah enemies charged him with aiding and abetting the enemy. Again, a case could be made against him based on appearances.

There were five ways to take a walled city (see 2 Kings 25:1-4). The least violent and costly was by trickery. Apparently, Jeremiah's enemies were convinced that the prophet was an agent of Nebuchadnezzar, and that his words concerning the certainty of Jerusalem's fall were a ruse to convince the city's defenders to lay down their arms and open the city gates.

Only through the intervention of the eunuch Ebed-Melech (Jeremiah 37:7-13) and the private doubts of King Zedekiah (Jeremiah 38:14-26) was Jeremiah spared. In the end he was vindicated when Jerusalem fell in 587 B.C. (Jeremiah 38-39:2; 2 Kings 25:4).

2 Chronicles 7:14

If my people, which are called by my name, shall humble themselves, and pray, and seek my face, and turn from their wicked ways; then will I hear from heaven, and will forgive their sin, and will heal their land.

Psalm 122:6

Pray for the peace of Jerusalem; they will prosper who love thee.

Lesson Plan 218

The Book of Jeremiah

Chapters 40, 41, 42, 43, 44, & 45

Objective: To gain a good understanding of the Book of Jeremiah and to help each of us to realize the influence we have on others. Also, to determine the actions we can take to lead others toward God and not away from Him.

Objective Breakdown:

Introduction

2. Jeremiah's Given His Freedom Release	Jeremiah 40:1-6
3. Gedaliah Is Made Governor of Judah	Jeremiah 40:7-12
4. News of a Plot Against the Governor	Jeremiah 40:13-16
5. Gedaliah's Assassination	Jeremiah 41:1-10
6. Johanan Pursues the Assassin Ishmael	Jeremiah 41:11-18
7. The People Look for Divine Counsel	Jeremiah 42:1-6
8. God's Answer: Do Not Go to Egypt	Jeremiah 42:7-12
9. Death Will Punish Disobedience	Jeremiah 42:13-22
10. The People Take Jeremiah to Egypt	Jeremiah 43:1-7
11. Jeremiah Predicts Egypt's Downfall	Jeremiah 43:8-13
12. God Sends Word to the Israelites	Jeremiah 44:1-6
13. God's Wrath Is Against the Refugees	Jeremiah 44:7-14
14. The People Remain Obstinate	Jeremiah 44:15-19
15. Jeremiah Proclaims Punishment	Jeremiah 44:20-30
16. The Lord Makes a Promise to Baruch	Jeremiah 45:1-5

Introduction:

Jerusalem was partly destroyed in 606 B.C.; further devastated in 597 B.C.; finally burned and desolated in 586 B.C. Jeremiah lived through these terrible years, the close of the monarchy, the death and agony of a nation. Jeremiah during this period cried out that if the nation would repent God would save them from Babylon.

As Assyria had been the background of Isaiah's ministry, so Babylon was the background of Jeremiah's ministry.

The internal situation was that the Northern Kingdom had fallen (721 B.C.), and much of Judah. Judah had suffered reverse after reverse, till Jerusalem alone was left. Still Judah ignored the continued warnings of the prophets and grew harder and harder in their idolatry and wickedness. The hour of doom was ahead.

The international situation there was three cornered contests for world supremacy at play: Assyria, Babylon, and Egypt. For 300 hundred years Assyria, in the North Euphrates valley with Nineveh as its capital, had ruled the world; but now Assyria was growing weak. Babylon in the Southern Euphrates valley was becoming powerful. Egypt, in the Nile valley, which 1000 years earlier had been a world power and had declined, was again becoming ambitious. Babylon became the leading power about the middle of Jeremiah's ministry. It broke the power of Assyria (607 B.C.); and 2 years later crushed Egypt, in the battle of Carchemish (605 B.C.); and for 70 years ruled the world, the same 70 years as Jews captivity.

Contemporary Prophets:

Jeremiah, was one of the leading prophets that God had clustered around the destruction of Jerusalem.

Ezekiel, a fellow priest somewhat younger than Jeremiah was preaching in Babylon the same things that Jeremiah was preaching in Jerusalem. (Taken to Babylon 597 B. C.).

Daniel, man of royal blood taken to Babylon in 607 B. C.

Habakkuk and Zephaniah, helping Jeremiah in Jerusalem.

Nahum, at the same time was predicting the Fall of Nineveh.

Obadiah, at the same time was predicting the Ruin of Edom.

2 Chronicles 7:14

If my people, which are called by my name, shall humble themselves, and pray, and seek my face, and turn from their wicked ways; then will I hear from heaven, and will forgive their sin, and will heal their land.

Pray for the peace of Jerusalem; they will prosper who love thee.

Lesson Plan 219

The Book of Jeremiah

Chapters 46, 47, 48, 49, 50, 51, & 52

Objective: To gain a good understanding of the Book of Jeremiah and to help each of us to realize the influence we have on others. Also, to determine the actions we can take to lead others toward God and not away from Him.

Objective Breakdown:

Introduction

2.	Egypt Will Face Defeat at Carchemish	Jeremiah 46:1-12
3.	Nebuchadnezzar Will Beat the Egyptians	Jeremiah 46:13-24
4.	Israel Will Not Come to a Complete End	Jeremiah 46:25-28
5.	A Word Concerning the Philistines	Jeremiah 47:1-7
6.	A Prophecy Against Moab	Jeremiah 48:1-11
7.	Moab's Idols and Cities Will Be Broken	Jeremiah 48:12-25
8.	The Pride of Moab Will Be Brought Low	Jeremiah 48:26-34
9.	Moab Will Be Destroyed as a People	Jeremiah 48:35-47
10.	A Prophecy Against the Ammonites	Jeremiah 49:1-6
11.	A Prophecy Against the Edomites	Jeremiah 49:7-13
12.	Edom Will Resemble Sodom and Gormorrah	Jeremiah 49:14-22
13.	A Word Against Damascus	Jeremiah 49:23-27
14.	A Prophecy Against Kedar	Jeremiah 49:28-33
15.	A Prophecy Against Elam	Jeremiah 49:34-39
16.	A Prophecy Against Babylon	Jeremiah 50:1-7
17.	An Alliance Will Overthrow Babylon	Jeremiah 50:8-17

Introduction:

Baruch, Jeremiah's scribe, was a man of prominence with high ambitions (Chapter 45:5). He was recognized as having great influence with Jeremiah (Chapter 43:3).

Chapter 46 Egypt. A description of the defeat of the Egyptian Army at Carchemish (605 B.C.) in the middle period of Jeremiah's life (Chapter 46:1-12); and a later prophecy that Nebuchadnezzar would invade Egypt (Chapter 46:13-26). Over a hundred years earlier Isaiah prophesied Assyrian invasions of Egypt. Ezekiel also had something to say about Egypt (Ezekiel Chapter 19-32).

Chapter 47 The Philistines. This prophecy foretelling the desolation of Philistia by Babylon, was fulfilled 20 years later when Nebuchadnezzar took Judah. Other prophets who spoke regarding the Philistines were: Isaiah (Chapter 14:28-32); Amos (Chapter 1:6-8); Zephaniah (Chapter 2:4-7); Zechariah (Chapter 9:1-7).

Chapter 48 Moab. A picture of impending desolation of Moab. Moab helped Nebuchadnezzar against Judah, but later was devastated at his hands (582 B.C.).

Chapter 49 Ammon, Edom, Syria, Hazor, Elam. A prediction that Nebuchadnezzar would conquer these, which he did. Ammon under Ezekiel 25:1-11, Edom under Obadiah.

Chapter 50, 51 Prediction of the Fall of Babylon. The fall and perpetual desolation of Babylon is here predicted, in language matching the grandeur of the theme (Chapter 51:37-43); as Isaiah had done earlier (Isaiah 13:17-22). The Medes, leading a great company of nations, are named as the conquerors (Jeremiah chapters 50:9; 51:11, 27, 28). These two chapters pronouncing the doom of Babylon, were copied in a separate book, and sent to Babylon in a deputation headed by King Zedekiah, seven years before Nebuchadnezzar burned Jerusalem (Jeremiah 51:59-64). The book was to be read publicly and then solemn ceremony sunk in the Euphrates, with these words, "Thus shall Babylon sink, and not rise."

Chapter 52 Captivity of Judah. (See 2 Kings Chapters 24 & 25)

2 Chronicles 7:14

If my people, which are called by my name, shall humble themselves, and pray, and seek my face, and turn from their wicked ways; then will I hear from heaven, and will forgive their sin, and will heal their land.

Psalm 122:6

Pray for the peace of Jerusalem; they will prosper who love thee.

The Book of Lamentations

Scripture Focus Chapters 1-5

Objective: To gain insight on the book of Lamentations which is a funeral dirge, mourning the fall of Jerusalem in 587 B.C.

Objective Breakdown:

1. Introduction

2. The Lonely City   Chapter 1:1-6

3. The Cause of Jerusalem's Fall   Chapter 1:7-11

4. God Has Handed His People Over   Chapter 1:12-16

5. No One Comforts Zion   Chapter 1:17-22

6. Judah Feels the Wrath of God   Chapter 2:1-8

7. Jerusalem's Enemies Rejoice   Chapter 2:9-16

8. The Lord Has Kept His Promise   Chapter 2:17-22

9. Personal Experience of God's Anger   Chapter 3:1-12

10. God's Faithfulness Is Great   Chapter 3:13-27

11. "There May Yet Be Hope"   Chapter 3:28-39

12. The Answer Is to Turn Back to God   Chapter 3:40-51

13. A Plea for Justice   Chapter 3:52-66

14. A Punishment Worse Than Sodom's   Chapter 4:1-6

15. The Living Envy the Dead   Chapter 4:7-11

16. Jerusalem's Unbelievable Reduction   Chapter 4:12-16

17. There Was No Help for Jerusalem   Chapter 4:17-22

18. Desperate Conditions   Chapter 5:1-9

19. "Our Dance Has Turned into Mourning"   Chapter 5:10-22

Lesson Plan 220

The Book of Lamentations

Chapters 1, 2, 3, 4, & 5

Objective: To introduce us to the book of Lamentations which is a funeral dirge, mourning the fall of Jerusalem in 587 B.C.

Objective Breakdown:

1. Introduction

2. Lament Over Jerusalem   Lamentations 1:1-22

3. Judgment on Jerusalem   Lamentations 2:1-22

4. Hope Through the Lord's Compassion   Lamentations 3:1-66

5. Horrors of the Besieged City   Lamentations 4:1-22

6. Prayer for Restoration   Lamentations 5:1-22

Introduction:

People can fall into serious trouble by failing to consider the consequences of their actions. The people of Judah failed to think through the consequences of their choices (Lamentations 1:9). For generations they ignored the law's warning against idolatry, oppressing the poor, cheating in business, relying on foreign governments (especially Egypt) for security, and other sins of public life. They maintained a pretense of worshiping the Lord by keeping up temple rituals, but reality was that they turned their backs on God (see Jeremiah's Sermon at the Temple at Jeremiah 7:2-4).

The Lord sent numerous prophets to warn His people of impending disaster, but the Judeans routinely ignored them (2 Chronicles 36:15-16). As a result, they were shocked when the Babylonians finally came and destroyed their way of life. Jeremiah was stunned, dazed, heartbroken, weeps with inconsolable grief over the horrors of the siege; desolate ruins; all due to their corporate sin and disobedience.

Is there a relationship that needs healing, a problem that needs to be solved, a habit that needs to be broken or established, or decision that needs to be made? Procrastination will only invite sudden disaster and ruin. Why not get started today on making changes—before it's too late?

The fall of Jerusalem seems to have come as a surprise to its people. Yet the real surprise is they did not recognize what was coming. Despite repeated warnings about the consequences of idolatry and other corporate sins, they were shocked when the Babylonians breached the walls (587 B.C.), sacked the city, and carried off its survivors into exile. The great devastation of Jerusalem is attributed to God's anger because this city's iniquity had become worse than Sodom (Lamentations 4:6). This tragic outcome need not have happened, but it in fact did fulfill God's Word (Lamentations 2:17), both ancient and recent.

2 Chronicles 7:14

If my people, which are called by my name, shall humble themselves, and pray, and seek my face, and turn from their wicked ways; then will I hear from heaven, and will forgive their sin, and will heal their land.

Psalm 122:6

Pray for the peace of Jerusalem; they will prosper who love thee.

The Book of Ezekiel

Scripture Focus Chapters 1-48

Objective: To gain insight on the life of Ezekiel the Prophet and Priest, his prophecies on Jerusalem and the surrounding nations of Judah.

Objective Breakdown:

1. Introduction

2. Ezekiel Sees Four Creatures in a Vision   Chapter 1:1-9

3. The Four Creatures Are Described   Chapter 1:10-14

4. Movement by Wheels and Wings   Chapter 1:15-25

5. Ezekiel Sees the Glory of the Lord   Chapter 1:26-28

6. Ezekiel's Call as a Prophet   Chapter 2:1-8

7. Ezekiel Is Commanded to Eat a Scroll   Chapter 2:9-10

8. Ezekiel Is Commanded to Eat a Scroll (cont.)   Chapter 3:1-9

9. The Prophet Goes to the Captives   Chapter 3:10-15

10. A Watchman for Israel   Chapter 3:16-21

11. Israel Is a Rebellious House   Chapter 3:22-27

12. The Siege of Jerusalem Is Portrayed   Chapter 4:1-8

13. An Object Lesson Predicting Famine   Chapter 4:9-17

14. Ezekiel Shaves His Head   Chapter 5:1-10

15. Pestilence, Famine, and Sword   Chapter 5:11-17

16. Israel's Idols Will Be Destroyed   Chapter 6:1-7

17. Those Who Escape Will Remember God   Chapter 6:8-14

18. Judgment on Israel Is Near   Chapter 7:1-9

19. God's Wrath Will Fall on Everyone   Chapter 7:10-18

20. Riches Will Not Save Anyone   Chapter 7:19-22

Lesson Plan 221

The Book of Ezekiel

Chapter 1

Objective: To learn about the life and times of Ezekiel the Prophet and Priest, his prophecies on Jerusalem and the surrounding nations of Judah.

Objective Breakdown:

1. Introduction

2. Ezekiel Sees Four Creatures in a Vision

3. The Four Creatures Are Described

4. Movement by Wheels and Wings

5. Ezekiel See the Glory of the Lord

Introduction:

In 594 B.C., the Babylonian King Nebuchadnezzar deported King Jehoiachin and 10,000 of Jerusalem's best and brightest citizens to Babylon (See "King Jehoichin's Captivity" at Ezekiel 1:2). Probably included among this group was a young priest-in-training named Ezekiel. About four years later, God called this man to be his prophet to the Jews already taken into captivity.

This was a uniquely difficult assignment. What could Ezekiel say that would turn the hearts of these exiles back to the Lord? Fear of being captured and resettled was no longer a factor. Still, they needed to be reminded that their circumstances were the result of God's judgment, which was far from over. Jerusalem would soon be destroyed, and their captivity would last for a least half a century more. This message is given in Ezekiel 4-24.

The second major theme of Ezekiel's prophecies is that God was also going to judge the Gentile nations surrounding Judah—Ammon, Moab, Edom, Philistia, Tyre, Sidon, and Egypt. These warning are given in Ezekiel 25-32.

In the final portion of the book of Ezekiel 33-48, there is a word of hope: God would eventually restore His people to their land. Ezekiel's famous vision of the dry bones coming to life (Ezekiel 37) forms part of that promise. The same theme is continued in Ezekiel 40-48, which describes the restoration of the temple and the renewal of sacrifices and authentic worship.

One of the most important messages that Ezekiel gave to the exiles had to do with individual responsibility. One is responsible for one's own sin before a Holy God. Some of exiles believed that it was up to future generations to pay for the consequences of their sins. Ezekiel changed this sort of thinking by declaring that **"the soul who sins shall die"** (Ezekiel 18:20). He underscored the need for everyone to make a personal decision to follow the Lord. No one can depend on the faith of ancestors to gain acceptance with God.

Ezekiel Sees Four Creatures in a Vision	Chapter 1:1-9
The Four Creatures Are Described	Chapter 1:10-14
Movement by Wheels and Wings	Chapter 1:15-25
Ezekiel See the Glory of the Lord	Chapter 1:26-28
God's Blessing on Israel	(Numbers 6:24-27)
Jabez's Prayer to the Lord	(1 Chronicles 4:10)

2 Chronicles 7:14

If my people, which are called by my name, shall humble themselves, and pray, and seek my face, and turn from their wicked ways; then will I hear from heaven, and will forgive their sin, and will heal their land.

Psalm 122:6

Pray for the peace of Jerusalem; they will prosper who love thee.

Lesson Plan 222

The Book of Ezekiel

Chapters 2, 3, & 4

Objective: To learn about the life, times, mission, and prophetic insights of Ezekiel the Prophet and Priest, his prophecies on Jerusalem and the surrounding nations of Judah.

Objective Breakdown:

1. Introduction

2. Ezekiel's Call as a Prophet

3. Ezekiel is Commanded to Eat a Scroll

4. The Prophet Goes to the Captives

5. A Watchman for Israel

6. Israel is a Rebellious House

7. The Siege of Jerusalem Is Portrayed

8. An Object Lesson Predicting Famine

Introduction:

Last week we read Ezekiel's vision of living creatures (Chapter 1:1-28). We also seen the description of these creatures (see Chapter 1:1-28), but we didn't really know who these creatures really were. Well, these magnificent being are later identified in Ezekiel Chapter 10:20, as the Cherubim Angels of high-ranking order. They make their appearance on three distinct occasions in the word of God:

a) In the Garden of Eden, to keep Adam from the Tree of Life after his sin (Genesis 3:22- 24).

b) To Ezekiel here in Babylon (Chapter 1:1-28).

c) In Heaven, during John's vision (Revelation 4:6-8).

The duties of these living creatures are to: a) guard and vindicate the righteousness of God (Genesis 3:24; Exodus 26:1; Ezekiel 36:8, 35); b) symbolize the mercy of God (Exodus 25:22; 37:9); c) aid in the administration of the government of God (1 Samuel 4:4; Psalms 80:1; Psalms 99:1; Ezekiel 1:22, 27).

Note: There is another kind of special angel called the Seraphim, (see Isaiah 6:1-7). Also where

does the Book of Ezekiel fit into the scheme of the Old Testament organization and with fellow prophets?

Ezekiel's Call as a Prophet	Chapter 2:1-5
Ezekiel is Commanded to Eat a Scroll	Chapter 2:6-8 & Chapter 3:1-9
The Prophet Goes to the Captives	Chapter 3:10-15
A Watchman for Israel	Chapter 3:16-21
Israel is a Rebellious House	Chapter 3:22-27
The Siege of Jerusalem Is Portrayed	Chapter 4:1-8
An Object Lesson Predicting Famine	Chapter 4:9-17

2 Chronicles 7:14

If my people, which are called by my name, shall humble themselves, and pray, and seek my face, and turn from their wicked ways; then will I hear from heaven, and will forgive their sin, and will heal their land.

Psalm 122:6

Pray for the peace of Jerusalem; they will prosper who love thee.

Lesson Plan 223

The Book of Ezekiel

Chapters 5, 6, & 7

Objective: To learn about the life, times, mission, and prophetic insights of Ezekiel the Prophet.

Objective Breakdown:

1. Introduction

2. Shaves His Head   Chapter 5:1-10

3. Pestilence, Famine, and Sword   Chapter 5:11-17

4. Israel's Idols Will Be Destroyed   Chapter 6:1-7

5. Those Who Escape Will Remember God   Chapter 6:8-14

6. Judgment On Israel Is Near   Chapter 7:1-9

7. God's Wrath Will Fall on Everyone   Chapter 7:10-18

8. Riches Will Not Save Anyone   Chapter 7:19-22

9. Disaster Will come Upon Disaster   Chapter 7:23-27

Introduction:

Nebuchadnezzar destroyed Jerusalem in three stages. First, in 605 B.C., he overcame Jehoiakim and carried off key hostages including Daniel and his friends. Second, in 597 B.C., the rebellion of Jehoiakim and Jehoiachin brought further punishment; and Nebuchadnezzar made Jerusalem submit a second time. He carried off ten thousand hostages including Jehoiachin and Ezekiel. Third, in 586 B.C., Nebuchadnezzar destroyed the city after a long siege and disrupted all of Judah. If the "thirtieth year" in 1:1 refers to Ezekiel's age, he was twenty-five years old when he received his prophetic commission (1:2, 3). This means he was about seventeen when Daniel was deported in 605 B.C. so that Ezekiel and Daniel were about the same age. Both men were about 20 years younger than Jeremiah who was ministering in Jerusalem.

According to this chronology, Ezekiel was born in 622 B.C., deported to Babylon in 597 B.C., prophesied from 592 B.C. to at least 567 B.C., and died about 560 B.C. Thus, he overlapped the end of Jeremiah's ministry and the beginning of Daniel's ministry. By the time Ezekiel arrived in Babylon, Daniel was well known; and Daniel is mentioned three times in Ezekiel's prophecy (14:14, 20; 28:3). His active ministry lasted for a least twenty-two years and his book was probably completed by 565 B.C.

Shaves His Head	Chapter 5:1-10
Pestilence, Famine, and Sword	Chapter 5:11-17
Israel's Idols Will Be Destroyed	Chapter 6:1-7
Those Who Escape Will Remember God	Chapter 6:8-14
Judgment On Israel Is Near	Chapter 7:1-9
God's Wrath Will Fall on Everyone	Chapter 7:10-18
Riches Will Not Save Anyone	Chapter 7:19-22
Disaster Will come Upon Disaster	Chapter 7:23-27

2 Chronicles 7:14

If my people, which are called by my name, shall humble themselves, and pray, and seek my face, and turn from their wicked ways; then will I hear from heaven, and will forgive their sin, and will heal their land.

Psalm 122:6

Pray for the peace of Jerusalem; they will prosper who love thee.

Lesson Plan 224

The Book of Ezekiel

Chapters 8, 9, 10, & 11

Objective: To learn about the life and times of Ezekiel the Prophet and Priest, his prophecies on Jerusalem and the surrounding nations of Judah.

Objective Breakdown:

1. Introduction

2. Ezekiel Goes in a Vision to Jerusalem   Chapter 8:1-5

3. Abominations in the Temple   Chapter 8:6-18

4. Judgment Falls on the Idolaters   Chapter 9:1-11

5. Ezekiel's Vision of Four Cherubim   Chapter 10:1-13

6. God's Glory Leaves the Temple   Chapter 10:14-22

7. Ezekiel Speaks in the Temple   Chapter 11:1-13

8. God Will Regather Israel   Chapter 11:14-21

9. Ezekiel Is Returned to Babylon   Chapter 11:22-25

Introduction:

We are likely to focus on the spectacular vision of the cherubim and the wheels within wheels. But the real story in this passage is the Lord's departure from His temple at Jerusalem (Ezekiel 10:18). Given the history and significance of the temple, nothing could be more tragic for Judah.

The Temple was designed by David and built by Solomon to be the "house of the Lord" (2 Chronicles 5:1). When it was completed, God blessed the magnificent structure by filling it with His Glory and Presence (2 Chronicles 5:14). From then on, the temple was regarded as a hallowed symbol that stood for God (2 Chronicles 6:20).

Yet now Ezekiel saw God departing from the temple. There is little wonder why. The people had turned the "House of the Lord" into a house of idolatrous abominations. As a result, God decided to leave His Temple and go "far away" from His people (Ezekiel 8:5-17; also see Ezekiel 11:23). Clearly the end of Judah was at hand.

Note: Even though God departed from the temple. He did not completely abandon His people. He scattered them throughout the world, but also assured those who feared Him that He would be a "little sanctuary" for them wherever they went. This is verified in Ezekiel 11:16.

2 Chronicles 7:14

If my people, which are called by my name, shall humble themselves, and pray, and seek my face, and turn from their wicked ways; then will I hear from heaven, and will forgive their sin, and will heal their land.

Psalm 122:6

Pray for the peace of Jerusalem; they will prosper who love thee.

Lesson Plan 225

The Book of Ezekiel

Chapters 12, 13, 14, & 15

Objective: To learn about the life, times, mission, and prophetic insights of Ezekiel the Prophet.

Objective Breakdown:

1. Introduction

2. Ezekiel Digs Through the Wall   Chapter 12:1-7

3. The Digging Is Explained   Chapter 12:8-16

4. A Warning that God's Judgment Is Near   Chapter 12:17-28

5. A Word Against False Prophets   Chapter 13:1-9

6. False Prophecies Will Crumble and Fall   Chapter 13:10-16

7. Lies of False Prophetesses Will Fail   Chapter 13:17-23

8. Elders with Idols in Their Hearts   Chapter 14:1-11

9. One's Righteousness Cannot Save Others   Chapter 14:12-23

10. The Lesson of the Outcast Vine   Chapter 15:1-8

Introduction:

Mercy to the repentant. God's forgiveness has always required repentance on the part of sinners. It did in ancient times; it still does today.

In Ezekiel's vision of Jerusalem, the Lord commanded angelic executioners to place a special mark on the foreheads of those who were moved to repentance over the "abominations" being committed in the city. The rest were to be slain (Ezekiel 9:4-7). The justification for the slaughter was that the sins of the wicked–bloodshed and perversity (Idolatry) were "exceedingly great" (Ezekiel 9:9). By contrast the citizens who demonstrated a deep concern for holiness were shown mercy.

This vision recalls a similar judgment in Egypt, in which the Lord killed the first-born children of the Egyptians but spared the Hebrew households that had marked their doorposts with blood (Exodus 12:1-36). In both cases God marked out those to whom He would show mercy on the basis of their heart attitude toward Him.

It is interesting to note that the "mark" referred to by Ezekiel is the Hebrew letter taw, the last letter of the Hebrew alphabet. Today, taw is the equivalent of "T" but in Jeremiah day it was written like an "X" and was often used as a signature (Job 31:35). Early Christians pointed out the similarity between Ezekiel's "mark" and the sign of the cross. Both indicated God's mercy and redemption of sinners.

The judgment foreseen in Ezekiel's vision applies to people today. It demonstrates that God shows mercy, but He always looks for repentance. Those who resist Him and remain committed to sin can expect His wrath. But those who "sigh and cry" over their own sins and the sins of others will know His comfort and forgiveness (See James 4:8-10).

2 Chronicles 7:14

If my people, which are called by my name, shall humble themselves, and pray, and seek my face, and turn from their wicked ways; then will I hear from heaven, and will forgive their sin, and will heal their land.

Psalm 122:6

Pray for the peace of Jerusalem; they will prosper who love thee.

Lesson Plan 226

The Book of Ezekiel

Chapters 16 & 17

Objective: To learn about the life and times of Ezekiel the Prophet and Priest, his prophecies on Jerusalem and the surrounding nations of Judah.

Objective Breakdown:

1. Introduction

2. Abandoned Jerusalem Was Adopted by God   Chapter 16:1-7

3. God's Covenant Love   Chapter 16:8-14

4. Yet Jerusalem Has Been Unfaithful   Chapter 16:15-26

5. The Degenerate Heart of a Harlot   Chapter 16:27-34

6. Jerusalem Will Be Abused and Humiliated   Chapter 16:35-43

7. Jerusalem Outdoes Her Wicked Sisters   Chapter 16:44-52

8. God's Covenant Will Prevail   Chapter 16:53-63

9. The Parable of the Eagles and the Vine   Chapter 17:1-10

10. The Parable Interpreted   Chapter 17:11-18

11. Israel's Exaltation Is Predicted   Chapter 17:19-24

Introduction:

The allegory of the two eagles and the vine is used to show he futility of the nation's dependence on foreign powers. The first eagle, Nebuchadnezzar, had gone to Lebanon, which represented Jerusalem. Though he took the highest branch of the cedar (Ezekiel 17:3), meaning that he took the king and the nobles into captivity (597 B.C.), yet he left the seed of the land (Ezekiel 17:5) or a remnant. They, in turn appealed to another eagle (Ezekiel 17:7) which was Egypt. This description refers to Zedekiah's vain attempt to get military assistance from Egypt. This alliance forced Nebuchadnezzar to return later to Jerusalem and destroy it (586 B.C.).

In Ezekiel chapter 17:22-24, **I will take the highest branch**: The Lord is the speaker, and He here promises to be like an eagle Himself. Yet He will take a branch, one of the Davidic lines, and plant it upon the highest mountain (i.e., reestablish the kingdom to Israel).

In Ezekiel chapter 18:2 **The fathers have eaten sour grapes, and the children's teeth are set on edge** was evidently a well-known proverb (Jeremiah 31:29-30). The point is that the children suffer for their parents' sins. However, this proverb was not true in the case of Israel, and the Lord tells them that they cannot use the proverb anymore. Evidently the people thought they were suffering unjustly for their ancestors' sins. Although there is an element of truth in the statement that the children suffer as a consequence of the parent's sins (Exodus 20:5; 34:6, 7; Deuteronomy 5:9), it could not be applied here. The proverb was being used as a lame excuse for their own sinful condition. Rather, the Lord say, "The soul that sinneth, it shall die. The son shall not bear the iniquity of the father" (Ezekiel 18:20). Thus, Ezekiel preserves in proper balance the tragic consequences of sin and the principle of individual accountability.

2 Chronicles 7:14

If my people, which are called by my name, shall humble themselves, and pray, and seek my face, and turn from their wicked ways; then will I hear from heaven, and will forgive their sin, and will heal their land.

Psalm 122:6

Pray for the peace of Jerusalem; they will prosper who love thee.

Lesson Plan 227

The Book of Ezekiel

Chapters 18, 19, & 20

Objective: To learn about the life and times of Ezekiel the Prophet and Priest, his prophecies on Jerusalem and the surrounding nations of Judah.

Objective Breakdown:

1. Introduction

2. The Sinner and the Just Contrasted   Chapter 18:1-9

3. The Rebellious Son Shall Surely Die   Chapter 18:10-13

4. The Righteous Son Shall Surely Live   Chapter 18:14-18

5. Individual Responsibility for Sin   Chapter 18:19-24

6. The Lord's Way Is Fair   Chapter 18:25-32

7. The Parable of the Lioness   Chapter 19:1-9

8. The Parable of the Vine   Chapter 19:10-14

9. The Lord Brought Israel Out of Egypt   Chapter 20:1-9

10. Israel resisted God in the Wilderness   Chapter 20:10-26

11. God's People Became Idolaters   Chapter 20:27-36

12. God Will Deal with His Wayward People   Chapter 20:37-44

13. There will Be Fire in the Forest   Chapter 20:45-49

Introduction:

There is little doubt that parents can have a profound and lasting influence, for better or for worse, on their children's development and outlook on life. That is why the Bible strongly exhorts parents to raise their children accordingly to Godly values and principles. But Scripture seems to refrain from holding parents completely responsible for the ultimate state of their children. Sooner or later, the children must assume responsibility for their own choices and actions.

Ezekiel recognized the tendency to blame parents. Actually, given their situation, the children of Ezekiel's day had much about which to complain. They were coming of age as exiles in a foreign land because their parents and grandparents had forsaken the Lord. So, they kept alive a popular saying about the children's troubles coming from their parents (Ezekiel 18:2).

But Good declared that His people should stop talking that way (Ezekiel 18:3). He spoke at length about the fact that sin and righteousness are not inherited. **One reaps what one sows.** Individuals will be held responsible for their choices and behavior in regard to matters of idolatry (Ezekiel 18:6, 12, 15), the use or abuse of money (Ezekiel 18:7-8, 13, 16-17), and the treatment of the poor (Ezekiel 18:7, 12, 16-17).

The same principle holds true today. No matter how bad a start you may feel that your family has given you, God calls you to accept responsibility for your own life. Even with a troubled background, you can share in the Lord's forgiveness, healing, and righteousness. God delights in fresh starts and invites you to make one in Him.

2 Chronicles 7:14

If my people, which are called by my name, shall humble themselves, and pray, and seek my face, and turn from their wicked ways; then will I hear from heaven, and will forgive their sin, and will heal their land.

Psalm 122:6

Pray for the peace of Jerusalem; they will prosper who love thee.

Lesson Plan 228

The Book of Ezekiel

Chapters 21, 22, & 23

Objective: To learn about the life and times of Ezekiel the Prophet and Priest, his prophecies on Jerusalem and the surrounding nations of Judah.

Objective Breakdown:

Ezekiel Sighs Over Jerusalem's Ruin	Chapter 21:1-17
A Fork in the Road	Chapter 21:18-27
A Sword Against the Ammonites	Chapter 21:28-32
Jerusalem the Bloody City	Chapter 22:1-5
Law Violators Defile the City	Chapter 22:6-16
Israel Has Become Dross	Chapter 22:17-22
No One to Stand in The Gap	Chapter 22:23-31
The Tale of Two Sisters	Chapter 23:1-10
Judah Outdoes Her Sister's Harlotry	Chapter 23:11-21
Judah's Lovers Will Turn Against Her	Chapter 23:22-27
Judah Will Go the Way of Samaria	Chapter 23:28-39
Judgment for Spiritual Adultery	Chapter 23:40-49

Introduction:

Did God really have to allow the Babylonians to destroy Jerusalem and disperse His people throughout the Middle East? Yes! Nearly one thousand years before these events, the Lord made a solemn, binding covenant with Israel. The covenant stipulated that persistent rebellion against Him must result in foreign invasion, the devastation of Israelites' cities, and exile in a foreign land. Thus, the Lord would have broken an oath if He had not executed judgment on His wayward people (Ezekiel 20:23; Lamentations 2:17; Leviticus 26; Deuteronomy 27-28).

The sins of Jerusalem. Over and over Ezekiel names sins of Jerusalem: defiles herself with idols, sheds blood, profanes the Sabbath, practices robbery, promiscuous adultery; and the princes, priests, and prophets are ravening wolves after dishonest gain.

Oholah and Oholibah. Two sisters, insatiable in their lewdness. This a parable of Israel's idolatry. Oholah is Samaria; Oholibah is Jerusalem. Both have grown old in their adulteries. Again and again the relation between husband and wife is used to represent the relation between God and his people (see Chapter 16). Promiscuous adultery must have been very wide spread (see Chapter 16:32; Chapter18:6, 11 and 15; Chapter 22:11; Chapter 23:43; Jeremiah Chapter 5:7 and 8; Chapter 7:9; Chapter 9:2; Chapter 23:10 and 14; Chapter 29:23).

2 Chronicles 7:14

If my people, which are called by my name, shall humble themselves, and pray, and seek my face, and turn from their wicked ways; then will I hear from heaven, and will forgive their sin, and will heal their land.

Psalm 122:6

Pray for the peace of Jerusalem; they will prosper who love thee.

Lesson Plan 229

The Book of Ezekiel

Chapters 24, 25, & 26

Objective: To learn about the life and times of Ezekiel the Prophet and Priest, his prophecies on Jerusalem and the surrounding nations of Judah.

Objective Breakdown:

1.   Introduction

2. A Pot Begins to Boil   Chapter 24:1-8

3. The Heat Consumes the Impurities   Chapter 24:9-14

4. Ezekiel May Not Mourn His Wife's Death   Chapter 24:15-27

5. A Prophecy Against Ammon   Chapter 25:1-7

6. Moab Will Be Judged   Chapter 25:8-11

7. God's Fury Will Be on Edom   Chapter 25:12-14

8. Vengeance Will Be on Philistia   Chapter 25:15-17

9. Tyre Will Be Destroyed   Chapter 26:1-14

10. A Lamentation for Tyre   Chapter 26:15-21

Introduction:

Symbolic of the destruction of Jerusalem, now at hand. The rust on the pot represented the bloodshed and immorality of the city. The death of Ezekiel's wife (verses 15-24). This was the day that the siege of Jerusalem began (verses 1, 18; II Kings 25:1): a heart-rendering sign to the exiles that their beloved Jerusalem, was now to be taken from them. Silence was imposed on Ezekiel till news came of the fallen city, 3 years later (verses 27; Chapter 33:21, 22).

Chapter 25. Concerns four nations: Ammon, Moab, Edom, & Philistia. These four nations were Judah's closest neighbors, who rejoiced at Judah's destruction by Babylon. Ezekiel here predicts for them the same fate as did Jeremiah (Jeremiah 27:1-7). Nebuchadnezzar subdued the Philistines when he took Judah, and four years later invaded Ammon, Moab, and Edom.

Chapter 26. The visions of doom of Tyre were given to Ezekiel in the same year that Jerusalem fell, that is the 11th year (Ezekiel 26:1). Tyre will be destroyed.

Chapter 26:1-14. A lamentation for Tyre. Then all the princes of the sea will come down from their thrones, lay aside their robes, and take off their embroidered garments; they will clothe themselves with trembling; they will sit on the ground, tremble every moment, and be astonished at you. And they will take up lamentation for you and say to you: "How you have perished. O one inhabited by sea fearing men, O renowned city, who was strong at sea, She, and her inhabitants, who caused their terror to be on all her inhabitants! Now the coast lands by the sea are troubled by your departure." (Ezekiel 26:15-21).

2 Chronicles 7:14

If my people, which are called by my name, shall humble themselves, and pray, and seek my face, and turn from their wicked ways; then will I hear from heaven, and will forgive their sin, and will heal their land.

Psalm 122:6

Pray for the peace of Jerusalem; they will prosper who love thee.

God's Blessing on Israel   (Numbers 6:24-27)

Jabez's Prayer to the Lord   (1 Chronicles 4:10)

Lesson Plan 230

The Book of Ezekiel

Chapters 27, 28, & 29

Objective: To learn about the life and times of Ezekiel the Prophet and Priest, his prophecies on Jerusalem and the surrounding nations of Judah.

Objective Breakdown:

1. Introduction

2. The Beauty and Splendor of Tyre   Chapter 27:1-11

3. Tyre's Great Commerce   Chapter 27:12-24

4. Tyre's Shipping Will Come to a Halt   Chapter 27:25-36

5. The Fall of the Prince of Tyre   Chapter 28:1-10

6. A Lamentation for The King of Tyre   Chapter 28:11-19

7. A Prophecy Against Sidon   Chapter 28:20-23

8. Regathered Israel Shall Dwell Safely   Chapter 28:24-26

9. A Word Against Pharaoh   Chapter 29:1-7

10. Egypt Will Become a Minor Kingdom   Chapter 29:8-16

11. Nebuchadnezzar Will Conquer Egypt   Chapter 29:17-21

Introduction:

The Book of Ezekiel is divided into four parts: Part (I) is the commission of Ezekiel Chapters 1-3; Part (II) Judgment on Judah Chapters 4-24; Part (III) Judgment on the Gentiles (Chapters 25-32); Part (IV) Restoration of Israel Chapters (33-48).

As we will see Tyre and Sidon were two Phoenician seaports cities about 25 miles apart on the coast of the Mediterranean Sea. For the most part, Israel had a good relationship with these cities. The Phoenician king, Hiram, was a trading partner of both David and Solomon. He provided building materials as well as skilled tradesmen to help build the temple and Solomon's palace complex in the city of Jerusalem.

Why, then, did the prophet Ezekiel utter such bitter words against Tyre (Ezekiel 26)? It was probably because of the taunting attitude Tyre demonstrated when the nation of Judah was overrun by the Babylonians in 586 B.C. (Ezekiel 26:2). Judah's collapse meant that the Phoenicia was a region with little competition in central Palestine. Their trade monopoly complete, Tyre and Sidon rejoiced. Their insatiable greed and prideful attitude led Ezekiel to issue his bitter condemnation. When Ezekiel spoke these words, the cities of Tyre and Sidon had no peers on the Mediterranean shores. As early as 1000 B.C. the two cities had emerged as important population centers. As the leader of a group of small city states, Sidon first grew into prominence in trade. After a time, it was eclipsed by Tyre which established an empire based on maritime trade. The ships of Tyre sailed as far away as Great Britain and North Africa on trading ventures. The Greek conqueror Alexander the great built a causeway to the offshore city and destroyed it in 332 B.C.

2 Chronicles 7:14

If my people, which are called by my name, shall humble themselves, and pray, and seek my face, and turn from their wicked ways; then will I hear from heaven, and will forgive their sin, and will heal their land.

Psalm 122:6

Pray for the peace of Jerusalem; they will prosper who love thee.

| God's Blessing on Israel | (Numbers 6:24-27) |
| Jabez's Prayer to the Lord | (I Chronicles 4:10) |

Words of Comfort for the Soul

Ephesians 4:29, Let no corrupt word proceed out of your mouth, but what is good for necessary edification, that it may impart grace to the hearers.

Ephesians 4:30, Do not grieve the Holy Spirit of God, by whom you were sealed for the day of redemption.

Ephesians 4:31, Let all bitterness, wrath, anger, clamor, and evil speaking be put away from you, with all malice.

Ephesians 4:32, Be kind to another, tenderhearted, forgiving one another, even as God in Christ forgave you.

Lesson Plan 231

The Book of Ezekiel

Chapters 30, 31, 32, & 33

Objective: To learn about the life and times of Ezekiel the Prophet and Priest, his prophecies on Jerusalem and the surrounding nations of Judah.

Objective Breakdown:

Introduction:

Chapters 29, 30, 31, 32 predicts & reflects Nebuchadnezzar's invasion of Egypt and Egypt's reduction to a place of minor importance for all future time. Nebuchadnezzar invaded and plundered Egypt 572 and 568 B.C. Egypt never recovered its former glory, and since has played a very minor part in world history, fulfilling in a very real sense of Ezekiel's prophecy that it would be "the basest of kingdoms" (Chapter 29:15).

Ezekiel's prophecy of Pharaohs' broken arms (Ezekiel 30:20-26) probably came about a year after the Egyptians sent an army north during the Babylonian siege of Jerusalem (588 B.C.) (Jeremiah 37:5). The Babylonians briefly retreated, causing some to in Jerusalem to assume that the siege had ended, and that the security of the city now lay in an alliance with the Egyptians.

In Jerusalem, Jeremiah spoke out strongly against these false hopes (Jeremiah 37:6-10). Likewise, in Tel Abib, Ezekiel's parable warned the Judean exiles that Egypt soon would be neutralized. Its Pharaoh, probably Hophra (see Jeremiah 44:30), would have his arms "broken" a powerful image of powerlessness.

Both prophet's words were fulfilled. Shortly after returning to capture Jerusalem, Nebuchadnezzar's troops traveled south to Egypt, where they found a new king in power, Ahmose II. He was the victor in a civil war that had ended Hophra's life.

2 Chronicles 7:14

If my people, which are called by my name, shall humble themselves, and pray, and seek my face, and turn from their wicked ways; then will I hear from heaven, and will forgive their sin, and will heal their land.

Psalm 122:6

Pray for the peace of Jerusalem; they will prosper who love thee.

Lesson Plan 232

The Book of Ezekiel

Chapters 34, 35, & 36

Objective: To learn about the life and times of Ezekiel the Prophet and Priest, his prophecies on Jerusalem and the surrounding nations of Judah.

Objective Breakdown:

1. Introduction

Introduction:

Leaders should care. Much has been written in recent years about effective managers focusing on customers, markets, trends, quality, succession, marketing, teamwork, and commitment. These and other factors are important, sometimes vitally so. But Ezekiel's prophecy concerning Leaders of Israel (Ezekiel 34:1-2) points out one more critical factor: if the people one is leading are neglected or suffering, one's qualifications to lead are in question.

The "Shepherds" of Israel received a "performance review" from God, and it was not good. The leaders were spending most of their energies feeding themselves instead of the flock (Ezekiel 34:2-8), and they were giving them nothing but leftovers (Ezekiel 34:18-19). Not only were they neglecting the least powerful and most vulnerable among the people—the weak, the sick, the broken, and the refugees–they were actually taking advantage of them (Ezekiel 34:4-6, 21). There was only one remedy for this situation—to remove the leaders from leadership (Ezekiel 34:9-10). God Himself heal the hurting, restore the scattered, and feed His flock (Ezekiel 34:11-16).

Centuries later, Jesus prescribed "shepherd leadership" for one of His followers (John 21:15-19), as the good Shepherd, Jesus had modeled this approach by laying down His life for the sheep (John 10:17).

A new Spirit. The prospects of God placing His own Spirit within His people to help them walk in His ways (Ezekiel 36:26-27) was an exciting new development. The Holy Spirit inspired Old Testament believers to pursue holiness, and from time to time He came upon certain leaders in way that gave them extraordinary power. But He was not a permanent resident in God's people as He is today. So, Ezekiel's vision of an indwelling Spirit must have filled his listeners with anticipation.

2 Chronicles 7:14

If my people, which are called by my name, shall humble themselves, and pray, and seek my face, and turn from their wicked ways; then will I hear from heaven, and will forgive their sin, and will heal their land.

Psalm 122:6

Pray for the peace of Jerusalem; they will prosper who love thee.

God's Blessing on Israel   (Numbers 6:24-27)

Lesson Plan 233

The Book of Ezekiel

Chapters 37, 38, & 39

Objective: To learn about the life and times of Ezekiel the Prophet and Priest, his prophecies on Jerusalem and the surrounding nations of Judah.

Objective Breakdown:

Introduction

The Valley of Dry Bones	Chapter 37:1-8
The Bones Are Given Life	Chapter 37:9-14
Ezekiel Joins Two Sticks to Each Other	Chapter 37:15-23
An Everlasting Covenant of Peace	Chapter 37:24-28
A Prophecy Against Gog	Chapter 38:1-9
Gog Will Come Against Israel	Chapter 38:10-17
The Lord Will Assert His Sovereignty	Chapter 38:18-23
The Israelites Will Plunder Gog's Army	Chapter 39:1-10
Seven Months to Bury the Dead	Chapter 39:11-16
A Sacrificial Meal for Birds and Beasts	Chapter 39:17-20
Israel's Restoration to the Land	Chapter 39:21-29

Introduction:

The Book of Ezekiel can be divided into 4 sections:

Section a. Commission of Ezekiel (Chapters 1-3);

Section b. Judgment on Judah (Chapters 4-24);

Section c. Judgment on Gentiles (Chapters 25-32);

Section d. Restoration of Israel (Chapters 33-48).

The land of Israel is to be re-inhabited. Although desolate, it will one day become like the garden of Eden (Chapter 36:25). It will be populated with and by penitent Judah and Israeli Jews (Chapter 36:10, 31). This will be for the Glory of God's own name (Chapter 36:22, 32).

In Chapter 37, the vision of dry bones: we see a vision of the national resurrection of scattered Israel, a return to their own land. We see the reunion of Judah and Israel, under the reign of an everlasting Prince called David (Chapter 37:24-26). It is a plain forecast of the conversion of the Jews to Christ; as Paul also foretold in Romans (Chapter11:15, 25, 26). This vision which Ezekiel sees is for the whole house of Israel...both Judah and Israel...the two Kingdoms reunited after 2900 plus years, and again known as the nation of Israel with its capital as Jerusalem.

2 Chronicles 7:14

If my people, which are called by my name, shall humble themselves, and pray, and seek my face, and turn from their wicked ways; then will I hear from heaven, and will forgive their sin, and will heal their land.

Psalm 122:6

Pray for the peace of Jerusalem; they will prosper who love thee.

God's Blessing on Israel   (Numbers 6:24-27)

Lesson Plan 234

The Book of Ezekiel

Chapters 40 & 41

Objective: To learn about the life and times of Ezekiel the Prophet and Priest, his prophecies on Jerusalem and the surrounding nations of Judah.

Objective Breakdown:

1. Introduction

2. Man with A Measuring Rod   Chapter 40:1-6

3. The Eastern Gateway to the Temple   Chapter 40:7-16

4. The Outer Court   Chapter 40:17-19

5. The Northern Gateway to the Temple   Chapter 40:20-23

6. The Southern Gateway to The Temple   Chapter 40:24-27

7. The Gateway of the Inner Court   Chapter 40:28-46

8. The Inner Court and the Vestibule   Chapter 40:47-49

9. Dimensions of the Sanctuary   Chapter 41:1-4

10. The Side Chambers on the Wall   Chapter 41:5-12

11. Dimensions and Design of the Temple   Chapter 41:13-26

Introduction:

April, 572 B.C. Passover time, 14 years after the destruction of Jerusalem. Ezekiel's second vision-journey to Jerusalem, the first having been 19 years earlier (Chapter 8:1, 3), on a mission of doom for the city. This to give specifications for its reconstruction, dealing largely with the Temple details.

This vision was not fulfilled in the Return from Babylon. Evidently it is a prediction of the Messianic Age.

Some interpret it literally, as meaning that the Twelve Tribes will one day again inhabit the land, and be distributed as here indicated, that the Temple will be rebuilt literally in all particulars as here specified, and that will be a literal animal sacrifice. They call it "The Millennial Temple."

Others interpret it figuratively, taking the vision to a metamorphic preview of the whole Christian Era, under the imagery of a revived, restored, and glorified nation.

This Temple of Ezekiel's Vision with its courts, arrangements, and furnishings, roughly, though with some variations follow the general plan of Solomon's Temple.

God was to "dwell in this Temple forever" (Chapter 43:7). This language can scarcely be predicated of a literal material Temple. It must be a figurative representation of something; for Jesus, in John 4:21-24, abrogated Temple worship; and in heaven there will be no Temple (Revelation 21:22).

2 Chronicles 7:14

If my people, which are called by my name, shall humble themselves, and pray, and seek my face, and turn from their wicked ways; then will I hear from heaven, and will forgive their sin, and will heal their land.

Psalm 122:6

Pray for the peace of Jerusalem; they will prosper who love thee.

Words of Comfort for the Soul

Ephesians 4:29, Let no corrupt word proceed out of your mouth, but what is good for necessary edification, that it may impart grace to the hearers.

Ephesians 4:30, Do not grieve the Holy Spirit of God, by whom you were sealed for the day of redemption.

Ephesians 4:31, Let all bitterness, wrath, anger, clamor, and evil speaking be put away from you, with all malice.

Ephesians 4:32, Be kind to another, tenderhearted, forgiving one another, even as God in Christ forgave you.

Lesson Plan 235

The Book of Ezekiel

Chapters 42, 43, & 44

Objective: To learn about the life and times of Ezekiel the Prophet and Priest, his prophecies on Jerusalem and the surrounding nations of Judah.

Objective Breakdown:

1. Introduction

2. The Chambers for the Priest   Chapter 42:1-14

3. Outer Dimensions of the Temple   Chapter 42:15-20

4. The Lord Claims the Temple for Himself   Chapter 43:1-9

5. Ezekiel Told to Record the Design   Chapter 43:10-17

6. Consecrating the Altar   Chapter 43:18-27

7. The Lord's Gate Must Remain Shut   Chapter 44:1-5

8. The Rebellious May Not Enter the Temple   Chapter 44:6-14

9. Regulations for the Priest   Chapter 44:15-24

10. The Lord is The Priest's Inheritance   Chapter 44:25-31

Introduction:

Times of great loss or suffering can provide a valuable opportunity for reflection and self-examination. For example, the loss of a loved one often brings back vivid memories that five insights into the meaning of the person's life. In a similar way, Ezekiel's vision of the new temple appears to have been intended as a reminder of Solomon's temple, which had been the center of Judah's spiritual life and cultural identity. For centuries, that temple had stood as a powerful symbol of God's abiding presence. Now it was gone.

Yet God did not leave His people without hope. Through Ezekiel, He told them that He had plans for an entirely new temple. He described these plans in the most exacting detail (Ezekiel 40-42). What was the point of this elaborate description? In effect, they were to measure themselves with the same level of precision with which God was designing the new temple (Ezekiel 43:10-11).

The same principle applies to believers today. In our darkest moments, in times of great loss or fear, God would have us pursue insight and self-examination. We can harness our thoughts and feelings as the exiles of Judah were challenged to through Ezekiel's description of the Temple.

Note: Solomon anticipated that foreigners from all over the world would be drawn to the temple that he built. So, he asked God to honor their prayers so that people all over the earth would come. Solomon's prayer of dedication for the temple at Jerusalem showed that Israel's God was a God for all nations. And as Jesus pointed out in Isaiah 56:7 and Mark11:17 that Israel was to be a blessing to the **nations** and a light showing the way to the one true God (Genesis 12:1-3; Isaiah 51:4).

Unique Features of the Millennial Temple Several articles and objects present in the temples of Moses, Solomon, and Herod will be absent from the millennial temple. These are:

There will be no veil. This was torn in two from the top to bottom (Matthew 27:51) and will not appear in the temple. There will be no barrier to keep man from the glory of God.

There will be no table of shrew bread. This will not be needed, for the Living Bread Himself will be present.

There will be no lamp stands. These will not be needed either, since the Light of the World Himself will personally shine forth.

There will be no Ark of the Covenant. This will also be unnecessary since the Shekinah Glory Himself will hover over all the world.

The east gate will be closed. This gate shall be shut, and no man shall enter by it; because the Lord God of Israel shall enter by it; therefore, it shall be shut (Ezekiel 44:2)

Note: It was from the eastern gate that the glory of God departed from for the last time in the Old Testament (Ezekiel 10:18, 19). By sealing the gate God reminds all those within that His glory will never again depart from His people.

2 Chronicles 7:14

If my people, which are called by my name, shall humble themselves, and pray, and seek my face, and turn from their wicked ways; then will I hear from heaven, and will forgive their sin, and will heal their land.

Psalm 122:6

Pray for the peace of Jerusalem; they will prosper who love thee.

Lesson Plan 236

The Book of Ezekiel

Chapters 45 & 46

Objective: To learn about the life and times of Ezekiel the Prophet and Priest, his prophecies on Jerusalem and the surrounding nations of Judah.

Objective Breakdown:

1. Introduction

2. A Holy District   Chapter 45:1-8

3. Weights, Measures and Offerings   Chapter 45:9-17

4. The Feast Will Be Kept Again   Chapter 45:18-25

5. Worship Rituals Are Prescribed   Chapter 46:1-11

6. Offerings and Gifts of the Prince   Chapter 46:12-24

Introduction:

Holiness—it is not just a place. For many the word "holy" brings to mind special places such as cathedrals and temples. It would be easy to limit our concept of holiness to such concrete examples, especially when we see so many such cases in the Old Testament. In various times throughout their history, God called the Israelites to dedicate various places (and persons) in a way that would remind God's people that they were His own. Certain monuments, the tabernacle, the temple, and even certain mountains, along with some leaders, the priests, and the prophets were designated as "holy," consecrated, or set apart to the Lord.

This pattern was continued in Ezekiel's vision of the new temple, access to which was to be highly restricted (Ezekiel 44:1-19). Likewise, a certain "holy district" was to be established in the restored land (Ezekiel 45:1-5).

So, holiness was attached to certain places, but we shouldn't forget that the call to holy living is not confined to one place or another. All life is to be holy, no matter where one is. Ezekiel urges some down to earth practices of holiness:

Stop the use of violence and oppression (Ezekiel 45:9).

Cease the pattern of evicting people (Ezekiel 45:9).

Restore honest dealing in business, using standards of value that have integrity and can be trusted (Ezekiel 45:10-12).

Donate a percentage of each business transaction to God, whether one is a prince or one of the common people (Ezekiel 45:13-17).

Restore the six-day work week, and protect the Sabbath rest, with the prince with the providing substantially for this observance (Ezekiel 46:1-15).

Mark all life with monthly festivals and celebrations that include everyone (Ezekiel 45:18-25).

Provide an area for the common people, for homes and common space (Ezekiel 48:15-20).

Name each of the commercial centers—the exits or gates of the city—after a portion of the citizenry (tribes).

Name the city itself "THE LORD IS THERE," reflecting a very inclusive view of holiness: everything that goes on there pertains to the Lord (Ezekiel 48:35).

2 Chronicles 7:14

If my people, which are called by my name, shall humble themselves, and pray, and seek my face, and turn from their wicked ways; then will I hear from heaven, and will forgive their sin, and will heal their land.

Psalm 122:6

Pray for the peace of Jerusalem; they will prosper who love thee.

Lesson Plan 237

The Book of Ezekiel

Chapters 47 & 48

Objective: To learn about the life and times of Ezekiel the Prophet and Priest, his prophecies on Jerusalem and the surrounding nations of Judah.

Objective Breakdown:

1. Introduction

2. The River of Life from the Sanctuary   Chapter 47:1-12

3. The Borders of the Land   Chapter 47:13-23

4. The Lands Are Assigned to Tribes   Chapter 48:1-8

5. Lands Governed by Priest & Levites   Chapter 48:9-14

6. Common Lands   Chapter 48:15-20

7. Lands for the Prince   Chapter 48:21-22

8. Lands for the Remaining Tribes   Chapter 48:23-29

9. The Gates of the City   Chapter 48:30-35

Introduction:

Ezekiel a priest and a prophet, ministers during the darkest days of Judah's history: the seventy-year period of Babylonian captivity. Carried to Babylon (597 B.C.) before the final assault on Jerusalem (588 B.C. & destroyed in 586 B.C.), Ezekiel uses prophecies, parables, signs, and symbols to dramatize God's message to His exiled people. Though they are like dry bones in the sun, God will reassemble them and breathe life into the nation once again.

Ezekiel was the son of Buzi (Ezekiel 1:3) had a wife who died as a sign to Judah when Nebuchadnezzar began his final siege on Jerusalem (Ezekiel 24:16-24). Like Jeremiah, he was a priest who was called to be a prophet of the Lord. His prophetic ministry shows a priestly emphasis in his concern with the temple, priesthood, sacrifices, and Shekinah (Glory of God). Ezekiel was privileged to receive a number of visions of the power and plan of God, and he was careful and artistic in his written presentation.

Ezekiel was about 25 years old when he was deported to Babylon in 590 B.C., prophesied from 592 B.C.

to at least 570 B.C., and died about 560 B.C. Thus, he overlapped the end of Jeremiah's ministry and the beginning of Daniel's ministry.

In today's lesson, chapters 47 and 48, we see the River of life from the Sanctuary (chapter 47:1-12); The Borders of the Land (chapter 47:13-23); The Lands Which Are Assigned to Tribes (chapter 48: 1-8); Lands Governed by Priest & Levites (chapter 48:9-14,); Common Lands (chapter 48:15-20); Lands for The Prince (chapter 48:21-22); Lands for The Remaining Tribes (chapter 48:23-29); and The Gates of the City (chapter 48:30-35). This is a divine road map for the future of Israel and their existence in the Millennium. Ezekiel is a powerful book of prophecy, teachings and promises to the Jewish people and to the world.

2 Chronicles 7:14

If my people, which are called by my name, shall humble themselves, and pray, and seek my face, and turn from their wicked ways; then will I hear from heaven, and will forgive their sin, and will heal their land.

Psalm 122:6

Pray for the peace of Jerusalem; they will prosper who love thee.

The Book of Daniel

Scripture Focus Chapters 1-12

Objective: To gain an understanding and insight on the Book of Daniel, his prophecies, and visions, and who ultimately became the most powerful Jew and prophet of the Jewish exile.

Objective Breakdown:

1. Introduction

2. Daniel and His Friends Are Deported   Chapter 1:1-7

3. The Steward Agrees to a Test   Chapter 1:8-14

4. The Four Young Men Get Top Grades   Chapter 1:15-21

5. Who Can Interpret the King's Dream?   Chapter 2:1-13

6. The Lord Reveals the Dream to Daniel   Chapter 2:14-23

7. Daniel Is Brought Before the King   Chapter 2:24-30

8. Daniel Describes the Dream   Chapter 2:31-35

9. The Interpretation of the Dream   Chapter 2:36-45

10. Daniel and His Friends Are Promoted   Chapter 2:46-49

11. Nebuchadnezzar Erects a Golden Image   Chapter 3:1-7

12. Daniel's Friends Will Not Bow Down   Chapter 3:8-18

13. Thrown into the Fiery Furnace   Chapter 3:19-25

14. The Three Men Exit the Furnace Unhurt   Chapter 3:26-30

15. Nebuchadnezzar Has Another Dream   Chapter 4:1-9

16. A Mighty Tree Chopped Down   Chapter 4:10-18

17. Daniel Interprets the King's Dream   Chapter 4:19-27

18. The Prediction Comes to Pass   Chapter 4:28-36

19. A Hand Interrupts Belshazzar's Feast   Chapter 5:1-9

20. Daniel Is Brought in to Interpret   Chapter 5:10-16

Lesson Plan 238

The Book of Daniel

Chapters 1 & 2

Objective: To gain an understanding and insight on the Book of Daniel, his prophecies and visions, and who ultimately became the most powerful Jew and prophet of the Jewish exile.

Objective Breakdown:

1. Introduction

2. Daniel & His Friends Are Deported

3. The Steward Agrees to a Test

4. The Four Young Men Get Top Grades

5. Who Can Interpret the King's Dream?

6. The Lord Reveals the Dream to Daniel

7. Daniel is Brought Before the King Daniel Describes the Dream

8. The Interpretation of the Dream

9. Daniel and His Friends Are Promoted

Introduction:

Babylon, scene of Daniel's ministry, was the wonder city of the ancient world. Situated in the cradle of the human race, near the Garden of Eden region; built around the Tower of Babel, the first seat of the empire and a favorite residence of Babylonians, Assyrian, and Persian kings, even of Alexander the Great. Babylon was brought to the zenith of its power and glory in the days of Daniel, by Nebuchadnezzar, who during his 45 years reign never wearied of building and beautifying its palaces and temples.

The size of Babylon: Ancient historian said that its wall was 60 miles around, 15 miles on each side, 300 feet high, 80 feet thick, extending 35 feet below the ground so that enemies could not tunnel under the walls. The bricks were one-foot square and 3 or four inches thick. The walls were protected by wide and deep moats canals. There were 250 towers on the wall, guard rooms for soldiers, 100 gates of brass. The city was divided by the Euphrates into two almost equal parts, both banks guarded by brick walls all the way, with 25 gates connecting streets, ferry boats, one bridge on stone piers ½ mile long and 30 feet wide with drawbridges which were removed at night. There was also a tunnel under the river, 15 feet wide and 12 feet high.

The Great temple of Marduk (Bel) adjoining the Tower of Babylon (Babel) was the most renowned sanctuary in all the Euphrates valley. It contained a golden image of Bel and a golden table which together weighed no less than 50,000 pounds. At the top were golden images of Bel and Ishtar, 2 golden lions, a golden table 40 feet long and 15 wide and a human figure of solid gold 18 feet high. Truly Babylon was a city of gold (Isaiah 14:4). The city had 53 temples and 180 altars to Ishtar.

Daniel & His Friends Are Deported	Chapter 1:1-7
The Steward Agrees to a Test	Chapter 1:8-14
The Four Young Men Get Top Grades	Chapter 1:15-21
Who Can Interpret the King's Dream	Chapter 2:1-13
The Lord Reveals the Dream to Daniel	Chapter 2:14-23
Daniel is Brought Before the King Daniel	Chapter 2:24-30
Daniel Describes the Dream	Chapter 2:31-35
The Interpretation of the Dream	Chapter 2:36-45
Daniel and His Friends Are Promoted	Chapter 2:46-49

2 Chronicles 7:14

If my people, which are called by my name, shall humble themselves, and pray, and seek my face, and turn from their wicked ways; then will I hear from heaven, and will forgive their sin, and will heal their land.

Psalm 122:6

Pray for the peace of Jerusalem; they will prosper who love thee.

Words of Comfort for the Soul

Ephesians 4:29, Let no corrupt word proceed out of your mouth, but what is good for necessary edification, that it may impart grace to the hearers.

Ephesians 4:30, Do not grieve the Holy Spirit of God, by whom you were sealed for the day of redemption.

Ephesians 4:31, Let all bitterness, wrath, anger, clamor, and evil speaking be put away from you, with all malice.

Ephesians 4:32, Be kind to another, tenderhearted, forgiving one another, even as God in Christ forgave you.

Romans Road to Salvation

1. Romans 3:23, For all have sinned and fall short of the glory of God.

2. Romans 6:23, For the wages of sin is death, but the free gift of God is eternal life in Christ Jesus our Lord.

3. Romans 5:8, But God demonstrates His own love toward us, in that while we were yet sinners, Christ died for us.

4. Romans 10:9, that if you confess with your mouth Jesus as Lord and believe in your heart that God raised Him from the dead, you shall be saved.

5. Romans 10:13, for "Whoever will call upon the Name of the Lord will be saved."

**** As God's ambassadors: If you are not happy with what is happening in your country call your Senators and House Representatives and let them know.

U.S. Congress Switchboard 202-225-3121. Ask to speak to your representative.

U.S. Senate Switchboard 202 224- 3121. Ask to speak to your representative.

Lesson Plan 239

The Book of Daniel

Chapters 3 & 4

Objective: To gain an understanding and insight on the Book of Daniel, his prophecies and visions, and who ultimately became the most powerful Jew and prophet of the Jewish exile.

Objective Breakdown:

1. Introduction

2. Nebuchadnezzar Erects a Golden Image	Chapter 3:1-7
3. Daniel's Friends Will Not Bow Down	Chapter 3:8-18
4. Thrown into the Fiery Furnace	Chapter 3:19-25
5. Three Men Exit the Furnace Unhurt	Chapter 3:26-30
6. Nebuchadnezzar Has Another Dream	Chapter 4:1-9
7. A Mighty Tree Chopped Down	Chapter 4:10-18
8. Daniel Interprets the King's Dream	Chapter 4:19-27
9. The Prediction Comes to Pass	Chapter 4:28-37

Introduction:

The Book of Daniel divides into two sections. Chapters 1 through 6 give a biographical and historical narrative of the highlights in the lives of Daniel and three other Jewish captives, Shadrach, Meshach, and Abed-Nego.

Chapters 7-12 record visions of future events that were given Daniel by the Lord, beginning in about 553 B.C. Daniel is the only known prophet to have lived almost all his entire life in pagan society. Probably born in Jerusalem, he was deported to Babylon in 605 B.C. where he was immediately placed in a re-education program to prepare him for service in the very government which destroyed Jerusalem. Eventually he became probably the most powerful Jew of the exile and its aftermath. He served at least three kings and two governments in a career of nearly 70 years and is a powerful role model for people of faith who live and work in secular societies today.

As for the prophecies of Daniel, they are often seen as a panoramic overview of world history from

Daniel's time until the second coming of Christ (although see all of the fulfillment of his prophecies in the events of the centuries closely following his own time). No matter how one interprets Daniel's visions, they point to the fundamental truth that God is the God of the nations. He is ultimately in control of history, sovereignty, appointing and replacing rulers, and through them orchestrating international events to accomplish His purposes.

2 Chronicles 7:14

If my people, which are called by my name, shall humble themselves, and pray, and seek my face, and turn from their wicked ways; then will I hear from heaven, and will forgive their sin, and will heal their land.

Psalm 122:6

Pray for the peace of Jerusalem; they will prosper who love thee.

God's Blessing on Israel   (Numbers 6:24-27)

Words of Comfort for the Soul

Ephesians 4:29, Let no corrupt word proceed out of your mouth, but what is good for necessary edification, that it may impart grace to the hearers.

Ephesians 4:30, Do not grieve the Holy Spirit of God, by whom you were sealed for the day of redemption.

Ephesians 4:31, Let all bitterness, wrath, anger, clamor, and evil speaking be put away from you, with all malice.

Ephesians 4:32, Be kind to another, tenderhearted, forgiving one another, even as God in Christ forgave you.

Romans Road to Salvation

Romans 3:23, For all have sinned and fall short of the glory of God.

Romans 6:23, For the wages of sin is death, but the free gift of God is eternal life in Christ Jesus our Lord.

Romans 5:8, But God demonstrates His own love toward us, in that while we were yet sinners, Christ died for us.

Lesson Plan 240

The Book of Daniel

Chapters 5 & 6

Objective: To gain an understanding and insight on the Book of Daniel, his prophecies and visions, and who ultimately became the most powerful Jew and prophet of the Jewish exile.

Objective Breakdown:

1. Introduction

2. A Hand Interrupts Belshazzar's Feast   Chapter 5:1-9

3. Daniel Is Brought in to Interpret   Chapter 5:10-16

4. The Prophet Recalls Nebuchadnezzar   Chapter 5:17-21

5. The End of Belshazzar's Kingdom   Chapter 5:22-31

6. Darius Signs an Idolatrous Decree   Chapter 6:1-9

7. Daniel Is Thrown into a Den of Lions   Chapter 6:10-17

8. The Lord Protects Daniel   Chapter 6:18-24

9. A New Decree: "Fear the God of Daniel"   Chapter 6:25-28

Introduction: Babylon, scene of Daniel' ministry, was the wonder city of the ancient world. Situated in the cradle of the human race, near the Garden of Eden region; built around the Tower of Babel, the first seat of the empire and a favorite residence of Babylonians, Assyrian, and Persian kings, even of Alexander the Great. Babylon was brought to the zenith of its power and glory in the days of Daniel, by Nebuchadnezzar, who during his 45 years reign never wearied of building and beautifying its palaces and temples.

The size of Babylon: Ancient historian said that its wall was 60 miles around, 15 miles on each side, 300 feet high, 80 feet thick, extending 35 feet below the ground so that enemies could not tunnel under the walls. The bricks were one-foot square and 3 or four inches thick. The walls were protected by wide and deep moats canals. There were 250 towers on the wall, guard rooms for soldiers, 100 gates of brass. The city was divided by the Euphrates into two almost equal parts, both banks guarded by brick walls all the way, with 25 gates connecting streets, ferry boats, one bridge on stone piers ½ mile long and 30 feet wide with drawbridges which were removed at night. There was also a tunnel under the river, 15 feet wide and 12 feet high.

The Great temple of Marduk (Bel) adjoining the Tower of Babylon (Babel) was the most renowned sanctuary in all the Euphrates valley. It contained a golden image of Bel and a golden table which together weighed no less than 50,000 pounds. At the top were golden images of Bel and Ishtar, 2 golden lions, a golden table 40 feet long and 15 wide and a human figure of solid gold 18 feet high. Truly Babylon was a city of gold (Isaiah 14:4). The city had 53 temples and 180 altars to Ishtar.

2 Chronicles 7:14

If my people, which are called by my name, shall humble themselves, and pray, and seek my face, and turn from their wicked ways; then will I hear from heaven, and will forgive their sin, and will heal their land.

Psalm 122:6

Pray for the peace of Jerusalem; they will prosper who love thee.

Some Similarities Between the Book of Daniel and the Book of Revelation

Captivity

Daniel in Babylon   John in Patmos

Prophet

Daniel was a Prophet   John was an Apostle & Prophet

Visions

Daniel saw the Time of the End   John saw end-times

Daniel 2:34   Revelation 19

Survived Temple Destruction

Solomon's Temple BC 586   Herod's Temple AD 70

Served Under Various Leaders

Daniel under 4 Kings   John under 4 Emperors

(2 Babylonian-2Medes/Persians)

Seal the Book/Do Not Seal the Book

Daniel told to seal the Book   John told not to seal the Book

Note:

The Book of Daniel is incomplete without the Book of Revelation. Daniel did not see the Mark of the Beast; False prophet; beheading of people; the image of the beast that speaks. Daniel wrote for the nation of Israel and John wrote for the Church and the nation of Israel.

Daniel and John both saw the world's final kingdom. Daniel 4:3; 9:27 & Revelation 11:15.

Daniel and John both saw a time frame of seven years. Daniel 12:7 & Revelation 12:14.

Daniel and John saw a final rule for 42 months. Daniel 12:7 & Revelation 12:4.

Daniel and John both saw a final dictator. Daniel 8:23 & Revelation 13:1-2

Daniel & John saw final kingdom as a Beast. Daniel 7:7 & Revelation 13:1-2

Daniel & John saw time of Great Tribulation. Daniel 12:1 & Revelation 7:14

Daniel & John saw Great Trouble for Israel & Jews. Daniel 12:1 & Revelation 12:17

Daniel & John saw Michael intervene. Daniel12:1 & Revelation 12:7

Daniel & John saw 10,000 X 10,000 & K's x K's. Daniel 7:10 & Revelation 5:11

Daniel & John saw books open in Heaven. Daniel 7:10 & Revelation 20:12

Daniel & John saw the return of the Messiah. Daniel 7:13, 14 & Revelation 19:11-14

Daniel & John saw the Messiah coming in the clouds. Daniel 7:13 & Revelation 1:7

Daniel & John saw the beast burning in the flames. Daniel 7:11 & Revelation 19:20

Daniel & John saw **the Saints take over** the Kingdom on Earth. Daniel 7:22 & Revelation 20:4

Daniel & John saw an everlasting Kingdom that would not end. Daniel 7:18 & Revelation 21:1-4

Daniel & John both saw empires that would affect Israel and Jerusalem. Daniel Chapter 12 & Revelation Chapters12 & 13.

Daniel & John both saw into the Throne Room of God. Daniel 7:9 & Revelation 20:4

Daniel & John both saw Ten Kings accompanying the Beast. Daniel 7:24 &17:12

Daniel & John both lived into their late nineties.

Things That Daniel Did Not See

Daniel did not see the false prophet. Revelation 13:11; 16:13; 19:20; 20:10

Daniel did not see the Mark of the Beast. Revelation 13:8

Daniel did not see the Beheading of People. Revelation 20:4

Daniel did not see the Image of the Beast. Revelation 13:14-15

Daniel did not see the New Jerusalem. Revelation Chapters 21 & 22

2 Chronicles 7:14

If my people, which are called by my name, shall humble themselves, and pray, and seek my face, and turn from their wicked ways; then will I hear from heaven, and will forgive their sin, and will heal their land.

Psalm 122:6

Pray for the peace of Jerusalem; they will prosper who love thee.

Some Thoughts on Our Future with God

Five Pictures of God's Ultimate World Order

A. It Will Be a Time of Peace One thousand years of peace (Psalm 72:7) Nations will not make war against each other (Micah 4:3).

B. It Will Be a Time of Prosperity The wilderness and waste lands shall bloom abundantly; there will be streams in the desert (Isaiah 35:1-2).

C. It Will Be a Time of Purity Justice will be pure, no conflicting or competing ideologies (Zechariah 13:2).

D. It Will Be a Time of Prolonged Life Persons who are 100 years old will be considered young (Isaiah 65:20). There will be rapid multiplication of the human race. (Jeremiah 30:19b).

E. It Will Be a Time of Personal Joy God will multiply joy among the Nations (Isaiah 9:3). The whole Earth will break forth in singing (Isaiah 14:7). Tears will be wiped away (Isaiah 25:8-9). New songs will be sung (Isaiah 42:10-12).

WOW!!

Lesson Plan 241

The Book of Daniel

Chapters 7 & 8

Objective: To learn of the courage and convictions that Daniel displayed in one of the most Godless cultures of the ancient world.

Objective Breakdown:

1. Introduction

2. Daniel Has a Vision of Four Beasts   Chapter 7:1-8

3. Daniel Has a Vision of the Lord   Chapter 7:9-14

4. Daniel Asks What It All Means   Chapter 7:15-20

5. The Vision Is Explained   Chapter 7:21-28

6. A Vision of a Ram and a Goat   Chapter 8:1-7

7. The Exalted Horn   Chapter 8:8-14

8. Gabriel Arrives to Explain the Vision   Chapter 8:15-22

9. A Wicked King Shall Rise and Fall   Chapter 8:23-27

Introduction:

This is a continuation of the prophecy of chapter 2, which was uttered 60 years earlier: "two aspects of one grand scheme of history," Four World Empires, and then the Kingdom of God. In chapter 2, these are represented by an Image with a Head of Gold, a Breast of Silver, Thighs of Brass, and Feet of Iron, broken in pieces by a Stone. In this chapter these same Four World Empires are represented as a Lion, a Bear, a Leopard, and a Terrible Beast.

These Four World Empires are commonly taken to be Babylon, Persia, Greece, and Rome (see chapter 2), representing a period from Daniel to Christ. These Beasts seem to form the basis of the imagery of the Seven-Headed, Ten Horned Beast of Revelation 13.

The "Ten Horns" of the Fourth Beast (24) are taken to be the ten kingdoms into which the Roman Empire was resolved. The "Other Horn" (8, 20, 24, 25), which should arise among the Ten Horns, is a combination of the Leopard Beast and Lamb Beast of Revelation 13. The "three kings" which he displaced (8, 24), are thought to refer to Lombard's, Ravenna, and Rome, which were handed over to the Popes as the beginning of their Temporal Kingdom, (A.D. 754).

2 Chronicles 7:14

If my people, which are called by my name, shall humble themselves, and pray, and seek my face, and turn from their wicked ways; then will I hear from heaven, and will forgive their sin, and will heal their land.

Psalm 122:6

Pray for the peace of Jerusalem; they will prosper who love thee.

God's Blessing on Israel   **(Numbers 6:24-27)**

Jabez's Prayer to the Lord   **(1 Chronicles 4:10)**

Words for Comfort of the Soul

Ephesians 4:29, Let no corrupt word proceed out of your mouth, but what is good for necessary edification, that it may impart grace to the hearers.

Ephesians 4:30, Do not grieve the Holy Spirit of God, by whom you were sealed for the day of redemption.

Ephesians 4:31, Let all bitterness, wrath, anger, clamor, and evil speaking be put away from you, with all malice.

Ephesians 4:32, Be kind to another, tenderhearted, forgiving one another, even as God in Christ forgave you.

Philippians 4:6, Be anxious for nothing, but in everything by prayer and supplication, with thanksgiving, let your requests be made known to God; and the peace of God, which surpasses all understanding, will guard your hearts and minds through Christ Jesus.

Road to Salvation

1. Romans 3:23, For all have sinned and fall short of the glory of God.

2. Romans 5:12, Therefore, just as through one-man sin entered the world, and death through sin, and thus death spread to all men, because all sinned.

3. Ephesians 2: 8, 9, For by Grace you have been saved through faith, and not of yourselves; it is a gift of God, not of works, lest anyone should boast.

4. Romans 6:23, For the wages of sin is death, but the free gift of God is eternal life in Christ Jesus our Lord.

5. Romans 5:8, But God demonstrates His own love toward us, in that while we were yet sinners, Christ died for us.

6. Titus 3:4, 5, 6, But when the kindness and the love of God our Savior toward man appeared, not by works of righteousness which we have done, but according to His mercy He saved us, through the washing of regeneration and renewing of the Holy Spirit whom he poured out on us abundantly through Jesus Christ our Savior for having been justified by His grace we should become heirs according to the hope of eternal life.

7. John 3:16, For God so loved the world that He gave His only begotten Son, that whosoever believes in Him should not perish but have everlasting life.

8. John 14:6, Jesus said to him, "I am the way, the truth, and the life. No one comes to the father except through me."

9. 1 John 10:13, He who believes in the Son of God has the witness in himself; he who does not believe God has made him a liar, because he has not believed the testimony that God has given of His Son. And this is the testimony: that God has given us eternal life, and this life is in His Son. He who has the Son has life; he who does not have the Son of God does not have life. These things I have written to you who believe in the name of the son of God, that you may know that you have eternal life, and that you may continue to believe in the name of the Son of God.

10. Romans 10:9, that if you confess with your mouth Jesus as Lord and believe in your heart that God raised Him from the dead, you shall be saved.

11. Romans 10:13, for "Whoever will call upon the Name of the Lord will be saved."

Lesson Plan 242

The Book of Daniel

Chapters 9, 10, 11, & 12

Objective: To gain an understanding and insight on the Book of Daniel, his prophecies and visions, and who ultimately became the most powerful Jew and prophet of the Jewish Exile.

Objective Breakdown:

Introduction:

God's line of defense. One of the most popular topics of speculation in recent years has been the subject of angels. Many books have been published on them claiming to have first accounts of experiences with angels. But as always, the Bible must remain our authority on the supernatural.

Daniel chapter 10 is an important passage pertaining to angels. Daniel records a vision in which an archangel Michael describes as "one of the chief princes," which is said to defend the nation of Israel from the "princes" (probably evil angels) of Persia and Greece (Daniel 10-21). Later, during the end times, Michael will help to deliver Israel from all her enemies (Daniel (12:1).

The Bible presents angels as real beings and provides little information about them, but for the most part it leaves them veiled in mystery. Apparently, God wants us to know that realty extends beyond our normal perceptions, yet He does not want us to know too much about it. However, He does lift the veil and allows humans to catch a glimpse of the spiritual activity and warfare taking place around us. Daniel saw some of that reality and was overwhelmed and troubling about it (Daniel 7:15; 8:27; 10:15-16). On the other hand, Elisha experienced it and found it reassuring (2 Kings 6:16–17).

As you develop your understanding and beliefs about angelic forces, good and evil, cosmic battles in the heavens, and other topics of the supernatural, be sure they accord with Scripture. Sensational stories and wild speculations may make for interesting reading, but ultimately truth is at stake. God revelation in Scripture can help us sort it out.

2 Chronicles 7:14

If my people, which are called by my name, shall humble themselves, and pray, and seek my face, and turn from their wicked ways; then will I hear from heaven, and will forgive their sin, and will heal their land.

Psalm 122:6

Pray for the peace of Jerusalem; they will prosper who love thee.

God's Blessing on Israel   (Numbers 6:24-27)

"The Lord bless you and keep you; The Lord make his face Shine upon you, and be gracious to you, and give you peace. So, they shall put My name on the children of Israel, and I will bless them."

Jabez's Prayer to the Lord   (I Chronicles 4:10)

Words for Comfort of the Soul

Ephesians 4:29, Let no corrupt word proceed out of your mouth, but what is good for necessary edification, that it may impart grace to the hearers.

Ephesians 4:30, Do not grieve the Holy Spirit of God, by whom you were sealed for the day of redemption.

Ephesians 4:31, Let all bitterness, wrath, anger, clamor, and evil speaking be put away from you, with all malice.

Ephesians 4:32, Be kind to another, tenderhearted, forgiving one another, even as God in Christ forgave you.

Philippians 4:6, Be anxious for nothing, but in everything by prayer and supplication, with thanksgiving, let your requests be made known to God; and the peace of God, which surpasses all understanding, will guard your hearts and minds through Christ Jesus.

The Book of Hosea

Scripture Focus Chapters 1-14

Objective: To gain an understanding on the book of Hosea which provides us insight and comparison of the unfaithfulness of Gomer, Hosea's wife, and the unfaithfulness of Israel to God.

Objective Breakdown:

1. Introduction

2. Hosea Marries a Prostitute   Chapter 1:1-9

3. The Israelites Will Be Reunited   Chapter 1:10-11

4. God Calls Israel an Adulteress   Chapter 2:1-5

5. God's Judgment Is Promised   Chapter 2:6-15

6. A Day of Reconciliation Is Coming   Chapter 2:16-23

7. Hosea Buys His Wife Out of Prostitution   Chapter 3:1-5

8. God's Charge Against Israel   Chapter 4:1-10

9. The Idolatry of Israel   Chapter 4:11-19

10. Impending Judgment on Israel and Judah   Chapter 5:1-7

11. Assyria Will Not Be Any Help   Chapter 5:8-15

12. A Call to Repentance   Chapter 6:1-11

13. A Nation of Thieves and Scoffers   Chapter 7:1-7

14. Israel Rebels Despite God's Efforts   Chapter 7:8-16

15. Israel Seeks Other Rulers and Gods   Chapter 8:1-10

16. Israel Forgets His Maker   Chapter 8:11-14

17. Israel Will Be Sent Among the Gentiles   Chapter 9:1-9

18. The Sorrow of Wandering Israel   Chapter 9:10-17

19. God's Judgment on Idolatry   Chapter 10:1-8

20. A Harvest of Rebellion   Chapter 10:9-15

Lesson Plan 243

The Book of Hosea

Chapters 1, 2, 3, & 4

Objective: To gain an understanding on the book of Hosea which provides us insight and comparison of the unfaithfulness of Gomer, Hosea's wife, and the unfaithfulness of Israel to God.

Objective Breakdown

1. Introduction

2. Hosea Marries a Prostitute   Chapter 1:1-9

3. The Israelites Will Be Reunited   Chapter 1:10-11

4. God Calls Israel an Adulteress   Chapter 2:1-5

5. God's Judgment Is Promised   Chapter 2:6-15

6. A Day of Reconciliation Is Coming   Chapter 2:16-23

7. Hosea Buys His Wife Out of Prostitution   Chapter 3:1-5

8. God's Charge Against Israel   Chapter 4:1-10

9. The Idolatry of Israel   Chapter 4:11-19

Introduction:

The prophet Hosea proclaimed his prophecies to the northern kingdom of Israel during the 30 years before Samaria fell and the nation was taken into captivity by Assyrians (722 B.C.). These were years of temporary prosperity for Israel, even though four of the six kings who reigned during this period were assassinated in the midst of their affluence, the people were rejecting God and turning to idolatry as never before.

At the command of the Lord, Hosea endured the infidelity f his wife as the basis for a message about God's love for wayward Israel (Hosea 1:1-2:5). The book sometime refers to the nation as Ephraim, which was the largest tribe among the ten tribes of the northern kingdom (Hosea 5:3, 5,11,13).

Popular culture often describes love in terms of passion, sexuality, or blind devotion. By this measure, love is a little more than an uncontrollable attraction toward another person that ebbs and flows unconsciously. This sort of "love" looks for its own gain and can walk away if its demands and needs go unmet or unsatisfied.

By contrast, God called Hosea to pursue a radically different kind of love, one based on a conscious choice to be committed to someone else for her benefit, regardless of her response to that gift (Hosea 3:1-3). That is how God is committed to Israel. Hosea marriage was an illustration of God's marriage to the spiritually adulterous nation of Israel.

2 Chronicles 7:14

If my people, which are called by my name, shall humble themselves, and pray, and seek my face, and turn from their wicked ways; then will I hear from heaven, and will forgive their sin, and will heal their land.

Psalm 122:6

Pray for the peace of Jerusalem; they will prosper who love thee.

Lesson Plan 244

The Book of Hosea

Chapters 5, 6, 7, & 8

Objective: To gain an understanding on the book of Hosea which provides us insight and comparison of the unfaithfulness of Gomer, Hosea's wife, and the unfaithfulness of Israel to God.

Objective Breakdown

1. Introduction

2. Impending Judgment on Israel and Judah   Chapter 5:1-7

3. Assyria Will Not Be Any Help   Chapter 5:8-15

4. A Call to Repentance   Chapter 6:1-11

5. A Nation of Thieves and Scoffers   Chapter 7:1-7

6. Israel Rebels Despite God's Efforts   Chapter 7:8-16

7. Israel Seeks Other Rulers and Gods   Chapter 8:1-10

8. Israel Forgets His Maker   Chapter 8:11-14

Introduction:

Hosea's marriage was extraordinary in that he was called to marry a wife of harlotry (Hosea 1:2). Gomer's background (Hosea's wife) is unknown, but it may also be that she had been unfaithful to a previous husband, or she may have been a known prostitute. It may also be that she was one of the temple prostitutes believed to be part of the idolatrous rites then practiced in Israel.

Whatever Gomer's background, she was a powerful symbol of Israel's spiritual adultery against the Lord (Hoses 2:2). The nation had departed almost entirely from worship as prescribed by the LAW. Instead, people had adopted the religions around them, particularly the Canaanites, Phoenicians, and Moabites. Canaanite religion was essentially a fertility cult in which ritual sexual intercourse with prostitutes is believed to have played a major role.

God rejected these Canaanites practices calling them what they were—harlotries. The Lord, not the Canaanite god Baal, was Ruler over the land and Israel's faithful Lover and forgotten Provider of bounty (Hosea 2:8).

Like Israel, Gomer left her loving husband and returned to her life as a harlotry. Apparently, she ended up in the slave market, where Hosea redeemed her for 15 shekels and some barley (Hosea 3:2). This was a fairly minor cost in terms of value, merely the common price of a slave (see Exodus 21:32). But it was a great sacrifice of love on Hosea's part. The prophet was mirroring the love of God for his prodigal people and symbolizing the reconciliation that would take place (Hosea 3:4-5).

Spiritual adultery is still a danger for God's people today. The New Testament likens the relationship between believers and Christ to marriage (Ephesians 5:25-33). When Christians turn away and adopt beliefs, values, practices, and rituals that are unworthy of Him, they commit the same sort of "harlotries" as ancient Israel committed against the Lord (2 Corinthians 11:2-4).

2 Chronicles 7:14

If my people, which are called by my name, shall humble themselves, and pray, and seek my face, and turn from their wicked ways; then will I hear from heaven, and will forgive their sin, and will heal their land.

Psalm 122:6

Pray for the peace of Jerusalem; they will prosper who love thee.

Lesson Plan 245

The Book of Hosea

Chapters 9, 10, 11, 12, 13, & 14

Objective: To gain an understanding on the book of Hosea which provides us insight and comparison of the unfaithfulness of Gomer, Hosea's wife, and the unfaithfulness of Israel to God.

Objective Breakdown:

1. Introduction

2. Israel Will Be Sent Among the Gentiles   Chapter 9:1-9

3 The Sorrow of Wandering Israel   Chapter 9:10-17

4. God's Judgment on Idolatry   Chapter 10:1-8

5. A Harvest of Rebellion   Chapter 10:9-15

6. God's Continuing Love for His People   Chapter 11:1-12

7. God's Continuing Love for His People (cont.) Chapter 12:1

8. The Lord Charges Judah Also   Chapter 12:2-14

9. Relentless Judgment on Israel   Chapter 13:1-8

10. The Wind of the Lord from the East   Chapter 13:9-16

11. Repentance Will Lead to Reconciliation   Chapter 14:1-9

Introduction:

Corrupted and half-baked. Those who speak of a moral and spiritual decline in society might want to borrow a page from the Book of Hosea. The prophet denounced ancient Israel by heaping up metaphors that sound like what is being said about modern culture. He described Ephraim (Israel) as:

Corrupted (Hosea 7:8). Israel mixed itself with surrounding nations by allowing their pagan religions to corrupt its religious and spiritual life. In doing so God's people violated the First and Second Commandments (Exodus 20:3-4). They also formed political alliances to prop up their defenses rather than relying on the Lord (see 2 Kings 16:5-6).

Half-baked (Hosea 7:8). An unturned cake is like a pancake that is burned on one side and gooey on the other. Israel was half-baked in that its prosperity under Jeroboam II was purely material and not at all spiritual. Its vapid, self-absorbed culture had nothing significant to offer.

Weakened and feeble (Hosea 7:9). The aliens (Hebrew, zarim) mentioned by Hosea were foreign "allies" such as Assyria and Egypt who seemed to be friends but were actually enemies (2 Kings15:17-20; 17:3-4). These nations devoured Israel's strength by requiring heavy payments and tribute. Yet this aging process occurred imperceptibly of about 40 years, so the Israelites hardly even noticed that the loss of power.

Arrogant (Hosea 7:10). Despite the many reversals that took place between the prosperous reign of Jeroboam II (793-753 B.C.) and the foolish reign of Hoshea, Israel's last king (732-722B.C.), the nation lived an illusion of strength and virility. The people arrogantly resisted the Lord right up to the end of their kingdom (2 Kings 17:13-18).

No nation can survive very long when its activity turns away from God.

2 Chronicles 7:14

If my people, which are called by my name, shall humble themselves, and pray, and seek my face, and turn from their wicked ways; then will I hear from heaven, and will forgive their sin, and will heal their land.

Psalm 122:6

Pray for the peace of Jerusalem; they will prosper who love thee.

The Book of Joel

Scripture Focus Chapters 1-3

Objective: To gain insight on the book of Joel and its message that we need to pass on to our children and grandchildren and future generations what God has done for us.

Objective Breakdown:

1. Introduction

2. An Invasion of Locusts   Chapter 1:1-7

3. A Lament for the Land   Chapter 1:8-20

4. The Day of the Lord   Chapter 2:1-11

5. A Call for Repentance   Chapter 2:12-17

6. The Land Will Be Renewed   Chapter 2:18-27

7. God Will Pour Out His Spirit   Chapter 2:28-32

8. God's Judgment Against the Nations   Chapter 3:1-8

9. The Lord Will Destroy His Enemies   Chapter 3:9-17

10. Judah Will Be Preserved   Chapter 3:18-21

Lesson Plan 246

The Book of Joel

Chapters 1, 2, & 3

Objective: To gain insight on the book of Joel and its message that we need to pass on to our children and grandchildren and future generations what God has done for us.

Objective Breakdown:

1. Introduction

2. An Invasion of Locusts   Joel 1:1-7

3. A Lament for the Land   Joel 1:8-20

4. The Day of the Lord   Joel 2:1-11

5. A Call for Repentance   Joel 2:12-17

6. The Land Will Be Renewed   Joel 2:18-27

7. God Will Pour Out His Spirit   Joel 2:28-32

8. God's Judgment Against the Nations   Joel 3:1-8

9. The Lord Will Destroy His Enemies   Joel 3:9-17

10. Judah Will Be Preserved   Joel 3:18-21

Introduction:

God wants His people to pass on to their children, their grandchildren, and even to generations yet unborn the story of what God has done (Joel 1:3). God wants no one to fall into condemnation and come under His judgment. He warns people ahead of time so that they will recognize their sin and experience the Godly sorrow that leads to repentance (Joel 2:12-17).

There is a close connection between the redemptive work of God and the creative work of God. He cares about the land as well as the people who live on it (Joel 2:18). The name Joel means: the Lord is God.

The Book of Joel describes a dark and frightening event known as the "Day of the Lord" (Joel 2:1-2; also see Joel 1:15). The doom and gloom of that judgment are all-encompassing: fields and pastures ravaged by locust as if burned to the ground (Joel 2:3-5), death steals upon the cities (Joel 2:6-9), and even the cosmos itself trembles (Joel 2:10-11). The "Day of the Lord" can relate to three different meanings in Joel:

1) a coming of judgment for Israel (Joel 1:15; 2:1-11);

2) a coming day of restoration for Israel (Joel 2:28-32); and

3) a coming day of judgments for the nations (Joel 3:1-21).

Yet all of this terror is intended to bring about repentance (Joel 2:12-17), which results in the renewal of the land and the restoration of its inhabitants (Joel 2:18-27); and the signs of hope will outshine all previous disasters (Joel 2:25). The creation will be in full bloom, the rains will fall again, the threshing floors will be full of grain, the vats will overflow with oil and wine, and households will be satisfied and ringing praise. Ultimately the world will experience a spectacular renewal (Joel 2:28-32). And as we consider the state of the world today and its prospect for the future, we should lay hold of God's promise of hope. "Whoever calls on the name of the Lord shall be saved" (Joel 2:32).

2 Chronicles 7:14

If my people, which are called by my name, shall humble themselves, and pray, and seek my face, and turn from their wicked ways; then will I hear from heaven, and will forgive their sin, and will heal their land.

Psalm 122:6

Pray for the peace of Jerusalem; they will prosper who love thee.

The Book of Amos

Scripture Focus Chapters 1-9

Objective: To gain an understanding of the prophecies and warnings of judgment that Amos addressed to the Northern Kingdom of Israel (around 760 B.C.) for its idolatry, injustice, corruption, and oppression of the poor.

Objective Breakdown:

1. Introduction

2. God's Judgment on Damascus and Gaza — Chapter 1:1-8

3. God's Judgment on Tyre, Edom, and Ammon — Chapter 1:9-15

4. God's Judgment on Moab and Judah — Chapter 2:1-5

5. God's Judgment on Israel — Chapter 2:6-16

6. Israel's Iniquities Will Be Punished — Chapter 3:1-10

7. An Adversary Will Devour the Nation — Chapter 3:11-15

8. Rich Women of Samaria Are Denounced — Chapter 4:1-8

9. The People Ignored God's Discipline — Chapter 4:9-13

10. A Lamentation for Israel — Chapter 5:1-3

11. "Seek Me and Live" — Chapter 5:4-15

12. The Day of the Lord Will Be Fearsome — Chapter 5:16-27

13. The People Are Too Much at Ease — Chapter 6:1-8

14. Total Destruction Is Coming — Chapter 6:9-14

15. Locusts, Fire, and a Plumb Line — Chapter 7:1-9

16. The Priest Amaziah Opposes Amos — Chapter 7:10-17

17. A Basket of Fruit — Chapter 8:1-8

18. Days of Darkness and Mourning — Chapter 8:9-14

19. There Will Be No Hiding from God — Chapter 9:1-4

20. Israel Will Be Scattered — Chapter 9:5-10

21. A Promise of Restoration — Chapter 9:11-15

Lesson Plan 247

The Book of Amos

Chapters 1 & 2

Objective: To give us insight on the judgment of God when He is dealing with disobedience and to gain an understanding of the prophecies and warnings of judgment that Amos addressed to the Northern Kingdom of Israel (around 760 B.C.) for its idolatry, injustice, corruption, and oppression of the poor.

Objective Breakdown:

1. Introduction

2. God's Judgment on Damascus and Gaza   Chapter 1:1-8

3. God's Judgment on Tyre, Edom, and Ammon   Chapter 1:9-15

4. God's Judgment on Moab and Judah   Chapter 2:1-5

5. God's Judgment on Israel   Chapter 2:6-16

Introduction:

The name Amos means "Burden Bearer." Amos was a prophet of Judah, the Southern Kingdom, with a message to Israel, the Northern Kingdom during the reigns of Uzziah King of Judah and Jeroboam II, King of Israel. Amos' prophecy occurred about 751 B.C.

Home of Amos

Tekoa was the home of Amos located 10 miles South of Jerusalem and 5 miles from Bethlehem on an elevation of 2700 feet overlooking the wilderness of Judea. This is thought to be the same region where eight centuries later John the Baptist grew to manhood. Amos was not a priest or a professional prophet. He was a herdsman and a dresser of sycamore trees.

Jeroboam's reign (Northern Kingdom) had been very successful. The Kingdom had been considerably enlarged (2 Kings 14:23-29). Israel was in the high tide of prosperity; but brazen in its idolatry and reeking in moral rottenness: a land of Swearing, Stealing, Injustice, Oppression, Robbery, Adultery and Murder.

It had been some 200 years since the ten tribes had set up the Northern Kingdom, with Calf-Worship as its religion (2 Kings 12:25-33). During part of this time Baal-Worship also had been adopted and many of the abominable practices of Canaanite Idolatry were still rampant. Meantime God had sent Elijah, and

Elisha and Jonah, but to no avail. Israel hardened in its idolatry and wickedness and was now speeding on to its ruin. God sent Amos and Hosea in a final effort to stay the nation in its mad dash for death.

Amos' Contemporaries

Amos, as a boy probably had known Jonah and may have heard tell of his visit to Nineveh. Possibly too he may have known of Elisha and may have heard of him tell of his association with Elijah. Elisha and Jonah were passing off the stage as Amos was coming on. Joel also may have been his contemporary or near predecessor. Hosea was a co-worker with Amos and was the younger. As Amos was closing his work, Isaiah and Micah were beginning theirs.

Doom of Israel and neighbor nations, Phoenicia, Edom, Ammon, Moab, Judah, and Israel. He then centers his attention on Israel. He arranges each nation under the same formula, "for three transgressions, yea for four specifying their particular transgressions. "Captivity" is one of the key words of the book of Amos and within 50 years these predictions were fulfilled.

God's Judgment on Damascus and Gaza	Chapter 1:1-8
God's Judgment on Tyre, Edom, and Ammon	Chapter 1:9-15
Gods Judgment on Moab and Judah	Chapter 2:1-5
God's Judgment on Israel	Chapter 2:6-16

2 Chronicles 7:14

If my people, which are called by my name, shall humble themselves, and pray, and seek my face, and turn from their wicked ways; then will I hear from heaven, and will forgive their sin, and will heal their land.

Psalm 122:6

Pray for the peace of Jerusalem; they will prosper who love thee.

Lesson Plan 248

The Book of Amos

Chapters 3 & 4

Objective: To give us insight on the judgment of God when He is dealing with disobedience and to gain an understanding of the prophecies and warnings of judgment that Amos addressed to the Northern Kingdom of Israel (around 760 B.C.) for its idolatry, injustice, corruption, and oppression of the poor.

Objective Breakdown:

1. Introduction

2. Israel' Iniquities Will Be Punished   Chapter 3:1-10

3. An Adversary Will Devour the Nation   Chapter 3:11-15

4. Rich Women of Samaria Are Denounced   Chapter 4:1-8

5. The People Ignored God's Discipline   Chapter 4:9-13

Introduction: _

Amos's description of Israel is sobering, if not downright frightening. They do not know to do right. Wickedness overflows the nation like a mighty river. As a result, the people are drowning in sin. They can no longer tell right from wrong. There is no longer any **national conscience**.

A) Samaria, capital of the northern Kingdom, was situated on a hill 300 feet high, in a vale of surprising beauty, surrounded on three sides by mountains, as impregnable as it was beautiful. Its palatial residences had been built out of the blood of the poor (Amos 2:6, 7; 3:10; 5:11; 8:4-7) with a heartlessness that would shock even heathen Egyptians and Philistines (Amos 9-10).

B) Bethel (3:14) where Amos was speaking (Amos 7:13) was the religious center of the northern kingdom, 12 miles north of Jerusalem where Jeroboam I set up a Golden calf (I Kings 12:25-33), which was still there (Hosea 13:2). To this degenerate center of idolatry came Amos with the final warning: prepare to meet your God.

C) Pampered ladies of Samaria (4:1-3) were living in sumptuous indulgence on gains squeezed out of the poor, "Cows of Bashan" (Amos 4:1) or fatted animals waiting for slaughter. Within a few years they were taken away "with hooks." Assyrians literally lead their captives away with hooks through the lip.

D) A nation is on the verge of collapse when good and evil look the same. If questions of right and wrong no longer enter the people's minds, then that nation is in desperate trouble. Has the nation lost its conscience? Do people call good bad and bad good?

The Kingdom lasted 120 years: Saul 40 years (Acts 13:21); David 40 years (II Samuel 5:4); Solomon 40 years (I Kings 11:42). After the death of Solomon, the Kingdom was Divided: Ten Tribes forming the Northern Kingdom called "Israel;" Judah and Benjamin forming the Southern Kingdom called "Judah." The Northern Kingdom lasted a little over 200 years and was destroyed by Assyria, 721 B.C. The Southern Kingdom lasted a little over 300 years and was destroyed by Babylon about 600 years B.C.

The Secession of the Ten Tribes was of God (1 Kings 11:11, 31; 12:15); a punishment for the apostasy of Solomon, and a lesson to Judah.

Religion of the Northern Kingdom

Jeroboam, founder of the Northern Kingdom adopted calf worship, the religion of Egypt, as the state religion. God worship had come to be identified with Judah and the family of David. The calf came to stand as a symbol of Israel's independence of Judah. Jeroboam rooted calf worship so deeply that it was not swept away until the fall of the Kingdom by the Assyrians in 721 B.C. Every one of the 19 kings of the Northern Kingdom followed the worship of the golden calf. Some of them also served Baal, but none of them ever attempted to bring the people back to God.

Religion of the Southern Kingdom

God-worship: though most of the kings served idols and walked in the evil ways of the kings of Israel; some of Judah's kings served God, and at times there were great reformations in Judah. On the whole, however, in spite of repeated warnings, Judah sank lower and lower in the horrible practice of Baal worship and other Canaanite religions, till there was no remedy.

2 Chronicles 7:14

If my people, which are called by my name, shall humble themselves, and pray, and seek my face, and turn from their wicked ways; then will I hear from heaven, and will forgive their sin, and will heal their land.

Psalm 122:6

Pray for the peace of Jerusalem; they will prosper who love thee.

Lesson Plan 249

The Book of Amos

Chapters 5 & 6

Objective: To give us insight on the judgment of God when He is dealing with disobedience to gain an understanding of the prophecies and warnings of judgment that Amos addressed to the Northern Kingdom of Israel (around 760 B.C.) for its idolatry, injustice, corruption, and oppression of the poor.

Objective Breakdown:

1. Introduction

2. A Lamentation for Israel   Chapter 5:1-3

3. Seek Me and Live   Chapter 5:4-15

4. The Day of the Lord Will Be Fearsome   Chapter 5:16-27

5. The People Are Too Much at Ease   Chapter 6:1-8

6. Total Destruction Is Coming   Chapter 6:9-14

Introduction:

The decimation of Israel. Amos's prediction that Israelite cities under God's judgment would lose 90 percent of their people (Amos 5:3) gives new meaning to the word decimate. The term comes from the Latin word decimare, which means to remove or destroy by one-tenth. The Roman army (among others) practiced decimation on units of soldiers which had committed a major crime, such as mutiny. One tenth of the offenders was chosen by lot for execution.

But we see that instead of every tenth person being killed, one out of ten would be spared. This would leave a handful of survivors to bury the dead. Amos's grim prophecy was fulfilled when Sargon II of Assyria destroyed the cities of Israel (722 B.C.), bringing an end to Israelite kingdom (2 Kings 17:5-6). Most of the survivors were deported to Assyria, while Israel was repopulated with outsiders (2 Kings 17: 6, 24 see Jeremiah 9:16).

Amos's description of Israel is sobering if not downright frightening—they do not know to do right (Amos 3:10). Wickedness overflows the nation like a river. As a result, the people are drowning in sin. They no longer can tell right from wrong. There is no longer a national conscience.

A nation is on the verge of collapse when good and evil look the same. When a question of right and wrong never evens enters the people's minds, then that nation is in desperate trouble. In Israel's case, the enemies were waiting just around the corner (Amos 3:11-12).

Has our nation lost its conscience? Do people call good bad and bad good? Or can we really tell right from wrong? Or worse, do questions of morality concern them? As God's ambassadors we can challenge people to consider their ways and apprise them of their responsibility to fear God. Although we may not be received well, God will honor us for standing up for righteousness.

2 Chronicles 7:14

If my people, which are called by my name, shall humble themselves, and pray, and seek my face, and turn from their wicked ways; then will I hear from heaven, and will forgive their sin, and will heal their land.

Psalm 122:6

Pray for the peace of Jerusalem; they will prosper who love thee.

Lesson Plan 250

The Book of Amos

Chapters 7, 8, & 9

Objective: To give us insight on the judgment of God when He is dealing with disobedience and to gain an understanding of the prophecies and warnings of judgment that Amos addressed to the Northern Kingdom of Israel (around 760 B.C.) for its idolatry, injustice, corruption, and oppression of the poor.

Objective Breakdown:

Introduction

Locust, Fire, and a Plumb Line	Chapter 7:1-9
The Priest Amaziah Opposes Amos	Chapter 7:10-17
A Basket of Fruit	Chapter 8:1-8
Days of Darkness and Morning	Chapter 8:9-14
There Will Be No Hiding from God	Chapter 9:1-4
Israel Will Be Scattered	Chapter 9:5-10
A Promise of Restoration	Chapter 9:11-15

Introduction:

The name Amos means "Burden Bearer." Amos was a prophet of Judah, the Southern Kingdom, with a message to Israel, the Northern Kingdom during the reigns of Uzziah King of Judah (787-735 B.C.) and Jeroboam II, King of Israel (790-749 B.C.). Amos prophecy occurred about 751 B.C.

Home of Amos

Tekoa was the home of Amos located 10 miles South of Jerusalem and 5 miles from Bethlehem on an elevation of 2700 feet overlooking the wilderness of Judea. This is thought to be the same region where eight centuries later John the Baptist grew to manhood. Amos was not a priest or a professional prophet. He was a herdsman and a dresser of sycamore trees.

Jeroboam's reign (Northern Kingdom) had been very successful. The Kingdom had been considerably enlarged (II Kings 14:23-29). Israel was in the high tide of prosperity; but brazen in its **idolatry and reeking in moral rottenness: a land of Swearing, Stealing, Injustice, Oppression, Robbery, Adultery**

and Murder.

It had been some 200 years since the ten tribes had set up the Northern Kingdom, with calf-worship as its religion (II Kings 12:25-33). During part of this time Baal-Worship also had been adopted and many of the abominable practices of Canaanite idolatry were still rampant. Meantime God had sent Elijah, and Elisha and Jonah, but to no avail. Israel hardened in its idolatry and wickedness and was now speeding on to its ruin. God sent Amos and Hosea in a final effort to stay the nation in its mad dash to God's judgment.

Amos' Contemporaries

Amos's, as a boy probably had known Jonah and may have heard tell of his visit to Nineveh. Possibly too he may have known of Elisha and may have heard of him tell of his association with Elijah. Elisha and Jonah were passing off the stage as Amos was coming on. Joel also may have been his contemporary or near predecessor. Hosea was a co-worker with Amos and was the younger. As Amos was closing his work, Isaiah and Micah were beginning theirs.

Doom of Israel and Neighbor Nations

Amos starts with a general impeachment of the whole region, **eight nations, Syria, Philistia, Phoenicia, Edom, Ammon, Moab, Judah, and Israel.** He then centers his attention on Israel. He arranges each nation under the same formula, "for three transgressions, yea for four specifying their particular transgressions. "Captivity" is one of the key words of the book of Amos and within 50 years these predictions were fulfilled.

Chapter 1: We learn of God's judgment on the eight nations. Syria, Philistia, Phoenicia,

Edom, Ammon, Moab, Judah, & Israel (Amos 1:6 through Amos 2:6-16).

Chapter 2: We found that Israel was selling the righteous for silver and the poor for a pair

of sandals (Amos 2:6).

Chapter 3: We learn that a nation will be on the verge of collapse when good and evil

look the same, when right and wrong no longer enter the people's mind.

Chapter 4: We see the rich women of Samaria Denounced ("you cow of Bashan").

Chapter 5: A Lamentation for Israel (90% of their men will fall in battle).

Chapter 6: We see that the people's lifestyle did not include God. All pleasure

oriented.

Locust, Fire, and a Plumb Line   Chapter 7:1-9

Note: We Must always BE LOYAL & OBEDIENT TO GOD!!

2 Chronicles 7:14

If my people, which are called by my name, shall humble themselves, and pray, and seek my face, and turn from their wicked ways; then will I hear from heaven, and will forgive their sin, and will heal their land.

Psalm 122:6

Pray for the peace of Jerusalem; they will prosper who love thee.

The Book of Obadiah

Scripture Focus Chapter 1

Objective: To gain an understanding of the Lord's judgment on Edom in the shortest book of the Old Testament.

Objective Breakdown:

1. Introduction

2. The Lord Will Bring Down Edom   Chapter 1:1-4

3. Edom Will Be Robbed and Plundered   Chapter 1:5-9

4. Edom Rejoiced About Judah's Downfall   Chapter 1:10-14

5. God's People Will Be Blessed   Chapter 1:15-21

Lesson Plan 251

The Book of Obadiah

Chapter 1

Objective: To gain an understanding of the Lord's judgment on Edom in the shortest book of the Old Testament.

Objective Breakdown:

1. Introduction

2. The Lord Will Bring Down Edom   Chapter 1:1-4

3. Edom Will Be Robbed and Plundered   Chapter 1:5-9

4. Edom Rejoiced About Judah's Downfall   Chapter 1:10-14

5. God's People Will Be Blessed   Chapter 1:15-21

Introduction:

The name Obadiah means worshiper of the Lord or servant. Obadiah, the shortest book in the Old Testament, tell a big story that spans the Bible from the time of the patriarchs to the last days of the Old Testament, and even into the early days of the New Testament. What begins in the womb as a rivalry between twins; matures into a long-standing feud between two nations—Israel and Edom. One way to understand the book is to see it in terms of a five-act historical drama.

Act 1: The birth of two nations. In many ways, Obadiah actually begins in Genesis with the account of Jacob grabbing the heel of his brother Esau as they emerge from their mother's womb (Genesis 25:24-26). Jacob continues his grasping, scheming ways by obtaining the family's birthright and father's blessing which were Esau's (Genesis 25:27-34; 27:1-40). For several years Jacob takes refuge from his vengeful brother, but eventually they are reconciled. Esau settles in Edom and gives rise to the Edomites (Genesis 36:1-43). Jacob remains in Canaan and gives rise to the nation of Israel. Thus, the stage is set for the fulfillment of the Lord's word to Rebekah that the "older shall serve the younger" (Genesis 25:23).

Act II: As the Israelites come from Egypt and travel along the King's Highway bound for Moab and Canaan, they arrive at a portion of the road controlled by Edom. Moses petitions for a right of safe passages, but he and his people are turned away (Numbers 20:14-21). The Israelites are forced to take a longer, southern route, resulting in many more hardships and setbacks.

Act III: The Israelites take control of Canaan and eventually establish a kingdom. Their first king, Saul, harasses the Edomites (1 Samuel 14:47). Then King David tries to exterminate them (2 Samuel 8:13-14; 1 Kings 11:15-16). Then another king, Solomon, exploits their land (2 Samuel 9:26-28). These oppressions occur despite a prohibition in the Law against "abhorring" the Edomites (Deuteronomy 23:7-8). The feud continues into the time of the divided kingdom. During the reign in Judah of Jehoshaphat, the armed forces of Edom, Moab, and Amon form an alliance and for the shallows of the Dead Sea to stage a sneak on Judah (2 Chronicles 20:22-23). Later Edom rebels against King Jehoram (2 Kings 8:20-22). Later still, King Amaziah of Judah slaughters 10,000 Edomites, as if in remembrance of David (2 Kings 14:2; 2 Chronicles 25:11-25).

Act IV: The Edomites gloat. With the passage of time, the Lord begins to punish His people for their persistent rebellion against His law, and especially for their idolatries. The Assyrian Empire rises and eventually overruns Israel (722 B.C.). Then the Babylonians take control and gradually take Judah into captivity. Finally, Jerusalem is viciously destroyed following a long siege (587 B.C.). The Edomites react to Judah's downfall with great celebration (Psalms 137:7). They gloat over Jerusalem's destruction and deride the survivors. They gradually nibble away at Judah's territory during the years of Babylonian domination, they gladly occupy more of its land by permission of Nebuchadnezzar. It may be this attitude of gloating that Obadiah condemns in his prophecy. Certainly, Jeremiah alludes to this period when he predicts that soon it will be Edom's turn for judgment (Jeremiah 49:17-18; Lamentation 4:21).

Act V: In an ironic postscript to the Old Testament record, the Edomites are eventually driven out of Edom by the Nabateans, a tribe from northern Arabia. The refugees settle in the Negev, south of Judah, where they come to be called Idumeans. In the second century B.C. They are subdued by a Maccabean Jew named John Hyrcanus, who compels them to be circumcised. One of the descendants of the Idumeans proselytes is Herod, a politically astute leader whom the Romans install as "king" of Judea (37-4 B.C.). His family runs Jewish Palestine for the Romans until the destruction of Jerusalem in A.D. 70.

Lessons learned. Nations are ultimately brothers and sisters, and conflicts between nations are ultimately deep-rooted conflicts between family. What begins as a rivalry between two brothers ends up a perpetual feud between two nations.

2 Chronicles 7:14

If my people, which are called by my name, shall humble themselves, and pray, and seek my face, and turn from their wicked ways; then will I hear from heaven, and will forgive their sin, and will heal their land.

Psalm 122:6

Pray for the peace of Jerusalem; they will prosper who love thee.

The Book of Jonah

Scripture Focus Chapters 1-4

Objective: To get an understanding of the prophet who survived being swallowed by a large   fish before preaching a message of repentance to people in Nineveh.

Objective Breakdown:

1. Introduction

2. Jonah Tries to Get Away from God   Chapter 1:1-9

3. Jonah Asks to Be Thrown into the Sea   Chapter 1:10-16

4. Jonah in the Belly of a Great Fish   Chapter 1:17

5. Jonah in the Belly of a Great Fish (cont.)   Chapter 2:1-10

6. Nineveh Repents   Chapter 3:1-10

7. Jonah's Anger and God's Compassion   Chapter 4:1-11

Lesson Plan 252

The Book of Jonah

Chapters 1, 2, 3, & 4

Objective: To learn to love people you dislike and to get an understanding of the prophet who survived being swallowed by a large fish before preaching a message of repentance to people in Nineveh.

Objective Breakdown:

1. Introduction

2. Jonah Tries to Get Away from God   Chapter 1:1-9

3. Jonah Asks to be Thrown into the Sea   Chapter 1:10-16

4. Jonah in the Belly of a Great Fish   Chapter 1:17-2:10

5. Nineveh Repents   Chapter 3:1-10

6. Jonah's Anger and God's Compassion   Chapter 4:1-11

Introduction:

Nineveh was a prominent Assyrian city on the east bank of the Tigris River about 280 miles north of Babylon. It was founded by Nimrod, along with Rehoboth Ir, Calah, and Resen (Genesis 10:11-12), forming a massive quadrangle 60 mile wide.

It rivaled Babylon for beauty and splendor with its royal palaces, temples, broad streets, public gardens, and impressive library containing more than 26,000 clay tablets—one of the largest in the ancient world.

Defended by an outer wall and an inner wall 100 feet high and fifty foot wide. It was irrigated by the Khasr River, whose flow was controlled by a dam built by Sennacherib (705-681 B.C.), and also by a large water aqueduct that carried water from a second dam 30 miles away.

Target of prophecies by Zephaniah (Zephaniah 2:13-15) and Nahum (Nahum 1:1; 3:1), who warned of the city's ultimate destruction. Nineveh was destroyed in 612 B.C. by a siege of Babylonians, Scythians, and Medes who penetrated its defenses when sudden floods eroded the walls. Nineveh quickly became a mound of ruins.

Jonah played a part as a prophet toward the end of Israel's existence as a nation. His story has an important part in God's story because in the middle of all the judging and deporting, worshiping other gods, God gave him a message for the enemies of Yahweh. God offered people who did not know Him the same deal He offered the people He had chosen for His own centuries before. Jonah's sermon was only one sentence long: "Forty more days and Nineveh will be overturned" (Jonah 3:4), but it had the impact of a weeklong Billy Graham crusade that had come to town.

Jonah felt happy to share the Good News with his own people, but it irked him to know that those who were not God's chosen would get the same reward for their repentance as would Israel. In the end, God taught him a lesson about God's Grace and mercy and concern for all people, not just those who are "His."

2 Chronicles 7:14

If my people, which are called by my name, shall humble themselves, and pray, and seek my face, and turn from their wicked ways; then will I hear from heaven, and will forgive their sin, and will heal their land.

Psalm 122:6

Pray for the peace of Jerusalem; they will prosper who love thee.

The Book of Micah

Scripture Focus Chapters 1-7

Objective: To gain insight on the prophet Micah and his prophecies concerning Samaria and Jerusalem.

Objective Breakdown:

1. Introduction

2. Samaria Will Become a Heap of Ruins   Chapter 1:1-7

3. Mourning for the People's Misfortune   Chapter 1:8-16

4. The Israelites Will Pay for Their Sins   Chapter 2:1-9

5. False Prophets and the True Shepherd   Chapter 2:10-13

6. God Denounces Wicked Leaders   Chapter 3:1-4

7. False Prophets Will Be Judged   Chapter 3:5-12

8. A Vision of Restoration   Chapter 4:1-8

9. Exile Will Feel Like Birth Pangs   Chapter 4:9-13

10. A Shepherd Will Come from Bethlehem   Chapter 5:1-5a

11. A Shepherd Will Come from Bethlehem (cont.)   Chapter 5:5b

12. The Assyrians Will Be Repelled   Chapter 5:6

13. Israel Will Be Scattered   Chapter 5:7-9

14. God Will Have Vengeance   Chapter 5:10-15

15. God's Complaint Against His People   Chapter 6:1-7

16. What the Lord Requires   Chapter 6:8

17. Israel's Injustice Will Be Punished   Chapter 6:9-16

18. Violence and Betrayal Fill the Land   Chapter 7:1-7

19. Jerusalem Will Be Restored   Chapter 7:8-13

20. God Will Again Show Compassion   Chapter 7:14-20

Lesson Plan 253

The Book of Micah

Chapters 1, 2, 3, & 4

Objective: To gain insight on the Prophet Micah and his prophecies concerning Samaria and Jerusalem.

Objective Breakdown:

1. Introduction

2. Samaria Will Become a Heap of Ruins   Chapter 1:1-7

3. Mourning for the People's Misfortune   Chapter 1:8-16

4. The Israelites Will Pay for Their Sins   Chapter 2:1-9

5. False Prophets and the True Shepherd   Chapter 2:10-13

6. God Denounces Wicked Leaders   Chapter 3:1-4

7. False Prophets Will Be Judged   Chapter 3:5-12

8. A Vision of Restoration   Chapter 4:1-8

9. Exile Will Feel Like Birth Pangs   Chapter 4:9-13

Introduction:

The three kings of Micah. Micah delivered his prophecies to Judah under three different kings (Micah 1:1). Two feared and served the Lord, the other did not. Here are the men who set the pace for the nation to which Micah was called to speak:

Jotham (750-735 B.C.) came to power even before he was formally crowned King, when his father Uzziah (also known as Azariah) was found to be a leper (2 Kings 15:5; 2 Chronicles 26:1). Like his father Jotham feared God. He extended the holdings of Judah, built, and fortified several cities; and fought off the Ammonites (2 Kings 15:32-38; 2 Chronicles 27:1-9).

Ahaz (735-715 B.C.) the son of Jotham was an evil ruler (2 Chronicles 28:1). Following his father's death, he reinstituted the practice of idolatry, including child sacrifice, and began serving the gods of the Syrians after they and the Israelites slaughtered and captured hundreds of thousands of his people (2 Chronicles 28:1-25). He appealed to the Assyrians for help during the time of trouble, causing Judah to become a tributary to Tiglath-Pileser. As a result, Ahaz began serving Assyrian idols (2 Kings 16:1-18), and not even Isaiah's warnings could cause him to change his ways (Isaiah 7:10-17).

Hezekiah (Isaiah 715-686 B.C.) was one of the outstanding rulers of Judah, despite his background as Ahaz's son (see 2 Chronicles 29:1). He combined exceptional faith with vigorous political leadership and spiritual reforms (2 Kings 18-20; 2 Chronicles 29-32). Two notable incidents in his life were surviving a siege of Assyrian troops sent by King Sennacherib, and miraculously recovering from a terminal illness (Isaiah 38:1-8).

2 Chronicles 7:14

If my people, which are called by my name, shall humble themselves, and pray, and seek my face, and turn from their wicked ways; then will I hear from heaven, and will forgive their sin, and will heal their land.

Psalm 122:6

Pray for the peace of Jerusalem; they will prosper who love thee.

Lesson Plan 254

The Book of Micah

Chapters 5, 6, & 7

Objective: To gain insight on the prophet Micah and his prophecies concerning Samaria and Jerusalem.

Objective Breakdown:

Introduction:

What would you say about a country where justice is for sale, truth depends on what you can afford and spirituality I determined by your ability to pay? You might say that such a country has sold its soul. When even the moral values of a culture are defined in terms of money, then the society is in deep trouble.

Judah was a deeply troubled society in Micah's day. Three categories of leaders—the Judges, the priests, and the prophets—had put their services up for sale (Micah 3:11). The issue was not that they were being paid: obviously they needed money to live. But they corrupted their offices by allowing money to distort their leadership. Rather than say what was true and right they said whatever they were paid to say. They grew wealthy from their positions, but their integrity went bankrupt. Do we recognize anything in our current culture similar to this?

The amazing thing is that these leaders believed the Lord would continue to underwrite their hypocrisy. They brushed off the warnings of an impending invasion by a foreign army that Micah and other prophets were giving "Is not the Lord among us?" They replied, "no harm can come upon us." But they were sorely mistaken. The Lord had written them off in their impenitence. He was not about to allow them to go on violating His law and still enjoy peace and affluence.

Do you see any parallels between ancient Judah and our own society today?

2 Chronicles 7:14

If my people, which are called by my name, shall humble themselves, and pray, and seek my face, and turn from their wicked ways; then will I hear from heaven, and will forgive their sin, and will heal their land.

Psalm 122:6

Pray for the peace of Jerusalem; they will prosper who love thee.

The Book of Nahum

Scripture Focus Chapters 1-3

Objective: To gain insight on the Prophet Nahum in his denouncing the entire culture of the bloody city of Nineveh and their sins against God and humanity.

Objective Breakdown:

1. Introduction

2. God Will Have His Way   Chapter 1:1-11

3. God Will Cut Off Judah's Enemies   Chapter 1:12-15

4. Nineveh Besieged   Chapter 2:1-7

5. The Lord Stands Against Nineveh   Chapter 2:8-13

6. "Woe to the Bloody City"   Chapter 3:1-7

7. Nineveh Will Fall Like Thebes   Chapter 3:8-13

8. God's Challenge to Assyria   Chapter 3:14-19

Lesson Plan 255

The Book of Nahum

Chapters 1-3

Objective: To gain insight on the Prophet Nahum in his denouncing the entire culture of the bloody city of Nineveh and their sins against God and humanity.

Objective Breakdown:

1. Introduction

2. God Will Have His Way   Chapter 1:1-11

3. God Will Cut Off Judah's Enemies   Chapter 1:12-15

4. Nineveh Besieged   Chapter 2:1-7

5. The Lord Stands Against Nineveh   Chapter 2:8-13

6. "Woe to the Bloody City"   Chapter 3:1-7

7. Nineveh Will Fall Like Thebes   Chapter 3:8-13

8. God's Challenge to Assyria   Chapter 3:14-19

Introduction:

Nahum's prophecy was given sometime between 663 and 612 B.C. The Middle East was dominated during that period by Assyria, whose capital was Nineveh. Possibly speaking from southern Judah, the prophet Micah predicted the city's downfall, which eventually occurred at the hands of the Babylonians, Medes, and Scythians (Nahum 2:6-8). To illustrate what Nineveh's fall would be like, Nahum pointed to No-Amon (Thebes) in Egypt (Nineveh 3: 8-10), a well defended city which the Assyrians had destroyed. Nahum's world was essentially the same as that of his predecessor Jonah.

Even the patience of God has its limits. He will not allow sin to go unchecked forever. Sooner or later, He will deal with evil and those who commit it, and when He does, His wrath is likely to come rather swiftly. Sometimes in judgment God Removes His restraining hand, exposing people and nations to their own unbridled destruction of each other.

Nahum denounced Nineveh as the "bloody city," an indication of how notorious the Assyrians were for their crimes against humanity. As Micah's prophecy draws to a close, he begins a psalm or hymn of praise (Micah 7:8), praising the Lord for His watchful protection over His people. Looking into the future Micah can foresee a time of restoration, when the Lord will gather His people Israel as a shepherd gathers his sheep (Micah 7:14) and the ruined city of Jerusalem will stand again (Micah 7:11-12).

2 Chronicles 7:14

If my people, which are called by my name, shall humble themselves, and pray, and seek my face, and turn from their wicked ways; then will I hear from heaven, and will forgive their sin, and will heal their land.

Psalm 122:6

Pray for the peace of Jerusalem; they will prosper who love thee.

The Book of Habakkuk

Scripture Focus Chapters 1-3

Objective: To gain an understanding of Habakkuk and the impact of the Lord's declaration to him that "the just shall live his faith."

Objective Breakdown:

1. Introduction

2. Habakkuk Cries Out to God   Chapter 1:1-4

3. God Is Raising Up the Chaldeans   Chapter 1:5-11

4. The Prophet Questions God   Chapter 1:12-17

5. The Prophet Questions God (cont.)   Chapter 2:1

6. The Just Shall Live by Faith   Chapter 2:2-4

7. A Taunt Against Judah's Enemy   Chapter 2:5-17

8. Idolaters Will Feel God's Wrath   Chapter 2:18-20

9. Habakkuk's Psalm   Chapter 3:1-9

10. God Fights for His People   Chapter 3:10-16

11. "I Will Rejoice in the Lord"   Chapter 3:17-19

Lesson Plan 256

The Book of Habakkuk

Chapters 1, 2, & 3

Objective: To gain an understanding of Habakkuk and the impact of the Lord's declaration to him that "the just shall live his faith."

Objective Breakdown:

1. Introduction

2. Habakkuk Cries Out to God   Chapter 1:1-4

3. God Is Raising Up the Chaldeans   Chapter 1:5-11

4. The Prophet Questions God   Chapter 1:12-17

5. The Prophet Questions God (cont.)   Chapter 2:1

6. The Just Shall Live by Faith   Chapter 2:2-4

7. A Taunt Against Judah's Enemy   Chapter 2:5-17

8. Idolaters Will Feel God's Wrath   Chapter 2:18-20

9. Habakkuk's Psalm   Chapter 3:1-9

10. God Fights for His People   Chapter 3:10-16

11. "I Will Rejoice in the Lord"   Chapter 3:17-19

Introduction:

Questioning God. Some people believe that human beings should never question the ways of God. Some even feel that it borders on sin to ask God, "Why?" But the Book of Habakkuk counters that idea. It is filled with a prophet's perplexing questions—and the Lord's penetrating answers. God never seems to reproach His servant for asking too many fundamental questions:

Why does the Lord seem so unresponsive to injustice and violence that Habakkuk sees around him (Habakkuk 1:2-3)?

How can God use the vicious, oppressive idolatrous Babylonians (Chaldeans) to judge His people (Habakkuk 1:12-17)?

Habakkuk was not unlike many people today who are troubled by world around them. They too, sometimes wonder, where is God? Why doesn't He do something about all the pain and suffering, the injustice, and oppression, the wars and diseases that destroy humanity? If He is there, why doesn't He speak? If He is powerful, why doesn't He act? If He is loving, why doesn't He intervene? Habakkuk shows that questions like these are as old as the seventh century B.C.

Well so are the answers. While God may not explain everything to our satisfaction—nor are we capable of understanding everything He has told us—He assures us just as He assured Habakkuk, that His ways are just and righteous. "The just shall live by faith" (Habakkuk 2:4). This truth applies universally, as Paul and other writers of the New Testament realized (Romans 1:17, Galatians 3:11; Hebrews 10:38). In the end the ultimate answer is to trust God.

2 Chronicles 7:14

If my people, which are called by my name, shall humble themselves, and pray, and seek my face, and turn from their wicked ways; then will I hear from heaven, and will forgive their sin, and will heal their land.

Psalm 122:6

Pray for the peace of Jerusalem; they will prosper who love thee.

The Book of Zephaniah

Scripture Focus Chapters 1-3

Objective: To gain an understanding and insight of Zephaniah's warning of imminent judgment to the nation of Judah, focusing on what he called "the Day of the Lord."

Objective Breakdown:

1. Introduction

2. A Vision of Utter Destruction   Chapter 1:1-6

3. The Day of the Lord's Sacrifice   Chapter 1:7-9

4. Jerusalem Will Experience Punishment   Chapter 1:10-18

5. A Call to Repentance   Chapter 2:1-3

6. Judgment on the Philistines   Chapter 2:4-7

7. Judgment on Moab and Ammon   Chapter 2:8-11

8. Judgment on Ethiopia and Assyria   Chapter 2:12-15

9. Jerusalem Has Rebelled Despite Warnings   Chapter 3:1-7

10. A Remnant Will Be Restored   Chapter 3:8-13

11. The People Will Have God in Their Midst   Chapter 3:14-20

Lesson Plan 257

The Book of Zephaniah

Chapters 1, 2, & 3

Objective: To remind God's people that they are to resist pride and seek Him in humility.

Objective Breakdown:

1. Introduction

2. A Vision of Utter Destruction   Chapter 1:1-6

3. The Day of the Lord's Sacrifice   Chapter 1:7-9

4. Jerusalem Will Experience Punishment   Chapter 1:10-18

5. A Call to Repentance   Chapter 2:1-3

6. Judgment on the Philistines   Chapter 2:4-7

7. Judgment on Moab and Ammon   Chapter 2:8-11

8. Judgment on Ethiopia and Assyria   Chapter 2:12-15

9. Jerusalem Has Rebelled Despite Warnings   Chapter 3:1-7

10. A Remnant Will Be Restored   Chapter 3:8-13

11. The People Will Have God in Their Midst   Chapter 3:14-20

12. Need for Humility   Chapter 1:12-15

13. Call to Humility   Chapter 2:1-3

14. Benefits of Humility   Chapter 3:11-12

Introduction:

The Minor Prophets

The last twelve books of the Old Testament are known today as the Minor Prophets. The name was intended to distinguish them from the four "major" (that is longer) prophetic books

Isaiah 66, Jeremiah 52, Ezekiel 48, and Daniel 12.

In modern culture, where bigger is seen as better, and where celebrity is taken for significance, anything called "minor" is subtly thought of as less important. Thus, the Minor Prophets are sometimes treated as the "minor league" prophets, as if those who wrote them were on God's "second team."

That would be a grave misperception. There is nothing minor about these books. On the contrary, they play a major role in declaring God's Word not only to the Israelites and other nations of the world, but to us as well. By reading them, we gain additional perspective on the sins that God hates, and the faith that He honors.

The Minor prophets include: Hosea, Joel, Amos, Obadiah, Jonah, Micah, Nahum, Habakkuk, Zephaniah, Haggai, Zechariah, and Malachi.

The Minor prophets include:			Message to:
Hosea	14 chapters	Time Frame 760-700 B.C.	Israel
Joel	3 chapters	Time Frame 835 B.C.	Judah
Amos	9 chapters	Time Frame 760-753 B.C.	Israel
Obadiah	1 chapter	Time Frame 840 B.C.	Edom
Jonah	4 chapters	Time Frame 760 B.C.	Israel
Micah	7 chapters	Time Frame 735-710 B.C.	Israel & Judah
Nahum	3 chapters	Time Frame 660 B.C.	Nineveh
Habakkuk	3 chapters	Time Frame 607 B.C.	Judah
Zephaniah	**3 chapters**	**Time Frame 630 B.C.**	**Judah**
Haggai	2 chapters	Time Frame 520 B. C.	Jerusalem
Zechariah	14 chapters	Time Frame 520-470 B.C.	Jerusalem
Malachi	4 chapters	Time Frame 432-425 B.C.	Jerusalem

The main theme of the Book of Zephaniah is the Coming Day of the Lord. God was going to judge all the earth, including Judah, for its sins and idolatry. The coming Day of the Lord would be more than a day of defeat for Judah's enemies. That day also would bring judgement against Jerusalem, and Judah as well and against all others who sinned against the Lord (Zephaniah 1:1-2:3).

The Day of the Lord would be a day of judgment against those nations that surrounded Judah and who had been enemies of God's people: Philistia to the West, Moab and Ammon to the east, Ethiopia to the South, and Assyria to the northeast (Zephaniah 2:4-3:8).

The Day of the Lord was not just a day of Judgment. God also promised deliverance and restoration to those who called on the name of the Lord in repentance and humility. God would restore His people after the judgment. But greater than that fact was God's promise of future deliverance and restoration of all God's people at the final Day of the Lord. People of any age (era) can escape God's judgment if they resist their pride and seek the Lord in humility (Zephaniah 3:9-20).

2 Chronicles 7:14

If my people, which are called by my name, shall humble themselves, and pray, and seek my face, and turn from their wicked ways; then will I hear from heaven, and will forgive their sin, and will heal their land.

Psalm 122:6

Pray for the peace of Jerusalem; they will prosper who love thee.

Psalm 66:18-20

18. If I regard iniquity in my heart, the Lord will not hear me:

19. But verily God hath heard me; he hath attended to the voice of my prayer.

20. Blessed be God, which hath not turned away my prayer, nor his mercy from me.

The Book of Haggai

Scripture Focus Chapters 1-2

Objective: To remind God's people that they are to give priority to carrying out His work and to learn of the "earth shattering events" that will rock the nations of the world that Haggai had prophesied.

Objective Breakdown:

1. Introduction

2. Haggai Urges Rebuilding of the Temple   Chapter 1:1-11

3. Work on God's House Is Renewed   Chapter 1:12-15

4. The Lord Affirms His Presence   Chapter 2:1-9

5. Turn from Uncleanness and Be Blessed   Chapter 2:10-19

6. A Promise to Zerubbabel   Chapter 2:20-23

Lesson Plan 258

The Book of Haggai

Chapters 1 & 2

Objective: To remind God's people that they are to give priority to carrying out His work and to learn of the "earth shattering events" that will rock the nations of the world that Haggai had prophesied.

Objective Breakdown:

1. Introduction

2. Haggai Urges Rebuilding of the Temple   Chapter 1:1-11

3. Work on God's House is Renewed   Chapter 1:12-15

4. The Lord Affirms His Presence   Chapter 2:1-9

5. Turn from Uncleanness and Be Blessed   Chapter 2:10-19

6. A Promise to Zerubbabel   Chapter 2:20-23

Introduction:

Unfinished business. Spiritual growth is often likened to a journey. A person comes to faith and the begins walking with God, step by step, year by year, traveling into ever-higher regions of spiritual maturity. However, for many people, the journey seems to diminish along the way.

The people in Jerusalem in Haggai's day had an unfinished project around 538 B.C. they had returned from Babylon and had enthusiastically laid a foundation for a new temple with great fanfare. Yet two years into the project, the work came to a standstill. The reasons why may or may not have been legitimate, but for16 years nothing more was done. The people went about the rest of their lives, making a living, establishing families, building houses, setting up businesses—but the temple remained unfinished.

Finally, the Lord sent the prophet Haggai to tell the people to consider their ways and get back to work on the temple (Haggai 1:6-8). They needed to complete what they started. Not only did their spiritual lives depend on it, but their physical lives as well (Haggai 1:9-11).

Whatever steps are needed to get your spiritual life back on track, you need to finish your spiritual journey (Hebrews 6:11).

The Minor prophets include: Hosea, Joel, Amos, Obadiah, Jonah, Micah, Nahum, Habakkuk, Zephaniah,

Haggai, Zechariah, and Malachi

The Minor prophets include: Message to:

Hosea	14 chapters	Time Frame	760-700 B.C.	Northern Kingdom
Joel	3 chapters	Time Frame	835 B.C.	Judah
Amos	9 chapters	Time Frame	760-753 B.C.	Northern Kingdom
Obadiah	1 chapter	Time Frame	840 B.C.	Edom
Jonah	4 chapters	Time Frame	760 B.C.	Nineveh
Micah	7 chapters	Time Frame	735-710 B.C.	Northern & Southern Kingdoms
Nahum	3 chapters	Time Frame	660 B.C.	Nineveh
Habakkuk	3 chapters	Time Frame	607 B.C.	Southern Kingdom
Zephaniah	3 chapters	Time Frame	630 B.C.	Southern Kingdom
Haggai	**2 chapters**	**Time Frame**	**520 B.C.**	**Jerusalem**
Zechariah	14 chapters	Time Frame	520-470 B.C.	Jerusalem
Malachi	4 chapters	Time Frame	432-425 B.C.	Jerusalem

Haggai's name means "seed of Babylon," perhaps indicating that he was born during captivity.

The Book of Haggai consists of two chapters and covers the time frame of 520 B.C. He delivered four messages encouraging the leaders and people of Jerusalem to finish rebuilding the temple. His first message addressed to Zerubbabel and Joshua asked why the Israelites had built their houses but failed to build God's House. Haggai diagnosed the peoples lack of physical necessities as God's judgment for their having the wrong priority. God stirred up the spirits of Zerubbabel and Joshua and the people. They began work on the temple, assured of God's presence among them (Haggai 1:1-15).

The prophets second message was a word of encouragement (Haggai 2:1-9). The third message began with two questions: (1) can holiness in one object be transferred to another object? The answer was "no." (2) can uncleanness in one object be transferred to another object? The answer was "yes." The prophet's point was that the people of Israel had become defiled spiritually and therefore whatever they did or offered to the Lord was defiled. They resumed building the temple and God promised to bless them with a bountiful harvest (Haggai 2:10-19). The fourth message was a promise that God would establish a new kingdom and would bless Zerubbabel.

Haggai's job appears to have been to keep the leaders of Jerusalem and their "employees" focused not only on the actual rebuilding project, but on the value and importance of serving God rather than merely pursuing a comfortable lifestyle for themselves (Haggai 1:6-9). He essentially called them to a long-term view of life and work rather than a concern for immediate, short-term outcomes.

Evaluate your Priorities	Chapter 1:7-9
Follow Godly Leaders	Chapter 1:12-15
Experiencing Life's Fullness	Chapter 2:15-19

The prophet Haggai acted like a consultant for God in helping the stalled project of rebuilding the temple to get going again. His entire "contract" called for about four months of work, as follows:

August 29 520 B.C. presented status report of the situation and helped the people to see why failure to complete the temple was a problem (Haggai 1:1-11).

Reaffirmed the Lord's commitment to help the people; construction was restarted (Haggai 1:12-15).

Reviewed the long-term significance of the project, promising that the new temple would have greater glory than the old; this message brought hope and encouragement to the project team and its leaders (Haggai 2:1-9).

Announcing that God would start blessing the people again in light of the work being accomplished (Haggai 2:10-19).

Presented a message to Zerubbabel concerning God's plan to "shake heaven and earth," and the news that Zerubbabel was chosen as a part of God's purpose (Haggai 2:20-23).

2 Chronicles 7:14

If my people, which are called by my name, shall humble themselves, and pray, and seek my face, and turn from their wicked ways; then will I hear from heaven, and will forgive their sin, and will heal their land.

Psalm 122:6

Pray for the peace of Jerusalem; they will prosper who love thee.

Psalm 66:18-20

18. If I regard iniquity in my heart, the Lord will not hear me:

19. But verily God hath heard me; he hath attended to the voice of my prayer.

20. Blessed be God, which hath not turned away my prayer, nor his mercy from me.

The Book of Zechariah

Scripture Focus Chapters 1-14

Objective: To gain an understanding and insight of Zechariah's vision of a New Jerusalem, the activity of Angels and the accuser of God's people—Satan.

Objective Breakdown:

Lesson Plan 259

The Book of Zechariah

Chapters 1, 2, 3, & 4

Objective: To gain an understanding and insight of Zechariah's vision of a New Jerusalem, the activity of Angels and the accuser of God's People—Satan.

Objective Breakdown:

1. Introduction

2. Zechariah Urges Repentance from Sin   Chapter 1:1-6

3. A Man Riding Among Myrtle Trees   Chapter 1:7-17

4. Four Horns and Four Craftsmen   Chapter 1:18-21

5. A Man Measuring Jerusalem   Chapter 2:1-13

6. Joshua the High Priest Before the Lord   Chapter 3:1-10

7. A Lampstand and Two Olive Trees   Chapter 4:1-14

Introduction:

Zechariah envisioned a new Jerusalem without walls. This would have been unthinkable in Zechariah's day, a city without walls was a city without defense. Indeed, at the time of Zechariah's prophecy (519 B.C.), Jerusalem was in great distress and reproach (Nehemiah 1:3) because its walls were still in ruin from the siege of the Babylonians about 70 years earlier.

Walls imply a hostile world, a world divided into them and us. So, with God pledging Himself to be a wall of fire around her (Zechariah 2:5) the safety of the new Jerusalem would be safe. No wonder so many people want to live there (Zechariah 2:5), the safety of the new Jerusalem will be secure. Zechariah's vision is consistent with the prophecies of Isaiah, Haggai, and other prophets who foresaw God's new kingdom as a place that would be open to anyone from any background (Isaiah 66:18-23; Haggai 2:6-7). The nations and families of the earth will come together and re-inhabit the Holy city in safety (Zechariah 14:10-11; 16-17).

The reality of Angels. The book of Zechariah contains more references to angels than almost any other book of the Old Testament. The Bible indicates that angels are neither figurative nor mythological, but real spiritual beings who serve God and His people. However, there is one angel who has fallen and has taken one third of the angels of Heaven with him. His name is Lucifer or Satan. He is our mortal enemy and the enemy of God's people.

Who is Satan (Zechariah 3:1-2)? Scripture instructs us about the nature and activity of this evil angel, who is ceaselessly opposed to God, God's creation, and God's people. God wants us to be aware and be alert so that we are not caught off guard by his schemes.

He is called "the devil," means false witness or malicious accuser. This term occurs 35 times in the New King James translation of the Bible, always in the New Testament. Satan regularly accuses believers before God, seeking to tear down their sense of well-being and wear down their strength through guilt (Job1:6-11; Ephesians 4:27; 6:11; Revelation 12:10).

Satan specializes in deceit (Genesis 3:1-7), sometimes masquerading as angel of light as though he is representing God (2 Corinthians 11:14). He is the father of lies (John 8:44). Paul and John further illuminate this characteristic deception (1 Timothy 3:6-7; Revelation 20:10).

Satan is a tempter, seeking to draw people into activities that are disobedient to God and destructive to them (Matthew 4:1-11; 1 Corinthians 10:13; 1 Thessalonians 3:5). Satan has a great deal of influence on this world. Three times Jesus described him in Scripture as the ruler of this world (John 12:31; 14:30; 16:11). Paul used similar expressions (2 Corinthians 4:4; Ephesians 2:2).

How then should we respond to this dangerous enemy?

We need to remind ourselves that Satan has been defeated by the death and resurrection of Christ, and therefore we need not to submit or fear him (Hebrews 2:14-15; 1 John 3:8; Revelation 20:10). Our Lord Jesus Christ is familiar with his enticements and has met him head on and won (Luke 4:1-13; Hebrews 4:15).

We are to resist the Satan at all times. He will flee when we do that (James 4:7; 1 Peter 5:8-9).

2 Chronicles 7:14

If my people, which are called by my name, shall humble themselves, and pray, and seek my face, and turn from their wicked ways; then will I hear from heaven, and will forgive their sin, and will heal their land.

Psalm 122:6

Pray for the peace of Jerusalem; they will prosper who love thee.

Lesson Plan 260

The Book of Zechariah

Chapters 5, 6, 7, & 8

Objective: To gain an understanding and insight of Zechariah's vision of a New Jerusalem, the activity of Angels and the accuser of God's People—Satan.

Objective Breakdown:

1	Introduction	
2.	A Flying Scroll	Chapter 5:1-4
3.	A Woman in a Basket	Chapter 5:5-11
4.	Four Chariots	Chapter 6:1-8
5.	A Symbolic Crowning of the High Priest	Chapter 6:9-15
6.	Fasting Should Be for the Lord's Sake	Chapter 7:1-7
7.	True Justice Is What the Lord Wants	Chapter 7:8-14
8.	Glory Is Predicted for Jerusalem	Chapter 8:1-10
9.	A Day of Blessing and Plenty Is Coming	Chapter 8:11-17
10.	The Nations Will Honor the Jews	Chapter 8:18-23

Introduction:

The parables of Zechariah. A parable is a truth wrapped in a memorable story of word pictures. It could be fictional, dramatized, or a result of a vision. Jesus gave much of His teachings through parables so did many of the Old Testament prophets, including Zechariah. He saw eight visions which can be understood much like parables:

A Man and Horses Among the Myrtle Trees (Zechariah1:8-17) indicating that the Lord would again be merciful to Jerusalem.

The Four Horns and Four Craftsmen (Zechariah 1:18-20) showed that the Babylonians and others who scattered Judah would be cast out.

The Man with a Measuring Line (Zechariah 2:1-2) promised that God would be a protective wall of fire around Jerusalem.

The Cleansing of Joshua's garments (Zechariah 3:1-10) illustrated the redemptive work that God would do for His people.

The Golden Lampstand and Olive Trees (Zechariah 4:1-14) symbolized the way the Lord was going to empower His people by the Holy Spirit.

The Flying Scroll (Zechariah 5:1-4) indicated that dishonesty is cursed.

The Woman in the Basket (Zechariah 5:5-11) illustrated thee removal of wickedness.

The Four Chariots (Zechariah 6:1-8) showed that the spirits off Heaven would execute judgment on the whole earth.

Note:

Jeremiah and Ezekiel were two other prophets who used parables to communicate their message (Jeremiah 18:1-10; Ezekiel 15:1-8).

2 Chronicles 7:14

If my people, which are called by my name, shall humble themselves, and pray, and seek my face, and turn from their wicked ways; then will I hear from heaven, and will forgive their sin, and will heal their land.

Psalm 122:6

Pray for the peace of Jerusalem; they will prosper who love thee.

Lesson Plan 261

The Book of Zechariah

Chapters 9, 10, 11, & 12

Objective: To gain an understanding and insight of Zechariah's vision of a New Jerusalem, the activity of Angels and the accuser of God's People—Satan.

Objective Breakdown:

1. Introduction

2. Judgment on Many Cities Is Spoken   Chapter 9:1-8

3. A King Will Come to Jerusalem   Chapter 9:9-13

4. God Will Defend His People   Chapter 9:14-17

5. The Lord Provides and Protects   Chapter 10:1-8

6. God's People Will Return to the Land   Chapter 10:9-12

7. The Ruin of Lebanon and Bashan   Chapter 11:1-3

8. Prophecy of Shepherds   Chapter 11:4-12

9. "Woe to the Worthless Shepherd"   Chapter 11:13-17

10. Jerusalem Will Withstand Attack   Chapter 12:1-9

11. The Spirit of Grace Will Be Poured Out   Chapter 12:10-14

Introduction:

True fasting means true justice. God never allows formal religious observances to take the place of practical everyday godliness. As He pointed out through the prophet Zechariah, spiritual disciplines such as fasting, as important as they can be, make little impression on God if at the same time one's lifestyle lacks justice, mercy, and compassion (Zechariah 7:5,9).

In Babylon the people had imposed two fasts on themselves. One occurred in the fifth month (Ab, or July-August) to commemorate the destruction of the temple (2 Kings 25:8-9). The other occurred in the seventh month (Tishri, or September-October) to commemorate the assassination of Gedaliah, the appointed governor of Judah after Babylon destroyed Jerusalem (Jeremiah 1:1-3). Neither of these fasts were required by the Lord, but that was not why the Lord rebuked the people.

The Lord challenged the returnees for substituting empty religion—whether through fasting or feasting—for true spirituality (Zechariah 7:5-7), like their forebears (Isaiah 58:1-9), they followed the forms of religious ritual without the substance of a godly lifestyle.

The same challenge exists for believers today. Attendance at church, Bible reading, prayer, sharing one's faith—as crucial as these are—need to be matched by a lifestyle of integrity and Christ-like character, especially in one's dealings with others. Otherwise, they become empty rituals that leave one open to self-deception and hypocrisy.

2 Chronicles 7:14

If my people, which are called by my name, shall humble themselves, and pray, and seek my face, and turn from their wicked ways; then will I hear from heaven, and will forgive their sin, and will heal their land.

Psalm 122:6

Pray for the peace of Jerusalem; they will prosper who love thee.

Lesson Plan 262

The Book of Zechariah

Chapters 13 & 14

Objective: To gain an understanding and insight of Zechariah's vision of a New Jerusalem, the activity of Angels and the accuser of God's people—Satan.

Objective Breakdown:

1. Introduction

2. Idols Will Be Cut Off   Chapter 13:1-6

3. The Refining of God's People   Chapter 13:7-9

4. The Lord Will Split the Mount of Olives   Chapter 14:1-5

5. The Lord Will Reign Over All the Earth   Chapter 14:6-9

6. Safety for Jerusalem   Chapter 14:10-11

7. The City's Enemies Will Panic   Chapter 14:12-15

8. The World Will Worship the Lord   Chapter 14:16-21

Introduction:

Anticipating the Good Shepherd, the Lord Jesus Christ. Zechariah envisioned that a Good Shepherd would replace the bad ones that plagued Israel (Zechariah 11:16-17). However, the Good Shepherd would initially be rejected, and His sheep would be scattered (Zechariah 13:7). These prophecies were fulfilled in New Testament times by Jesus, the Good Shepherd (John 10:1; 1 Peter 5:4).

Prophecies of the Messiah in Zechariah:

Prophecy	New Testament Fulfillment
The Ruler on the Throne (Zechariah 2:10-13)	Revelation 5:13; 6:9; 21-24; 22:1-5
A Holy Priesthood (Zechariah 3:8)	John 2:19-21; Ephesians 2:20-21;
1 Peter 2:5	A Heavenly High Priest
Hebrews 4:4; 8:1-2	

The Ruler on a Donkey	Matthew 21:4-5
The Price 30 Pieces of Silver (Zechariah 11:12-13)	Matthew 26:14-15
The Silver Used to Buy a Potter's Field	Mathew 27: 9 (Zechariah 11:13)
Piercing of the Messiah's Body (Zechariah 12:10)	John 19:34, 37
Wounding of the Savior & Scattering of the Sheep	Mathew 26: 31; John 16:32
	(Zechariah 13:1; 6-7)

2 Chronicles 7:14

If my people, which are called by my name, shall humble themselves, and pray, and seek my face, and turn from their wicked ways; then will I hear from heaven, and will forgive their sin, and will heal their land.

Psalm 122:6

Pray for the peace of Jerusalem; they will prosper who love thee.

The Book of Malachi

Scripture Focus Chapters 1-4

Objective: To gain an understanding and insight of Malachi's prophecies concerning the Lord's purposes for all nations and Gentile people.

Objective Breakdown:

1. Introduction

2. Israel Questions God's Love   Chapter 1:1-5

3. God Asks Where His Honor Is   Chapter 1:6-8

4. God's Name Has Been Profaned   Chapter 1:9-14

5. Wicked Priests Are Denounced   Chapter 2:1-9

6. The Treachery of Infidelity   Chapter 2:10-17

7. The Lord Will Send His Messenger   Chapter 3:1-5

8. The People Are Robbing God   Chapter 3:6-10

9. God Hears Those Who Fear Him   Chapter 3:11-18

10. The Sun of Righteousness Shall Arise   Chapter 4:1-6

Lesson Plan 263

The Book of Malachi

Chapters 1 & 2

Objective: To gain insight on the book of Malachi and his concern about corrupt priests abusing their responsibility to serve the Lord and the people.

Objective Breakdown:

1. Introduction

2. Israel's Questions God's Love   Chapter 1:1-5

3. God Asks Where His Honor Is   Chapter 1:6-8

4. God's Name Has Been Profaned   Chapter 1:9-14

5. Wicked priest Are Denounced   Chapter 2:1-9

6. The Treachery of Infidelity   Chapter 2:10-17

Introduction:

Malachi, a prophet in the days of Nehemiah, directs his message of judgment to a people plagued with corrupt priests, wicked practices, and a false sense of security in their privilege relationship with God. Malachi probes deeply into their problems of hypocrisy, infidelity, mixed marriages, divorce, false worship, and arrogance. So sinful has the nation become that God's Word to the people had no impact. For four hundred years after Malachi's ringing condemnations, God remains silent. Only with the coming of John the Baptist (Malachi 3:1) does God again communicate to His people through a prophet's voice.

The Book of Malachi is the prelude to four hundred years of prophetic silence, broken by the words of the next prophet, John the Baptist, "Behold! The Lamb of God who takes away the sins of the world!" (John 1:29). John predicts the coming of the messenger who will clear the way before the coming of the Lord (Malachi 3:1; Isaiah 40:3). John the Baptist later fulfills this prophecy.

Malachi as the last prophetic voice of the Old Testament, peered across the centuries of time when the events spoken of by him and the prophets who proceeded him, would be filled in the person of Jesus Christ. The Jews of the fifth century B.C. longed for the day of their national and spiritual restoration. But when was it to come? Malachi announced that God must first send Elijah the prophet to prepare the way (Malachi 3:1; 4:5, 6). Malachi began his prophecy with the reassuring words "I have loved you, says the Lord" (Malachi 1:2). He then reminded the Jews of their obligation, in the meantime, to respond to God with actions that would show their love for Him (Malachi 1:7; 2:10; 17; 3:8, 13). In this way Malachi prepared the Jews to wait in obedient expectation for their coming Messiah.

2 Chronicles 7:14

If my people, which are called by my name, shall humble themselves, and pray, and seek my face, and turn from their wicked ways; then will I hear from heaven, and will forgive their sin, and will heal their land.

Psalm 122:6

Pray for the peace of Jerusalem; they will prosper who love thee.

Lesson Plan 264

The Book of Malachi

Chapters 3 & 4

Objective: To gain insight on the book of Malachi and his concern about corrupt priests abusing their responsibility to serve the Lord and the people.

Objective Breakdown:

1. Introduction

2. The Lord Will Send His Messenger   Chapter 3:1-5

3. The People Are Robbing God   Chapter 3:6-10

4. God Hears Those Who Fear Him   Chapter 3:11-18

5. The Sun of Righteousness Shall Rise   Chapter 4:1-6

Introduction:

God the father of all. The fatherhood of God applies in general sense to everyone since all men and women created by God in His image. Thus, their creature hood is derived from His fatherhood. This fact is demonstrated by Hebrews 12:9, which speaks of God as the father of spirits (Numbers 16:22; Ecclesiastes 12:7). Paul even agrees with a heathen poet that all men are God's offspring (Acts 17:28). God is also the father as the sustainer of life. Every person is an object of his fatherly care (Matthew 18:10) and is a candidate for His kingdom (Luke 18:16). Further, God is not willing that any should perish (Matthew18:14; 1 Timothy 2:4). Even when men and women reject God, He still provides for them as He does believers with rain, fruitful seasons, food, and gladness (Matthew 5:45; Acts 14:17).

The Scripture always reflect that God is our partner in the covenant of marriage. He handcrafted Eve for Adam from his side and gave her to him (Genesis 2:21, 22). He stated their union reflected the plural nature of the Godhead (Genesis 1:27). He promised the redemption of the human race from sin through the offspring of their union (Genesis 3:16). God ordained the family as the institution through which He would pass along truth of His Word from generation to generation (Deuteronomy 6:4-9). Christian marriage objectifies the presence and role of God in marriage by making its solemn vows to Him, the core of the wedding ceremony. In other word as the Prophet Malachi tells us God hates divorce (Malachi 2:16).

Note:

In closing the Book of the Old Testament, God is not happy with the USA (United States of America) nor for that matter with the rest of the world. As His ambassadors we should be doing a better job. In Isaiah chapter 45:7 God tells us that He creates calamity. The reason He does this, is to get us to refocus our attention on Him and turn from our wicked ways. Just look at what is happening in our society across the country in the last several years. His patience is running out!! So please join us in praying the below prayers. Thank You.

2 Chronicles 7:14

If my people, which are called by my name, shall humble themselves, and pray, and seek my face, and turn from their wicked ways; then will I hear from heaven, and will forgive their sin, and will heal their land.

Psalm 122:6

Pray for the peace of Jerusalem; they will prosper who love thee.

Supplemental Resources

The Doctrine of Mankind and the Doctrine of Angels

Objective: To gain some understanding of terrestrial (earthly) and celestial (spiritual) life doctrines.

Objective Breakdown:

1. Introduction

2. What Are Angels and Why do they Exist

3. What Is Mankind

4. Why Did God make Mankind

5. What is Mankind's Future/Destiny

Introduction:

The most incredible part of creation is the creation of angels and the creation of mankind. I always thought that the creation of Angels occurred during the six days of creation because it says in Genesis 2:1, "Thus the heavens and the earth, and all the host of them, were finished. And on the seventh day God ended His work which He had done and rested on the seventh day from all His work which He had done. Then God blessed the seventh day and sanctified it because in it He rested from all his work which God had created and made.

I naturally assumed that angels were created during the six days of creation, until it was brought to my attention that in Job chapter 38:4-7, that the angels shouted for joy when the foundations or cornerstones of the earth were laid, indicating that angels were existing when the foundation or cornerstones of the earth were thus laid. This teaching by many theologians suggests that angels existed before the creation week. So be it. If their existence occurred before the six days of creation, I will find out when I get home, until then, I will accept the premise that they existed prior to the foundations or laying of the cornerstone of the earth.

Why were they created or why do they exist so let's look at their nature:

What are Angels and what is their Nature?

    a. My understanding from the Word of God is that they are spiritual and masculine celestial beings (existing in the Heavens).

    b. They are invisible beings but can manifest themselves to be visible. Their normal practice is to remain invisible.

    c.   They are innumerable. They may be as many as stars in the Heavens. They are presented to men as unaccountable.

    d.   They possess individual personalities; intelligence, will, and emotions.

    e.   They are superior to man.

        1. They are stronger than man

        2. They are smarter than man

        3. They are swifter than man

    f.   They are inferior to God

        1. They are not omnipresent (theological term referring to be everywhere).

        2. They are not omnipotent (theological term referring to referring to all powerful)

        3. They are not omniscient (theological term referring to all superior knowledge).

Why do angels exist? They exist because God wanted order and format in His creation. They are His warriors, His messengers, and His administrative executives to carry out His desires. This is clearly defined in the reading and understanding of God's Word stated in the Scriptures.

Let us look at mankind; What is Mankind? Mankind is the ultimate in all creation. Mankind is finest and most important of all His creation. So great that God sacrificed His only son so that He could spend and **share eternity** with mankind as His family, in love, honor and glory. Thank God for such a glorious opportunity.

Man, or mankind was made from the dust of the ground, and God breathed into his nostrils the breath of life; and man became a living soul (Genesis 2:7). And let us not forget woman which came from man's side: "And God caused a deep sleep to fall upon Adam, and he slept: and God took one of his ribs and closed up the flesh thereof; and the rib which the Lord God had taken from man, made he a woman, and brought her unto the man. And Adam said: "This is now bone of my bones and flesh of my flesh; She shall be called Woman, because she was taken out of Man (Genesis 2:21-23)." This is the next best thing that happened to man besides the first best thing which is salvation, and the forgiveness of sin, by the Grace of God.

Why did God make mankind? God made man because He had so much love that he wanted to share it with His family of mankind. He made mankind in the image of Almighty God's image...the Trinity: body, soul, and spirit, which will live forever, and forever, and forever. When Jesus entered mankind (Philippians 2:7), He showed us the way we were to grow, and we became His adopted brothers and sisters. God has no grandchildren; we are all Jesus' brothers and sisters in the family of mankind. He paid the penalty for our sins, past, present, and future, at the cross. What love!! Wow!! Wow!!

Mankind's future/destiny. Mankind has a great future. His future and destiny is the New Jerusalem (Revelation 21:9-27) where the Garden of Eden will be restored and there will be no more tears (Revelation 21:4), no more death (Revelation 21:4), no more pain (Revelation 21:4), no more insecurity (Revelation 21:25), no more night (Revelation 21:25), no more sickness (Revelation 22:2), no more sin (Revelation 22:2), no more curse (Revelation 22:2), no more Satan (Revelation 20:10), no more thirst (Revelation 7:16), no more hunger (Revelation 7:16), no more heat (excessive sunburn) (Revelation 7:16), no more condemnation (John 5:24), and no more corruption (1 Corinthians 15:24).

We can look forward to an inheritance incorruptible, undefiled, and faded not away, reserved in Heaven for us (1 Peter 1:4). We can also look forward to Glory (John 17:24), Beauty (Psalm 50:2), Devine Light (Isaiah 60:19, 20), Unity (Ephesians 1:10), Perfection (1 Corinthians 13:10), Joy (Psalms 16:11), Eternity (John 3:15), Righteousness (2 Peter 3:15), Service (Revelation 7:15), and Rewards (Matthew 5:11,12). What a Heavenly Jackpot!!

What an unbelievable opportunity, what an unbelievable future, what an unbelievable destiny all for accepting and embracing the full meaning of John 14:6 which states: "I am the way, the truth, and the life, no one comes to the father except through me."

2 Chronicles 7:14

If my people, which are called by my name, shall humble themselves, and pray, and seek my face, and turn from their wicked ways; then will I hear from heaven, and will forgive their sin, and will heal their land.

Psalm 122:6

Pray for the peace of Jerusalem; they will prosper who love thee.

Ancient Israel's Divided Kingdoms: Israel Ephraim or the Northern Kingdom and Judah the Southern Kingdom

Objective: To gain an understanding of what caused the succession in Israel, resulting in the divided kingdoms of Ancient Israel into the Northern Kingdom and Judah into the Southern Kingdom.

Objective Breakdown:

1. Introduction

2. Rulers of the Northern Kingdoms

3. Rulers of the Southern Kingdoms

4. Future Prophecies of a Reunited Kingdom of Israel

5. Fulfillment of these Prophecies in Our Day

Introduction: David and Solomon presided over the golden days of the Israelite empire. David is remembered as a man after God's own heart (1 Samuel 13:14; 16:70) and Solomon as the wisest man who ever lived (1 Kings 3:12; 4:29-32; 10:3, 6-7, 24).

Yet as impressive as these two rulers were, they violated the express commandments of the law regarding Kings (Deuteronomy 17:16-17): they both had multiple wives (2 Samuel 3:2-5; 5:13;1 Kings 11:1-3), and Solomon multiplied horses, silver, and gold (2 Samuel 10:14-15, 22-23, 28-29).

Solomon has 700 hundred wives and 300 hundred concubines. The wives were acquired mostly through political marriages (see 2 Samuel 3:13-14). These wives not only complicated domestic lives, but also tended to turn their hearts away from God, particularly in the case of Solomon. This was the very reason that God warned against this practice.

Likewise importing the horses from Egypt, Solomon was symbolically returning Israel to bondage. God had delivered the people from the Egyptian in the days of Moses, and He warned them never to "return" there by making alliances.

The Lord took Solomon's fall into idolatry so seriously that He offered to give most of the nation of Israel to Jeroboam (see 1 Kings 11:9-13; 31-39). However, God out of His regard for David, waited to after Solomon's death (and Israel's civil war) to take the ten tribes of the North and give them to Jeroboam as their first ruler. The remaining two tribes (Judah and Benjamin) remained in the South and became known as the Southern Kingdom and Rehoboam, Solomon's son, as their first ruler.

The Northern Kingdom became known as Israel or Ephraim and lasted for 210 years (931-721 B.C.) before going into captivity by the Assyrians in 721 B.C.). The Northern Kingdom under Jeroboam offered to serve Rehoboam if Rehoboam would lighten the heavy tax burden that he was imposing on the Northern tribes, but Rehoboam listened to the council of members of his generation rather than the council of his father's generation and refused to lighten the tax burden but rather increased the burden of heavier taxation. Thus, succession of the ten Northern tribes to rulership under Jeroboam.

The Southern Kingdom became known as Judah and lasted for 325 years (931-606 B.C.) before going into captivity by Nebuchadnezzar.

Rulers of the Northern Kingdom referred to as Israel and Ephraim were:

Jeroboam	Dates 931-909 B.C.	Duration 22 years
Nadab	Dates 910-908 B.C.	Duration 2 years (son of Jeroboam)
Baasha	Dates 908-885 B.C.	Duration 24 years
Elah	Dates 885-883 B.C.	Duration 2 years (son of Baasha)
Zimri	Dates 885 B.C.	Duration 7 days
Omri	Dates 885-873 B.C.	Duration 12 years
Ahab	Dates 874-852 B.C.	Duration 22 years
Ahaziah	Dates 853-851 B.C.	Duration 2 years
Jehoram	Dates 852-840 B.C.	Duration 12 years
Jehu	Dates 841-813 B.C.	Duration 28 years
Jeh0ahaz	Dates 814-797 B.C.	Duration 17 years
Jehoash	Dates 798-785 B.C.	Duration 16 years
Jeroboam II	Dates 793-752 B.C.	Duration 41 years
Zechariah	Dates 753 B.C.	Duration 6 months
Shallum	Dates 751 B.C.	Duration 1 month
Menahem	Dates 752-742 B.C.	Duration 10 years
Pekahiah	Dates 742-740 B.C.	Duration 2 years
Pekah	Dates 740-732 B.C.	Duration 20 years
Hoshea	Dates 732-721 B.C.	Duration 9 years

The Northern Kingdom was referred to as Israel and Ephraim.

o. It began in 931 B.C.

o. First ruler was Jeroboam

o. Last ruler was Hoshea

o. Total number of rulers were 19

o. Not one was saved

o. Consisted of ten tribes

o. Capital was Samaria

o. Captured by the Assyrians in 721 B.C.

o. No return from captivity

o. Lasted 210 years; 931–721 B.C.

A little further insight into the Northern Rulers:

1. Jeroboam

DATES 931-909   DURATION 22 YEARS

SCRIPTURE 1 KINGS 11:26-14:20;

2 CHRONICLES 9:29-13:22

He served as a cabinet member under Solomon but fled to Egypt to escape the king's wrath.

He led the revolt of the ten tribes at Shechem.

His false religion caused Israel to sin.

His pagan altar was destroyed, his arm paralyzed, and his son stricken by God due to his sin.

He was defeated in battle by Abijam, the second king of the south.

He was stricken with a plague from God and died.

2. Nadab

DATES 910-908   DURATION 2 YEARS

SCRIPTURE 1 KINGS 15:25-28

He was the son of Jeroboam.

He was assassinated by a rebel named Baasha.

3. Baasha

DATES 909-885   DURATION 24 YEARS

SCRIPTURE 1 KINGS 15:27-16:7;

2 CHRONICLES 16:1-6

He killed Nadab and thus fulfilled Ahijah the prophet's prediction. Compare 1 Kings 14:4 with 15:29.

He fought with Asa (third king of the south) and built a wall to cut off trade to Jerusalem.

His seed was predicted to suffer the same judgment as that of Jeroboam.

4. Elah

DATES 885-883   DURATION 2 YEARS

SCRIPTURE 1 KINGS 16:6-14

He was the son of Baasha.

He was assassinated by a soldier rebel while drunk.

5. Zimri

DATES 885   DURATION 7 DAYS

SCRIPTURE 1 KINGS 16:9-20

He fulfilled prophecy by slaughtering Baasha's seed.

He was trapped by rebel soldiers in his own palace, resulting in a fiery suicidal death.

6. Omri

DATES 885-873   DURATION 12 YEARS

SCRIPTURE 1 KINGS 16:15-28

He made Samaria the northern capital.

He was the most powerful king up to his time.

He arranged the marriage of his son Ahab to Jezabel.

7. Ahab

DATES 874-852   DURATION 22 YEARS

SCRIPTURE 1 KINGS 16:28-22:40;

2 CHRONICLES 18:1-34

He married Jezebel.

His Baal-worshiping practices caused a great famine to fall upon the land.

He was allowed to defeat the Syrians on two occasions to prove a point.

He tricked godly King Jehoshaphat (fourth king of Judah) into a twofold compromise—matrimonial and military.

His death for his many sins was predicated by three prophets (1 Kings 20:42; 21:19; 22:17, 28).

The death of Jezebel, his wife, was also predicted by Elijah.

He experienced a brief (but temporary) fox-hole type conversion (1 Kings 21:29).

He was killed in a battle with Syria.

8. Ahaziah

DATES 853-851   DURATION 2 YEARS

SCRIPTURE 1 KINGS 22:40-2 KINGS 1:18;

2 CHRONICLES 20:35-37

He was the oldest son of Ahab and Jezebel.

He persuaded Jehoshaphat to enter into a ship-building enterprise with him at Ezion-Geber.

He suffered a severe fall (which proved fatal) in his palace in Samaria.

He turned to the pagan god Baal-Zebub for healing.

He was rebuked for this by Elijah, whom he unsuccessfully attempted to arrest.

9. Jehoram

DATES 852-840   DURATION 12 YEARS

SCRIPTURE 2 KINGS 3:1-9:25;

 2 CHRONICLES 22:5-7

He was the youngest son of Ahab and Jezebel.

He persuaded Jehoshaphat to ally with him against Syria.

Elisha the prophet performed a miracle (for Jehoshaphat's sake) which won the battle.

Elisha later helped Jehoram by warning him of several planned Syrian ambushes.

Elisha would, however, prevent him from slaughtering some supernaturally blinded Syrian troops.

He was on the throne when Naaman came to be healed of leprosy.

He was on the throne when God used four lepers to save Samaria from starvation.

He was finally murdered by Jehu in the Valley of Jezreel.

10. Jehu

DATES 841-813   DURATION 28 YEARS

SCRIPTURE 2 KINGS 9:1-10:36;

 2 CHRONICLES 22:7-12

He was anointed by a messenger from Elisha.

He was known for his bloodletting. He executed Judah's King Ahaziah (not to be confused with Ahab's oldest son), grandson of Jehoshaphat. He killed the northern king Jehoram, Jezabel, Ahab's seventy sons, relatives, and friends, forty-two royal princes of Judah the Baal-worshipers

11. Jehoahaz

DATES 814-797   DURATION 17 YEARS

SCRIPTURE 2 KINGS 13:1-9

He was the son of Jehu.

He saw his army almost wiped out by the Syrians.

He experienced a brief period of remorse over his sins, but apparently not genuine repentance.

12. Jehoash

DATES 798-782   DURATION 16 YEARS

SCRIPTURE 2 KINGS 13:10-14:16;

 2 CHRONICLES 25:17-24

He visited Elisha on his deathbed.

He defeated Amaziah (sixth king of Judah) on the battlefield.

He related one of the two Old Testament fables to ridicule the arrogant claims of Amaziah.

He plundered Jerusalem, taking many hostages and much wealth.

13. Jeroboam II

DATES 793-752   DURATION 41 YEARS

SCRIPTURE 2 KINGS 14:23-29

He ruled longer than any other northern king.

He was one of the most powerful kings of the north.

He recovered much of Israel's lost territory.

14. Zechariah

DATES 753   DURATION 6 MONTHS

SCRIPTURE 2 KINGS 14:29-15:12

He was the great-great-grandson of Jehu, and fourth ruler in his dynasty.

He was murdered by a rebel names Shallum, thus fulfilling God's prophecy against Jehu. See 2 Kings 10:30; 14:29; 15:8-12

15. Shallum

DATES 752   DURATION 1 MONTH

SCRIPTURE 2 KINGS 15:10-15

1. He was murdered by a cruel soldier names Menahem.

16. Menahem

DATES 752-742   DURATION 10 YEARS

SCRIPTURE 2 KINGS 15:14-22

2 CHRONICLES 22:7-12

1. He was one of Israel's most brutal dictators.

2. He bought off Assyrian king Tiglath-Pileser with a two-million dollar bribe.

17. Pekahiah

DATES 742-740   DURATION 2 YEARS

SCRIPTURE 2 KINGS 15:22-26

1. He was the son of Menahem.

2. He was killed by his army commander, Pekah.

18. Pekah

DATES 740-732   DURATION 20 YEARS

SCRIPTURE 2 KINGS 15:27-31;

2 CHRONICLES 28: 5-8

1. Only eight years are in view here (740-732). It is thought that the first twelve years (752-740) were shared by co-regency arrangement with both Menahem and Pekahiah.

2. He joined Syria in an unsuccessful attempt to punish Judah for their refusal to team up against Assyria.

3. He saw Assyria capture some of Israel's northern and eastern cities.

4. He was assassinated by Hoshea.

19. Hosea

DATES 732-721   DURATION 9 YEARS

SCRIPTURE 2 KINGS 15:30-17:6

1. He was Israel's final king.

2. He joined with Egypt in rebelling against Assyria.

3. For this he was imprisoned in Assyria.

3. Rulers of the Southern Kingdom:

Rehoboam	Dates 931-914 B.C.	Duration 17 years
Abijam	Dates 914-911 B.C.	Duration 3 years
Asa	Dates 911-870 B.C.	Duration 41 years
Jehoshaphat	Dates 873-848 B.C.	Duration 25 years
Joram	Dates 853-845 B.C.	Duration 8 years
Ahaziah	Dates 841 B.C.	Duration 1 year
Athaliah	Dates 841-835 B.C.	Duration 6 years
Joash	Dates 835-795 B.C.	Duration 40 years

Amaziah	Dates 796-767 B.C.	Duration 29 years
Uzziah	Dates 792-740 B.C.	Duration 52 years
Jotham	Dates 750-736 B.C.	Duration 16 years
Ahaz	Dates 735-719 B.C.	Duration16 years
Hezekiah	Dates 716-687 B.C.	Duration 29 years
Manasseh	Dates 697-642 B.C.	Duration 55 years
Amon	Dates 643-641 B.C.	Duration 2 years
Josiah	Dates 641-610 B.C.	Duration 31 years
Jehoahaz	Dates 609 B.C.	Duration 3 months
Jehoiakim	Dates 609-598 B.C.	Duration 11 years
Jehoiachin	Dates 508 B. C.	Duration 3 months
Zedekiah	Dates 597-586 B. C.	Duration 11 years

The Southern Kingdom was referred to as Judah.

o. It began in 931 B.C.

o. First ruler was Rehoboam

o. Last ruler was Zedekiah

o. Total number of rulers were twenty

o. Eight were saved

o. Consisted of two tribes

o. Capital was Jerusalem

o. Captured by the Babylonians in 606 B.C.

o. Three separate returns from captivity

o. Lasted 325 years: 931-606 B.C.

A little further insight into the Southern Rulers:

Southern Rulers

1. Rehoboam

DATES 931-914   DURATION 17 YEARS

SCRIPTURE 1 KINGS 11:42-14:31;

2 CHRONICLES 9:31-12:16

He was the son of Solomon.

His stupidity and tactlessness sparked the civil war.

He had eighteen wives and sixty concubines.

His favorite wife was Maachah, the evil daughter of Absalom.

He sees his capital, Jerusalem, invaded by Shishak, Pharaoh of Egypt.

2. Abijam

DATES 914-911   DURATION 3 YEARS

SCRIPTURE 1 KINGS 14:31-15:8;

2 CHRONICLES 13:1-22

He defeated (by supernatural intervention) the northern king Jeroboam on the battlefield.

In spite of God's help, he degenerated into a wicked king.

3. Asa

DATES 911-870   DURATION 41 YEARS

SCRIPTURE 1 KINGS 15:8-14;

2 CHRONICLES 14:1-16:14

He was Judah's first saved king.

He led Judah in a revival.

He was a great builder.

He saw God answer his prayer by delivering Jerusalem from a massive Ethiopian attack (2 Chronicles 14:11).

He deposed Maacah (his grandmother) because of her idolatry.

He later backslid and threw into prison a prophet who had rebuked his sin.

He died of a foot disease, which problem he refused to take to God.

4. Jehoshaphat

DATES 873-848   DURATION 25 YEARS

SCRIPTURES 1 KINGS 22:41-50;

2 CHRONICLES 17:1-20:37

He instituted a national religious education program by sending out teachers of the Word of God.

He later marred his testimony by compromising with three ungodly northern kings.

He appointed a religious director and a civil director, thus recognizing the separation of church and state.

When Jerusalem was threatened by a massive Moabite invasion, God heard his prayer and supernaturally intervened.

5. Joram

DATES 853-845   DURATION 8 YEARS

SCRIPTURES 2 KINGS 8:16-24;

2 CHRONICLES 21:1-20

He married Athaliah, daughter of Ahab and Jezebel.

He began his reign by murdering his six brothers.

He received a posthumous message from Elijah predicting judgment upon him because of his wicked and murderous reign.

He was attacked and defeated by the Philistines and Arabians.

He died of a horrible disease and was unmourned at the funeral.

6. Ahaziah

DATES 841   DURATION 1 YEAR

SCRIPTURE 2 KINGS 8:24-9:29;

2 CHRONICLES 22:1-9

He was the son of Joram and Athaliah.

He was killed by Jehu (tenth northern king).

7. Athaliah

DATES 841-835   DURATION 6 YEARS

SCRIPTURE 2 KINGS 11:1-20;

2 CHRONICLES 22:1-23:21

At the death of Ahaziah, her son, she took over the throne of Judah, slaughtering all the royal seed but one (Joash) who was hidden from her.

After a rule of six years, she herself was executed.

8. Joash

DATES 835-795   DURATION 40 YEARS

SCRIPTURE 2 KINGS 11:1-12:21;

2 CHRONICLES 22:10-24:27

He alone had survived Athaliah's bloody purge.

For a while he lived for God, but later became a cruel tyrant.

He sanctioned the stoning of Judah's own high priest, Zechariah, who had fearlessly rebuked the sin among the people.

He was executed by his own palace guard.

9. Amaziah

DATES 796-767   DURATION 29 YEARS

SCRIPTURE 2 KINGS 14:1-20;

2 CHRONICLES 25:1-28

He was a good king for a while, executing the killers of his father, Joash.

He was rebuked by a prophet for hiring some mercenary Israeli soldiers to help him fight against Edom.

He reluctantly dismissed these paid soldiers and, with God's help, defeated Edom with his own soldiers.

He foolishly brought back some of the Edomite gods for worshiping purposes.

The reckless king then declared war on northern Israel and was soundly defeated.

10. Uzziah

DATES 792-740   DURATION 52 YEARS

SCRIPTURE 2 KINGS 15:1-7;

2 CHRONICLES 26:1-23

He was a mighty warrior and builder.

He attempted, however, to intrude into the office of the priesthood and was punished for this by leprosy.

11. Jotham

DATES 750-736   DURATION 16 YEARS

SCRIPTURE 2 KINGS 15:32-38;

2 CHRONICLES 27:1-9

He was a good king.

He built the upper gate of the Temple and erected fortresses and towers.

He defeated his enemies and received huge annual tribute from them.

12. Ahaz

DATES 735-719   DURATION 16 YEARS

SCRIPTURE 2 KINGS 16:1-20;

2 CHRONICLES 28:1-27

He was perhaps the second worst king of Judah.

He sacrificed his own children to devil gods.

He was the first person to hear about the virgin birth. (See Isaiah 7:1-25)

He ordered the construction of a pagan Assyrian altar and placed it in the Temple to appease Tiglath-Pileser.

13. Hezekiah

DATES 716-687   DURATION 29 YEARS

SCRIPTURE 2 KINGS 18:1-20:21;

2 CHRONICLES 29:1-32:33

He was Judah's second-best king and the richest of all.

He repaired the Temple, organized an orchestral group, and appointed a Levitical singing choir.

He carried out the greatest Passover celebration since Solomon.

He saw the death angel defeat the Assyrian enemies which had surrounded Jerusalem.

He was supernaturally healed of a terminal disease and given an additional fifteen years to live.

He added fifteen Psalms to the Old Testament Canon.

He foolishly showed the wealth of Judah to some nosy Babylonian ambassadors.

14. Manasseh

DATES 697-642   DURATION 55 YEARS

SCRIPTURE 2 KINGS 21:1-18;

2 CHRONICLES 33:1-20

He ruled longer than any other king of north or south.

He was the most wicked king of all.

He experienced the new birth while in an enemy prison.

15. Amon

DATES 643-641   DURATION 2 YEARS

SCRIPTURE 2 KINGS 21:19-26;

2 CHRONICLES 33:21-25

He was wicked like his father, Manasseh, but did not repent as did his father.

He was executed by his own household servants.

16. Josiah

DATES 641-610   DURATION 31 YEARS

SCRIPTURE 2 KINGS 22:1-23:30;

2 CHRONICLES 34:1-35:27

He was the godliest king since David.

He was Judah's last godly king.

The book of Moses was accidentally discovered among the debris in the Temple at the beginning of his reign.

He used this to lead Judah in a great revival.

He also conducted a larger Passover celebration than that of Hezekiah his great-grandfather.

He fulfilled a three-hundred-year-old prophecy. Compare 1 Kings 13:1, 2 with 2 Kings 23:15.

He was killed in a battle with the Egyptians.

17. Jehoahaz

DATES 609   DURATION 3 MONTHS

SCRIPTURE 2 KINGS 23:31-33;

2 CHRONICLES 36:1-4

He was the middle son of Josiah.

He was deposed after only ninety days by the Pharaoh who had killed his father.

He was carried into Egyptian captivity where he eventually died.

18. Jehoiakim

DATES 609-598   DURATION 11 YEARS

SCRIPTURE 2 KINGS 23:34-24:5;

2 CHRONICLES 36:5-7

He was the oldest brother of Jehoahaz.

He was put on the throne by the Egyptian Pharaoh.

He was later made vassal by Nebuchadnezzar after the Babylonians had defeated the Egyptians.

He was totally materialistic and self-centered. He can be considered Judah's third worst king.

He murdered the innocent and often persecuted Jeremiah.

He burned a copy of a part of God's Word. (See Jeremiah 36:22-32.)

He experienced the first of three fearful "visits" Nebuchadnezzar made to the city of Jerusalem.

During this visit (606 B.C.) Daniel and other Hebrew young people were carried off into captivity.

9. At his death he received the burial of an ass, as Jeremiah had predicted.

19. Jehoiachin

Dates 598   Duration 3 Months

SCRIPTURE 2 KINGS 24:6-16;

2 CHRONICLES 36:8-10

1. He was the son of Jehoiakim and grandson of Josiah.

2. He incurred a curse from God, stating that his sons would not sit upon Judah's throne.

3. Both Ezekiel (19:5-9) and Jeremiah (22:24-26) predicted that he would be carried off into Babylonian captivity.

4. This happened during Nebuchadnezzar's second visit (597 B.C.) to Jerusalem. Ezekiel was also carried away at this time.

5. He eventually died in Babylon.

20. Zedekiah

Dates 597-586   Duration 11 Years

SCRIPTURE 2 KINGS 24:17-25:30;

2 CHRONICLES 36:11-21

1. He was the youngest son of Josiah and uncle to Jehoiachin.

2. Jeremiah was persecuted during his reign.

3. He rebelled against Babylon along with Egypt.

4. He was captured, blinded, and carried off into Babylon by Babylonian captivity by Nebuchadnezzar.

5. Jerusalem was burned to the ground and the temple destroyed at this time.

Note: Source of the information on the Northern and Southern kings obtained from Dr. Willmington's *Guide to the Bible*...Liberty University.

4. Future Prophecies for a reunited kingdom of Israel. Here is what the Scriptures tells us:

Israel's New Heart and Spirit

Ezekial 11:14 Again the word of the LORD came unto me, saying,

Ezekial 11:15 Son of man, thy brethren, *even* thy brethren, the men of thy kindred, and all the house of Israel wholly, *are* they unto whom the inhabitants of Jerusalem have said, Get you far from the LORD: unto us is this land given in possession.

Ezekial 11:16 Therefore say, Thus saith the Lord GOD; Although I have cast them far off among the heathen, and although I have scattered them among the countries, yet will I be to them as a little sanctuary in the countries where they shall come.

Ezekial 11:17 Therefore say, Thus saith the Lord GOD; I will even gather you from the people, and assemble you out of the countries where ye have been scattered, and I will give you the land of Israel.

Ezekial 11:18 And they shall come thither, and they shall take away all the detestable things thereof and all the abominations thereof from thence.

Ezekial 11:19 And I will give them one heart, and I will put a new spirit within you; and I will take the stony heart out of their flesh, and will give them an heart of flesh:

Ezekial 11:20 That they may walk in my statutes, and keep mine ordinances, and do them: and they shall be my people, and I will be their God.

Israel Gathered in Security

Ezekial 28:25 Thus saith the Lord GOD; When I shall have gathered the house of Israel from the people among whom they are scattered, and shall be sanctified in them in the sight of the heathen, then shall they dwell in their land that I have given to my servant Jacob.

Ezekial 28:26 And they shall dwell safely therein, and shall build houses, and plant vineyards; yea, they shall dwell with confidence, when I have executed judgments upon all those that despise them round about them; and they shall know that I *am* the LORD their God.

Prophecy to the Mountains of Israel

Ezekial 36:1 Also, thou son of man, prophesy unto the mountains of Israel, and say, Ye mountains of Israel, hear the word of the LORD:

Ezekial 36:2 Thus saith the Lord GOD; Because the enemy hath said against you, Aha, even the ancient high places are ours in possession:

Ezekial 36:3 Therefore prophesy and say, Thus saith the Lord GOD; Because they have made *you* desolate, and swallowed you up on every side, that ye might be a possession unto the residue of the heathen, and ye are taken up in the lips of talkers, and *are* an infamy of the people:

Ezekial 36:4 Therefore, ye mountains of Israel, hear the word of the Lord GOD; Thus saith the Lord GOD to the mountains, and to the hills, to the rivers, and to the valleys, to the desolate wastes, and to the cities that are forsaken, which became a prey and derision to the residue of the heathen that *are* round about;

Ezekial 36:5 Therefore thus saith the Lord GOD; Surely in the fire of my jealousy have I spoken against the residue of the heathen, and against all Idumea, which have appointed my land into their possession with the joy of all *their* heart, with despiteful minds, to cast it out for a prey.

Ezekial 36:6 Prophesy therefore concerning the land of Israel, and say unto the mountains, and to the hills, to the rivers, and to the valleys, Thus saith the Lord GOD; Behold, I have spoken in my jealousy and in my fury, because ye have borne the shame of the heathen:

Ezekial 36:7 Therefore thus saith the Lord GOD; I have lifted up mine hand, Surely the heathen that *are* about you, they shall bear their shame.

Ezekial 36:8 But ye, O mountains of Israel, ye shall shoot forth your branches, and yield your fruit to my people of Israel; for they are at hand to come.

Ezekial 36:9 For, behold, I *am* for you, and I will turn unto you, and ye shall be tilled and sown:

Ezekial 36:10 And I will multiply men upon you, all the house of Israel, *even* all of it: and the cities shall be inhabited, and the wastes shall be builded:

Ezekial 36:11 And I will multiply upon you man and beast; and they shall increase and bring fruit: and I will settle you after your old estates, and will do better *unto you* than at your beginnings: and ye shall know that I *am* the LORD.

Ezekial 36:12 Yea, I will cause men to walk upon you, *even* my people Israel; and they shall possess thee, and thou shalt be their inheritance, and thou shalt no more henceforth bereave them *of men*.

Ezekial 36:13 Thus saith the Lord GOD; Because they say unto you, Thou *land* devourest up men, and hast bereaved thy nations;

Ezekial 36:14 Therefore thou shalt devour men no more, neither bereave thy nations any more, saith the Lord GOD.

Ezekial 36:15 Neither will I cause *men* to hear in thee the shame of the heathen anymore, neither shalt thou bear the reproach of the people any more, neither shalt thou cause thy nations to fall any more, saith the Lord GOD.

I Will Put My Spirit Within You

Ezekial 36:22 Therefore say unto the house of Israel, Thus saith the Lord GOD; I do not *this* for your sakes, O house of Israel, but for mine holy name's sake, which ye have profaned among the heathen, whither ye went.

Ezekial 36:23 And I will sanctify my great name, which was profaned among the heathen, which ye have profaned in the midst of them; and the heathen shall know that I *am* the LORD, saith the Lord GOD, when I shall be sanctified in you before their eyes.

Ezekial 36:24 For I will take you from among the heathen, and gather you out of all countries, and will bring you into your own land.

Ezekial 36:25 Then will I sprinkle clean water upon you, and ye shall be clean: from all your filthiness, and from all your idols, will I cleanse you.

Ezekial 36:26 A new heart also will I give you, and a new spirit will I put within you: and I will take away the stony heart out of your flesh, and I will give you an heart of flesh.

Ezekial 36:27 And I will put my spirit within you, and cause you to walk in my statutes, and ye shall keep my judgments, and do *them.*

Ezekial 36:28 And ye shall dwell in the land that I gave to your fathers; and ye shall be my people, and I will be your God.

Ezekial 36:29 I will also save you from all your uncleanness: and I will call for the corn, and will increase it, and lay no famine upon you.

Ezekial 36:30 And I will multiply the fruit of the tree, and the increase of the field, that ye shall receive no more reproach of famine among the heathen.

Ezekial 36:31 Then shall ye remember your own evil ways, and your doings that *were* not good, and shall loathe yourselves in your own sight for your iniquities and for your abominations.

Ezekial 36:32 Not for your sakes do I *this,* saith the Lord GOD, be it known unto you: be ashamed and confounded for your own ways, O house of Israel.

Ezekial 36:33 Thus saith the Lord GOD; In the day that I shall have cleansed you from all your iniquities I will also cause *you* to dwell in the cities, and the wastes shall be builded.

Ezekial 36:34 And the desolate land shall be tilled, whereas it lay desolate in the sight of all that passed by.

Ezekial 36:35 And they shall say, This land that was desolate is become like the garden of Eden; and the waste and desolate and ruined cities *are become fenced, and* are inhabited.

Ezekial 36:36 Then the heathen that are left round about you shall know that I the LORD build the ruined *places, and* plant that that was desolate: I the LORD have spoken *it,* and I will do *it.*

Ezekial 36:37 Thus saith the Lord GOD; I will yet *for* this be inquired of by the house of Israel, to do *it* for them; I will increase them with men like a flock.

Ezekial 36:38 As the holy flock, as the flock of Jerusalem in her solemn feasts; so shall the waste cities be filled with flocks of men: and they shall know that I *am* the LORD.

I Will Be Their God, They Shall Be My People

Ezekial 37:16 Moreover, thou son of man, take thee one stick, and write upon it, For Judah, and for the children of Israel his companions: then take another stick, and write upon it, For Joseph, the stick of Ephraim, and *for* all the house of Israel his companions:

Ezekial 37:17 And join them one to another into one stick; and they shall become one in thine hand.

Ezekial 37:18 And when the children of thy people shall speak unto thee, saying, Wilt thou not shew us what thou *meanest* by these?

Ezekial 37:19 Say unto them, Thus saith the Lord GOD; Behold, I will take the stick of Joseph, which *is* in the hand of Ephraim, and the tribes of Israel his fellows, and will put them with him, *even* with the stick of Judah, and make them one stick, and they shall be one in mine hand.

Ezekial 37:20 And the sticks whereon thou writest shall be in thine hand before their eyes.

Ezekial 37:21 And say unto them, Thus saith the Lord GOD; Behold, I will take the children of Israel from among the heathen, whither they be gone, and will gather them on every side, and bring them into their own land:

Ezekial 37:22 And I will make them one nation in the land upon the mountains of Israel; and one king shall be king to them all: and they shall be no more two nations, neither shall they be divided into two kingdoms any more at all:

Ezekial 37:23 Neither shall they defile themselves any more with their idols, nor with their detestable things, nor with any of their transgressions: but I will save them out of all their dwelling places, wherein they have sinned, and will cleanse them: so shall they be my people, and I will be their God.

Ezekial 37:24 And David my servant *shall be* king over them; and they all shall have one shepherd: they shall also walk in my judgments, and observe my statutes, and do them.

Ezekial 37:25 And they shall dwell in the land that I have given unto Jacob my servant, wherein your fathers have dwelt; and they shall dwell therein, *even* they, and their children, and their children's children for ever: and my servant David *shall be* their prince for ever.

Ezekial 37:26 Moreover I will make a covenant of peace with them; it shall be an everlasting covenant with them: and I will place them, and multiply them, and will set my sanctuary in the midst of them for evermore.

Ezekial 37:27 My tabernacle also shall be with them: yea, I will be their God, and they shall be my people.

Ezekial 37:28 And the heathen shall know that I the LORD do sanctify Israel, when my sanctuary shall be in the midst of them for evermore.

Fulfillment of these Prophecies in Our Day

754

On May 14, 1948, Israel became a nation and on December 6, 2017, President Trump formally recognized Jerusalem as the capital of Israel. Today Jewish people from all over the world continue to return to Israel, where cities that once were destroyed by their enemies have been rebuilt and where the soil is bursting with fruit, trees, and flowers, just as the prophet Ezekiel had foretold.

We can now recognize the fulfillment of God's Word before our very eyes (daily) and in our lifetime.

And yes, there is a great future for the nation of Israel and its people. It will be the capital of the World during the Millennium and with the Lord Jesus Christ as the Supreme ruler! We Love You Lord Jesus, Your Father and Your Holy Spirit, Amen!! and Amen!!

www.ingramcontent.com/pod-product-compliance
Lightning Source LLC
Chambersburg PA
CBHW082006140626
46553CB00020B/2427